Emotional and Behavioural Difficulties Associated with Bullying and Cyberbullying

Bullying affects the lives of many children: some are victims, some take part in bullying others, and many are, to a greater or lesser extent, onlookers or witnesses of bullying behaviours. Usually seen as something that happens in schools and amongst peers, the advent of cyberbullying by mobile phones and via the internet, primarily in this century, has seen such cases of bullying increase and traditional forms of the behaviour evolve.

This book considers the effects of bullying and cyberbullying on children. It looks at the different roles that are present within bullying and the different effects that it can have on a child's development of psychosomatic problems, self-esteem, friends and loneliness, school satisfaction, and family relations. It focuses on several key aspects of this type of intimidation and considers topics including traditional bullying, the situation of immigrant children in relation to bullying and victimization, cyberbullying in young people, and emotional and behavioural correlates of cyberbullying.

This book was originally published as a special double issue of *Emotional and Behavioural Difficulties.*

Peter K. Smith is Emeritus Professor of Psychology at the Unit for School and Family Studies at Goldsmiths College, University of London, UK. His research interests are in social development, school bullying, play, and grandparenting. Previous publications include *Children and Play* (2010), *Understanding Children's Development* (2011) and *Bullying in Schools: How Successful can Interventions be?* (2004).

Emotional and Behavioural Difficulties Associated with Bullying and Cyberbullying

Edited by
Peter K. Smith

Routledge
Taylor & Francis Group
LONDON AND NEW YORK

First published 2014
by Routledge

2 Park Square, Milton Park, Abingdon, Oxfordshire OX14 4RN
711 Third Avenue, New York, NY 10017

Routledge is an imprint of the Taylor & Francis Group, an informa business

First issued in paperback 2018

British Library Cataloguing in Publication Data
A catalogue record for this book is available from the British Library

ISBN13: 978-0-415-63498-4 (hbk)
ISBN13: 978-1-138-37708-0 (pbk)

Typeset in Times New Roman
by Taylor & Francis Books

Publisher's Note
The publisher accepts responsibility for any inconsistencies that may have arisen during the conversion of this book from journal articles to book chapters, namely the possible inclusion of journal terminology.

Contents

Citation Information vii

Introduction
Peter K. Smith 1

1. Listening to children's voices: moral emotional attributions in relation to primary school bullying
Dawn Jennifer and Helen Cowie 6

2. Profiling social, emotional and behavioural difficulties of children involved in direct and indirect bullying behaviours
H. Smith, K. Polenik, S. Nakasita and A. P. Jones 19

3. Associations between types of involvement in bullying, friendships and mental health status
Grace Skrzypiec, Phillip T. Slee, Helen Askell-Williams and Michael J. Lawson 34

4. Peer groups and victimisation among native and immigrant adolescents in Norway
Hildegunn Fandrem, Dagmar Strohmeier and Kolbrun Asta Jonsdottir 48

5. Emotional problems and victimisation among youth with national and international migration experience living in Austria and Turkey
Dagmar Strohmeier and Aysun Dogan 61

6. From cyberbullying to electronic aggression: typology of the phenomenon
Jacek Pyżalski 79

7. The perception of cyberbullying in adolescent victims
Anna Ševčíková, David Šmahel and Mlada Otavová 92

8. Emotional and behavioural problems in the context of cyberbullying: a longitudinal study among German adolescents
Anja Schultze-Krumbholz, Anne Jäkel, Martin Schultze and Herbert Scheithauer 102

9. Moral disengagement and emotional and social difficulties in bullying and cyberbullying: differences by participant role
Sebastian Wachs 119

10. Cyberbullying victimisation in adolescence: relationships with loneliness and depressive mood
Dorit Olenik-Shemesh, Tali Heiman and Sigal Eden 133

11. Predictors of victimisation across direct bullying, indirect bullying and cyberbullying
Antonella Brighi, Annalisa Guarini, Giannino Melotti, Silvia Galli and Maria Luisa Genta 147

12. Victims' perceptions of traditional and cyberbullying, and the psycho-social correlates of their victimisation
Marilyn Campbell, Barbara Spears, Phillip Slee, Des Butler and Sally Kift 161

13. Peer victimisation and depressive symptoms: can specific coping strategies buffer the negative impact of cybervictimisation?
Katja Machmutow, Sonja Perren, Fabio Sticca and Françoise D. Alsaker 174

14. Does the association with psychosomatic health problems differ between cyberbullying and traditional bullying?
Linda Beckman, Curt Hagquist and Lisa Hellström 192

15. Problem behaviours, traditional bullying and cyberbullying among adolescents: longitudinal analyses
Leanne Lester, Donna Cross and Thérèse Shaw 206

Index 219

Citation Information

The chapters in this book were originally published in *Emotional and Behavioural Difficulties*, volume 17, issue 3-4 (September-December 2012). When citing this material, please use the original page numbering for each article, as follows:

Introduction
Introduction
Peter K. Smith
Emotional and Behavioural Difficulties, volume 17, issue 3-4 (September-December 2012) pp. 223-227

Chapter 1
Listening to children's voices: moral emotional attributions in relation to primary school bullying
Dawn Jennifer and Helen Cowie
Emotional and Behavioural Difficulties, volume 17, issue 3-4 (September-December 2012) pp. 229-241

Chapter 2
Profiling social, emotional and behavioural difficulties of children involved in direct and indirect bullying behaviours
H. Smith, K. Polenik, S. Nakasita and A.P. Jones
Emotional and Behavioural Difficulties, volume 17, issue 3-4 (September-December 2012) pp. 243-257

Chapter 3
Associations between types of involvement in bullying, friendships and mental health status
Grace Skrzypiec, Phillip T. Slee, Helen Askell-Williams and Michael J. Lawson
Emotional and Behavioural Difficulties, volume 17, issue 3-4 (September-December 2012) pp. 259-272

Chapter 4
Peer groups and victimisation among native and immigrant adolescents in Norway
Hildegunn Fandrem, Dagmar Strohmeier and Kolbrun Asta Jonsdottir
Emotional and Behavioural Difficulties, volume 17, issue 3-4 (September-December 2012) pp. 273-285

Chapter 5

Emotional problems and victimisation among youth with national and international migration experience living in Austria and Turkey
Dagmar Strohmeier and Aysun Dogan
Emotional and Behavioural Difficulties, volume 17, issue 3-4 (September-December 2012) pp. 287-304

Chapter 6

From cyberbullying to electronic aggression: typology of the phenomenon
Jacek Pyżalski
Emotional and Behavioural Difficulties, volume 17, issue 3-4 (September-December 2012) pp. 305-317

Chapter 7

The perception of cyberbullying in adolescent victims
Anna Ševčíková, David Šmahel and Mlada Otavová
Emotional and Behavioural Difficulties, volume 17, issue 3-4 (September-December 2012) pp. 319-328

Chapter 8

Emotional and behavioural problems in the context of cyberbullying: a longitudinal study among German adolescents
Anja Schultze-Krumbholz, Anne Jäkel, Martin Schultze and Herbert Scheithauer
Emotional and Behavioural Difficulties, volume 17, issue 3-4 (September-December 2012) pp. 329-345

Chapter 9

Moral disengagement and emotional and social difficulties in bullying and cyberbullying: differences by participant role
Sebastian Wachs
Emotional and Behavioural Difficulties, volume 17, issue 3-4 (September-December 2012) pp. 347-360

Chapter 10

Cyberbullying victimisation in adolescence: relationships with loneliness and depressive mood
Dorit Olenik-Shemesh, Tali Heiman and Sigal Eden
Emotional and Behavioural Difficulties, volume 17, issue 3-4 (September-December 2012) pp. 361-374

Chapter 11

Predictors of victimisation across direct bullying, indirect bullying and cyberbullying
Antonella Brighi, Annalisa Guarini, Giannino Melotti, Silvia Galli and Maria Luisa Genta
Emotional and Behavioural Difficulties, volume 17, issue 3-4 (September-December 2012) pp. 375-388

Chapter 12

Victims' perceptions of traditional and cyberbullying, and the psychosocial correlates of their victimisation

Marilyn Campbell, Barbara Spears, Phillip Slee, Des Butler and Sally Kift

Emotional and Behavioural Difficulties, volume 17, issue 3-4 (September-December 2012) pp. 389-401

Chapter 13

Peer victimisation and depressive symptoms: can specific coping strategies buffer the negative impact of cybervictimisation?

Katja Machmutow, Sonja Perren, Fabio Sticca and Françoise D. Alsaker

Emotional and Behavioural Difficulties, volume 17, issue 3-4 (September-December 2012) pp. 403-420

Chapter 14

Does the association with psychosomatic health problems differ between cyberbullying and traditional bullying?

Linda Beckman, Curt Hagquist and Lisa Hellström

Emotional and Behavioural Difficulties, volume 17, issue 3-4 (September-December 2012) pp. 421-434

Chapter 15

Problem behaviours, traditional bullying and cyberbullying among adolescents: longitudinal analyses

Leanne Lester, Donna Cross and Thérèse Shaw

Emotional and Behavioural Difficulties, volume 17, issue 3-4 (September-December 2012) pp. 435-447

Introduction

Peter K. Smith

Bullying affects the lives of many children in school. Some are victims, some take part in bullying others, and many are, to a greater or lesser extent, onlookers or witnesses of bullying behaviours. Considered as a systematic abuse of power, bullying can be seen as an infringement of the rights of a child to a happy and productive life, inside and outside school (Greene 2006). Usually seen as something that happens in schools and amongst peers, the advent of cyberbullying by mobile phones and via the internet, primarily in this century, has seen bullying spread to the 'global playground' (Li, Cross and Smith 2012).

Although some bullying can be seen as very severe and pathological, the extent of bullying in schools suggests that much of it is within the normal range of behaviours. Indeed for some children who bully others there can be payoffs, in terms of for example demonstration of power and status in the peer group. This does not make such behaviours any less undesirable, from the point of view of general welfare of young people and the positive environment of a school or other venue where children meet. It is well established that bullying can have many negative consequences, especially for the victims of course, but more widely for all involved (Arseneault, Bowes and Shakoor 2009).

Cyberbullying now takes up an appreciable fraction of all bullying in young people, and it has its own distinctive characteristics (Smith 2012). For example, it is primarily indirect rather than face-to-face, and may be anonymous; the perpetrator does not usually see the victim's reaction, at least in the short term; the breadth of the potential audience is increased; and it is difficult to escape from, as the victim may be sent messages to their mobile or computer, or access nasty website comments, wherever they are. Cyberbullying too has negative consequences, and these are often thought to be worse than for traditional bullying, due to the characteristics above. However this is not necessarily the case, and there is a lively debate about the importance of cyberbullying, its definition and its consequences (Bauman, Walker and Cross 2012).

This special issue on bullying and cyberbullying contains many new research findings relevant to the effects of bullying and cyberbullying. These are mainly cross-sectional studies, so it is most prudent to talk about emotional and behavioural correlates, although three studies present longitudinal data where more direct causal relations can be inferred. The collection is truly international, with data sets from 12 countries represented in the 15 articles, reflecting the widespread interest and concern about bullying and cyberbullying. The collection starts with five papers primarily on traditional forms of bullying, including two focussing on bullying in immigrant children, a relatively new but clearly important topic. Two papers then introduce the topic of cyberbullying, with new perspectives on the kinds of phenomena involved. The remaining eight papers examine correlates or consequences of cyberbullying, often with traditional bullying as a comparison.

Jennifer and Cowie, in the first article, used semi-structured interviews in two primary schools in England. Pictorial vignettes depicting a hypothetical story of peer bullying were employed, showing bully, victim, and follower characters. Pupils were asked about the moral emotions that characters might be feeling (as other), and then how they might feel in that situation (as self). Worry and shame were often attributed to the victim, and also to the follower, whether as other or as self. Interestingly, pride was often attributed to the bully as other, but again shame and worry to bully as self. The authors discuss the findings in relation to the role of peers in addressing school bullying, and school-based interventions to facilitate self-awareness and empathy in children.

Smith, Polenik, Nakasita and Jones report data from three primary schools in England. They used a questionnaire-based design, assessing social inclusion and both direct and indirect types of bullying behaviour to identify pupils involved in either direct, indirect, both or neither types of bullying. Measures of social competence and self-perception were obtained from both pupils and teachers. While all children involved in bullying others were more likely to be socially rejected, and those involved in both direct and indirect bullying were at greatest risk, the authors found that most associations were stronger for direct bullying; those who only bullied indirectly showed weaknesses in self-perception, but no teacher-rated problems. The implications for early identification of children at risk of becoming bullies are discussed.

Skrzypiec, Slee, Askell-Williams and Lawson worked with adolescents from three South Australian secondary schools, looking at the adjustment and mental health status of victims, bullies and bully-victims. Besides gender, they also took account of friendship status as a possibly important factor. They found that young people involved in bullying, and particularly bully-victims, had more difficulties, but that having good friends was a protective factor. Some gender differences were also found. Like the previous study, these authors used the Strengths and Difficulties Questionnaire (SDQ), and they too recommend the possible benefits of early identification of pupils in difficulty; as well as explicit teaching of strategies for promoting friendships, especially for victims.

The next two papers discuss the situation of immigrant children in relation to bullying and victimization; the acculturative stress model predicts that they will be more vulnerable in this respect. Fandrem, Strohmeier, and Jonsdottir report data from adolescents in a multicultural urban Norwegian secondary school, many from immigrant backgrounds. They looked carefully at the friendship groups in the 10 classes, using a procedure called social cognitive mapping, based on peer nominations of who is friends with whom; this enabled them to identify 42 peer groups, many being ethnically mixed. The number of victims was not related to the ethnic composition of these groups. However across the whole sample, victimization was experienced more by immigrant adolescents. Surprisingly, in this sample victimization was not correlated strongly with depressive symptoms (which were self-assessed).

In the second paper on this topic, Strohmeier and Dogan report data from adolescents aged 12 and 15 years in a large number of schools in Austria and Turkey. They compared levels of peer victimization, and emotional difficulties, in five groups: in Turkey, non-migrant Turks, and national migrants; and in Austria, non-migrant Austrians, and first generation and second generation international migrants from Turkey. Immigrant status was not clearly related to victimization, and in fact the non-migrant Austrian group had the highest victimization score. However national and first generation (but not second generation) international migrants had higher levels of depression and social anxiety and lower levels of self esteem compared to non-migrant Austrians. National and first generation international migrants who had high levels of social anxiety and depression also tended to have high levels of victimization; so the authors conclude that acculturative stress can be a risk factor for peer victimization.

The next two papers introduce aspects of cyberbullying in young people. Typologies of cyberbullying usually consider the medium used (e.g. text message, email, social networking site), or the content of the material (e.g. threat, denigration, embarrassing pictures).

However Pyżalski takes a novel approach by identifying the varied targets of cyber attacks, which, aside from classmates known offline, can include people known only from the Internet, celebrities, teachers, totally unknown individuals or whole groups of people. This typology was based on qualitative interviews, but the author then presents data from a large quantitative survey on Polish 15-year-olds, revealing a broad spectrum of targets of cyber aggression. Correlations of the extent of cyber attacks, and specifically cyberbullying, show associations with attitudes toward school, peer norms, negative relations in the family, norms concerning online behaviour at school/home, pro-aggressive beliefs, and level of self-esteem, with negative peer norms emerging as the strongest factor.

In a study in the Czech Republic, Ševčíková, Šmahel, and Otavová carried out interviews with 16 cyber-victimised participants aged 15 to 17 years. They were interested in how victims perceived these attacks and how harmful they were. Threats from an unknown online perpetrator led to greater feelings of harm than attacks from a known person from the real world. Other aspects such as collective perpetration, and onlookers being personally identifiable, increased perceptions of harm, as did cyberbullying being associated with traditional bullying. This small but detailed qualitative study suggests that the type and situational context of cyber attacks appears to influence how the victim perceives this and thus attempts to cope.

The remaining papers focus on the emotional and behavioural correlates of cyberbullying, often providing data for traditional bullying as a comparison. Schultze-Krumbholz, Jäkel, Schultze and Scheithauer report on data from five middle schools in Germany. They examined both internalising and externalising problems in relation to cyberbullying roles – cyberbullies, cybervictims, and cyberbully-victims compared to non-involved students – using both cross-sectional and longitudinal analyses. There were no significant differences in internalising problems, but externalising problems were higher in all three cyberbullying groups compared to those who were non-involved. The cross-sectional data showed some interesting different effects by gender for changes over time.

In another study in Germany, in four secondary schools, Wachs examined both traditional bullying and cyberbullying roles, focusing especially on moral disengagement in the perpetrators of bullying. As is commonly found, many students involved in cyberbullying were also involved in traditional bullying, but those involved in cyberbullying showed greater moral disengagement than those involved in traditional bullying. Wachs examined some other aspects, finding that feeling lonely and unpopular or friendless appeared to be risk factors for being a victim (traditional or cyber), whereas high satisfaction with school was a protective factor. The author discusses enhancement of empathy and the development of a positive school culture as important aspects for prevention and intervention.

In a study in three Israeli secondary schools, Olenik-Shemesh, Heiman and Eden examined the association between being a victim of cyberbullying or traditional bullying, and loneliness and depressive mood. Both kinds of victimization predicted loneliness (both emotional and social), but only cyber victimization was significantly linked to depressive mood. This study too points out the importance of developing adolescents' ability to establish close intimate relationships, and avoid both the feelings and actual experiences of loneliness, as protective factors against victimization of any kind.

Brighi, Guarini, Melotti, Galli and Genta report data from pupils drawn from 39 secondary schools in central Italy. They examined school climate, self-esteem (global, family and peer), and loneliness with parents and peers, in relation to three kinds of victimization: traditional direct, traditional indirect and cyber. Loneliness in relations with peers, and a negative perception of school climate, significantly predicted victimization. There were some age and gender effects, and although effects of cyber victimization were similar to those of traditional victimization, lower self-esteem in family relationships was a predictor of cyber victimization for males, while loneliness with parent was a predictor for females. This study points up the aspect of family involvement as another factor in tackling victimization.

Campbell, Spears, Slee, Butler and Kift analyse data from a large-scale study of pupils aged 9 to 19 years from 29 schools in three Australian states. They focus on comparing victims' perceptions of the harshness and impact of bullying by traditional and by cyber means. Their findings were intriguing; on the one hand, traditional victims felt that their experience was more harsh, cruel and impactful than cyber victims; but when the authors examined mental health correlates (using the SDQ and a depression scale), cyber victims reported more social difficulties and higher anxiety levels and depression than did traditional victims.

Machmutow, Perren, Sticca and Alsaker report findings from a longitudinal study of pupils in 12 Swiss schools. They examined depression in relation to both traditional and cyber victimization, together with coping. Both traditional and cyber victimization were associated with higher levels of depression, and cyber victimization predicted increases in depression by the second time point. Coping strategies rated as helpless were associated with more depression. Over time, support seeking from peers and family were associated with reduced depression, but assertive coping strategies with increased depression.

The study by Beckman, Hagquist and Hellström involved pupils from 16 secondary schools in Sweden. Both traditional and cyber bullies, victims and bully-victims were compared to non-involved pupils, as regards psychosomatic problems. Generally, the results show non-involved children to have the least problems, and bully-victims the most. No statistically significant differences in psychosomatic problems were found between cyberbullying and traditional bullying, either for victims, or bullies; both predicted greater psychosomatic problems, but neither more strongly than the other.

Finally, Lester, Cross and Shaw use some longitudinal data from pupils at 11 secondary schools in South Australia, to analyse the relationships between traditional bullying, cyberbullying and engagement in antisocial problem behaviours. Levels of traditional victimization and perpetration at the beginning of secondary school predicted levels of engagement in problem behaviours two years later; although cyberbullying also predicted engaging in problem behaviours, it did not represent an independent risk factor over and above levels of traditional victimization and perpetration. The authors suggest that it remains important to focus on interventions to reduce traditional bullying, even when cyberbullying is a concern.

Many of these studies indicate the complexity of examining the emotional and behavioural correlates of bullying and cyberbullying. We need to consider different types of bullying (at least, direct, indirect and cyber), different roles (at least, bully, victim and bully-victim), and different kinds of outcome (such as psychosomatic problems, self-esteem, friends and loneliness, school satisfaction, family relations). Assessments may come from self, peers, or more rarely teachers or parents. There may be age effects, gender effects, and cultural effects. Concurrent associations may not always be the same as those suggested by longitudinal trends. Some common themes emerge: bully and victim roles are usually associated with enhanced problems, with bully-victims often most at risk. Cyberbullying is associated with such problems, but not necessarily more so than traditional forms of bullying.

Interventions to reduce bullying have a history of some 30 years now, and have some success (Ttofi and Farrington 2011). Interventions to reduce cyberbullying can draw on these but are still being developed and evaluated. Hopefully the research studies here, and others available and to come, can suggest foci for intervention and help us to reduce the suffering that bullying brings to the lives of too many young people.

Acknowledgements

Much of the work for this special issue was facilitated by COST Action IS0801 on Cyberbullying https://sites.google.com/site/costis0801/

References

Arseneault, L., L. Bowes, and S. Shakoor. 2009. Bullying victimization in youths and mental health problems: 'Much ado about nothing?' *Psychological Medicine* 29: 1–13.

Bauman, S., J. Walker, and D. Cross (eds). 2012. *Principles of cyberbullying research: Definition, measures, and methods*. Phila, PA: Routledge.

Greene, M.B. 2006. Bullying in schools: A plea for a measure of human rights. *Journal of Social Issues* 62: 63–79.

Li, Q., D. Cross, and P.K. Smith (eds). 2012. *Cyberbullying in the global playground: Research from international perspectives*. Chichester: Wiley-Blackwell.

Smith, P.K. 2012. Cyberbullying and cyber aggression. In *Handbook of school violence and school safety: International research and practice*, ed. S.R. Jimerson, A.B. Nickerson, M.J. Mayer and M.J. Furlong, 93–103. New York: Routledge.

Ttofi, M.M. and D.P. Farrington. 2011. Effectiveness of school-based programs to reduce bullying: a systematic and meta-analytic review. *Journal of Experimental Criminology* 7: 27–56.

Listening to children's voices: moral emotional attributions in relation to primary school bullying

Dawn Jennifer[a] and Helen Cowie[b]

[a]*Research Unit, Business Affairs, Department for Communities and Social Inclusion, Adelaide, South Australia, Australia;* [b]*Faculty of Health and Medical Sciences, University of Surrey, Surrey, UK*

This study explored 10- and 11-year-old students' ($N = 64$) moral emotional attributions in relation to other and self in peer-to-peer bullying scenarios in primary school. Data were gathered using one-to-one semi-structured interviews facilitated by the use of a series of pictorial vignettes depicting a hypothetical story of peer bullying. The results demonstrated that worry and to a lesser extent shame were most often attributed to the other as victim character, indifference and pride to the other as bully character, and worry and shame to the other as follower character. Participants mostly attributed worry to self as victim, shame and worry to self as bully, and shame to self as follower. The findings are discussed in relation to the role of peers in addressing school bullying, such as through peer support. There are implications for school-based interventions to address bullying that facilitate self-awareness and empathy in children and young people as a means of addressing such behaviour.

Introduction

Research on general attitudes to peer-to-peer bullying suggest that the majority of children are opposed to such behaviour and supportive of victims (e.g. Boulton and Underwood 1992). Not only do children judge that it is morally wrong to hurt others or to treat others unfairly, they also perceive that aggression is wrong and harmful (Murray-Close, Crick, and Galotti 2006; Shaw and Wainryb 2006). In addition, children of all ages are likely to be critical of behaviours that target others' well-being (Shaw and Wainryb 2006). Nevertheless, substantial numbers of primary school children report being bullied, and bullying others, on a regular basis (Shaughnessy and Jennifer 2007). More worryingly, sadistic types of bullying have emerged as a subtype of aggression, suggesting that some children experience positive arousal from inflicting harm on another (Bosacki, Marini, and Dane 2006). Research into school bullying that focuses on the area of moral reasoning could have important implications for interventions that reduce and prevent such conduct (Menesini et al. 2003).

A few studies have investigated children's understanding of others' emotions in relation to peer-to-peer school bullying. In a cross-national study using pictorial vignettes, participants from Portugal and Spain, aged 9, 11 and 13 years, were interviewed regarding their emotional attributions to other and self as the bully and the victim characters (del Barrio et al. 2003). Participants attributed rejected (55%), sad (49%), and ashamed and afraid (13% each) to other as victim. Similar emotional attributions were made to self as victim. In terms of other as bully, happy (60%), pride (27%) and guilt (8%) were attributed. In contrast, almost half of the sample reported that they would feel guilt (45%) as the bully and, to a lesser extent, happiness (17%) and pride (11%).

These findings regarding bullies and moral development are supported by the results from another European study, which explored bullies', victims' and outsiders' feelings in relation to the task of putting themselves into the role of the bully in a bullying situation (Menesini et al. 2003). The study focused on emotions of moral responsibility (guilt and shame) and emotions of moral disengagement (indifference and pride). Compared with victims and outsiders, bullies attributed higher levels of moral disengagement emotions to the bully in the bullying scenario. Analysis of specific mechanisms of moral disengagement revealed that bullies possessed a main profile of egocentric reasoning. The authors suggest that, when putting themselves into the role of the bully, personal motives and the benefits of bullying behaviour were sufficient to justify negative and antisocial behaviours.

Using a set of pictorial vignettes, Ttofi and Farrington (2008) asked 10–12-year-olds questions about the emotions they would have felt, including anger, shame, remorse or guilt, if they were in the position of the child in the vignette. Two types of shaming – disintegrative shaming and integrative shaming – had different effects on the ways in which the children anticipated managing shame. Children who scored high on disintegrative shaming scored high on maladaptive forms of shame management. Disintegrative shaming relates to rejecting parenting styles, usually associated with the suppression of empathy. The authors acknowledge the difficulty involved in enhancing children's moral competence by working with emotions of shame and guilt, but they propose that the management of emotions and behaviour is closely bound to the social context and the quality of relationships, both in the family and within the peer group. This study confirms the role of school in promoting moral values through restorative practices and through the teaching of emotional literacy.

Since research evidence suggests that the social group context within which bullying takes place both promotes and sustains bullying behaviour (Salmivalli 2010), a major limitation of the previous research is the focus on emotional moral attributions to the bully, or the bullies as a homogeneous group, and the victim, to the exclusion of other individuals involved in bullying. It is important to give attention to the wider social group context that influences whether aggressive behaviour between group members will occur (DeRosier et al. 1994). For example, bystanders in the bullying context have been described as 'those who watch, avert their eyes, pretend not to notice, egg on protagonists, stand on the outskirts, and provide an audience' (Hazler 1996, 19). Research by Salmivalli et al. (1996) suggests that bystanders play a number of roles in the bullying episode from simply providing an audience to becoming actively involved in the interaction between the bully and the victim. Hazler (1996) observes that bystanders make up the majority in any given bullying situation, yet they receive the least research attention and their potential contribution to influence such situations goes largely unnoticed.

In terms of moral reasoning, Jones, Manstead, and Livingstone (2011), using a text-message bullying scenario with 10–11-year-olds, indicated the key role played by the group in shaping how children respond to bullying. They found that pride following a bullying episode was associated with affiliation with the bullying group and concluded that group identification influences the individual's response to a group-relevant event. Their findings indicate that children value the protection provided by affiliation with a dominant group of peers. This group affiliation plays a powerful role in whether members resist or support the aggressive intentions of others, also influences the group-based emotions of pride, shame and anger experienced as a consequence, and highlights the roles other than perpetrator and target that children play in the bullying process (Salmivalli 1999).

Therefore, the main aim of the present study was to explore children's emotional attributions and moral reasoning in relation to primary school bullying, and their understanding of the bullying relationship. Here we report the results concerning the nature of the relationship portrayed in the story, the moral emotional experiences attributed to characters in the story, and how children related to and empathised with the characters' emotional states.

Method

Design

One-to-one interviews were carried out using a semi-structured interview schedule devised to capture children's knowledge and reasoning about school bullying facilitated by the use of a series of pictorial vignettes depicting a hypothetical story of peer-to-peer bullying adapted from the Scripted-CArtoon Narrative of Bullying (SCAN) drawings (Almeida et al. 2001). Data were collected during 2003/04.

Participants

Letters were mailed to all primary and secondary school head teachers in a south-west London (UK) local authority inviting them to participate in the study. Following telephone conversations with several prospective schools, two primary schools agreed to participate. A principle of consent was adopted that required the active consent of the child and the passive consent of the adult (Thomas and O'Kane 1998). Head teachers sent a letter to parents seeking 'opt-in' consent for their child to be approached to participate. Following this, all students from year 6 were invited to participate in the study at an introduction session; all consented to take part (66 children). However, not all volunteers were available to participate owing to absence at the time of data collection; the final sample consisted of 64 participants, 30 males (47%) and 34 females (53%), aged 10–11 years.

Materials

The pictorial vignettes were adapted and modified for a UK sample from the SCAN drawings (Almeida et al. 2001) developed in Europe. The vignettes were redesigned by a young art student to reflect the UK sample in terms of primary school age, ethnic diversity and primary school culture (i.e. the wearing of school uniform). The intention of the story illustrated by the drawings was to convey the idea of an imbalance of power and repeated aggressive behaviours such that the interpretation of the story was in terms of intentional and hurtful actions, rather than isolated or irregular events. The set of 14 A4-size drawings included one neutral vignette, followed by nine vignettes (depicting mean and unpleasant behaviours) performed by one individual or by a group of peers (see Figure 1 for an example). A short caption describing the content of the vignette was included with each (e.g. 'She sees the other children playing a game and wants to join in'; see Table 1 for a summary). The remaining four vignettes completed the set of drawings, each representing a different outcome to the story in terms of distinct roles taken by adults and peers (optimistic: the children all play together; pessimistic: the victim remains alone; peer social

Figure 1. An example of one of the pictorial vignettes (female version).

Table 1. Content of the 10 pictorial vignettes.

Behaviour	Caption
1. Neutral	The girl is new to the school and it's her first day.
2. Social exclusion	She sees the other children playing a game and wants to join them.
3. Teasing	She is wearing a different uniform and the other children start teasing her about it.
4. Physical obstruction	The school day is over and when she is leaving the classroom she gets blocked by a classmate.
5. Attack on personal possessions	During playtime the other children get together and grab her schoolbag and start to pull out her books.
6. Real damage to personal possessions	She gets to her table and finds her book torn and notices one of her classmates walking away holding a pair of scissors.
7. Group physical attack	On the way to the classroom she gets pushed over by the other children and falls down. Her books are all over the floor, but the others walk away.
8. Coercion	The other children get together and hold out a cigarette, telling her to smoke.
9. Blackmail	The children grab her and threaten to harm her if she doesn't steal money from another child.
10. Social isolation	She stands alone behind a tree, away from the playground and from the other children.

support: the victim seeks the support of a peer; and adult social support: the victim seeks the support of an adult). A masculine and a feminine version of the same story were used for males and females, respectively. Where necessary, captions were re-written to address anomalies arising from translation into English, and to incorporate idiomatic vocabulary; for example, in vignette 5, 'recess' was changed to 'playtime'; and in vignette 7, 'ground' was changed to 'floor'.

To assess the modifications to the vignettes, pre-test interviews were carried out with 12 participants from the main sample. The majority of these participants (82%) described the nature of the relationship as bullying. The remaining 18% described the behaviours as aggression, without explicitly mentioning bullying. This was the intended outcome and supported the effectiveness of vignettes to study children's constructions of bullying in school (Ojala and Nesdale 2004). The data from the pre-test interviews were analysed along with the data from the main study.

During presentation of the vignettes, participants were interviewed using a semi-structured interview schedule devised to capture children's knowledge and reasoning about bullying in school (del Barrio et al. 2003). This included questions about narrative and causal attributions (e.g. 'After looking carefully at the drawings, what would you say is happening in the story, from the beginning to the end?'; 'What do you think is happening with this girl/boy? [pointing to one character in two or three different drawings, then another character, etc.]); moral emotional attributions (worry, shame, indifference, pride) to the characters in the story (e.g. 'Can anyone in this story feel ashamed? Why?'); and moral emotional attributions to self in the role of the characters (e.g. 'And if you were one of these boys/girls could you also feel ashamed? [pointing to the characters in turn]. Why?'). Interview questions were re-written to incorporate idiomatic vocabulary where necessary. In addition, in consideration of bullying from a wider social group context, questions relating to the role of characters other than the bully and the victim were included in the interview schedule. The full interview schedule can be obtained from the first author on request.

Procedure

Interviews were conducted during lesson time by the first author, each lasting approximately 20 minutes. Each interview commenced with standardised instructions regarding the general nature of the interview, confidentiality, anonymity and the right to withdraw, and ended with a debriefing, including resources for outside support should the need arise. With the agreement of all participants, audio tape recordings were collected for later transcription.

The first 10 drawings, which conveyed temporal and space continuity for the various mean and unpleasant behaviours, were laid out on a table one by one, in ascending order (see Table 1). The researcher did not enter into discussion with participants regarding the script headings. If any doubts were verbalised by the participant the researcher avoided personal interpretation; rather, children were probed about what they thought might be happening in the particular drawing. At no point did the interviewer introduce the terms 'bullying', 'aggression', 'victim', 'bully/ies' or 'follower'. Following presentation of the drawings, participants were interviewed using the semi-structured interview schedule. The final stage of the interview required the presentation of the four story outcomes, which were displayed in a randomised order to control for order of presentation effects.

Data analysis

Methods of data analysis and representation were adopted that would respect children's rights to freedom of participation and freedom of expression (UN 1989), and that would ensure that the children's voices were heard and represented (Mauthner and Doucet 1998). Thus, audio tape recordings were transcribed verbatim and analysis of the interview transcripts was carried out using a qualitative approach to content analysis as described by Millward (2000) and Woods, Priest, and Roberts (2002). A coding system was derived from the interview schedule with additional conceptual codes arising from a closer inspection of each interview transcript (Millward 2000). Previously coded data were revisited periodically to check the stability of the coding over time (Cavanagh 1997).

To address concerns regarding researcher subjectivity, and in order that the process of research might be tracked (McKechnie 2002), a research journal was maintained throughout the study. Awareness of events during data collection, and of researcher feelings, insights and interpretations, together with decisions regarding methodology, data analysis and ethical dilemmas (Miles and Huberman 1994), were recorded to facilitate consideration of the phenomenon under study, as well as the ways in which researcher assumptions and behaviour might have impacted on the investigation. These issues were discussed regularly by the two authors.

Results

The majority of participants (89%) described the nature of the relationship depicted in the vignettes as bullying. They clearly identified a victim role and a group of bullies with a dominant leader. They also perceived a role, which primarily reflected their perception of a tentative, yet supportive, character in the bullying process, variously constructed as a 'follower', 'tagger' and 'back-up bully' and henceforward referred to as 'follower'.

Moral emotional attributions to the victim character

The victim character was most often characterised by worry. A major theme that emerged for this attribution related to the notion of fear of threat or harm from the bullies: 'Because she knows that every day something horrible is going to happen' (female). Another key theme that emerged was in terms of the victim's anticipation of future danger or harm from the bullies, with the most common concern related to the continuation and escalation of the bullying: 'Um, I think he feels worried, the one who's getting bullied . . . 'cos he's not sure at any stage if they're gonna really, really beat him up, or like they're going to spoil his life at school' (male).

The victim character was also characterised, to a lesser extent, by shame, more usually by males. According to participants' responses, the main reasons for this attribution were the victim's actual experience of being bullied and the notion that the victim had offended the bullies (broken up the bully group, done something bad to the bullies, hurt the bullies' feelings, said something wrong to the bullies). Feeling humiliated was cited as another reason for attributing shame to the victim, usually in terms of being laughed at or for falling over. Shame was also attributed to the victim in terms of difference, usually due to his or her appearance.

Moral emotional attributions to self as the victim character

Self in the role of victim was most often characterised by worry, with participants' main explanation for this attribution in terms of fear of harm. Anticipation of future harm or danger was also mentioned when taking the role of the victim, in terms of the continuation of the bullying and anticipation of what might happen next. A number of participants expressed concern that the bullying might get worse.

Moral emotional attributions to the bully character

Pride was commonly attributed to the bully character, with engagement in bullying the victim cited as the main reason. For example, one girl reasoned: 'Those three might be feeling proud . . . 'cos they're doing something to someone else'. This theme was further illustrated by responses from some participants who suggested that being mean or hurtful or upsetting the victim was a reason to feel proud. One girl explained: 'Because she gets pleasure, I think, out of doing this to people, it's just some people get pleasure out of hurting other people'. A number of responses suggested that the bullies were feeling proud for being the leader of the bully group. For example, one boy stated: 'Because he's leading the whole organisation' and a female participant said: 'I think the blonde haired girl's feeling proud because she's got a little gang around her'. Feeling proud was also attributed to the bullies in terms of feeling 'big', 'cool' and 'hard'; for example, one boy reasoned that the blond boy felt proud: 'Because he's done most of the stuff and he thinks that doing that is going to make him all cool and Mr Nice Guy'. Not caring was also cited as a reason for the bully to feel proud.

Indifference was also commonly attributed to the bully character, with participants mentioning this character's role as the bully and engagement in bullying the victim as the main reason for their attribution. For example, one girl reasoned: 'Because they're not the ones that are, like, being bullied, like, they're the ones that are the bullies'. A number of responses suggested that the bullies were making the victim do things, hinting at a power imbalance. For example, one boy said, 'Because they don't really care, they're just trying to vandalise everything he has and annoy him and try to make him do bad things and they might even be trying to get him into trouble'. This theme was further illustrated by another boy who articulated his response in terms of a power imbalance: 'Because like they're in control . . . like bullying him, yeah, and they realise that he's quite weak and they gang up on him and they can, like, do whatever they want'.

Feeling indifferent was also attributed to the bullies in terms of their familiarity with bullying others, for example, one boy said, 'Because he's the one probably, like, in the story, like, the best at doing it because he's done it so many times before'. This notion was further demonstrated by a response from a girl who replied, 'Because she's the one that's doing it and people who usually get into the habit of doing things like this they just think it's alright to do it 'cos they're powerful and they're popular and they just think it's alright to do stuff like this to them'. This response also alludes to the perception that popularity permits the opportunity to bully others.

A number of responses were constructed in terms of the bully feeling indifferent because he or she felt 'big' or 'cool' or was telling the other two what to do because he or she was the leader of the gang. Furthermore, participants attributed feeling indifferent to the bully in terms of feeling confident that there would not be any repercussions to the bully's behaviour. For example, one girl said, 'they know that they won't get in trouble'. One male said, ''Cos he thinks that he can get away with it and blame it on him, he's got someone to blame'.

Moral emotional attributions to self as the bully character

In contrast, shame was most commonly attributed to self in the role of bully, typically in terms of the bullying behaviours perpetrated against the victim. A number of participants mentioned that they would feel ashamed after the event.

To a lesser extent, worry was attributed to self in the role of bully, the main reason being for fear of the consequences of bullying, that is, the victim would either tell someone or they would 'get caught' and 'get into trouble' ('expulsion', 'exclusion', 'suspension'). A number of participants were concerned that, as a consequence of engaging in bullying behaviours, self in the role of bully would themselves be bullied either by the victim's siblings or by another group.

Moral emotional attributions to the follower character

Participants characterised the follower as someone who 'tags along with' the bullies, someone who is 'not really doing that much', someone who is 'following them, doing nothing' or someone 'who's trying to fit in'. Accordingly, worry was attributed to the follower in terms of this character not being fully engaged in the bullying. Whether this indicated that participants were worried for the follower for not playing a bigger part in the bullying episode or for only playing a small part was unclear. For example, one girl said, ''Cos they're not really doing anything . . . because they might not be, like, into bullying her . . . they might be the ones who are feeling sorry for her'. On the other hand, another girl suggested: 'I think that little one there is worried because she's not really doing much, she's just laughing and stuff, and I think that she thinks, like, I'm not going to really get involved in it that much, I'm just going to laugh about it'.

The follower character was also characterised by shame, with the main reason given for this attribution being this character's ambivalence regarding their participation in the bullying. Primarily, shame was attributed to the follower in terms of being involved but not really wanting to be involved. For example, one girl said, 'Because, like, she doesn't really want to be a bully or anything like that'. Additionally, in terms of questioning his or her part in the bullying, one girl said, ''Cos she's just looking away she might think in her head I shouldn't have done that, I shouldn't have done that to the new girl'. Other reasons cited included participating in the bullying while knowing that such behaviour was wrong. For example, one girl said: 'Because she knows that they shouldn't be doing it'.

A number of female participants reasoned that their engagement in bullying was as a form of protection against becoming the next victim. As one girl said, 'She's feeling a bit ashamed that she has to do this but she still wants to be safe because she knows she won't get bullied if she can stay best friends with the bullies'. Less specifically, shame was attributed to the follower for being involved with the bully group; for example, one girl stated, 'Yeah, she's been looking at what they're doing and feeling ashamed that she ever joined the gang'. A number of participants suggested that the follower knew what it was like for the victim because they had themselves experienced bullying, for example, one girl suggested, 'Because she might have been bullied before and she can know what it feels like 'cos she wears glasses'.

Moral emotional attributions to self as the follower character

In taking the role of the follower, participants overwhelmingly cited ambivalence regarding this character's participation in the bullying as the main reason. Primarily, responses were framed in terms of self in the role of follower feeling ashamed for being coerced into participating, or assisting against their better judgement. For example, one boy said: ''Cos the blond one's like telling me what to do and sometimes them bullies, like, they are all, like, if the head one says "yeah I'm gonna beat you up" and then the other two goes "yeah, yeah, we're going to beat you up" they all agree with what he says'. A number of participants suggested that they would feel ashamed because they would not really want to participate in the bullying. For example, one boy replied, 'Because, like, I wouldn't want to, I would, like, I don't want to bully them, these guys are pushing me into bullying'. Others explained that they would feel ashamed for not helping the victim; for example, one boy suggested: 'Because whatever you do you have to help others'. Some participants questioned their role in the bullying; for example, one female replied: 'Because I would be thinking to myself that why am I trying to impress the other children, I should be running my own life, welcoming the new girl, not being mean to her'.

Discussion

In attributing moral emotions to the hypothetical protagonists in the pictorial vignettes, the victim character was most often characterised by worry and to a lesser extent shame; the bully character by pride and indifference; and the follower character by worry and shame. In stepping into the role of each of the characters in the hypothetical story, participants mostly cited worry in taking the role of the victim and shame in taking the role of the follower, attributions similar to those attributed to the hypothetical victim and follower. On the other hand, when stepping into the role of the bully, participants attributed shame and worry to the self, attributions that contrasted with the emotions of pride and indifference previously ascribed to the hypothetical bully in the story.

That participants attributed a positive emotion such as pride to the bully character is consistent with previous research (del Barrio et al. 2003). This might suggest recognition that the expression of pride in a bullying situation brings social success for the bullies in terms of personal and social gains and advantages and an awareness of a lack of consideration of the consequences for the victims (Jones, Manstead, and Livingstone 2011; Menesini et al. 2003).

The attribution of negative emotions (worry, shame) to the victim character is also consistent with previous research (del Barrio et al. 2003), with participants perceiving the bullying behaviours depicted to be threatening and harmful. This resonates with Olweus' (1994) definition of bullying in terms of repetition and imbalance of power. The attribution of worry to the victim suggests that participants saw a power imbalance between the victim and the bullies and perceived the physical, emotional or social well-being of the victim to be under threat and/or attack, such that the victim was perceived to be unable to defend him- or herself.

The characterisation of the follower as worried and ashamed is illuminating. This has not been previously documented and the present findings enhance knowledge regarding children's understandings of others' moral emotions that go beyond the bully/victim dyad to include the wider social group within which bullying takes place. While participants' responses demonstrate the follower's concern for the victim (feeling sorry, worrying about the continuation of the bullying, worrying about the intensity of the bullying), their responses also suggest an awareness that the follower feared the personal consequences of their bullying behaviour more than they feared the consequences of their actions on the victim (Menesini et al. 2003). Indeed, some of the participants in this study perceived the follower's behaviour to be justified, because it offered protection against becoming the next victim, suggesting that such behaviour was deemed personally and socially acceptable through a process of moral disengagement, that is, in terms of personal gain (Bandura 1999). Conversely, some participants' citing of empathic reasons for attributing worry to the follower suggests an attitude of moral responsibility toward the victim (Menesini et al. 2003).

When participants were asked whether they could feel worried, ashamed, indifferent or proud if they were one of the characters in the hypothetical story, they mostly cited worry in taking the role of the victim, shame and to a lesser extent worry in taking the role of the bully, and shame in taking the role of the follower. When taking the role of the victim and the follower, participants' self attributions were similar to those for a hypothetical victim and a hypothetical follower; this suggests that they share these characters' feelings, that is, they empathise with the emotional states of both the victim and the follower in the story (Eisenberg 2000). On the other hand, when stepping into the role of the bully, participants attributed shame and worry to the self, attributions that contrast with the emotions of moral disengagement (pride, indifference) ascribed to the hypothetical bully. This finding concurs with previous research that has shown that children attribute more negative emotions to the self as aggressor than to a hypothetical aggressor (del Barrio et al. 2003; Keller et al. 2003). This suggests that participants were able to differentiate themselves from the hypothetical bully and reject the bully's moral disengagement regarding the bullying behaviours (Keller et al. 2003).

The present study offers ideas for strategies and policies to address the issue of bullying in real-life situations. Boulton et al. (1999) found that having at least one good friend at school is a fundamental resource. It can be a very effective strategy if the bullied pupil starts a process of making new friends in order to cope with bullying. Our participants indicated a capacity to feel empathy for the victim in a range of bullying scenes. The school can facilitate this process by establishing a system of buddying to offer emotional support to vulnerable pupils and to give the befrienders the opportunity to find practical ways to demonstrate the empathy for the victim that they might otherwise feel unable to express.

At a wider level, peer support systems have been shown to heighten awareness of the impact of bullying on individuals' emotions and to foster a sense of moral responsibility in the whole school (Cowie 2011). Cowie and Smith (2010) demonstrate how systems of peer support not only help individuals to deal with the emotional impact of rejection and social exclusion at the hands of peers but also create a more positive ethos in the school community as a whole. They identify evidence-based strategies, including training programmes in active listening, peer mediation and befriending, to address emotions of distress, anger and fear. The capacity of peer supporters to listen and learn facilitates the recognition and effective management of emotions and is germane to the development of a caring school community.

Lessons on challenging group norms that condone abusive behaviour could directly address the emotions of bullies, followers and bystanders by, for example, exploring the reasons why some children might feel pride in bullying others or being associated with perpetrators' actions. Working with classroom groups may be a strong part of the solution by indicating that members of the peer group can work collectively to overcome bullying and to buffer its negative effects on the emotions and sense of moral engagement in the school community. By enabling children to explore emotions aroused by bullying situations they can be given the opportunity to reflect on how these feelings arise, where the origins of guilt and shame are situated and how collectively they can work to resist aggressive behaviour that targets vulnerable peers. Activities that use narrative approaches to raise awareness about bullying (Cowie and Jennifer 2008), for example, would provide a foundation for emotional literacy in the whole school grounded in real-life concerns of the children themselves.

Finally, our research indicates the importance of working with peer group relationships as a fundamental way of addressing the issue of bullying. The findings support the view that members of the peer group may play a role in the development of bullying behaviour. This affirms the need for schools to establish a whole-school approach with a range of systems and interventions in place for tackling all forms of bullying and social exclusion. This suggests that action against bullying should be part of a much wider concern within the school to foster self-awareness and understanding of group processes within an emotionally literate community. Learning to regulate emotions and navigate relationships is an essential developmental task if children and young people are to cope with the complex array of situations, some very stressful, that they will inevitably encounter in their lives.

There were a number of limitations with the use of pictorial vignettes as a means of facilitating one-to-one interviews. In the first instance, participants' responses to the interview questions were about how they believed they would feel or act in a hypothetical bullying situation and, as such, may not have accurately reflected how they would behave in actuality (Barter and Renold 2000; Schoenberg and Ravdal 2000). In this study, therefore, participants' responses can only be considered as representative of how they might behave or feel in an actual bullying situation. Furthermore, it should be borne in mind that participants may have presented social desirable responses about, for example, self as bully, or responses that reflected their school's ethos and anti-bullying work, in an attempt to appear prosocial in front of the researcher.

Associated with the issue of pictorial vignettes versus real-life bullying experiences was the portrayal of bullying behaviours and bullying scenarios in the hypothetical story. The pictorial vignettes used depicted a range of types of bullying behaviours including direct physical, direct verbal and indirect verbal bullying behaviours, with same-gender versions of the story presented to participants. Nevertheless, the content of the pictorial vignettes was problematic for a number of reasons. First, while a masculine and a feminine version of the hypothetical story were used, by intention and design, the pictorial vignettes did not provide for the notion of mixed gender bullying identified in the literature. Shaughnessy and Jennifer (2007) found that whereas girls rarely bullied boys, girls experienced bullying from both boys and girls. Therefore, future research may want to take into account scenarios depicting mixed gender bullying. In addition, the types of bullying behaviours portrayed in the pictorial vignettes did not include cyberbullying. Future research might consider featuring pictorial vignettes that illustrate cyberbullying, such as through the use of mobile phones and the Internet.

The employment of a semi-structured interview schedule is worthy of comment. While the use of a semi-structured interview enables the modification, omission or addition of questions according to what the interviewer considers appropriate in a given interview situation, such an approach entails the relative control of the researcher over the whole process (Robson 2002). On reflection, it could be argued that one of the primary limitations of employing a semi-structured interview schedule was that the researcher–participant interaction might have been influenced by the school context in terms of the adult–child discourse patterns established in the classroom (Robinson and Kellett 2004). For example, schoolchildren are used to teachers and other adults initiating a discussion or conversation, often with a question, in which they are expected to provide a response, followed by feedback from the adult (Westcott and Littleton 2005). Thus, when interacting with an adult researcher in the school context, participants in the present study might have had an expectation of how to respond to an interview situation based on their prior experience in the classroom. Future research may consider employing a less structured interview format to facilitate a shared and co-constructed process, through which children could create their accounts regarding school bullying actively and meaningfully (Westcott and Littleton 2005). Actively involving children in the design and implementation of such research as co-researchers or peer researchers may help to remove such contextual expectations.

In conclusion, while this paper makes no claims to generalisability to wider populations, nevertheless, this study allowed for in-depth exploration of moral emotional attributions in relation to primary school bullying from the child's perspective. The results generally concur with previous research, supporting the notion of participant roles in the bullying process. In addition, the findings regarding moral attributions to the follower role are novel and suggest opportunities for future research. The findings also suggest implications for school-based interventions to address bullying. It may be prudent for interventions to focus on fostering emotionally healthy interpersonal relationships that include components such as understanding moral values, understanding emotional states and strategies for building empathy. Furthermore, it is apparent that researchers and practitioners need to take into account the perspectives of the children themselves if anti-bullying work is to be effective.

Acknowledgements

The authors would like to thank the children and schools for taking part in this study, the reviewers for their constructive feedback on earlier drafts of this paper, and A. Almeida for kindly allowing the use of the SCAN.

References

Almeida, A., C. del Barrio, M. Marques, H. Gutiérrez, and K. van der Meulen. 2001. A script-cartoon narrative of bullying in children and adolescents: A research tool to assess cognitions, emotions and coping strategies in bullying situations. In *Prevention and control of aggression and the impact on its victims*, ed. M. Martinez, 161–8. New York: Kluwer Academic/Plenum Publishers.

Bandura, A. 1999. Moral disengagement in the perpetration of inhumanities. *Personality and Social Psychology* 3: 193–209.

del Barrio, C., A. Almeida, K. van der Meulen, Á. Barrios, and H. Gutiérrez. 2003. Representaciones acerca del maltrato entre iguales, atribuciones emocionales y percepción de estrategias de cambio a partir de un instrumento narrativo: *SCAN*-Bullying. *Infancia y Aprendizaje* 26: 63–78.

Barter, C., and E. Renold. 1999. The use of vignettes in qualitative research. *Social Research Update* 25. http://sru.soc.surrey.ac.uk/SRU25.html (accessed December, 15, 2011).

Bosacki, S.L., Z.A. Marini, and A.V. Dane. 2006. Voices from the classroom: Pictorial and narrative representations of children's bullying experiences. *Journal of Moral Education* 35: 231–45.

Boulton, M.J., M. Trueman, C. Chau, C. Whitehand, and K. Amatya. 1999. Concurrent and longitudinal links between friendship and peer victimization: Implications for befriending interventions. *Journal of Adolescence* 22: 461–6.

Boulton, M.J., and K. Underwood. 1992. Bully/victim problems among middle school children. *British Journal of Educational Psychology* 62: 73–87.

Cavanagh, R. 1997. Content analysis: Concepts, methods and applications. *Nurse Research* 4, no. 3: 5–16.

Cowie, H. 2011. Peer support an intervention to counteract school bullying: Listen to the children. *Children and Society* 25: 287–92.

Cowie, H., and Jennifer, D. 2008. *New perspectives on bullying*. London: Open University Press.

Cowie, H., and P.K. Smith. 2010. Peer support as a means of improving school safety and reducing bullying and violence. In *Handbook of youth prevention science*, ed. B. Doll, W. Pfohl and J. Yoon, 179–95. New York: Routledge.

DeRosier, M.E., A.H.N. Cillessen, J.D. Coie, and K.A. Dodge. 1994. Group social context and children's aggressive behaviour. *Child Development* 65: 1068–79.

Eisenberg, N. 2000. Emotion, regulation, and moral development. *Annual Review of Psychology* 51: 665–97.

Hazler, R.J. 1996. Bystanders: An overlooked factor in peer on peer abuse. *Journal for the Professional Counselor* 11, no. 2: 11–21.

Jones, S.E., A.S.R. Manstead, and A.G. Livingstone. 2011. Ganging up or sticking together? Group processes and children's responses to text-message bullying. *British Journal of Psychology* 102: 71–96.

Keller, M., O. Lourenço, T. Malti, and H. Saalbach. 2003. The multifaceted phenomenon of 'happy victimizers': A cross-cultural comparison of moral emotions. *British Journal of Developmental Psychology* 21: 1–18.

Mauthner, N., and A. Doucet. 1998. Reflections on a voice-centred relational method: Analysing maternal and domestic voices. In *Feminist dilemmas in qualitative research: Public knowledge and private lives*, ed. J. Ribbens and R. Edwards, 117–46. London: Sage.

McKechnie, J. 2002. Children's voices and researching childhood. In *Children, welfare and the state*, ed. B. Goldson, M. Lavalette and J. McKechnie, 42–58. London: Sage.

Menesini, E., V. Sanchez, A. Fonzi, R. Ortega, A. Costabile, and G. Lo Feudo. 2003. Moral emotions and bullying: A cross-national comparison of differences between bullies, victims and outsiders. *Aggressive Behavior* 29: 515–30.

Miles, M.B., and M. Huberman. 1994. *Qualitative data analysis*. London: Sage.

Millward, L. 2000. Focus groups. In *Research methods in psychology*, ed. G.M. Breakwell, S. Hammond and C. Fife-Schaw, 303–24. London: Sage.

Murray-Close, D., N.R. Crick, and K.M. Galotti. 2006. Children's moral reasoning regarding physical and relational aggression. *Social Development* 15: 345–72.

Ojala, K., and D. Nesdale. 2004. Bullying and social identity: The effects of group norms and distinctiveness threat on attitudes towards bullying. *British Journal of Developmental Psychology* 22: 19–35.

Olweus, D. 1994. Annotation: Bullying at school: Basic facts and effects of a school based intervention program. *Journal of Child Psychology and Psychiatry* 35: 1171–90.

Robinson, C., and M. Kellett. 2004. Power. In *Doing research with children and young people*, ed. S. Fraser, V. Lewis, S. Ding, M. Kellett and C. Robinson, 81–96. London: Sage.

Robson, C. 2002. *Real world research*. 2nd ed. Oxford: Blackwell.

Salmivalli, C. 1999. Participant role approach to school bullying: Implications for interventions. *Journal of Adolescence* 22: 453–9.

Salmivalli, C. 2010. Bullying and the peer group: A review. *Aggression and Violent Behavior* 15: 112–20.

Salmivalli, C., K. Lagerspetz, K. Björkqvist, K. Österman, and A. Kaukiainen. 1996. Bullying as a group process: Participant roles and their relations to social status within the group. *Aggressive Behavior* 22: 1–15.

Schoenberg, N.E., and H. Ravdal. 2000. Using vignettes in awareness and attitudinal research. *International Journal of Social Research Methodology* 3: 63–74.

Shaughnessy, J., and D. Jennifer. 2007. *Mapping the statistics: Moving towards a shared understanding of the scale and nature of bullying and violence in schools across Birmingham LEA*. Roehampton University, Froebel College.

Shaw, L.D., and C. Wainryb. 2006. When victims don't cry: Children's understandings of victimization, compliance, and subversion. *Child Development* 77: 1050–62.

Thomas, N., and C. O'Kane. 1998. The ethics of participatory research with children. *Children and Society* 12: 336–48.

Ttofi, M.M., and D.P. Farrington. 2008. Reintegrative shaming theory, moral emotions and bullying. *Aggressive Behavior* 34: 352–68.

United Nations. 1989. *Convention on the rights of the child*. Geneva, Switzerland: UN. www.unicef.org/crc

Westcott, H.L., and K.S. Littleton. 2005. Exploring meaning in interviews with children. In *Researching children's experience: Approaches and methods*, ed. S. Greene and D. Hogan, 141–57. London: Sage.

Woods, L., H. Priest, and R. Roberts. 2002. An overview of three different approaches to the interpretation of qualitative data. Part 2: Practical illustrations. *Nurse Researcher* 10, no. 2: 43–51.

Profiling social, emotional and behavioural difficulties of children involved in direct and indirect bullying behaviours

H. Smith[a], K. Polenik[a], S. Nakasita[b] and A. P. Jones[a]

[a] *Unit for School and Family Studies, Department of Psychology, Goldsmiths, University of London, London, UK;* [b] *Psychology and Language Sciences, University College London, London, UK*

Being involved in bullying places a child at risk of poor psychosocial and educational outcomes. This study aimed to examine the profile of behavioural, emotional and social functioning for two subtypes of bullying: direct and indirect (relational). Pupils aged between 7 and 11 years completed sociometric measures of social inclusion and bullying behaviour to identify 192 pupils considered to be involved in either direct or indirect, both or neither type of bullying. These pupils and their teachers completed a battery of assessments relating to behaviour, social competence and self-perception. All bully groups experienced similar levels of significant social rejection. Direct and both groups showed the greatest number of behavioural, emotional and social difficulties, while the indirect group showed weaknesses in self-perception, but no teacher-rated problems. Understanding the behavioural, emotional and social correlates of bullying is of particular importance for early identification of children at risk of becoming bullies and for developing targeted interventions.

Introduction

Bullying has been defined as a subset of aggressive behaviour which involves intentional harm that is repeated over time, and where there is an imbalance of power between the bully and the victim (Rigby and Smith 2011). Some researchers have argued for the presence of two particular subtypes of bullying behaviour: direct (comprising physical and verbal aggression) and indirect (e.g. Scheithauer et al. 2006). While direct bullying is defined as involving face-to-face physical and verbal aggression, indirect bullying is more covert in nature and may occur via a third person (e.g. spreading malicious rumours, purposefully isolating others from social situations). The effects of bullying on its victims have been comprehensively researched (Hemphill et al. 2011; Jaana, Yueyan, and Guadelope 2011; Knack, Jensen-Campbell, and Baum 2011; Løhre et al. 2011) and bullying behaviour itself has also been found to be associated with a range of difficulties in children and adolescents; for example, conduct disorder, oppositional defiant disorder, attention deficit hyperactivity disorder (ADHD) and passive-aggressive personality disorder (Coolidge, DenBoer, and Segal 2003).

Children who bully at school have also been reported to have increased conduct problems and hyperactivity symptoms on the Strengths and Difficulties Questionnaire (SDQ; Goodman 1997) (e.g. Gini 2008; Viding et al. 2009; Wolke et al. 2000). However, as in much of the bullying literature, many studies have considered bullying as a single entity, without considering possible different outcomes for different subtypes of bullying behaviour. Wolke et al. (2000) examined direct and relational/indirect subtypes of bullying in almost 2000 British students aged between 6 and 9 years. Children who reported themselves as direct bullies had statistically greater scores on the total difficulties scale of the SDQ than did relational bullies. This group, and the group of children who took part in both direct and indirect bullying, also had greater conduct problems, hyperactivity symptoms and peer problems than relational bullies and children who did not bully. The finding that differences exist between these different subtypes of bullying behaviours suggests that these subtypes should be examined separately in future research.

Children who bully have been found to be more aggressive in terms of both reactive and proactive aggression compared to children who do not bully. Comparison children, including victims of bullying, appear to only show reactive aggression (Camodeca and Goossens 2005; Salmivalli and Nieminen 2002). Reactive aggression is defined as a defensive response to provocation, whereas proactive aggression is deliberate and provocative and may involve some pleasure or satisfaction (Crick and Dodge 1996). Although these studies compared bullies to victims and children who are both bullies and victims, direct and indirect bullying subtypes were not considered. As differences have previously been found between direct and indirect bullies in terms of behavioural difficulties on the SDQ, differences may also exist between these bullying subtypes for incidences of proactive and reactive aggression.

Children involved in bullying have also been reported to show greater levels of emotional difficulties. In particular, these individuals have been reported to show increased rates of depression, self-harm, suicide and suicidal ideation (Barker et al. 2008; Coolidge, DenBoer, and Segal 2003; Klomek et al. 2009; Salmon, James, and Smith 1998; Seals and Young 2003). As children's behavioural difficulties have been shown to differ between direct and indirect bullies, emotional difficulties related to different bullying subtypes also need to be explored.

Findings have been mixed with regard to the self-perceptions and self-esteem of children who bully. Using a measure of self-perception, Austin and Joseph (1996) reported that lower self-perception scores were associated with pupils in middle childhood who reported themselves to be bully–victims. However, those children in the 'bully-only' group did not differ from non-bully comparison pupils. Seals and Young (2003) reported no statistically significant differences in self-esteem of children who bully and children who do not, while others have reported those who bully to have lower self-esteem (Coolidge, DenBoer, and Segal 2003; O'Moore and Kirkham 2001). Using peer reports and exploring different subtypes of self-esteem, Salmivalli et al. (1999) found that young people who bully tend to be characterised by a type of self-esteem known as 'defensive egotism', a term used to describe individuals who have a grandiose and self-enhancing attitude and who are defensive in response to criticism. This was not the same as 'low self-esteem', but rather a group of young people whose sense of self appears sensitive to criticism.

In addition to the behavioural and emotional difficulties associated with bullying, associations have been found between school bullying and social functioning. Children who bully have been shown to have lower peer acceptance and greater peer rejection than those not involved in bullying behaviour (Dijkstra, Lindenberg, and Veenstra 2008). Furthermore, Viding et al. (2009) found that children who bully had increased peer problems and lower prosocial behaviour scores on the SDQ. However, it may be the case that the association between social rejection and bullying should be considered from a developmental perspective. During adolescence, some research has reported that those who bully do not fare less well than their peers on measures of popularity (Caravita, DiBlasio, and Salmivalli 2009). The nature of any social deficit that may play a role in bullying behaviours remains unclear, and two main theories have been postulated.

One theory core to our understanding of bullying behaviour is the Social Deficit Model (Crick and Dodge 1996). This suggests that children who bully lack social perspective-taking skills and are unable to form an accurate perception of the intentions and motivations of others. However, Sutton, Smith, and Swettenham (1999a) argue that this view relies on evidence from aggressive children or those with conduct disorders, rather than direct studies of bullying behaviour. They propose an opposing theory which suggests that children who bully actually have good social cognition skills and that this allows them to successfully manipulate others whilst avoiding detection (Sutton, Smith, and Swettenham 1999b). Sutton et al. make use of the 'theory of mind' paradigm to discuss social cognition in relation to bullying behaviour. Having a good theory of mind allows individuals to accurately attribute mental states to others and therefore to make sensible predictions about others' behaviour.

In support of their theory, Sutton, Smith, and Swettenham (1999b) found that at 8–11 years, 'bullies' scored higher than comparison peers on understanding social cognition and emotions in a social story task. However, 'bullies' were grouped as a single category in this study. It may be that indirect bullying requires a good theory of mind in order to manipulate the mental states of others, whereas a theory of mind may not be necessary for direct bullying behaviours. Again, this suggests differences in the profiles of direct and indirect bullies and supports the idea that bullying behaviour should be considered in terms of these subtypes.

One further consideration when profiling children involved in bullying is the gender of the 'bully'. There is a reported higher prevalence of males than females involved in bullying behaviour (Jolliffe and Farrington 2011; Rivers and Smith 1994; Wolke et al. 2000). However, it may be that boys and girls differ in terms of the type of bullying behaviour that they are involved in, and this higher male prevalence may reflect the fact that previous studies have predominantly studied direct bullies only. Girls may also bully but may be less direct and instead bully indirectly. It is important that gender differences are considered as this may help to explain some of the behavioural, emotional and social differences found between the different subtypes of bullying.

These adverse potential outcomes make it clear that effective interventions for bullying are important for both victims of bullying and children who bully others. The development of such intervention strategies requires a fine-grained understanding of the cognitive and affective profile of abilities and difficulties that underpin bullying behaviour. However, as previous research has shown, there appear to be many correlates of bullying behaviour and inconsistencies in the literature remain. It is unlikely that considering one single profile of a bully is sensible, and instead we should seek to consider different risk pathways to becoming a bully. This kind of research speaks to an ultimate aim of informing the development of interventions that relate directly to the profiles of strengths and weaknesses shown by children who are involved in different bullying subtypes.

This study set out to refine the understanding of the profiles associated with bullying by examining differences in teacher and self-reports of behaviour, social functioning and self-perception in a group of children who were rated by their peers as being involved in direct or indirect bullying behaviour, both or neither. In line with previous research, six specific hypotheses were formulated for investigation. We expect:

(1) A gender difference will be found in the proportion of males and females involved in direct and indirect bullying. Specifically, we expect more boys to be involved in direct bullying, and more girls to be involved in indirect bullying.
(2) Direct bullies (and children involved in both types of bullying) will be characterised by greater levels of behavioural problems (in terms of conduct problems, hyperactivity and aggression) than indirect bullies and a non-bully comparison group. Furthermore, we predict that direct bullies will report more reactive and proactive aggression than children who do not bully.
(3) Direct and indirect bullies (and those involved in both) will show greater levels of emotional difficulties than their peers who are not involved in bullying.
(4) Group differences in self-perception will be apparent, with children who are not involved in bullying having the most positive self-perception profile, and those who are involved in both to have the poorest.
(5) Children reported by their peers to be 'bullies' (direct, indirect, or children involved in both) will fare less well in terms of social acceptance, and will experience greater levels of social rejection than children not involved in bullying.
(6) Indirect bullies will not have social skills difficulties, but direct bullies (and children involved in both) will be less socially competent than indirect bullies and children not involved in bullying behaviour.

Method

The study employed a two-stage design with a proportion of pupils from stage 1 being asked to participate in stage 2.

Participants

Pupils in year groups 3–6 (aged between 7 and 11 years) were recruited from three local authority maintained mainstream primary schools in England. The three participating schools yielded 20 classes and 576 pupils, who were all invited to take part. Of these pupils, 512 took part in the first stage of the study. Pupils who did not take part were either absent from school on the day of assessment ($n = 36$), had recently left the school ($n = 6$) or had been withdrawn from the study by their parents or guardians ($n = 22$). No child was excluded owing to literacy or other difficulties.

Of the 512 pupils who took part in the first stage, 192 students were seen in stage 2, selected on the basis of peer nomination scores. Only one pupil who was recruited to stage 2 elected not to take part, while three others were away from school during the times that a researcher was available to work with them. Pupils from all age groups were recruited into stage 2: 58 from year 3, 45 from year 4, 31 from year 5 and 58 from year 6. The mean age for participants in stage 2 was 9 years 7 months (SD = 1 year 3 months) and 47.4% were female.

Procedure

Data were gathered during the academic year 2010/11. Parents of all year 3–6 pupils at participating schools were sent a letter containing information about the whole study and were asked to indicate by returning a form, telephone or email within two weeks if they did not want their child to take part. This opt-out consent was approved by the schools and was granted permission from the institutional research ethics committee. This opt-out method was included in order to gain maximum possible involvement in the whole-class sociometric stage of the study, which allowed the most accurate peer-reports of behaviour. Final consent to take part was given by the pupils' class teacher, and each pupil was made aware that they did not have to take part and that they could withdraw at any time.

During stage 1, participants took part in a whole-class exercise to complete the Social Inclusion Survey (Frederickson and Graham 1999) and the Guess Who measure (Frederickson and Graham 1999) (described below) with the research team and their teachers and classroom assistants to support pupils as necessary.

Nominations on the Guess Who sociometric measure were used to identify pupils recruited to participate in stage 2. The second stage of the study involved individual sessions with pupils who had fulfilled one of four criteria:

- Direct bully group: One-third or more of their classmates had nominated them as being involved with 'direct bullying behaviours';
- Indirect bully group: One-third or more of their classmates had nominated them as being involved with 'indirect bullying behaviours';
- Both direct and indirect bully group: One-third or more of their classmates had nominated them as being involved with both 'direct bullying behaviours' and 'indirect bullying behaviours';
- Comparison group: Fewer than 10% of their classmates had nominated them as being involved with both 'direct bullying behaviours' and 'indirect bullying behaviours'.

One member of the research team (AJ) was responsible for grouping the pupils as described above. This member of the team did not take part in stage 2, which was carried out by researchers who were blind to the pupils' bully group status. Teachers were also given a short pack of measures that they completed in their own time.

Measures

Information about participants' gender was collected from pupils at the beginning of the whole-class session, and age information was collected for participants taking part in stage 2.

Stage 1

Social inclusion survey (Frederickson and Graham 1999). This is a sociometric measure assessing how willing children are to associate with classmates at school. Children were asked to indicate how much they like to play with each classmate at school. The measure uses a forced-choice format in which children are presented with a list of classmates' names in the order they appear in the class register. Opposite each name are four response options: a question mark (to indicate any classmates they did not know well enough to decide how much they like to play with them – usually reserved for pupils who are very new to the class); a smiling face ('would be happy to play with'); a neutral schematic face ('don't mind whether they play with or not'); and a sad face ('rather not play with'). Any missing data were coded as 'don't know'. For each participant a proportion score of acceptance (or rejection) was calculated by dividing the number of smiling faces (or sad faces) received by the total number of ratings in categories other than 'don't know'. Test–retest reliabilities for acceptance and rejection have been reported at $\alpha = 0.70$–0.78 over a five-week period (Frederickson and Furnham 1998). This instrument also allows a measure of 'mutual friends', that is the number of peers that an individual reports as 'happy to play with' that also report that individual as being someone with whom they are 'happy to play with'.

'Guess Who' Social behaviour and bullying measure (Frederickson and Graham 1999). An unlimited nomination peer assessment measure adapted from Coie and Dodge (1983) was used where children were asked to identify anyone in their class who fitted each of the following behavioural descriptors:

- 'Sporty': this person is very good at sport. They can run pretty fast and they like to play games.
- 'Cooperates': this person is really good to have as part of your group because they are agreeable and cooperate. They join in, share and give everyone a turn.
- 'Direct bully': this person often picks on other people or hits them or teases them or does other nasty things to them for no good reason.
- 'Shy': this person is shy with other children, they always seem to work or play by themselves. It is hard to get to know this person.
- 'Indirect bully': this person who often tells stories about people, says things behind people's backs to make them lose their friends and leaves people out of things on purpose to be mean.
- 'Leader': this person gets chosen by the others as the leader. Other people like to have this person in charge.

A mixture of positive and negative descriptor items was included here so that 'bullying' and negative peer nominations were not the focus of the assessment. Data from these other descriptors are not included here.

Stage 2

Strengths and difficulties questionnaire (SDQ; Goodman 1997). This is a widely used and well-validated measure of adjustment and psychopathology in children (Goodman 2001). This study used the 25-item teacher-rated versions which both have five subscales: Prosocial behaviour, Conduct Problems, Hyperactivity, Emotional Symptoms, and Peer Problems. Internal consistencies in this study ranged from $\alpha = 0.69$ (peer problems) to 0.91 (hyperactivity), comparable to those reported by Goodman (2001) ($\alpha = 0.70$–0.88 for teachers).

Reactive and proactive aggression questionnaire (Raine et al. 2006). This is a 23-item measure designed to assess proactive and reactive aggressive acts in children and adolescents. Participants were asked to rate each item on a three-point scale of never, sometimes and often. Greater scores are indicative of greater aggression. This measure has been demonstrated to have good internal reliability and good construct validity (Raine et al. 2006). Internal consistencies for this study were $\alpha = 0.80$ for reactive aggression and $\alpha = 0.86$ for proactive aggression; these are comparable with alphas reported by Raine et al. (both $\alpha > 0.81$).

Social perception profile for children (Harter 1985). This widely used instrument covers five domains of self-competence together with an assessment of global self-worth. Subscales include the child's perception of their scholastic competence, social acceptance, athletic competence, physical appearance and behaviour conduct. The global self-worth scale taps the extent to which the child likes him- or herself as a person. The question format is designed to offset the tendency to give socially desirable responses by asking participants to decide which kind of child he or she is most like by presenting him/her with two contrasting alternatives (for example, 'some children often forget what they learn' as opposed to 'other children can remember things easily'). Having made that decision the child is asked to decide whether the description is 'sort of true' or 'really true' for them. Higher scores reflect higher perceived competence.

Social competence inventory (SCI; Rydell, Hagekull, and Bohlin 1997). This is a teacher-reported method of obtaining information about social skills and social functioning. It comprises 25 items, subdivided into two subscales measuring Prosocial orientation (e.g. 'Is often able to find solutions or compromises when involved in a conflict') and Social initiative (e.g. 'Often suggests activities and games to play with peers'). Greater scores are indicative of greater social competence. The SCI has good reported reliability and validity, and internal consistencies for this study ($\alpha = 0.86$ and 0.95 for social initiative and prosocial orientation) are comparable to those reported by Rydell, Hagekull, and Bohli (1997) ($\alpha = 0.91$ and 0.94, respectively).

Results

Out of the 512 initial participants in this study, 37 (7.2%) met our criteria for being involved in only direct bullying, 31(6.1%) for being involved in only indirect bullying, and 41 (8.0%) for being involved in both direct and indirect bullying. The comparison group ($n = 76$) all met the criteria of being nominated by less than 10% of their peers as being involved in either type of bullying behaviour.

Participant characteristics

A preliminary analysis was carried out to investigate age and gender differences in relation to the three bully types and the comparison group; these are shown in Table 1. Pupils did not significantly differ in age between the four groups. However, there was a significant association between gender and group status, $\chi^2(3) = 44.87, p < 0.001$, Cramer's $V = 0.48$. Many more males than females were rated as being direct bullies and many more females were rated as being indirect bullies. There were more males than females rated as being involved in both direct and indirect bullying behaviour, while the comparison group had a relatively even proportion of males and females.

A series of multivariate analyses of variance (MANOVAs) was carried out to examine bullying group and gender differences in each of the measures completed by teachers and

Table 1. Participant characteristics (age and gender) reported by group.

	Direct ($n = 37$)	Indirect ($n = 31$)	Both ($n = 41$)	Comparison ($n = 76$)	F
Age, mean (SD)	9 yrs 10 m (1 yr 4 m)	9 yrs 4 m (1 yr 4 m)	9 yrs 6 m (1 yr 4 m)	9 yrs 7 m (1 yr 2 m)	0.80 (ns)
Female (%) ($n = 91$)	10.80	90.30	39.10	53.80	

Notes: yrs: years; m: months; ns: not significant.

pupils' self-reports. All post-hoc investigations compare each group with every other group and are reported as having been corrected for multiple comparisons using Tukey's HSD test.

Strengths and difficulties questionnaire

On the SDQ, main effects of gender were reported for teacher ratings of conduct problems and hyperactivity; boys had greater levels of conduct problems and hyperactivity [Conduct Problems: mean (*M*) (males) = 2.88 (SD = 2.91); *M* (females) = 1.25 (SD = 1.85); Hyperactivity: *M* (males) = 3.09 (SD = 2.82); *M* (females) = 1.24 (SD = 1.95)].

Table 2 shows that children nominated as being involved either in direct bullying only or in both types of bullying had greater levels of conduct problems and hyperactivity symptoms than those involved in indirect bullying and comparison children. These groups were also rated as showing fewer prosocial behaviours. A main effect of the bullying group was observed for teacher-rated SDQ total difficulties, conduct problems, hyperactivity, peer problems and prosocial behaviour. There were no significant interaction effects with gender. Post-hoc comparisons revealed that children involved in direct bullying (direct) and children identified as being involved in both direct and indirect bullying (both) had significantly more total difficulties and conduct problems, and fewer prosocial behaviours, than children involved in indirect bullying (indirect) and the comparison group (comparison). The direct and both group had significantly more hyperactivity compared to all other groups. Direct and both groups did not differ significantly in terms of their SDQ profiles and the indirect group did not differ significantly from the comparison group. Post-hoc comparisons revealed no significant differences between the groups for peer problems.

Aggression

There were no significant main effects of gender for either reactive or proactive aggression. Table 2 shows that children nominated as being either involved in direct bullying only or both types of bullying had greater levels of self-reported proactive and reactive aggression than those involved in indirect bullying and comparison children. Significant group differences were found. The direct group had the highest total aggression scores and the highest scores on the proactive and reactive aggression subscales. The direct group was found to be significantly more aggressive than the indirect and comparison groups. The both group did not differ significantly from the direct or indirect group on any measure of aggression; however, the both group had significantly higher aggression total scores and proactive and reactive scores than the comparison group. There were no significant differences between the indirect and comparison groups on total aggression or proactive or reactive aggression subscales.

Self-perception

On the Social Perception Profiles, main effects of gender were reported for 'athletic competence' and 'social acceptance' subscales, where males self-rated more highly than females [Athletic Competence: *M* (males) = 3.17 (SD = 0.61); *M* (females) = 2.79 (SD = 0.73); Social Acceptance: *M* (males) = 3.14 (SD = 0.57); *M* (females) = 2.79 (SD = 0.73)].

There were significant differences between the groups on pupils' self-rated social perception. Neither the direct nor the indirect group differed from the comparison group on self-reported scholastic competence. However, both direct and indirect groups had

Table 2. Means and standard deviations (in parentheses) and tests of group difference on all reported measures by group.

	Direct	Indirect	Both	Comparison	F	Post-hoc
Conduct Problems	4.39 (2.79)	1.08 (1.44)	3.62 (2.47)	0.19 (0.46)	33.49***	D, B > I, C
Hyperactivity	4.37 (2.47)	0.96 (1.53)	4.03 (2.44)	0.26 (0.79)	38.59***	D, B > I, C
Emotional Symptoms	2.09 (2.50)	1.76 (2.48)	2.53 (2.61)	1.56 (2.41)	0.91	–
Peer Problems	2.74 (2.32)	1.92 (1.96)	2.76 (2.08)	1.47 (1.89)	3.05*	None after correction
Prosocial Behaviour	4.48 (2.13)	7.11 (1.86)	4.72 (2.34)	8.18 (2.01)	23.11***	C, I > D, B
Total Difficulties	13.59 (7.58)	5.72 (5.17)	12.95 (7.30)	3.47 (3.88)	22.15***	D, B > I, C
Proactive Aggression	5.75 (5.57)	2.25 (2.10)	4.88 (4.28)	1.7 (2.76)	8.16***	D > I, C; B > C
Reactive Aggression	11.67 (3.32)	7.48 (4.41)	10.15 (4.29)	7.13 (3.67)	9.02***	D > I, C; B > C
Total Aggression	17.42 (7.83)	9.73 (5.82)	15.03 (7.75)	8.83 (5.66)	11.27***	D > I, C; B > C
Scholastic Competence	2.71 (1.37)	2.31 (1.17)	2.12 (1.20)	2.71 (0.83)	3.34*	C > D, I
Social Acceptance	2.73 (1.13)	2.17 (1.33)	2.35 (1.31)	2.73 (.97)	2.47	–
Athletic Competence	2.76 (1.12)	2.00 (1.34)	2.71 (1.28)	2.59 (1.01)	2.98*	None after correction
Physical Appearance	3.00 (0.57)	2.74 (0.61)	2.98 (0.86)	3.16 (0.59)	2.99*	C > I
Behavioural Conduct	2.55 (0.70)	2.84 (0.64)	2.42 (0.82)	3.26 (0.63)	16.53***	C > D, I, B
Global Self-worth	3.15 (0.53)	2.97 (0.53)	2.89 (0.74)	3.29 (0.59)	4.81***	C > B
Whole Class: Acceptance	0.34 (0.13)	0.37 (0.17)	0.31 (0.15)	0.55 (0.16)	30.73***	C > D, I, B
Whole Class: Rejection	0.36 (0.17)	0.33 (0.20)	0.41 (0.22)	0.15 (0.13)	27.99***	D, I, B > C
Same-gender: Acceptance	0.56 (0.25)	0.61 (0.26)	0.44 (0.27)	0.70 (0.21)	11.15***	C > D, B
Same-gender: Rejection	0.20 (0.21)	0.16 (0.20)	0.26 (0.21)	0.07 (0.11)	13.27***	D, B > C
Mutual Friends	4.20 (2.83)	4.01 (3.59)	3.76 (3.14)	6.25 (3.75)	6.20**	C > D, I, B
Prosocial Orientation	2.66 (0.58)	3.45 (0.67)	2.67 (0.72)	3.70 (0.73)	14.44***	C, I > D, B
Social Initiative	3.48 (0.71)	3.51 (0.87)	3.44 (0.83)	3.35 (0.90)	0.19	–
Total Social Skills	2.92 (0.50)	3.47 (0.67)	2.93 (0.61)	3.59 (0.73)	6.95***	C > D, B

Notes: $^{*}p < 0.05$, $^{**}p < 0.01$, $^{***}p < 0.001$.

significantly lower scholastic competence ratings compared to the comparison group. Post-hoc tests revealed no significant differences between groups for social acceptance or athletic competence. Children grouped as indirect bullies had a significantly lower perception of their physical appearance compared to the comparison group. There were no other group differences on this subscale. All three of the 'bully' groups reported lower self-perceptions of their own behaviour than the comparison group, but there were no differences between the three bully subtypes. Pupils in the both group had significantly lower global self-worth than the comparison group, but there were no other group differences in terms of global self-worth.

Social acceptance and rejection

MANOVAs revealed no main effects of gender for social acceptance, rejection or the number of mutual friends that a participant had. Table 2 shows that the comparison groups were the most socially accepted and least socially rejected groups (by both whole-class and same-gender peer groups), while there were few differences in social acceptance and rejection between the three bullying groups. The same was also true for the number of mutual friends reported. Accordingly, a significant main effect of bullying group was demonstrated for both social acceptance and rejection and the number of mutual friends. For whole-class measures of social acceptance and social rejection, all three bully groups fared less favourably than the comparison group, with significant post-hoc tests indicating greater levels of social rejection and poorer levels of social acceptance. A similar finding was also reported for the number of mutual friends, with the three bully groups having significantly fewer mutual friends than comparison children. There was a significant interaction effect between gender and bully group for the social rejection outcome, where social rejection for pupils involved in indirect and both types of bullying was only significantly different from the comparison group for girls.

Social competence

There were no main effects of gender on teacher reports of either social competence or prosocial orientation. Table 2 shows that comparison children and children involved in indirect bullying had higher levels of teacher-reported prosocial orientation than the other two groups. There was a main effect of bullying group, where the direct group and the both group had significantly lower total social competence scores compared to the comparison group. However, the indirect group did not differ from the comparison group or the other bullying groups in terms of their total teacher-reported social competence. Children in the direct group did not differ from those in the both group in terms of prosocial orientation. However, the direct group and the both group had significantly lower prosocial orientation scores compared to the indirect group and the comparison group. The indirect group did not differ on prosocial orientation from the comparison group. There were no significant group differences on the teacher-rated social initiative subscale, neither were there any significant interaction effects for either variable.

Discussion

This study aimed to investigate the behavioural, emotional and social correlates of bullying behaviours in primary school children in order to refine bullying profiles for two bullying subtypes: direct and indirect bullying.

As expected, there were gender differences in the proportion of males and females reported to be involved in direct and indirect bullying. The ratio of males to females involved in direct bullying was approximately 9:1, while for indirect bullying, the opposite pattern was observed. These findings are consistent with previous studies (e.g. Rivers and Smith 1994; Wolke et al. 2000) and are also in line with the theory that boys are more overtly aggressive than girls, while some research suggests that girls show greater levels of relational style aggression (Crick and Grotpeter 1995; Card et al. 2008). Although there is a more even spread of boys and girls reported to be both direct and indirect bullies, more boys than girls were reported to be involved. Gender differences in the incidence of bullying behaviours offer a way to further explore the antecedents and causal processes specific to direct and indirect bullying behaviours, and may prove to be an avenue of research importance. However, it is interesting to note that there were very few outcomes that differed according to gender. Gender differences in teacher-reported conduct problems and hyperactivity are not unusual (Fontaine et al. 2009; Ullebø et al. 2012), although it is important to note that in this study, the mean scores for girls and boys were within the 'typical' range of the SDQ.

Our second hypothesis related to teacher- and self-reports of behaviour. Direct bullies and children involved in both types of bullying were reported by their teachers as having a greater number of conduct problems and hyperactivity symptoms compared to the other groups, while the indirect bullying group was indistinguishable from the comparison group on both of these dimensions. The same was also true for reactive and proactive aggression as reported by the children themselves. Behaviours such as aggression that are commonly considered under the domain of externalising difficulties may place a child at particular risk for direct bullying behaviours. It may be useful for interventions to focus on aggression reduction among this particular subset of children involved in bullying.

The finding that there were no significant group differences in terms of teacher-rated emotional symptoms was somewhat surprising, and contrary to our initial hypotheses. However, it may be the case that such difficulties were not sufficiently problematic to be reported by the children's teachers. Future work should aim to also obtain information from parents, who may be more aware of their children's emotional symptoms than teachers. Support was found for our hypothesis that children involved in bullying would have poorer self-perceptions. Both direct and indirect bullying groups self-reported poorer scholastic competence, and all bullying groups self-reported poorer behavioural control than the comparison group. Global self-worth was poorest for those children involved in both types of bullying. These findings support previous research in this area (Coolidge, DenBoer, and Segal 2003; O'Moore and Kirkham 2001).

Theories have been suggested to explain the link between poorer self-esteem and bullying behaviours, including bullying as a method of compensating for negative self-image; behaving dominantly in order to improve or to maintain one's own social status (Salmivalli et al. 1999). On the other hand, poor self-esteem may be a more direct consequence of bullying behaviours, where children become socially isolated and their self-esteem suffers as a function of this social rejection. In this study, pupils involved in both types of bullying reported lower global self-worth than comparison children. In terms of bullying subtypes, pupils who bullied only directly or only indirectly did not differ from the comparison group on self-perception, suggesting that it is children involved in both types of bullying who are at particular risk for poor emotional outcomes.

In line with previous research, bullies were less socially accepted and more socially rejected by peers compared to the comparison group. All three bullying groups also had fewer mutual friends than comparison children. There was a particular problem with social rejection for girls involved in indirect and both types of bullying. Social rejection is a particular risk factor for poor psychological adjustment and rejection tends to be stable over time, with negative associations shown as long term as 30 years later (Beeri and Lev-Wiesel 2011; Modin, Östberg, and Almquist 2011). Peer rejection can also be cumulative; children who are rejected by a majority of the peer group tend to be treated more negatively and become more isolated, contributing to ongoing risks for maladjustment (Buhs and Ladd 2001). The results of this study suggest that girls who are involved in indirect bullying during middle childhood may be at risk of social exclusion, and further work may need to consider how far social exclusion may contribute to escalation in these kinds of socially manipulative bullying behaviours among girls.

Further to these peer-rated difficulties in the domain of social inclusion; pupils in the direct bully group and those in the both group had the greatest difficulties in terms of teacher-reported prosocial orientation (i.e. tries to intervene in conflicts; gives compliments to peers) and prosocial behaviour (i.e. offering to help out, shares readily). There were no teacher reports of a general social skills deficit for children involved with indirect bullying, but poorer overall social competence scores were reported for children involved in direct bullying and both types of bullying. Given the previous literature by Sutton, Smith, and Swettenham (1999a, 1999b), it seems sensible to suggest that indirect bullies may not have a general social skills deficit. As noted by Sutton, Smith, and Swettenham (1999a), good social understanding is a requirement for the manipulation of others. It is interesting to note that children involved in indirect bullying were not considered to have a deficit in their prosocial behaviour. These individuals are likely to be aware of the social rules of a classroom, and are able to act in a prosocial manner.

As Sutton and colleagues point out, much of the evidence for the social deficit model (Crick and Dodge 1996) is based on work with children who have increased levels of aggressive behaviour and those who have a diagnosis of conduct disorder, which are both problems that tend to relate more to children involved in direct bullying behaviours. It may be that a social skills deficit, as proposed by the social deficit model, offers the best fit for children who are involved in direct bullying, while Sutton and colleagues' theory that some bullies have good social cognitive skills fits well for indirect bullying. Additional work directly comparing social–cognitive abilities between these two groups will be able to further explore this possibility that there is more than one route to becoming a 'bully'.

This study was able to make use of a large sample of children from which to draw peer-nominations of bullying behaviour. However, it did not include information on children's individual socio-economic status or any specific difficulties. All pupils were included in this study, regardless of ability or previous diagnoses, and it is quite likely that some of these children had diagnoses of ADHD or autism spectrum disorder (ASD). Our a priori reasoning for this was that we were specifically interested in the profiles of behavioural, emotional and social abilities that characterised the direct and indirect subtypes of bullying, which meant that excluding some children on the basis of a diagnosed psychiatric disorder would render our sample unrepresentative of children in mainstream school, and unrepresentative of children involved in bullying. Previous work has demonstrated that children with developmental disorders such as ADHD and ASD are often at risk for greater victimisation and bullying (Wiener and Mak 2009; Van Roekel, Scholte, and Didden 2010).

Understanding the underpinnings of bullying behaviours will allow more targeted interventions and, it is hoped, a reduction in peer rejection for these already vulnerable pupils. Future work should also focus on following pupils through their school career and examining the cumulative impact that social and emotional deficits, along with social rejection, may have on a child's perceived bullying behaviours. Related to this, one further limitation of this study is that bully–victims were not identified. Children in this category are often at risk of poor outcome, and understanding the risk factors for this type of behaviour is clearly important. It would be interesting to examine the prevalence of bully–victim status within the subtypes of direct and indirect bullying.

This study demonstrates differences in the profile of behavioural, emotional and social strengths and weaknesses in children who are perceived as being involved in direct or indirect bullying behaviours. As such, the findings from this study should be useful to those interested in interventions for bullying. Direct bullying behaviours appear to be more strongly associated with hyperactivity, aggression and poor social skills, while indirect bullying does not appear to be associated with increased aggression or conduct problems, but is associated with intact social skills and some weaknesses in self-perception. It is also of importance that indirect bullying appears to be a predominantly female phenomenon. Perhaps of most concern is the finding that children involved in both direct and indirect bullying are those who are at greatest risk of showing difficulties across the broad spectrum of behavioural, emotional and social functioning. Given the findings of this study and others, it seems sensible to suggest a profile-based approach to understanding bullying behaviours and developing interventions, taking into account profiles of strengths and weaknesses in the behavioural, emotional and social domains for direct and indirect bullying behaviours.

References

Austin, S., and S. Joseph. 1996. Assessment of bully/victim problems in 8–11 year olds. *British Journal of Educational Psychology* 66: 447–56.

Barker, E.D., L. Arseneault, M. Brendgen, N. Fontaine, and B. Maughan. 2008. Joint development of bullying and victimization in adolescence: Relations to delinquency and self-harm. *Journal of the American Academy of Child and Adolescent Psychiatry* 47: 1030–8.

Beeri, A., and R. Lev-Wiesel. 2011. Social rejection by peers: A risk factor for psychological distress. *Child and Adolescent Mental Health* DOI: 10.1111/j.1475-3588.2011.00637.x.

Buhs, E.S., and G.W. Ladd. 2001. Peer rejection as an antecedent of young children's school adjustment: An examination of mediating processes. *Developmental Psychology* 37: 550–60.

Camodeca, M., and F.A. Goossens. 2005. Aggression, social cognitions, anger and sadness in bullies and victims. *Journal of Child Psychology and Psychiatry* 46: 186–97.

Caravita, S., P. DiBlasio, and C. Salmivalli. 2009. Unique and interactive effects of empathy and social status on involvement in bullying. *Social Development* 18: 140–63.

Card, N., B.D. Stucky, G.M. Sawalani, and T.D. Little. 2008. Direct and indirect aggression during childhood and adolescence: A meta-analytic review of intercorrelations, gender differences, and relations to maladjustment. *Child Development* 79: 1185–229.

Coie, J.D., and K.A. Dodge. 1983. Continuity of children's social status: A five-year longitudinal study. *Merrill-Palmer Quarterly* 29: 261–82.

Coolidge, F.L., J.W. DenBoer, and D.L. Segal. 2003. Personality and neuropsychological correlates of bullying behavior. *Personality and Individual Differences* 36: 1559–69.

Crick, N.R., and K.A. Dodge. 1996. Social information-processing mechanisms in reactive and proactive aggression. *Child Development* 67: 993–1002.

Crick, N.R., and J.K. Grotpeter. 1995. Relational aggression, gender, and social–psychological adjustment. *Child Development* 66: 710–22.

Dijkstra, J.K., S. Lindenberg, and R. Veenstra. 2008. Beyond the class norm: Bullying behavior of popular adolescents and its relation to peer acceptance and rejection. *Journal of Abnormal Child Psychology* 36: 1289–99.

Fontaine, N., R. Carbonneau, F., Vitaro, E.D. Barker, and R.E. Tremblay. 2009. Research review: A critical review of studies on the developmental trajectories of antisocial behavior in females. *Journal of Child Psychology and Psychiatry* 50: 363–85.

Frederickson, N., and B. Graham. 1999. *Social skills and emotional intelligence: Psychology in education portfolio*. Windsor: NFER-Nelson.

Frederickson, N.L., and A.F. Furnham. 1998. Sociometric classification methods in school peer groups: A comparative investigation. *Journal of Child Psychology and Psychiatry* 39: 921–34.

Gini, G. 2008. Associations between bullying behaviour, psychosomatic complaints, emotional and behavioural problems. *Journal of Paediatrics and Child Health* 44: 492–7.

Goodman, R. 1997. The Strengths and Difficulties Questionnaire: A research note. *Journal of Child Psychology and Psychiatry* 38: 581–6.

Goodman, R. 2001. Psychometric properties of the Strengths and Difficulties Questionnaire. *Journal of the American Academy of Child and Adolescent Psychiatry* 40: 1337–45.

Harter, S. 1985. *Manual for the Self-Perception Profile for Children*. Denver, CO: University of Denver.

Hemphill, S.A., A. Kotevski, T.I. Herrenkohl, L. Bond, M.J. Kim, J.W. Toumbourou, and R.F. Catalano. 2011. Longitudinal consequences of adolescent bullying perpetration and victimisation: A study of students in Victoria, Australia. *Criminal Behavior and Mental Health* 21: 107–16.

Jaana, J., W. Yueyan, and E. Guadelope. 2011. Bullying experiences and compromised academic performance across the middle school grades. *Journal of Early Adolescence* 31: 152–73.

Jolliffe, D., and D.P. Farrington. 2011. Is low empathy related to bullying after controlling for individual and social background variables? *Journal of Adolescence* 34: 59–71.

Klomek, A.B., A. Sourander, S. Niemelä, K. Kumpulainen, J. Piha, T. Tamminen, F. Almqvist, and M.S. Gould. 2009. Childhood bullying behaviors as a risk for suicide attempts and completed suicides: A population-based birth cohort study. *Journal of the American Academy of Child and Adolescent Psychiatry* 48: 254–61.

Knack, J.M., L.A. Jensen-Campbell, and A. Baum. 2011. Worse than sticks and stones? Bullying is associated with altered HPA axis functioning and poorer health. *Brain and Cognition* 77: 183–90.

Løhre, A., S. Lydersen, B. Paulsen, M. Mæhle, and L.J. Vatten. 2011. Peer victimization as reported by children, teachers, and parents in relation to children's health symptoms. *BMC Public Health* 11: 278.

Modin, B., V. Östberg, and Y. Almquist. 2011. Childhood peer status and adult susceptibility to anxiety and depression. A 30-year hospital follow-up. *Journal of Abnormal Child Psychology* 39: 187–99.

O'Moore, M., and C. Kirkham. 2001. Self-esteem and its relationship to bullying behaviour. *Aggressive Behavior* 27: 269–83.

Raine, A., K. Dodge, R. Loeber, L. Gatzke-Kopp, D. Lynam, C. Reynolds, M. Stouthamer-Loeber, and J. Liu. 2006. The reactive–proactive aggression questionnaire: Differential correlates of reactive and proactive aggression in adolescent boys. *Aggressive Behavior* 32: 159–71.

Rigby, K., and P.K. Smith. 2011. Is school bullying really on the rise? *Social Psychology of Education* 14: 441–55.

Rivers, I., and P.K. Smith. 1994. Types of bullying behaviour and their correlates. *Aggressive Behavior* 20: 359–68.

Rydell, A.-M., B. Hagekull, and G. Bohlin. 1997. Measurement of two social competence aspects in middle childhood. *Developmental Psychology* 33: 824–33.

Salmivalli, C., A. Kaukiainen, L. Kaistaniemi, and K.M.J. Lagerspetz. 1999. Self-evaluated self-esteem, peer-evaluated self-esteem, and defensive egotism as predictors of adolescents' participation in bullying situations. *Personality and Social Psychology Bulletin* 25: 1268–78.

Salmivalli, C., and E. Nieminen. 2002. Proactive and reactive aggression among school bullies, victims and bully–victims. *Aggressive Behavior 28*: 30–44.

Salmon, G., A. James, and D.M. Smith. 1998. Bullying in schools: Self reported anxiety, depression, and self esteem in secondary school children. *British Medical Journal* 317: 924–5.

Scheithauer, H., T. Hayer, F. Petermann, and G. Jugert. 2006. Physical, verbal, and relational forms of bullying among German students: Age, trends, gender differences and correlates. *Aggressive Behavior* 32: 261–75.

Seals, D., and J. Young. 2003. Bullying and victimization: Prevalence and relationship to gender, grade level, ethnicity, self-esteem, and depression. *Adolescence* 38: 735–47.

Sutton, J., P.K. Smith, and J. Swettenham. 1999a. Bullying and 'theory of mind': A critique of the 'social skills deficit' view of anti-social behaviour. *Social Development* 8: 117–27.

Sutton, J., P.K. Smith, and J. Swettenham. 1999b. Social cognition and bullying: Social inadequacy or skilled manipulation? *British Journal of Developmental Psychology* 17: 435–50.

Ullebø, A.M., M.-B. Posserud, E. Heiervang, C. Obel, and C. Gillberg. 2012. Prevalence of the ADHD phenotype in 7- to 9-year-old children: Effects of informant, gender and non-participation. *Social Psychiatry and Psychiatric Epidemiology* 47: 763–9.

Van Roekel, E., R. Scholte, and R. Didden. 2010. Bullying among adolescents with autism spectrum disorders: Prevalence and perception. *Journal of Autism and Developmental Disorders* 40: 63–73.

Viding, E., E. Simmonds, K.V. Petrides, and N. Frederickson. 2009. The contribution of callous–unemotional traits and conduct problems to bullying in early adolescence. *Journal of Child Psychology and Psychiatry* 50: 471–81.

Wiener, J. and M. Mak. 2008. Peer victimization in children with attention-deficit/hyperactivity disorder. *Psychology in the Schools* 46: 116–31.

Wolke, D., S. Woods, L. Bloomfield, and L. Karstadt. 2000. The association between direct and relational bullying and behaviour problems among primary school children. *Journal of Child Psychology and Psychiatry* 41: 989–1002.

Associations between types of involvement in bullying, friendships and mental health status

Grace Skrzypiec, Phillip T. Slee, Helen Askell-Williams and Michael J. Lawson

Flinders Educational Futures Research Institute, School of Education, Flinders University, Adelaide, South Australia, Australia

The three-way relationship between types of involvement in bullying (as victim, bully or bully–victim), number of friends and mental health status is not well understood. This research aimed to establish whether the mental health status of victims, bullies and bully–victims would fall disproportionately into the abnormal range of the Strengths and Difficulties Questionnaire (SDQ); to examine the associations between gender and mental health status according to involvement in bullying; and to investigate the association between the type of students' involvement in bullying, friendship status and mental health status. A sample of 1313 adolescents, aged 12–15 years, drawn from three South Australian secondary schools, completed the SDQ and the Peer Relations Questionnaire (PRQ). Participants involved in bullying, particularly bully–victims, were more likely to be screened as 'abnormal' on the SDQ. The likelihood of obtaining an abnormal SDQ score decreased with an increased number of good friends, particularly for bully–victims. Mental health difficulties experienced by victims, bullies and bully–victims varied by gender. Recommendations are made concerning tailoring mental health promotion and early interventions to prevent mental health difficulties to the specific needs of identified subgroups of students involved in bullying, and explicit teaching of strategies for promoting friendships, especially for victims.

Introduction

Bullying is a common phenomenon amongst school students at various ages and year levels (Nansel et al. 2004). Children in victim, bully and bully–victim groups have poorer psychosocial outcomes (Gini and Pozzoli 2008). This has been shown to be particularly the case for children who are victims of bullying. Due et al. (2005) sampled 123,227 students aged 11, 13 and 15 years across 28 countries (in eastern and western Europe, Scandinavia, North America, Israel and Russia), and found a significant association between victimisation and psychological symptoms, such as feeling nervous, feeling 'low', loneliness and helplessness. Victims have also been found to be at a higher risk for psychosomatic complaints and depression than bullies (Fekkes, Pijpers, and Verloove-Vanhorick 2004; Juvonen, Graham, and Schuster 2003; Menesini et al. 2009; Veenstra et al. 2005).

The psychosocial adjustment of bullies is not well understood. Fekkes, Pijpers, and Verloove-Vanhorick (2004) did not find any significant association between being a bully and psychosomatic symptoms or depression. However, Kaltiala-Heino et al. (2000), in a study of over 26,000 Finnish adolescents, found that involvement in bullying was associated with a range of mental health problems such as anxiety, depression and psychosomatic symptoms. This was the case for both male and female victims, bullies and bully–victims. There was also an increased risk of co-morbidity of these mental disorders for youths involved with bullying compared to those not involved. Kumpulainen and Räsänen (2000) found that bullies are more likely than victims and non-involved students to display externalising symptoms such as conduct problems and hyperactive disorders. Juvonen, Graham, and Schuster (2003) suggested that rather than being associated with maladjustment, for preadolescent bullies, the issues stem from purely behavioural problems. A meta-analysis of 11 studies which examined the psychosomatic and psychological adjustment of young people involved in bullying, by Gini and Pozzoli (2008), found that irrespective of gender, bullies, victims and bully–victims fared worse than those not involved in bullying, and that victims and bully–victims were at higher risk of psychosomatic problems than bullies.

In a study of students aged 13–16 in secondary schools in the UK, Smith et al. (2004) used the teacher-informant SDQ (Goodman 1997) to profile the mental health status of victims and to investigate why some pupils became, or continued to be, victimised. The authors found that non-victims were the most well-adjusted students, while continuing victims showed significantly poorer SDQ scores compared to new victims or escaped victims. Continuing victims were also significantly more likely than the other groups to have fewer friends and to obtain high scores on the Emotional Symptoms and the Peer Problems subscales of the SDQ. Teachers also rated continuing victims high on the Conduct Problems and Hyperactivity subscales. However Smith et al. focused on victims, and did not use the SDQ to investigate bullies, nor did they identify or separate bully–victims from the victim group. The roles of bully or victim are not necessarily mutually exclusive, and students who are bully–victims are of interest in their own right (Nansel et al. 2004). The likely mix of victims and bully–victims in the victim groups in the Smith et al. study may have confounded some of the findings in that study. The Smith et al. study indicates that it may be useful to investigate further the development of different types of maladjustment experienced by victims, bullies and bully–victims. This is important because conduct problems and a tendency to be delinquent have been found to be more commonly associated with youths who bully others (Barker et al. 2008).

Gender differences

Gender differences in psychosocial adjustment in response to bullying have also been identified. Girls who are victimised are more likely than boys to react to bullying with emotional anxiety and depression (Bond et al. 2001; Kaltiala-Heino et al. 2000) and suicidal ideation (Lieberman, Poland, and Cassel 2008). Associated with this are differences in how girls and boys cope with bullying. For example, girls are more likely than boys to use productive coping strategies such as seeking social support from adults and peers, although only a small proportion of bullied students generally use these strategies overall (Skrzypiec et al. 2011). While such studies have examined gender differences amongst victims of bullying, studies which have also investigated gender differences in the psychosocial adjustment of bullies and also bully–victims have been limited in number. For example, the meta-analysis examining bullying and psychosomatic problems conducted by Gini and Pozzoli (2008) found that while all of the 11 studies they reviewed included an examination of victims, only a subgroup reported analyses for bullies (six) and bully–victims (five), and only two reported separate results for males and females.

Friendships

Poor peer relations are common amongst young people involved in bullying (Hodges and Perry 1999; Boulton and Smith 1994). However friendship is an important influence for the alleviation of psychosocial maladjustment during adolescence: friends provide validation of aspirations, trepidations and interests, and contribute to a general sense of social acceptance (Hodges et al. 1999; Prinstein, Boergers, and Vernberg 2001). Goldbaum et al. (2003) suggested that vulnerability to being victimised is more likely to occur where supportive friendship networks are lacking, and in such cases victims become susceptible to poorer health and depression. The number of friends held by a young person was found by Hodges, Malone, and Perry (1997) to be negatively correlated with victimisation, a finding reflected in other research where victims report that they have fewer friends than do their classmates, and are more lonely and less happy (Veenstra et al. 2005). Furthermore, Hodges, Malone, and Perry (1997) found that as a young person's number of friends increased maladjustment brought on by victimisation decreased. They argued that children with better social skills are more able to make and keep friends, and such friendships may act as a deterrent against victimisation, as well as a buffer against the emotional effects of being victimised.

Although friendship may act as a buffer against victimisation, to be effective, the friendship must be of good quality. This implies that the friendship should be reciprocal, and that friends should possess qualities such as being willing and able to support each other in the face of threats from bullies (Hodges et al. 1999). Bollmer et al. (2005) found that friendship quality played a role in reducing bullying behaviour, particularly when externalising problems were present in the potential bully. They suggested that quality friendships provide a model for good peer relations, and so reduce the likelihood that young people will engage in bullying.

The findings reported above suggest that young people who are victimised or who bully others are more likely to experience detrimental outcomes in terms of their physical well-being, mental health and social dispositions. Furthermore, outcomes for bully–victims may be worse than for students classified either as bullies or as victims (Menesini, Modena, and Tani 2009; Nansel et al. 2004). Bully–victims have been found to have fewer friends than bullies, to be more likely to be hyperactive, to be the most stigmatised by peers, and to have the highest probability of a psychiatric referral (Ireland and Power 2004; Nansel et al. 2004). Nansel et al. (2004, 734) regarded students in this bully–victim group as being in an 'especially high-risk group for emotional and social difficulties'.

It is important to investigate in more detail the patterns of association between students' type of involvement in bullying (as victim, bully or bully–victim), their friendships and their mental health status. In particular, while the SDQ has been used to assess the mental health of victims (Smith et al. 2004), the buffering or protective effect of friendships associated with the mental health status of victims, bullies and bully–victims has received limited attention. Thus, our first aim was to investigate the mental health status of students assigned to three separate groups involved in bullying, namely, victims, bullies and bully–victims. We sought to determine whether victims, bullies or bully–victims would fall disproportionately into the abnormal range of the SDQ or any of its subscales. Our second aim was to investigate any gender differences in the association between involvement in bullying and mental health status. Our third aim was to investigate the association between students' friendship status and their mental health status within the three bullying-involvement groups. This last aim would more precisely differentiate the role that friendship plays as a protective factor against poor mental health.

Method and procedure

All year 7, 8 and 9 (junior secondary) students from three metropolitan high schools in Adelaide, ranging in location from lower to upper middle socio-economic areas, completed a self-report questionnaire, 'Living and learning at school: Bullying at school' supervised by teachers during a specified session near the end of the 2007 school year. The schools were self-selected as part of their participation in a larger research project between the university and schools in that area. Ethics approvals for the research was received from the Flinders University Research Ethics Committee, and also from each school principal and the State Department of Education. Parental consent, as well as participant consent, was obtained prior to the administration of the questionnaire. The questionnaire consisted of the following sections:

- *Participant information*: year level, gender, age and the student's nomination of the number of good friends that he/she had at school.
- *Peer Relations Questionnaire (PRQ)* (Slee and Rigby 1993): This comprised 16 questions which measured students' tendency to be victimised (six questions), to bully (six questions) or to be prosocial (four questions) (the prosocial subscale is not reported in this paper); for example, 'I get called names by others' and 'I tell false stories or spread rumours about others'. Responses were invited on a four-point scale ranging from 'never', 'once in a while', 'pretty often' to 'very often'.
  Responses to the six items that measured victimisation in the PRQ were summed to obtain a 'tendency to be victimised' score for each participant. Similarly, summation of six PRQ bullying items resulted in a 'tendency to bully' score for each participant. For each subscale, possible scores ranged from 6 to 24. Only cases with complete victim and bully scores were included in further analyses. The tendency to bully and tendency to be victimised subscales were found to be reliable using Cronbach's alpha (victim subscale $\alpha = 0.88$; bully subscale $\alpha = 0.79$).
- *Strengths and Difficulties Questionnaire (SDQ)* (Goodman 1997): This included 25 questions which measured students' mental health status with response alternatives of 'not true', 'somewhat true' and 'certainly true', to items in the four difficulties subscales of Emotional Symptoms (e.g. 'I am often unhappy, downhearted or tearful'), Conduct Problems (e.g. 'I get very angry and often lose my temper'), Hyperactivity (e.g. 'I am restless. I cannot stay still for long'), Peer Problems (e.g. 'I am usually on my own') and the strength subscale Prosocial (e.g. 'I try to be nice to other people').

Participant characteristics

Surveys were available for 1388 students. The response rate was 80.9%. Of these, 1313 students provided complete demographic information as well as victim and bully scores (missing = 5.4%). Participants were 12–15 years old (mean = 13.4 years, SD = 0.94). Gender was well balanced (males 51.3%). Year 7 students were visiting the schools as the potential year 8 cohort in the upcoming academic year; they comprised the largest group (40.2%) compared to year 8 (31.9%) and year 9 (28.0%).

Identifying victims, bullies and bully–victims

Farrington and Loeber (2000) suggested that forming subgroups of response types can illustrate trends in a data set. For example, they used scores above the 75th percentile and below the 25th percentile to classify youths at risk of offending and not offending. We used a similar procedure in this study. Victims were identified as students whose scores were above the 75th percentile of the PRQ tendency to be victimised scores, while bullies were students whose scores were above the 75th percentile of the PRQ tendency to bully scores. Students whose scores were above the 75th percentile on both the tendency to bully, and the tendency to be victimised, scales were classified as bully–victims. The victim group comprised 135 students (10.3% of sample; 51.1% male), the bully group comprised 121 students (9.2% of sample; 76.9% male) and the bully–victim group comprised 114 students (8.7% of sample; 74.6% male). The 943 students who did not fall into these categories comprised the non-involved group (71.8% of sample; 45.3% male). The non-involved group is not included in the comparative statistical analyses of the other three groups since our aim was to investigate the mental health and friendship status of young people involved in bullying as victims, bullies or bully–victims.

Identifying mental health profiles

Since we were interested in investigating mental health status, participants were allocated to 'normal', 'borderline' and 'abnormal' ranges of mental health difficulties based upon Goodman's (2008) recommended classification groups (provided online at www.sdqinfo.com). Participants' responses to the SDQ showed highly skewed distributions; therefore, non-parametric tests were used to compare the scores of victims, bullies and bully–victims, as well as for comparisons between males and females. Cramer's *V* was used to calculate the effect size (ES) where chi-squared tests were undertaken. Eta squared [$\eta^2 = \chi^2/(N-1)$] was used to calculate ES where Kruskal–Wallis tests were used (Green and Salkind 2008). An ordinal measure of ES (the probability of superiority: PS $= U/mn$, where m, n = size of each group) was used, as well as Rosenthal's *r* (Rosenthal 1991), where Mann–Whitney U tests (used as alternative to the chi-squared test when the minimum expected cell count was less than 5) were used (Grissom and Kim 2005). Univariate general linear modelling (GLM) was undertaken where Levene's test suggested that the assumption of homogeneity of variance across variables was not severely violated. To account for the multiple tests of significance a stricter probability level of 0.01 was used (compared to the more typically reported 0.05). All analyses were carried out in SPSS 17.0.

Results

Differences between bully/victim/bully–victim groups by age and gender

Table 1 shows the incidence of victim, bully and bully–victim groups, by age and gender. Differences in the gender composition of the victim, bully and bully–victim groups were statistically significant [$\chi^2(2{,}370) = 23.6$, $p < 0.0001$, ES = 0.25], suggesting that males were more likely than females to be bullies and bully–victims.

Students in years 9 and 10 were more likely to be classified in the bully–victim group, while students in years 7 and 8 were more likely to be classified in the victim group [Kruskal–Wallis *H*, $\chi^2(2{,}370) = 34.4$, $p < 0.0001$, ES = 0.09]. Over two-thirds of students in the bully–victim group were aged 14 or 15 years, while over half of those students in the victim group were aged 12 or 13 years, being enrolled in corresponding earlier year levels 7 and 8.

Table 1. Incidence of victim, bully and bully–victim groups, by age and gender.

		12 years	13 years	14 years	15 years
Male	Non-involved group	76 (17.8)	169 (39.6)	124 (29.0)	58 (13.6)
	Victim group	19 (27.5)	26 (37.7)	19 (27.5)	5 (7.2)
	Bully group	19 (20.4)	33 (35.5)	30 (32.3)	11 (11.8)
	Bully–victim group	8 (9.4)	16 (18.8)	34 (40.0)	27 (31.8)
Female	Non-involved group	85 (16.5)	219 (42.4)	144 (27.9)	68 (13.2)
	Victim group	14 (21.2)	26 (39.4)	20 (30.3)	6 (9.1)
	Bully group	12 (42.9)	8 (28.6)	5 (17.9)	3 (10.7)
	Bully–victim group	3 (10.3)	9 (31.0)	10 (34.5)	7 (24.1)

Note: Data are shown as *n* (%).

Bullying and mental health

Students in the bully–victim group were more likely than students in the bully or victim groups to obtain scores that fell into the abnormal range of the Total SDQ, as well as two of the SDQ Difficulty subscales (i.e. Conduct Problems and Peer Problems) and the Prosocial scale. For the Emotional Symptoms scale, victims and bully–victims were more likely to score in the abnormal range.

Figure 1 illustrates the range of abnormal SDQ scores amongst victims, bullies and bully–victims, as well as for not involved students. The cut-off points suggested by Goodman (2008) were used to categorise students into the abnormal range of mental health strengths and difficulties. This included a score that was greater than 19 for Total

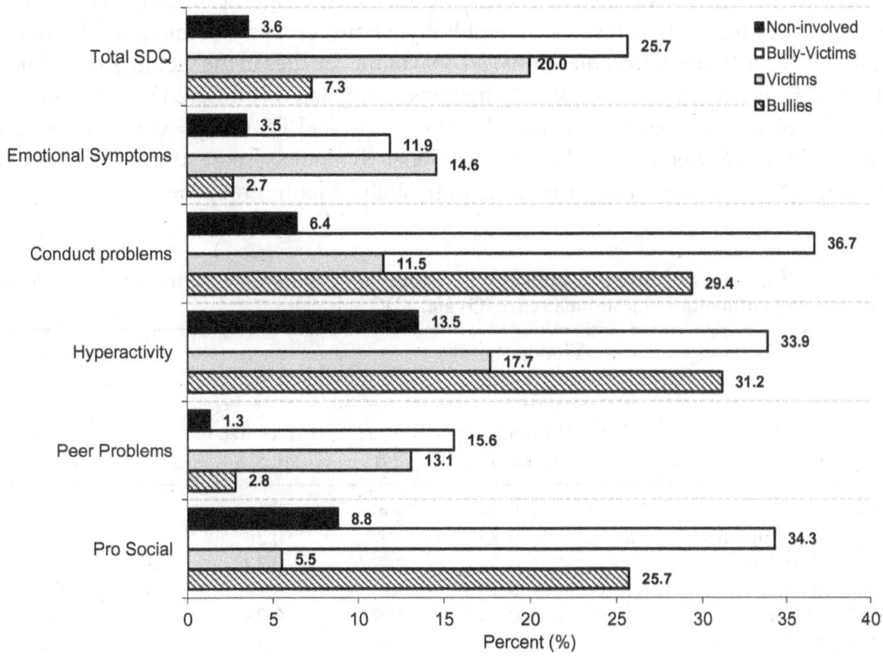

Figure 1. Proportion of non-involved, victims, bullies and bully–victims falling into the abnormal ranges of the total Strengths and Difficulties Questionnaire (SDQ) and SDQ subscales.

Difficulties, greater than 6 for Emotional Symptoms, greater than 4 for Conduct Problems, greater than 6 for Hyperactivity, greater than 5 for Peer Problems and less than 5 for Prosocial Behaviour. Students in the bully–victim group were most likely to have an abnormal Total SDQ score, with one-quarter (25.7%) of these students scoring above the abnormal cut-off point [$\chi^2(4{,}348) = 26.6$, $p < 0.0001$, ES = 0.20]. About one-third of students in the bully–victim group showed signs of Conduct Problems (36.7%) [$\chi^2(4{,}348) = 35.1$, $p < 0.0001$, ES = 0.23]. A small proportion of students in the bully–victim group (15.6%) had high Peer Problems scores [$\chi^2(4{,}348) = 25.0$, $p < 0.0001$, ES = 0.19] and over one-third (34.3%) obtained low Prosocial scores [$\chi^2(4{,}345) = 49.1$, $p < 0.0001$, ES = 0.27].

As shown in Figure 1, a significantly higher proportion (14.6%) of students in the victim group and bully–victim group (11.9%), compared to students in the bully group (2.7%), was assessed in the abnormal range of the Emotional Symptoms scale [Kruskal–Wallis, $\chi^2(2{,}349) = 37.6$, $p < 0.0001$, ES = 0.11]. Bully–victims and victims exhibited more signs of susceptibility to Emotional Symptoms and Peer Problems than bullies. Meanwhile, bully–victims, similarly to bullies, were more likely to be susceptible to Conduct Problems than victims, with a similar tendency for Hyperactivity. On the Prosocial scale, both bully–victims and bullies, particularly males, were likely to be less prosocial than victims.

As shown in Table 2, the groups differed significantly on all of the SDQ subscales with effect sizes that were small (< 0.3) to medium (< 0.5) (Cohen 1991).

Gender differences within the victim, bully and bully–victim groups

There were no statistically significant differences between males and females in each of the victim, bully and bully–victim groups on Total SDQ scores, Conduct Problems, Hyperactivity and Peer Problems. There were statistically significant differences between males and females within the victim and bully–victim groups on Emotional Symptoms. As illustrated in Table 3, over one-third (36.5%) of the females in the victim group obtained a borderline or abnormal Emotional Symptoms score, and this differed significantly from males [$U(67{,}63) = 1480.5$, $p < 0.01$, ES (r) = 0.26 and ES (PS) = 0.35, i.e. the probability of females obtaining a higher Emotional Symptoms score than males = 0.65]. Emotional Symptoms scores for females in the bully–victim group were also more likely

Table 2. Effect sizes of differences between victim, bully and bully–victim groups on the total Strengths and Difficulties Questionnaire (SDQ) and SDQ subscales.

	Victims and bully–victims		Bullies and victims		Bullies and bully–victims	
	p	Effect size (Cramer's V)	p	Effect size (Cramer's V)	p	Effect size (Cramer's V)
Total SDQ	**	0.24	*ns	0.19	****	0.31
Emotional Symptoms	ns	0.13	****	0.30	****	0.37††
Conduct Problems	****	0.38	****	0.27	ns	0.12
Hyperactivity	*ns	0.19	*ns	0.16	ns	0.04
Peer Problems	ns	0.04	****	0.28	****	0.32
Prosocial	****	0.43	****	0.37	ns	0.10

Notes: ns = not significant ($p > 0.05$), *ns = $p < 0.05$, ** $p < 0.01$, *** $p < 0.001$, **** $p < 0.0001$, † eta squared, †† Rosenthal's r.

Table 3. Proportion of male and female victims, bullies and bully–victims falling into different categories of the total Strengths and Difficulties Questionnaire (SDQ) and SDQ subscales.

		Victim group		Bully group		Bully–victim group	
		Male	Female	Male	Female	Male	Female
Total SDQ score	Normal	46 (68.7)	40 (63.5)	58 (70.7)	21 (77.8)	35 (43.8)	13 (44.8)
	Borderline	10 (14.9)	8 (12.7)	19 (23.2)	3 (11.1)	25 (31.2)	8 (27.6)
	Abnormal	11 (16.4)	15 (23.8)	5 (6.1)	3 (11.1)	20 (25.0)	8 (27.6)
Emotional Symptoms scale	Normal	60 (89.6)	40 (63.5)	80 (96.4)	27 (100.0)	71 (88.8)	22 (75.9)
	Borderline	3 (4.5)	8 (12.7)	0 (0.0)	0 (0.0)	2 (2.5)	1 (3.4)
	Abnormal	4 (6.0)	15 (23.8)	3 (3.6)	0 (0.0)	7 (8.8)	6 (20.7)
Conduct Problems scale	Normal	51 (76.1)	50 (79.4)	42 (51.2)	16 (59.3)	32 (40.0)	13 (44.8)
	Borderline	7 (10.4)	7 (11.1)	14 (17.1)	5 (18.5)	16 (20.0)	8 (27.6)
	Abnormal	9 (13.4)	6 (9.5)	26 (31.7)	6 (22.2)	32 (40.0)	8 (27.6)
Hyperactivity scale	Normal	45 (67.2)	45 (71.4)	46 (56.1)	14 (51.9)	44 (55.0)	15 (51.7)
	Borderline	10 (14.9)	7 (11.1)	12 (14.6)	3 (11.1)	8 (10.0)	5 (17.2)
	Abnormal	12 (17.9)	11 (17.5)	24 (29.3)	10 (37.0)	28 (35.0)	9 (31.0)
Peer Problems scale	Normal	40 (59.7)	39 (61.9)	68 (82.9)	25 (92.6)	45 (56.2)	17 (58.6)
	Borderline	18 (26.9)	16 (25.4)	12 (14.6)	1 (3.7)	23 (28.8)	7 (24.1)
	Abnormal	9 (13.4)	8 (12.7)	2 (2.4)	1 (3.7)	12 (15.0)	5 (17.2)
Prosocial scale	Normal	52 (78.8)	59 (95.2)	38 (46.3)	20 (74.1)	33 (41.8)	19 (65.5)
	Borderline	8 (12.1)	2 (3.2)	22 (26.8)	1 (3.7)	16 (20.3)	3 (10.3)
	Abnormal	6 (9.1)	1 (1.6)	22 (26.8)	6 (22.2)	30 (38.0)	7 (24.1)

Note: Data are shown as *n* (%).

to be higher than those of males in the bully–victim group [$U(80,29) = 803$, $p < 0.05$, ES (PS) = 0.35 and ES (r) = 0.24].

On the Prosocial subscale, males were generally more likely than females to be categorised as abnormal [$U(227,118) = 8869$, $p < 0.0001$, ES (PS) = 0.33 and ES (r) = 0.28). In the bully–victim group, males differed significantly from females [$U(79, 29) = 1507$, $p < 0.05$, ES (PS) = 0.66 and ES (r) = 0.24], with Prosocial scores that were generally indicative of poorer prosocial capabilities (see Table 3).

Friendship and mental health status

A univariate GLM analysis of Total SDQ scores found significant main effects between the three groups [$F(2,313) = 4.1$, $p < 0.05$] and number of good school friends [$F(3,313) = 2.97$, $p < 0.05$]. The more friends students reported having, the less likely was an abnormal or borderline Total SDQ score. There were no interaction effects. Post-hoc tests showed significant differences between having no friends at all and having two or three good friends ($p < 0.05$, ES = 0.27), or having many good friends ($p < 0.01$, ES = 0.21).

Victims, bullies and bully–victims with many friends were more likely to be categorised into the normal range of the Total SDQ than students reporting fewer friends, as displayed in Figure 2. Conversely, bully–victims and victims reporting no friends were more likely to be classified into the abnormal or borderline ranges on the Total SDQ. The findings suggest that friends may be particularly important for bully–victims, as the resulting mean score

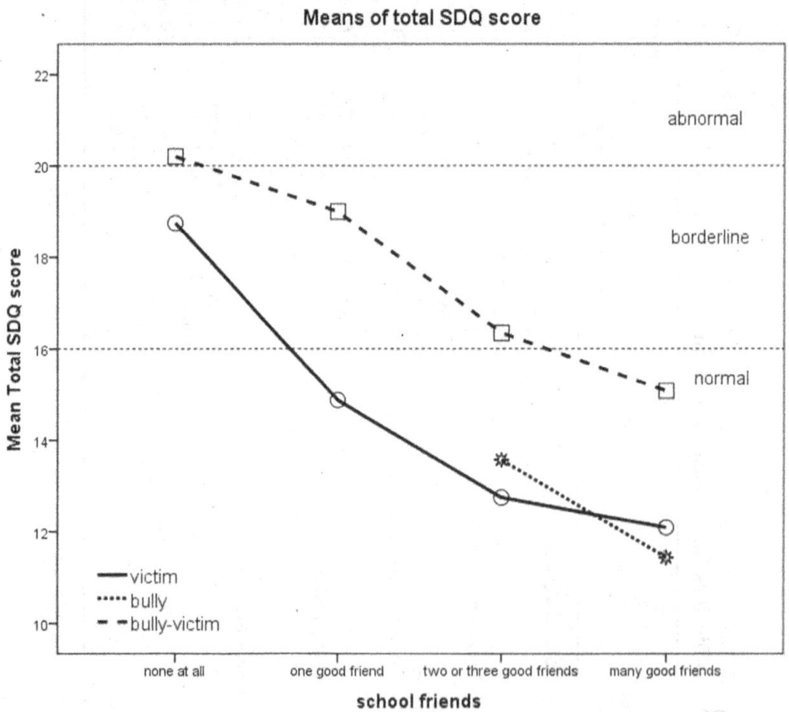

Figure 2. Means (calculated estimated marginal means) of total Strengths and Difficulties Questionnaire (SDQ) scores of victims, bullies and bully–victims and the number of student-nominated good school friends.

in Figure 2 for Total SDQ for this group moved into the normal range only when students reported having many friends. For victims, however, having at least one good friend may have been sufficient to provide a buffer against a higher Total SDQ score. Note that none of the students in the bully group reported having fewer than two or three good friends, although, as shown in Figure 1, about one-quarter of students in the bully group were assessed as having poor scores on the Prosocial scale.

Discussion

The findings of this study provide further support for suggested links between mental health problems and involvement in bullying (Rigby, Slee, and Martin 2007), particularly for students who are bully–victims. The precarious mental health state of those students who bully and who are also bullied is supported by the finding that bully–victims were more likely than victims or bullies to obtain scores in the abnormal range of the SDQ.

Approximately one-quarter of students in the bully–victim group, and one in five students in the victim group, scored in the abnormal range of the SDQ. These findings can be compared to statistics from the general population, where approximately one in seven adolescents in Australia are reported to experience mental health or behavioural difficulties (Sawyer et al. 2001). In the present study, about one in four students in the bully group and one in three students in the bully–victim group had scores which fell into the abnormal ranges of conduct problems, hyperactivity and prosocial problems. These findings flag the need for further attention to the mental health status of students involved in bullying – a view supported by Klomek et al. (2009) and by Lieberman and Cowan (2011, 13), who recommended that 'children and teens who are frequently involved in bullying behaviour either as victims or as perpetrators should be actively screened for mental health problems'. Identifying which students might require follow-up for mental health difficulties would be possible within school settings using instruments such as the PRQ in combination with the SDQ.

The profiling of students in the three groups, as shown in Table 1, indicates that conduct problems and prosocial problems (and hyperactivity to a lesser extent) were most likely to be associated with bullying, while emotional symptoms and peer problems were most likely to be associated with being victimised. Bully–victims shared identifiable characteristics with both victims and bullies. Showing similarity to the profiles of victims, bully–victims were more likely to show signs of emotional symptoms and peer problems. And showing similarity to the profiles of bullies, bully–victims were more likely to show signs of conduct problems and antisocial tendencies.

There were few differences between males and females within the different bully groups, although there was evidence that compared to males, female victims and bully–victims experienced more emotional symptoms, while male bully–victims were more likely than female bully–victims to have prosocial difficulties. Overall, there was evidence that prosocial difficulties were more commonly problematic for males than females in all of the victim, bully and bully–victim groups. These findings suggest that it may be beneficial to use interventions with female victims and bully–victims that focus on improving emotional coping strategies, while interventions that aim to improve the prosocial skills of males involved in bullying would assist males experiencing difficulties socialising with others.

The issue of friendship, and in particular the number of good friends reported by the different groups in this study, adds to existing research evidence suggesting that friendship may act as a protective factor against mental health difficulties. As illustrated in Figure 2, the likelihood of obtaining an abnormal Total SDQ score decreased with an increasing number of good friends for victim, bully and bully–victim groups. Our finding that none of the young people in the bully group reported having fewer than two or three good friends is out of step with Bollmer and colleagues' (2005) hypothesis of quality friends acting as role models for appropriate social behaviours. It may be that students in the bully group in our study overestimated the quality of their friendships; or, perhaps, that some young people are merely friends with bullies in order to avoid being victimised. However, the exact nature of *good* friendships was not made explicit in the present research, and it is not clear how participants may have interpreted the meaning of 'good friends'. Future research would benefit from follow-up interviews with victims, bullies and bully–victims to describe what they understand a 'good friend' to be, and what role a 'good friend' plays in bullying.

The differing SDQ subscale scores of students in the different types of bullying groups point strongly to the need to consider the aims and objectives of school-based bullying prevention and mental health promotion interventions. Whereas universal interventions tend to have aims that are useful for all students, the particular needs of identified victims, bullies and bully–victims may not be best served by universal programmes. A suite of more precisely targeted interventions seems warranted. Arguing this point, Fuchs (2006) stressed the importance of profiling relevant characteristics of subgroups of students, because, he suggested, allocating intervention resources mostly to generic whole group and/or individual student interventions fails to capitalise on the efficacy and efficiency of identifying common characteristics and needs of student subgroups. Future investigations that focus on different types of bullying, such as direct and indirect bullying, would also contribute to our understanding of the three-way relationship of bully involvement, mental health status and friendship. For example, a study by Viding et al. (2009) found that conduct problems and prosocial difficulties were more strongly associated with direct bullying.

The findings about the bully–victim group in the present study suggest two further hypotheses for investigation. First, it may be the case that bullies with emotional symptoms or peer problems might be susceptible to victimisation, while victims with conduct problems might respond by bullying others. Second, the patterns of differences among the three groups have relevance for considering the causal directions of bullying and mental health difficulties. Some researchers (Kaltiala-Heino et al. 2000; Kim et al. 2006) have noted that there is a lack of clarity about the direction of causality of this relationship. Kokkinos and Panayiotou (2004) suggested that psychological disturbances should be examined as possible causes of bullying, as people with mental health issues may be inclined to bully others, and that people with mental health issues may be bullied by others because of external signs of their mental health issues. An examination in this area would be particularly pertinent to bully–victims, who demonstrated greater tendencies towards mental health difficulties in the present study.

Limitations

This study included a South Australian sample of junior secondary school students and while there are no apparent reasons to consider that they were not typical youth in this group, the fact that they were not a random sample is a limitation of the study.

The SDQ has been used in this research in the manner suggested by Percy, McCrystal, and Higgins (2008). However, the limitations of the SDQ should be noted. The SDQ is only indicative of mental health disorders and may be more suited to clinical screening applications, as a pointer to further investigations, than as a single indicator of mental health status in general settings. Goodman et al. (2004) suggested setting higher cut-offs for categories in the SDQ if false positives are to be avoided, and future research could consider local norms, or norms suggested by Mellor (2005), to find appropriate cut-off points to determine categories for the population in question.

The data for this study were generated from self-reports. Goodman (2001) found that the self-report form of the SDQ was reliable and valid, and it can be predicted that students would be good informants about their own friendship and bully status. However, future research could triangulate assessments from other informants such as teachers and parents/guardians.

Conclusions

This study contributes to the literature on the relationship between mental health and bullying. The findings indicate that students who are involved in bullying are more likely to be classified as 'abnormal' on the Total SDQ and on its subscales, and this is particularly the case for bully–victims. This research also suggests that having friends may act as a protective factor against mental health difficulties for adolescents involved in bullying, particularly for victims, where the existence of (at least) one friend was associated with movement out of the difficulties score range on the SDQ. The different types of mental health difficulties experienced by males and females involved in bullying warrant targeted interventions relevant to the characteristics of subgroups of students.

Acknowledgements

This project was funded by an Australian Research Council Linkage Grant 2007–2009. Partners in the grant included Flinders University, the South Australian Department of Education and Children's Services and the Southern Schools of Adelaide.

References

Barker, E.D., L. Arseneault, M. Brendgen, N. Fontaine, and B. Maughan. 2008. Joint development of bullying and victimization in adolescence: Relations to delinquency and self-harm. *Journal of the American Academy of Child and Adolescent Psychiatry* 47: 1030–8.

Bollmer, J.M., R. Milich, M.J. Harris, and M.A. Maras. 2005. A friend in need: The role of friendship quality as a protective factor in peer victimization and bullying. *Journal of Interpersonal Violence* 20: 701–12.

Bond, L., J.B. Carlin, L. Thomas, K. Rubin, and G. Patton. 2001. Does bullying cause emotional problems? A prospective study of young teenagers. *British Medical Journal* 323: 480–4.

Boulton, M., and P.K. Smith. 1994. Bully/victim problems in middle school: Stability, self-perceived competence, peer perception, and peer acceptance. *British Journal of Developmental Psychology* 12: 315–29.

Cohen, J. 1991. A power primer. *Psychological Bulletin* 122: 155–9.

Due, P., B.E. Holstein, J. Lynch, F. Diderichsen, S.N. Gabhain, P. Scheidt, C. Currie, and the Health Behaviour in School-Aged Children Bullying Working Group. 2005. Bullying and symptoms among school-aged children: International comparative cross sectional study in 28 countries. *European Journal of Public Health* 15: 128–32.

Farrington, D.P., and R. Loeber. 2000. Some benefits of dichotomization in psychiatric and criminological research. *Criminal Behaviour and Mental Health* 10: 100–22.

Fekkes, M., F.I.M. Pijpers, and S.P. Verloove-Vanhorick. 2004. Bullying behavior and associations with psychosomatic complaints and depression in victims. *Journal of Pediatrics* 144: 17–22.

Fuchs, D. 2006. Cognitive profiling of children with genetic disorders and the search for a scientific basis of differentiated education. In *Handbook of educational psychology*. 2nd ed., ed. P.A. Alexander and P.H. Winne, 187–206. Mahwah, NJ: Erlbaum.

Gini, G., and T. Pozzoli. 2008. Association between bullying and psychosomatic problems: A meta-analysis. *Pediatrics* 123: 1059–65.
Goldbaum, S., W.M. Craig, D.J. Pepler, and J. Connolly. 2003. Developmental trajectories of victimization: Identifying risk and protective factors. *Journal of Applied School Psychology* 19: 139–56.
Goodman, R. 1997. The Strength and Difficulties Questionnaire: A research note. *Journal of Child Psychology and Psychiatry* 38: 581–6.
Goodman, R. 2001. Psychometric properties of the Strengths and Difficulties Questionnaire. *Journal of the American Academy of Child and Adolescent Psychiatry* 40: 1337–45.
Goodman, R. 2008. Scoring the SDQ. http://www.Sdqinfo.Com
Goodman, R., T. Ford, T. Corbin, and H. Meltzer. 2004. Using the Strengths and Difficulties Questionnaire (SDQ) multi-informant algorithm to screen looked-after children for psychiatric disorders. *European Child and Adolescent Psychiatry* 13: 1125–31.
Green, S.B., and N.J. Salkind. 2008. *Using SPSS for Windows and Macintosh: Analyzing and understanding data*. 5th ed. Upper Saddle River, NJ: Pearson Prentice Hall.
Grissom, R.J., and J.J. Kim. 2005. *Effect sizes for research: A broad practical approach*. Mahwah, NJ: Erlbaum.
Hodges, E.V.E., M. Boivin, F. Vitaro, and W.M. Bukowski. 1999. The power of friendship: Protection against an escalating cycle of peer victimization. *Developmental Psychology* 35: 94–101.
Hodges, E.V.E., M.J.J. Malone, and D.G. Perry. 1997. Individual risk and social risk as interacting determinants of victimization in the peer group. *Developmental Psychology* 33: 1032–9.
Hodges, E.V.E., and D.G. Perry. 1999. Personal and interpersonal antecedents and consequences of victimization by peers. *Journal of Personality and Social Psychology* 76: 677–85.
Ireland, J.L., and C.L. Power. 2004. Attachment, emotional loneliness, and bullying behaviour: A study of adult and young offenders. *Aggressive Behavior* 30: 298–312.
Juvonen, J., S. Graham, and M.A. Schuster. 2003. Bullying among young adolescents: The strong, the weak, and the troubled. *Pediatrics* 112: 1231–7.
Kaltiala-Heino, R., M. Rimpela, P. Rantanen, and A. Rimpela. 2000. Bullying at school – An indicator of adolescents at risk for mental disorders. *Journal of Adolescence* 23: 661–74.
Kim, Y.S., B. Leventhal, Y.J. Koh, A. Hubbard, and T. Boyce. 2006. School bullying and youth violence. Causes or consequences of psychopathological behaviour? *Archives of General Psychiatry* 63: 1035–41.
Klomek, A.B., A. Sourander, S. Niemela, K. Kumpulainen, J. Piha, T. Tamminen, F. Almqvist, and M.S. Gould. 2009. Childhood bullying behaviors as a risk for suicide attempts and completed suicides: A population-based birth cohort study. *Journal of the American Academy of Child and Adolescent Psychiatry* 48: 254–61.
Kokkinos, M., and G. Panayiotou. 2004. Predicting bullying and victimization among early adolescents: Associations with disruptive behavior disorders. *Aggressive Behavior* 30: 520–33.
Kumpulainen, K., and E. Räsänen. 2000. Children involved in bullying at elementary school age: Their psychiatric symptoms and deviance in adolescence. An epidemiological sample. *Child Abuse and Neglect* 24: 1567–77.
Lieberman, R., and K.C. Cowan. 2011. Bullying and youth suicide: Breaking the connection. *Principal Leadership*, October: 12–17.
Lieberman, R., S. Poland, and R. Cassel. 2008. Best practices in suicide intervention. In *Best practices in school psychology V: Vol. IV. Enhancing the development of wellness, social skills, and life competencies*, ed. A. Thomas and J. Grimes, Section V, 1457–73. Bethesda, MD: National Association of School Psychologists.
Mellor, D. 2005. Community norms for the Strengths and Difficulties Questionnaire in Australia. *Australian Psychologist* 40: 215–22.
Menesini, E., M. Modena, and F. Tani. 2009. Bullying and victimization in adolescence: Concurrent and stable roles and psychological health symptoms. *Journal of Genetic Psychology* 170: 115–33.
Nansel, T.R., W. Craig, M.D. Overpeck, G. Saluja, and W.J. Ruan. 2004. Cross-national consistency in the relationship between bullying behaviours and psychosocial adjustment. *Archives of Paediatric and Adolescent Medicine* 158: 730–5.
Percy, A., P. McCrystal, and K. Higgins. 2008. Confirmatory factor analysis of the adolescent self-report Strengths and Difficulties Questionnaire. *European Journal of Psychological Assessment* 24: 43–8.

Prinstein, M.J., J. Boergers, and E.M. Vernberg. 2001. Overt and relational aggression in adolescents: Social psychological adjustment of aggressors and victims. *Journal of Clinical Child Psychology* 30: 479–91.

Rigby, K., P.T. Slee, and G. Martin. 2007. Implications of inadequate parental bonding and peer victimization at school for adolescent mental health. *Journal of Adolescence* 30: 801–12.

Rosenthal, R. 1991. *Meta-analytic procedures for social research*. Newbury Park, CA: Sage.

Sawyer, M.G., F.M. Arney, P.A. Baghurst, J.J. Clark, B.W. Graetz, R.J. Kosky, B. Nurcombe, et al. 2001. The mental health of young people in Australia: Key findings from the child and adolescent component of the national survey of mental health and well-being. *Australian and New Zealand Journal of Psychiatry* 35: 806–14.

Skrzypiec, G., P.T. Slee, R. Murray-Harvey, and B. Pereira. 2011. School bullying by one or more ways: Does it matter and how do students cope? *School Psychology International* 32: 288–311.

Slee, P.T., and K. Rigby. 1993. Australian school children's self-appraisal of interpersonal relations: The bullying experience. *Child Psychiatry and Human Development* 23: 272–83.

Smith, P.K., L. Talamelli, H. Cowie, P. Naylor, and P. Chauhan. 2004. Profiles of non-victims, escaped victims, continuing victims and new victims of school bullying. *British Journal of Educational Psychology* 74: 565–81.

Veenstra, R., S. Lindenberg, A.J. Oldehinkel, A.F. De Winter, and F.C. Verhulst. 2005. Bullying and victimization in elementary schools: A comparison of bullies, victims, bully/victims, and uninvolved preadolescents. *Developmental Psychology* 41: 672–82.

Viding, E., E. Simmonds, K.V. Petrides, and N. Frederickson. 2009. The contribution of callous–unemotional traits and conduct problems to bullying in early adolescence. *Journal of Child Psychology and Psychiatry* 50: 471–81.

Peer groups and victimisation among native and immigrant adolescents in Norway

Hildegunn Fandrem[a], Dagmar Strohmeier[b] and Kolbrun Asta Jonsdottir[a]

[a] *Centre for Behavioural Research, University of Stavanger, Norway;* [b] *University of Applied Sciences Upper Austria, Austria*

Despite the rapid increase in immigration all over Europe and concerns expressed for the adjustment of immigrant children and young people, studies on peer victimisation among them are scarce. By combining the predictions of the acculturative stress model with the social–ecological perspective of peer victimisation, this study compared different forms of peer victimisation in native Norwegian and immigrant young people, and explored whether depressive symptoms and the ethnic composition of peer groups in multicultural classes were related to levels of victimisation. Victimisation and depressive symptoms were investigated with self-assessments. Social cognitive mapping was used to identify peer groups in classes. The sample comprised 97 native adolescents and 59 immigrant adolescents attending 10 grade 8, 9 and 10 classes in a multicultural urban Norwegian secondary school. In line with the predictions of the acculturative stress model, young immigrants reported higher global victimisation compared with native Norwegians. However, they did not differ regarding depressive symptoms. In total, 42 peer groups were identified; 26 were ethnically mixed. Taking into account the base rate of ethnically mixed peer groups in the sample, the number of victims was not related to their ethnic composition. Moreover, gender and immigrant status did not moderate the associations between depressive symptoms and victimisation. The study highlights the importance of investigating the ethnic composition of peer groups to understand better the dynamics of victimisation in multicultural classes.

Introduction

Despite the rapid increase in immigration all over Europe and concerns expressed for the adjustment of immigrant children and young people, studies on peer victimisation among them are scarce. It is well established that immigration is associated with poorer psychological health such as depression, loneliness or lower self-esteem (e.g. Berry et al. 2006; Sam et al. 2008). From the acculturative stress perspective (Berry 1997, 2006), immigration is an inherently stressful life event and causes psychological health problems when immigrants do not have appropriate skills and strategies to cope successfully with the stressors. These psychological health problems may operate as vulnerabilities for peer victimisation among young immigrants. It has been shown that psychological health problems operate not only as consequences but also as antecedents for peer victimisation (Card and Hodges 2008; Hodges and Perry 1999; Sweeting et al. 2006). Thus, according to the acculturative stress perspective, it is plausible to predict that young immigrants are more vulnerable to peer victimisation than native young people.

In Norway, studies suggest that about 5–10% of students are victimised by their peers weekly or more often (Roland and Idsøe 2001; Olweus 1991), with boys more often victimised than girls. Regarding immigrant status, the findings in Norway are sparse and controversial. While Fandrem, Strohmeier and Roland (2009) did not find any differences regarding the levels of peer victimisation between natives and immigrants using a large representative sample ($N = 2938$), Bakken and Nordahl (2003) found, in an even larger representative sample ($N = 10,527$), that young immigrants were at higher risk compared to native young people.

Such varying findings have been reported not only from Norway but also from other countries where studies on immigrants have been conducted. In some countries (e.g. Switzerland, the USA and Finland), the immigrant background of youth was found to be a risk factor for being victimised by peers (Graham and Juvonen 2002; von Grünigen et al. 2010; Strohmeier, Kärnä, and Salmivalli 2011), while in other countries (e.g. Austria) immigrant status and victimisation were unrelated or immigrant status was even a protective factor against victimisation (Stefanek et al. 2011; Strohmeier, Spiel, and Gradinger 2008).

Contextual factors that influence victimisation

Taking a social–ecological perspective, research has already identified several risk factors at the school or class level for peer victimisation (Swearer and Espelage 2004). It has been shown that peer victimisation varies considerably between classes (Atria, Strohmeier, and Spiel 2007). Kärnä and colleagues (2010) showed that 13% of variation in victimisation was explained by class effects. To better understand peer victimisation in multicultural classes, several studies have investigated the ethnic composition of classes to explain the variance in victimisation. The ethnic composition of classes is of high theoretical importance assuming that young people form peer groups along ethnic lines. This preference principle is called *homophily* and refers to the tendency whereby friendships between similar people occur at a higher rate than among dissimilar people (Zeng and Xie 2008).

However, the studies investigating the ethnic composition of classes have produced varied findings. In the USA Juvonen, Nishina, and Graham (2006) reported less peer harassment and higher feelings of safety among students in ethnically diverse classes compared with students in ethnically homogeneous classes; but studies in the Netherlands found that classes with a high proportion of ethnic minority students can have higher rates of victimisation (Verkuyten and Thijs 2002; Vervoort, Scholte, and Overbeek 2010). In Austria, Stefanek and colleagues (2011) found that the ethnic composition of classes and peer victimisation were unrelated. These inconsistent results may be explained by country-level factors such as the immigration history or policy in the countries investigated. However, it is also possible that the ethnic composition of classes is not the most proximal variable for understanding peer victimisation in multicultural classes. Therefore, the present study focused on peer groups.

The aim was to explore how many mixed ethnic peer groups are formed in multicultural classes and whether these mixed ethnic peer groups are characterised by more victimisation compared with ethnically homogeneous peer groups. This question was investigated in an explorative way, because it was not possible to draw conclusive hypotheses. Assuming that ethnic homophily would be a strong preference principle for forming peer groups, it was reasonable to expect more ethnically homogeneous than ethnically mixed peer groups. On the other hand, research has demonstrated that ethnic homophily is moderated by opportunity structures. It has been shown that the likelihood of successful interethnic exchange and ethnically mixed peer groups is higher when the percentage of same-ethnicity peers in the context is lower (Hallinan and Teixeira 1987). This 'opportunity hypothesis' would predict more ethnically mixed than ethnically homogeneous peer groups in our sample, because, in Norway, immigrants come from a huge variety of countries and it is not easy for them to affiliate exclusively with same-ethnicity peers in an average Norwegian school.

Peer groups and victimisation

Studies focusing on victims within peer groups are rare. Previous research has identified both intrapersonal and interpersonal characteristics of victimised young people (e.g. Salmivalli and Isaacs 2005; Strohmeier, Spiel, and Gradinger 2011). The most salient characteristics of victims are intrapersonal problems such as anxiety, low self-esteem and depressive symptoms, or interpersonal problems such as peer rejection. Another interpersonal aspect is that victims may also be aggressive themselves (Schwartz, Proctor, and Chien 2001). Aggressive victims may, however, also suffer from depression and low self-esteem. Furthermore, it has been shown that peers may have a negative bias towards rejected or aggressive classmates, i.e. rejected classmates are viewed as more responsible for their transgressions than well-liked peers (Hymel 1986). On the basis of these studies, we expected that victims might not often be found as members of peer groups, but might more often be isolated from peer groups in a class.

However, whether the victim is an immigrant or a native may influence whether he or she is a part of a peer group in the first place and of which peer group he or she is a member. To be accepted by native peers may be a particular challenge for young immigrants who are also acculturating into another culture (Berry et al. 2006). Therefore, it is possible that victimised immigrants are more often isolated, because they may have problems being accepted by native peers and are therefore also more likely to be targets of peer victimisation (Strohmeier, Spiel, and Gradinger 2011).

Depressive symptoms and victimisation

Victimisation is associated with a variety of intrapersonal problems and numerous studies have shown that depressive symptoms are a very relevant correlate (Davidson and Demaray 2007; Hawker and Boulton 2000; Riittakerttu and Fröjd 2011; Strohmeier, Spiel, and Gradinger 2011). Previous research in Norway suggests that young immigrants are more vulnerable to depressive symptoms than natives (Fandrem, Sam, and Roland 2009; Oppedal and Roysamb 2004; Pantzer et al. 2006; Sam 1997; Torgersen 2001). This vulnerability of young immigrants to depression has often been explained within a stress and coping acculturation framework (Berry 1997). Girls generally have more depressive symptoms than boys in adolescence and there is a dramatic increase in depression among girls during adolescence, but not among boys (Cyranowski et al. 2000; Kandel and Davies 1982).

Gender differences in depressive symptoms are moderated by immigrant status. Gender differences are larger between immigrant and native girls than between immigrant and native boys, and immigrant girls are most vulnerable (Fandrem, Sam, and Roland 2009). Studies investigating the associations between victimisation and depressive symptoms among immigrant and native girls and boys are sparse. Because gender and immigrant status were found to moderate the levels of depressive symptoms, our study explored whether the association between victimisation and depressive symptoms is moderated by immigrant status and gender. Thus, we wanted to find out whether the associations between depressive symptoms and victimisation are equally high between immigrant and native boys and girls. We conducted these analyses to explore gender-specific patterns. For this reason, we used a multiple group design to explore whether the correlations between victimisation and depressive symptoms differ between immigrant and native boys and girls.

The following research questions and hypotheses were the focus of this study:

(1) Are immigrant young people at higher risk for victimisation and depressive symptoms?
On the basis of the acculturative stress model (Berry 1997), we predicted that young immigrants would score higher in depressive symptoms compared with native young people. Assuming that challenges related with immigration or the status of being an immigrant might work as vulnerabilities for peer victimisation, we also predicted that immigrant youth would score higher in victimisation compared with native young people.

(2) To what extent is the ethnic composition of peer groups related to victimisation in multicultural classes?
Applying the social–ecological perspective of victimisation, we expected that the ethnic composition of peer groups would influence the number of victims within these groups. Owing to a very limited body of evidence, we were not able to formulate more specific hypotheses regarding the direction of the effects. Furthermore, we predicted that victimised immigrants might more often be isolates (members of no peer group) compared with natives.

(3) Do gender and being an immigrant moderate the associations between victimisation and depressive symptoms?
We investigated this question in an explorative way, because the two variables, gender and being an immigrant, have never been considered together in previous studies.

Method

Participants

The investigation was carried out in April 2007 in a Norwegian urban secondary school consisting of 262 students enrolled in 10 classes. The class sizes ranged from 21 to 28 students. The students were in grades 8, 9 and 10 (approximately 13, 14 and 15 years old, respectively). About 45% of the students enrolled in this school were immigrants. In nine out of the 10 classes the young immigrants constituted the numerical minority (see also Table 2).

Participation was based on written parental consent. The immigrant parents were offered the information letters in both Norwegian and their mother tongue. The overall response rate was 60%, so the final sample consisted of 156 students. Of these, 97 were native students (55 girls, 42 boys) and 59 were categorised as immigrants (34 girls, 25 boys). Either these young immigrants were born in a country other than Norway (first generation, 43) or one of their parents was born in another country (second generation, 16); 35 were from Pakistan, 11 from Somalia, five from Arabic countries, three from Vietnam, three from Turkey and two from Kosovo.

The school has a positive policy regarding the inclusion of immigrant students. For instance, immigrant students are encouraged to also take classes in their mother tongue. During the year of data collection the school was not involved in any structured anti-bullying programme.

Measures and procedure

In all classes, the questionnaires were administered by the class teachers, who told the students not to write their names on their questionnaire; instead, the class teacher gave them a code list, which included only the names of those students who were allowed to participate in the study. To ensure anonymity the students returned the filled-in questionnaire in a sealed envelope.

Victimisation/bullying

A standard definition of bullying was first given in the questionnaire (Roland 1999):

> We call it bullying or hassling when one or more students (together) are unfriendly or unpleasant to a student who cannot defend him- or herself easily. This could include kicking, hitting, or shoving the student. It is also bullying when students are teased or when students are shut out from others. When a student is exposed to bullying we say that he/she is victimised.

Four self-report items (one global, three specific) were used; those for victimisation were: This school year how often have you been: Bullied/hassled at school? Bullied/hassled at school by being teased? Bullied/hassled at school because you couldn't be with others, were isolated/shut out from others? Bullied/hassled at school by being hit, kicked, or shoved?

The four items for bullying others had corresponding wording, e.g.: This school year how often have you: Bullied/hassled others at school? The response options were 'never', 'now and then', 'weekly' and 'daily', scored 1, 2, 3 and 4, respectively.

For the investigation of level differences (analyses shown in Table 1), students' answers to the four victimisation items were treated both separately and as a scale that was formed by averaging across the items. The Cronbach's alphas of the scale were 0.84 and 0.82 for immigrant and native young people, respectively.

For the investigation of peer groups (analyses shown in Table 2), students with a score of 2 ('now and then') or above on the global question about victimisation were considered to be a victim and students with a score of 2 or above on the global question about bullying were considered to be a bully. This categorisation was used for three reasons. First, we did not want to restrict the categorisation of victims and bullies to those who were harassed at least weekly, because many regular victims and bullies would then have gone unreported. Second, the roughly corresponding term 'now and then' best corresponds to the answer option 'two or three times a month', which has been used as a cut-off point in many large-scale studies (summarised in Olweus 2003). Third, there was a need to have an inclusive cut-off criterion to be able to conduct the analyses owing to the sample size.

For the present analyses, students with a score of 2 or above on both bullying and victimisation were categorised as victims and not as bullies. Thus, the victim category presented in Table 2 also includes aggressive victims.

Depressive symptoms

This was a six-item scale covering emotional, cognitive, motivational and somatic symptoms in depression (Rosenhan and Seligman 1989). The items were adopted from the Hopkins Symptom Checklist (SCL-90) (Derogatis et al. 1974). The construct validity of this scale has previously been found to be good for both immigrant and native boys and girls (Fandrem, Sam, and Roland 2009). Students answered how much they had suffered from the different depressive symptoms over the past two weeks. The four response categories were 'not suffered, 'suffered a little', 'suffered somewhat' and 'suffered a lot' (coded from 0 to 3). The Cronbach's alphas of the scale were 0.85 and 0.86 for immigrants and natives, respectively.

Group affiliation

Social cognitive mapping (SCM) was used to identify which students affiliated with which in peer groups. The SCM procedure has been used extensively in investigating school social networks (Cairns, Perrin, and Cairns 1985; Ertesvaag 2002, 2003; Fandrem et al. 2010; Farmer and Cairns 1991). Students are instructed to nominate classmates in all groups they can think of from a given social unit (often the class), including groups they are part of themselves. Following the procedure developed by Cairns and his colleagues (Cairns, Perrin, and Cairns 1985; Cairns et al. 1996), the students in our study used a code list and reported as many groups as they could think of from their class. The questions they were asked were: Are there some students in your class who hang around together a lot? Who are they? These questions were asked before the questions about bullying/victimisation and depressive symptoms.

The procedure yields robust results even with low participation rates. To ensure validity and reliability, a 50% participation rate has been established as the standard (Cairns et al. 1995). The participation rate in the present study was 60%.

The software SCM version 4.0 was used to find peer groups within a class. This program uses a co-occurrence matrix of the number of nominations that each student received for being members of a peer group along with other particular peers to define individuals' level of centrality within the group. The degree of centrality of the individual ranges from *peripheral* to *nuclear*, with *secondary* in the middle. Peripheral members are infrequently nominated as being a member of the peer group, while the nuclear members are frequently nominated as being members of the peer group (for more specific details about the procedure, see Farmer et al. 1993).

Results

Levels of victimisation and depressive symptoms

The means and standard deviations are presented in Table 1. To test for the statistically significant differences between the immigrant and native boys and girls, a multivariate analysis of variance (MANOVA) was conducted, with gender and being an immigrant as independent variables and the four victimisation items, the victimisation score and the depressive symptoms score as the dependent variables. Application of a multivariate test using Pillai's criterion revealed a significant main effect *gender*, $F(5,143) = 9.20, p < 0.01$, $\eta^2 = 0.25$, and a significant main effect *immigrant status*, $F(5,143) = 3.23, p = 0.01, \eta^2 = 0.11$. The interaction effect *gender* × *immigrant status* was not significant, $F(5,143) = 2.14, p = 0.06, \eta^2 = 0.07$.

Table 1. Levels of victimisation and depressive symptoms.

	Native girls ($n = 53$)	Immigrant girls ($n = 33$)	Native boys ($n = 41$)	Immigrant boys ($n = 24$)
Global victimisation	1.13 (0.39)	1.15 (0.36)	1.34 (0.66)	1.79 (0.72)
Verbal victimisation	1.09 (0.30)	1.15 (0.36)	1.48 (0.84)	1.75 (0.74)
Social victimisation	1.19 (0.40)	1.15 (0.36)	1.24 (0.62)	1.16 (0.48)
Physical victimisation	1.00 (0.00)	1.00 (0.00)	1.24 (0.58)	1.25 (0.53)
Victimisation (score)	1.10 (0.19)	1.11 (0.24)	1.33 (0.58)	1.49 (0.52)
Depressive symptoms (score)	1.90 (0.70)	1.82 (0.79)	1.61 (0.56)	1.61 (0.55)

Note: Data are shown as mean (SD).

Follow-up univariate analyses revealed significant *gender* differences for the global, $F(1,147) = 22.19, p < 0.01, \eta^2 = 0.13$, verbal, $F(1,147) = 25.35, p < 0.01, \eta^2 = 0.15$, and physical items, $F(1,147) = 15.51, p < 0.01, \eta^2 = 0.10$, the victimisation score and the depressive symptoms score, $F(1, 147) = 5.16, p = 0.03, \eta^2 = 0.03$. Boys scored higher in the three victimisation items but lower in the depressive symptoms score compared with girls (for details see Table 1). Follow-up univariate analyses revealed significant *immigrant status* differences for the global victimisation item, $F(1,147) = 6.78, p = 0.01, \eta^2 = 0.04$. Young immigrants, especially immigrant boys, scored higher in global victimisation compared with their native counterparts. No differences between immigrants and natives were found for depressive symptoms (see Table 1).

Characteristics of the peer groups

In total, 42 groups were identified with the SCM procedure. With the exception of four *secondary* groups, i.e. groups in with individuals had a less central position, all the groups were *nuclear*, i.e. individuals had a central position in the peer group. In four out of the 10 classes there was overlap between groups; in two out of these four classes one pupil was a member of two groups, in the third class seven pupils were members of more than one group, and in the last class six pupils constituted a subgroup in a larger group of eight pupils.

A detailed illustration of the peer groups of one 9th grade class is shown in Figure 1. The class of 28 students had 14 girls and 14 boys, of whom six girls and four boys were immigrants. Two students were absent (both natives). This class is the class at the school with the most victims, five all together. The results from the SCM suggested four groups. All the groups where characterised as nuclear, and no student was a member of more than one group, indicating that there was no overlap between groups. There was no isolate in this class, so all the students were involved in a social structure. Three of the four groups were ethnically mixed. Unusually, each of the four groups included at least one victim. The biggest ethnically homogeneous group was the most problematic as it had three bullies and two victims.

Of the total of 42 groups, six were male groups, 14 were female groups and four were mixed gender groups. The number of students in the peer groups ranged from three to nine, except for four groups, which consisted of two members only. Only one student was not identified as member of a group, and was an isolate. This student was a native male and a victim. As shown in Table 2, 26 groups were ethnically mixed (i.e. groups with both natives and immigrants), and 16 groups were non-mixed or ethnically homogeneous (i.e. only natives, or only immigrants).

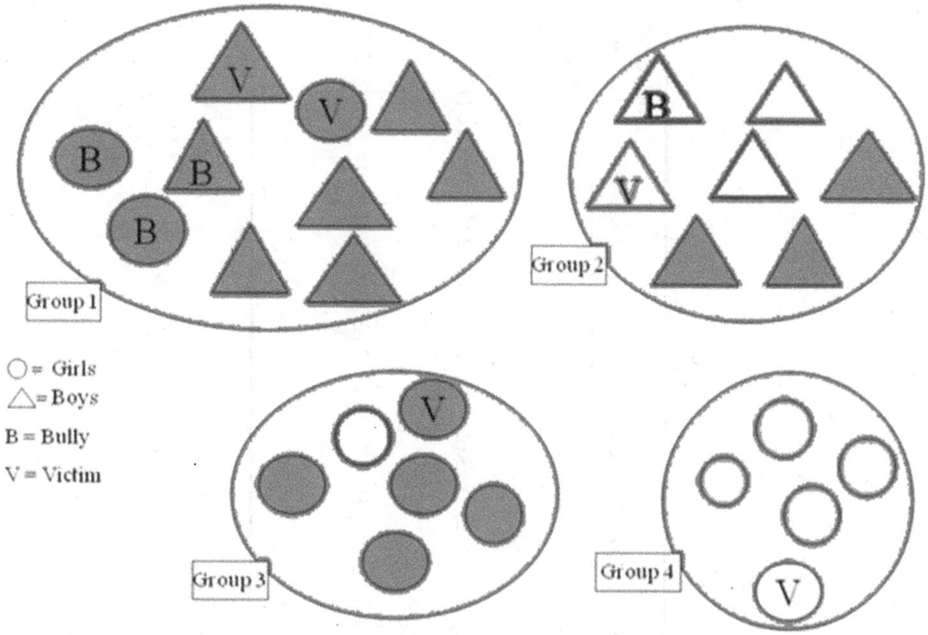

Figure 1. Descriptive results of peer groups in one class. Shaded students are native Norwegian, while white are immigrants.

Twenty (48%) peer groups – 12 ethnically mixed groups (46%) and eight non-mixed groups (50%) – included no victim; 15 (36%) peer groups – 10 mixed groups (39%) and five non-mixed (31%) – included one victim; and seven (16%) peer groups – four mixed groups (15%) and three non-mixed (19%) – had at least two victims. A 2 × 3 chi-squared test, $\chi^2(2) = 0.24$, $p = 0.89$, showed that the number of victims was not related to the ethnic composition of the groups.

Correlation between depressive symptoms and victimisation

The correlations between depressive symptoms and victimisation score were calculated, separately by gender and immigrant status. These were 0.07 (ns) for native boys, 0.07 for immigrant boys, −0.05 for native girls, and 0.26 for immigrant girls; none of these correlations was significant The association between depressive symptoms and victimisation was strongest among the immigrant girls, although the correlation did not differ significantly from that for native girls.

Discussion

From a theoretical perspective, this study breaks new ground by combining the predictions of the acculturative stress model (Berry 1997, 2006) with the social–ecological perspective (Swearer and Espelage 2004) to understand peer victimisation in young immigrants better. The study empirically investigated (1) whether immigrant status is a risk factor for peer victimisation and depressive symptoms in Norway, (2) whether the ethnic composition of peer groups as the most proximal contextual variable is related to victimisation

Table 2. Characteristics of the peer groups in the 10 classes.

	Class 1	Class 2	Class 3	Class 4	Class 5	Class 6	Class 7	Class 8	Class 9	Class 10	Total of all 10 classes
% of immigrants in the class	25	58.3	19	27.7	20	21.1	35.7	36	31.5	40	31.4
Number of peer groups	4	6	4	4	2	5	4	5	4	4	42
Number of mixed ethnic peer groups (with no/one/more than one victim)	3 (1/1/1)	4 (3/0/1)	2 (0/2/0)	4 (2/2/0)	1 (1/0/0)	3 (1/1/1)	2 (0/2/0)	3 (2/0/1)	2 (1/1/0)	2 (1/1/0)	26 (12/10/4)
Number of non-mixed peer groups (with no/one/more than one victim)	1 (0/0/1)	2 (1/1/0)	2 (2/0/0)	0	1 (0/1/0)	2 (0/2/0)	2 (0/1/1)	2 (1/0/1)	2 (2/0/0)	2 (2/0/0)	16 (8/5/3)

in multicultural classes, and (3) whether being an immigrant moderated the association between victimisation and depressive symptoms.

From the acculturative stress perspective (Berry 1997, 2006), immigration is an inherently stressful life event and causes psychological health problems when immigrants do not have appropriate skills and strategies to cope successfully with the stressors. These psychological health problems might operate as vulnerabilities for peer victimisation among young immigrants. Thus, irrespective of gender, it was predicted that young immigrants would score higher in victimisation and depressive symptoms compared with native young people. This prediction was confirmed for global victimisation, and thus is in line with the largest representative study in Norway (Bakken and Nordahl 2003), but for depressive symptoms it was not confirmed. The unexpected result for depressive symptoms may partly be explained by the data collection procedure. Because the questionnaire was only presented in Norwegian, we probably systematically excluded newly arrived immigrants who did not speak Norwegian well enough to answer the questions. The participating immigrants had probably already developed satisfactory language skills which might have facilitated successful coping with acculturative stress.

On the basis of a social–ecological perspective (Swearer and Espelage 2004) the ethnic composition of peer groups as the most proximal social context was explored via SCM to give a better understanding of peer victimisation in multicultural classes. The percentage of ethnically mixed groups (26 out of 42, or 62%) outnumbered the percentage of homogeneous immigrant or native groups (38%) in all of the 10 classes. This suggests a rather weak homophily bias for the students in this sample (Zeng and Xie 2008), and instead supports the prediction of the opportunity hypothesis (Hallinan and Teixeira 1987). In Norway it may not be easy for young immigrants to affiliate exclusively with other immigrant peers in an average Norwegian school. Contrary to our predictions, the victims in this multicultural school were not isolated because, except for one native male victim, they were all members of peer groups in their class. Moreover, when taking into account the base rate of ethnically mixed peer groups in the sample, the numbers of victims in each peer group was not related to their ethnic composition.

From the acculturative stress perspective (Berry 1997, 2006), it is reasonable to hypothesise that depressive symptoms mediate the link between being an immigrant and victimisation (Strohmeier, Kärnä, and Salmivalli 2011). To the best of our knowledge, the potential moderating effect of gender has not been empirically explored. Because gender and immigrant status were found to moderate the levels of depressive symptoms, this study explored whether the association between victimisation and depressive symptoms is moderated by being an immigrant and by gender. This question was investigated in an explorative way and these factors were not found to moderate the associations significantly.

Limitations of the study

A potential weakness of the study is that it was not possible to detect the response rate separately for immigrants and natives, because of the anonymity principle. Thus, we did not have any information about the immigrant status of those students who did not participate in the study on a class level. Moreover, the general response rate was quite low, as only 60% of eligible students participated. As a consequence, the network patterns in the classes may not be exact. Because the sample size was small and only 10 classes were investigated, it was not possible to apply more refined statistical analyses, such as hierarchical linear models. Thus, it was not possible to test empirically the importance of the opportunity structure for interethnic exchange at a class level. Instead, it was only possible to inspect the percentage of immigrant students in the 10 classes descriptively.

Another possible source of error is that the number of immigrants and natives may differ in different classes. Previous studies mostly used classes as the units for nominations (e.g. Estell, Farmer, and Cairns 2007). This was also the case in our study, as students were able to nominate students from their own class only. Except for one class, the immigrants were the numerical minority, while natives were the numerical majority. However, the number of immigrants and natives varied only slightly between classes.

Another limitation is due to the small sample size, which made it impossible to differentiate among immigrants. There might be differences inside the immigrant group depending on, for example, the place immigrants come from and the reason for their migration. However, the way of differentiating depends on the research question, and in this study we were interested in the role of acculturation, which is common for all immigrants. In addition, the reliance throughout on self-report measures is a limitation. The identification of victims could have been made more reliable by using several sources (peer and/or teacher report, in addition to self-report).

Another issue is that girls generally may be more willing to report emotional problems than boys (Fleming, Offord, and Boyle 1989; Philip and Segal 1969). This could influence the differences between natives and immigrants if one claimed that gender roles are much stronger in the eastern cultures represented in our sample (Nolen-Hoeksema 1990; Hofstede 1983). However, we did not find any differences between immigrant and non-immigrant girls in the present study.

The study would have had greater weight if it had sampled across a range of schools; then it would have been possible to generalise the findings, which would have strengthened the validity.

Scientific contribution and implications

Taken together, our findings highlight the importance of investigating the ethnic composition of peer groups to gain a better understanding of the dynamics of victimisation in multicultural classes. The focus on victims is generally important, as many studies, at least in Norway, mainly focus on the bullies. Further studies could contribute significantly to the existing literature by investigating the ethnic composition of peer groups in addition to opportunity structures at class level. Continued work on these issues, with diverse samples, is vital in developing effective intervention programmes, education and policy to achieve better integration of immigrant adolescents in Norwegian schools.

References

Atria, M., D. Strohmeier, and C. Spiel. 2007. The relevance of the school class as social unit for the prevalence of bullying and victimization. *European Journal of Developmental Psychology* 4: 372–87.

Bakken, A., and T. Nordahl. 2003. *Mobbing og sosial isolasjon i ungdomsmiljøene. Hva viser NOVAs ungsdoms- og skoleundersøkelser*. Oslo: NOVA.

Berry, J.W. 1997. Immigration, acculturation and adaptation. *Applied Psychology: An International Review* 46: 5–68.

Berry, J.W. 2006. Stress perspectives on acculturation. In *Acculturation psychology*, ed. D.L. Sam and J.W. Berry, 43–57. Cambridge: Cambridge University Press.

Berry, J.W., J.S. Phinney, D.L. Sam, and P. Vedder. 2006. Immigrant youth: Acculturation, identity, and adaptation. *Applied Psychology: An International Review* 55: 303–32.

Cairns, R.B., J.L. Garièpy, T. Kinderman, and M.C. Leung. 1996. *Identifying social clusters in natural settings*. Unpublished manuscript. University of North Carolina at Chapel Hill.

Cairns, R.B., M.C. Leung, L. Buchanan, and B.D. Cairns. 1995. Friendship and social networks in childhood and adolescence: Fluidity, reliability and interrelations. *Child Development* 66: 1330–5.

Cairns, R.B., J.E. Perrin, and B.D. Cairns. 1985. Social structure and social cognition in early adolescence: Affiliative patterns. *Journal of Early Adolescence* 5: 339–55.

Card, N., and E. Hodges. 2008. Peer victimization among schoolchildren: Correlations, causes, consequences, and considerations in assessment and intervention. *School Psychology Quarterly* 23: 451–61.

Cyranowski, J.M., E. Frank, E. Young, and M.K. Shear. 2000. Adolescent onset of the gender difference in lifetime rates of major depression. *Archives of General Psychiatry* 57: 21–7.

Davidson, L.S., and M.K. Demaray. 2007. Social support as moderator between victimization and internalizing–externalizing distress from bullying. *School Psychology Review* 36: 383–405.

Derogatis, L.R., R.S. Lipman, K. Rickels, E.H. Uhlenhuth, and L. Covi. 1974. The Hopkins Symptom Checklist (HSCL): A self-report symptom inventory. *Behavioral Science* 19: 1–15.

Ertesvåg, S.K. 2002. *Små gupper som sosial læringsaene. Ein kort longitudinell studie av trening av kommunikative dugleikar hjå elevar i 8. klasse*. Trondheim: NTNU.

Ertesvåg, S.K. 2003. Sosial status og sosialt nettverk i ei klasse med ein elev med multihandikap. *Nordisk tidsskrift for Spesialpedagogikk* 2: 53–65.

Estell, D.B., T.W. Farmer, and B.D. Cairns. 2007. Bullies and victims in rural African American youth: Behavioral characteristics and social network placement. *Aggressive Behavior* 33: 145–59.

Fandrem, H., S. Ertesvåg, D. Strohmeier, and E. Roland. 2010. Bullying and affiliation – A study of peer groups in native and immigrant adolescents in Norway. *European Journal of Developmental Psychology* 7: 401–18.

Fandrem, H., D.L. Sam, and E. Roland. 2009. Depressive symptoms among native and immigrant adolescents in Norway: The role of gender and urbanization. *Social Indicators Research* 92: 91–109.

Fandrem, H., D. Strohmeier, and E. Roland. 2009. Bullying and victimization among Norwegian and immigrant adolescents in Norway: The role of proactive and reactive aggressiveness. *Journal of Early Adolescence* 29: 898–923.

Farmer, T.W., and R.B. Cairns 1991. Social networks and social status in emotionally disturbed children. *Behavioural Disorders* 16: 288–98.

Farmer, T.W., C.B. Stuart, N.H. Lorch, and E. Field. 1993. The social behaviour and peer relations of emotionally and behaviourally disturbed pupils in residential treatment: A pilot study. *Journal of Emotional and Behavioural Disorders* 1: 223–234.

Fleming, J.E., D.R. Offord, and M.H. Boyle. 1989. Prevalence of childhood and adolescent depression in the community: Ontario Child Health Study. *British Journal of Psychiatry* 155: 647–54.

Graham, S., and J. Juvonen. 2002. Ethnicity, peer harassment, and adjustment in middle school: An exploratory study. *Journal of Early Adolescence* 22: 173–199.

von Grünigen, R., S. Perren, C. Nägele, and F. Alsaker. 2010. Immigrant children's peer acceptance and victimization in kindergarten: The role of local language competence. *British Journal of Developmental Psychology* 28: 679–97.

Hallinan, M., and R. Teixeira. 1987. Opportunities and constraints: Black–White differences in the formation of interracial friendships. *Child Development* 58: 1358–71.

Hawker, D., and M. Boulton. 2000. Twenty years' research on peer victimization and psychosocial maladjustment: A meta-analytic review of cross-sectional studies. *Journal of Child Psychology and Psychiatry and Allied Disciplines* 41: 441–55.

Hodges, E., and D.G. Perry. 1999. Personal and interpersonal antecedents and consequences of victimization by peers. *Journal of Personality & Social Psychology* 76: 677–85.

Hofstede, G. 1983. Dimensions of national cultures in fifty countries and three regions. In *Explanations in cross-cultural psychology*, ed. J. Deregowski, S. Dziurawiec and R. Annis, 335–55. Lisse: Swet & Zeitlinger.

Hymel, S. 1986. Interpretations of peer behaviour: Affective bias in childhood and adolescence. *Child Development* 57: 431–45.

Juvonen, J., A. Nishina, and S. Graham. 2006. Ethnic diversity and perceptions of safety in urban middle schools. *Psychological Science* 17: 393–400.

Kandel, D.B., and M. Davies. 1982. Epidemiology of depressed mood in adolescents. An empirical study. *Archives of General Psychiatry* 39: 1205–12.

Kärnä, A., M. Voeten, E. Poskiparta, and C. Salmivalli. 2010. Vulnerable children in varying classroom contexts: Bystanders' behaviors moderate the effects of risk factors on victimization. *Merrill-Palmer Quarterly* 56: 261–82.

Nolen-Hoeksema, S. 1990. *Sex-differences in depression*. Stanford, CT: Stanford University Press.

Olweus, D. 1991. Bully/victim problems among schoolchildren: Basic facts and effects of a school based intervention program. In *The development and treatment of childhood aggression*, ed. D.J. Pepler and K.H. Rubin, 411–48. Hillsdale, NJ: Lawrence Erlbaum.

Oppedal, B., and E. Roysamb. 2004. Mental health, life stress, and social support among young Norwegian adolescents with immigrant and host national background. *Scandinavian Journal of Psychology* 45: 131–44.

Pantzer, K., L. Rajmil, C. Tebé, F. Codina, V. Serra-Sutton, M. Ferrer, U. Ravens-Sieberer, M.-C. Simeoni, and J. Alonso. 2006. Health related quality of life in immigrants and native school aged adolescents in Spain. *Journal of Epidemiology and Community Health* 60: 694–8.

Philip, D.L., and B.E. Segal. 1969. Sexual status and psychiatric symptoms. *American Sociological Review* 34, no. 1: 58–72.

Riittakerttu, K.H., and S. Fröjd. 2011. Correlation between bullying and clinical depression in adolescent patients. *Adolescent Health, Medicine and Therapeutics* 2: 37–44.

Roland, E., and T. Idsøe. 2001. Aggression and bullying. *Aggressive Behavior* 27: 446–62.

Rosenhan, D.L., and M.E.P. Seligman. 1989. *Abnormal psychology*. 2nd ed. New York: W.W. Norton.

Salmivalli, C., and J. Isaacs. 2005. Prospective relations among victimization, rejection, friendlessness, and children's self- and peer-perceptions. *Child Development* 76: 1161–71.

Sam, D.L. 1997. Helse og helseatferd blant innvandrerungdom. In *Ungdom, livsstil og helsefremmende arbeid*, ed. K.-I. Klepp and L.E. Aarø, 88–99. Oslo: Universitetsforlaget.

Sam, D.L., P. Vedder, K. Liebkind, F. Neto, and E. Virta. 2008. Immigration, acculturation and the paradox of adaptation in Europe. *European Journal of Developmental Psychology* 5: 138–58.

Schwartz, D., L.J. Proctor, and D.H. Chien. 2001. The aggressive victim of bullying: Emotional and behavioral dysregulation as a pathway to victimization by peers. In *Peer harassment in school: The plight of the vulnerable and victimized*, ed. J. Juvonen and S. Graham, 147–174. New York: Guilford Press.

Stefanek, E., D. Strohmeier, R., Van de Schoot, and C. Spiel. 2011. Bullying and victimization in ethnically diverse schools: Risk and protective factors on the individual and class level. *International Journal of Developmental Science* 5: 73–84.

Strohmeier, D., A. Kärnä, and C. Salmivalli. 2011. Intrapersonal and interpersonal risk factors for peer victimization in immigrant youth in Finland. *Developmental Psychology* 47: 248–58.

Strohmeier, D., C. Spiel, and P. Gradinger. 2008. Social relationships in multicultural schools: Bullying and victimization. *European Journal of Developmental Psychology* 5: 262–85.

Swearer, S.M., and D.L. Espelage. 2004. Introduction: A social–ecological framework of bullying among youth. In *Bullying in American schools: A social–ecological perspective on prevention and intervention*, ed. D.L. Espelage and S.M. Swearer, 1–12. Mahwah, NJ: Lawrence Erlbaum.

Sweeting, H., R. Young, P. West, and G. Der. 2006. Peer victimization and depression in early–mid adolescence: A longitudinal study. *British Journal of Educational Psychology* 76: 577–94.

Torgersen, L. 2001. Sammenhengen mellom depressivt stemningsleie og relasjoner til foreldre. En studie av andregenerasjons pakistanske innvandrere og ungdommer av norsk opprinnelse. *Tidsskrift for norsk psykologiforening* 38: 640–8.

Verkuyten, M., and J. Thijs. 2002. Racist victimization among children in The Netherlands: The effect of ethnic group and school. *Ethnic and Racial Studies* 25: 310–31.

Vervoort, M.H.M., R.H.J. Scholte, and G. Overbeek. 2010. Bullying and victimization among adolescents: The role of ethnicity and ethnic composition of school class. *Journal of Youth and Adolescence* 39: 1–11.

Zeng, Z., and Y. Xie. 2008. A preference–opportunity–choice framework with applications to intergroup friendship. *American Journal of Sociology* 114: 615–48.

Emotional problems and victimisation among youth with national and international migration experience living in Austria and Turkey

Dagmar Strohmeier[a] and Aysun Dogan[b]

[a]*School of Applied Health/Social Sciences, University of Applied Sciences Upper Austria, Linz, Austria;* [b]*Ege University, Izmir, Turkey*

Young people with international migration experiences constitute an increasing proportion of the population in many European countries. In Austria, a substantial proportion of these international migrants come from Turkey. In Turkey, many adolescents are national migrants, having moved from the eastern part to the western part of the country. This study compares the impact of national and international migration experiences on the levels of emotional difficulties (depression, anxiety, loneliness and self-esteem) and peer victimisation, and tests whether emotional difficulties help to explain the associations between migration experiences and peer victimisation. In Austria, a total of 379 non-migrant Austrians, 82 first generation and 202 second generation international migrants from Turkey; and in Turkey, 990 non-migrant Turks and 501 national migrants participated; they were in two age cohorts (12 and 15 years). In line with the predictions of the acculturative stress model, national and first generation international migrants had higher levels of depression and social anxiety and lower levels of self esteem compared to non-migrant Austrians, while no differences were found for second generation international migrants. Unexpectedly, all four Turkish groups were less likely to be victimised compared to the non-migrant Austrian group. In line with the predictions, high levels of social anxiety and depression helped to explain high levels of victimisation, but only among youth who experienced resettlement (e.g. national and first generation international migrants), indicating that acculturative stress works as a risk factor for peer victimisation.

Introduction

In all industrialised countries there are rising numbers of children and youth who have migration experiences. While the migration experience of people who moved from one country to another country is defined as international, people who move within the same country are classified as national migrants (International Organization for Migration 2010). Migration is an inherently stressful life event because of resettlement and the challenges related with acculturation (Berry 2006). Several studies have investigated the behavioural and emotional difficulties of youth who have migrated internationally. It is well established that international migration is associated with poorer psychological health, including depression, loneliness and low self-esteem (e.g. Berry et al. 2006; Sam et al. 2008). However, very few studies (Aksel et al. 2007; Gün and Bayraktar 2008) have examined nationally migrated youth, although their numbers are increasing (International Organization for Migration 2010). To the best of our knowledge, no study has compared the impact of different kinds of national and international migration experiences regarding both the levels of, and the associations between, emotional difficulties and peer victimisation.

Victimisation experiences of nationally and internationally migrated youth

Studies considering victimisation of internationally migrated youth have produced varying findings. Most of these studies have found no differences between natives and migrant youth (Fandrem, Strohmeier, and Roland 2009; McKenney et al. 2006; Monks, Ortega-Ruiz, and Rodriguez-Hidalgo 2008). Some studies have found non-migrant youth to be at high risk for being victimised (Verkuyten and Thijs 2006), whereas other studies have found migrant youth to be at high risk for victimisation (Graham and Juvonen 2002; von Grünigen et al. 2009; Strohmeier, Kärnä, and Salmivalli 2011). Studies conducted in Austria have yielded more consistent results. In Austria, studies splitting internationally migrated youth according to their ethnic background showed that they were either at lower or at equal risk for being victimised by their peers compared to native youth (Bergmüller and Wiesner 2009; Strohmeier and Spiel 2003; Strohmeier, Atria, and Spiel 2005; Strohmeier, Nestler, and Spiel 2006; Strohmeier, Spiel, and Gradinger 2008). More specifically, adolescents with a Turkish background reported lower levels of victimisation compared to native youth and adolescents coming from the former Yugoslavia (Stefanek et al. 2011). However, to date no study has investigated the victimisation experiences of first and second generation Turkish migrant youth living in Austria.

Emotional difficulties of nationally and internationally migrated youth

International migration has been consistently identified as a risk factor for lower mental health among youth (Fandrem, Sam, and Roland 2009; Oppedal and Roysamb 2004; Stefanek et al. 2012). A study with a large cross-national sample of migrant and non-migrant youth aged 13–18 years living in Finland, the Netherlands, Norway, Portugal and Sweden showed that being a first generation migrant is associated with higher levels of emotional difficulties such as poor life satisfaction, depressive and somatic symptoms, anxiety and low self-esteem compared to non-migrant or second generation migrant youth (Sam et al. 2008). These higher levels of emotional difficulties in first generation migrant youth are often explained within a stress and coping acculturation framework (Berry 1997). This is due to the fact that resettlement leads to emotional difficulties when immigrants do not have appropriate skills and strategies to successfully cope with the stressors. Even though resettlement is also experienced by nationally migrated youth, studies examining the effects of national migration on emotional difficulties are scarce. Findings of these limited studies indicate that nationally migrated youth also showed emotional problems such as lower self-esteem and low levels of life satisfaction (Aksel et al. 2007; Gün and Bayraktar 2008) as well as high levels of anger and hostility (among girls) and high levels of generalised anxiety and obsessive compulsive symptoms (among boys) (Özen et al. 2001) compared to youth without any migration experience.

Associations between emotional difficulties and victimisation in nationally and internationally migrated youth

A large body of evidence indicates that depression, generalised and social anxiety, loneliness and low self-worth are related to peer victimisation (e.g. Hawker and Boulton 2000). Longitudinal studies support the idea that emotional difficulties such as depression, loneliness and anxiety are not only consequences but also potential vulnerabilities inviting peer victimisation (Card and Hodges 2008; Hodges and Perry 1999; Sweeting et al. 2006).

From an acculturative stress perspective, generational status is a very important variable to better understand the associations between emotional difficulties (depression, anxiety, loneliness and self-esteem) and peer victimisation. Being a first generation international migrant youth might be associated with emotional difficulties due to acculturative stress which, in turn, might work as a risk factor for peer victimisation. Exactly the same mechanism is expected for nationally migrated youth, because these youth have also experienced resettlement and acculturative stress. Thus, based on the acculturative stress model we assume the existence of the following mechanism: both national and international migration are associated with emotional difficulties due to acculturative stress. These emotional difficulties are expected to work as vulnerabilities for peer victimisation. Thus, high levels of emotional difficulties should help to explain high levels of victimisation among first generation international and national migrant youth. On the contrary, this particular mechanism is not expected to be present among second generation international migrant and native youth.

Beirens and Fontaine (2011) argued that in the literature acculturation and national background are often confounded, because internationally migrated youth are usually only compared with non-migrant youth born in the receiving country. Obviously such a design is limited, because it is not possible to know whether observed differences between the groups are due to differences in migration experiences or to different national or cultural backgrounds. To overcome such difficulties, non-migrant youth living in both the receiving country (Austria) and the sending country (Turkey) are included in the present study.

Migration situation in Austria

In 2010, 17.8% of the population were classified as international migrants in Austria (Statistik Austria 2010). Thirteen per cent were first generation migrants and 4.7% were second generation migrants. The three biggest groups migrated to Austria from the former Yugoslavia (31%), Germany (14%) and Turkey (13%); many people also migrated from eastern European countries (~14%), such as Poland, Romania, the Czech Republic and Hungary. Depending on the region in Austria, there is a huge variation of the percentage of migrants, with the biggest proportions (36%) present in Vienna. The migrant population is rather young: their average age is lower and their birth rate is higher than the native Austrian population (Statistic Austria 2010).

Migration situation in Turkey

Turkish people have been moving out of the country (international migration) or within the country (national migration) for many different reasons. International migration to Europe was launched at the beginning of 1960s when Turkish people were invited as 'guest workers'. The first legal agreement on workers' demands was signed between Turkey and Germany in 1961. Austria, Belgium and the Netherlands also requested workers and these agreements were signed in 1964 (Uslu and Cassina 1999). In the 1970s the majority of the first comers reunited with their family members and settled permanently in the host countries. In the 1980s the main reasons for migration included family reunification, marriage to Turkish migrants and political upheavals in Turkey (Icduygu and Sirkeci 1999). Today, a large number of second and third generation Turkish people are living in many European countries.

National migration within Turkey started in the 1950s, mainly because of population increase, land confiscations due to highway or dam constructions, high unemployment rates and natural disasters (Pazarlıoğlu 2007). In the mid-1980s and 1990s the reasons for national migration were heightened terrorism risk and forced migration by the government, especially from the eastern part of the country to the west. As people moved from rural areas to the cities, the proportion of the urban population increased from 24% in 1935 to 65% in 2000 (Özgür 2003; Sağlam 2006). İzmir (where part of the present study was carried out) is the third biggest city in Turkey with a population of over three million and has the second highest proportion of national migrants after Istanbul (Pazarlıoğlu 2007). In 2008, 111,255 national migrants moved to İzmir, meaning that the city welcomed 305 children, youth or adults every day from all over the country (Türkiye İstatistik Kurumu 2009).

The present study

The present study distinguishes between national as well as first and second generation international migration experiences. While nationally migrated youth moved within Turkey, first generation internationally migrated youth moved from Turkey to Austria, and second generation internationally migrated youth were born in Austria but their parents moved from Turkey to Austria. In addition, non-migrant youth living in both Austria and Turkey were included, to avoid confounding national background and migration experiences.

According to the acculturative stress perspective (Berry 1997), migration experiences both within and between countries are inherently stressful life events. However, the designs of the available studies are limited because usually (one or several groups of) internationally migrated youth are compared with non-migrant youth located in the receiving country. It is important to compare emotional difficulties and peer victimisation of nationally and internationally migrated youth with non-migrant youth located in both the receiving and the sending country to better understand the underlying mechanisms of peer victimisation among nationally and internationally migrated youth.

We predicted that both nationally and internationally migrated youth are more vulnerable regarding peer victimisation compared to native and second generation immigrant youth. This prediction was based on the acculturative stress perspective indicating that resettlement works as a risk factor for peer victimisation (Berry 1997, 2006). Based on this perspective, we also predicted that nationally and first generation internationally migrated youth would exhibit higher levels of emotional problems such as depression, anxiety, loneliness and low self-esteem compared to natives and second generation internationally migrated youth.

In addition, we investigated whether emotional problems help to explain the association between migration experiences and victimisation. More specifically, we tested whether first generation international and national migration experiences predict individual variation in emotional problems such as depression, anxiety, loneliness and low self-esteem and whether any of these problems further increase the risk for victimisation.

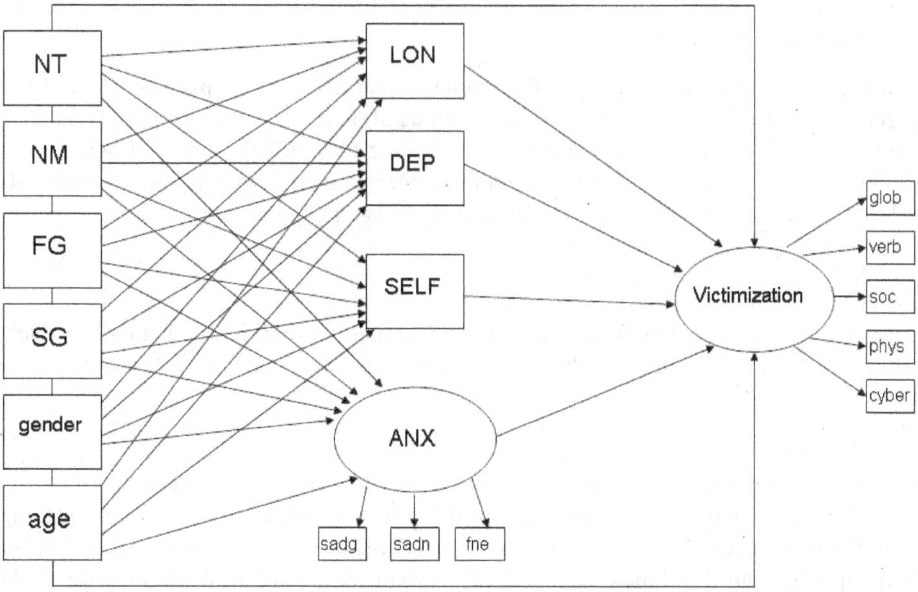

Figure 1. The initial model for predicting the direct and indirect effects of migration experiences on victimisation. NT: native Turks; NM: national migrants; FG: first generation international migrants; SG: second generation international migrants; LON: loneliness; DEP: depression; SELF: self-esteem; ANX: social anxiety; sadg: general social avoidance and distress; sadn: social avoidance and distress in new social situations; fne: fear of negative evaluation; victimisation: victimisation; glob: global victimisation; verb: verbal victimisation; soc: social victimisation; phys: physical victimisation; cyber: cybervictimisation.

The sample comprised of two age cohorts (12 and 15 years) living in Turkey and Austria. These age groups were chosen because victimisation peaks in preadolescence and declines during middle adolescence (Rigby 2002). Gender and age were included in the model to control for their potential effects because it is well known that they are both related to victimisation and emotional problems. As shown in Figure 1, we tested (1) whether migration experiences, gender and age are directly associated with emotional problems and victimisation, and (2) whether the four types of emotional problems are directly associated with victimisation. In addition (not shown in the model), we tested (3) whether there are indirect associations between migration experiences, emotional problems and victimisation.

Method

Design

Five groups of adolescents aged 12 and 15 years completed self-report questionnaires: in Austria, native Austrians (NA), Turkish youth with first generation international migration experience (FG) and Turkish youth with second generation international migration experience (SG); and in Turkey, native Turks (NT) with no migration experiences, and Turkish youth with national migration experience (NM). In both Austria and Turkey, participants were recruited in junior and high schools serving populations with international (Austria) and national (Turkey) migration experiences.

Measures

Demographic information

Adolescents were asked to indicate their gender, year of birth, the marital status of their parents, and the education and employment status of their father and mother. Adolescents were asked in which country and city (1) they were born, (2) their mother and (3) their father were born. Adolescents who migrated either nationally or internationally were also asked to indicate the reason for migration and their age at migration.

New media access

Adolescents were asked to indicate in a yes/no format whether they own a mobile phone, whether they have a computer at home and whether they have Internet access at home.

Victimisation

Five self-report items including a global question and four specific questions were used. For the present study it was important to find a term or phrase with a similar meaning in both the German and Turkish languages. It is difficult to translate the term 'being bullied' into German (Strohmeier et al. 2012). Several terms are available in German, but none of them is a fully appropriate translation of the English term 'bullying' (Smith et al. 2002). Similarly, several terms exist for 'being bullied' in Turkish (Ucanok, Smith, and Sertkaya Karasoy 2011). To avoid different interpretations in the two languages, the very concrete description 'being hurt or insulted' was used, as this phrase can easily be translated into both German and Turkish. Before presenting the items to the adolescents, the criteria of bullying behaviour, including hostile intent, power imbalance and repetition, were explained to the students. In the global question, the adolescents were asked: 'How often have you been hurt or insulted at school during this term?' The four specific questions were similar to the global one, except that they described one particular form of being bullied at the time, namely verbal, physical, social exclusion, and cyberbullying. The answers to all questions were given on a five-point Likert scale (1 = not at all, 2 = once or twice, 3 = once or twice a month, 4 = once or twice a week, 5 = nearly every day). In the analyses, adolescents' answers to the items were treated both separately and as a scale that was formed by averaging across the five items ($\alpha = 0.77$ for the whole sample).

Depression

The Child Depression Inventory (CDI) (Kovacs 1981) was used to measure adolescents' depressive symptoms. The CDI has previously been applied and validated in both the Turkish (Öy 1991) and German languages (Stiensmeier-Pelster, Schürmann, and Duda 2000). Participants responded to items on a three-point scale such as: 'I am sad once in a while', 'I am sad many times', 'I am sad all the time', or 'Nobody really loves me', 'I am not sure if anybody loves me', 'I am sure that somebody loves me' (reversed item); the reference period was the past two weeks. The scores for the 27 items formed a reliable scale and were averaged ($\alpha = 0.82$ for the whole sample).

Self-esteem

The Rosenberg Self-Esteem Scale (Rosenberg 1965) was used; this has previously been applied and validated in both Turkish (Çuhadaroğlu 1986) and German (Ferring and Filipp 1996). Participants responded on a four-point Likert-type scale (1 = I strongly disagree,

4 = I strongly agree) to 10 items such as 'I feel that I have a number of good qualities' and 'I feel that I am a person of worth, at least on an equal plane with others'. The scores formed a reliable scale and were averaged ($\alpha = 0.78$ for the whole sample).

Social anxiety

To assess social anxiety, 18 items from a questionnaire developed by La Greca and Lopez (1998) were used. Adolescents responded on a five-point Likert scale (1 = never, 5 = always). This scale has previously been applied and validated in both Turkish (Aydın and Tekinsav-Sutcu 2007) and German (Melfsen 1998; Melfsen and Florin 1997). The first subscale, reflecting *fear of negative evaluation*, included eight items, e.g. 'I worry about what others say about me'. The second subscale, tapping *general social avoidance and distress*, included four items, such as 'It's hard for me to ask others to do things with me'. The third subscale, measuring *social avoidance and distress in new social situations*, included six items, such as 'I get nervous when I meet new people'. The three subscales were reliable ($\alpha = 0.86$, 0.69 and 0.73, respectively) and were averaged for further analyses.

Loneliness

Loneliness was assessed with 16 items developed by Asher and Wheeler (1985) and Asher, Hymel and Renshaw (1984). This scale has been validated and previously used in Turkey (Tarhan 1996). The adolescents responded on a five-point Likert scale (1 = not at all true, 5 = always true) to items such as 'I can find a friend when I need one' or 'It's easy for me to make new friends at school' (reversed). The items formed a reliable scale and were averaged ($\alpha = 0.87$ for the whole sample).

Procedure

After permission had been obtained from the national and local authorities, parents and students, data were collected in 29 schools and 90 classrooms in Vienna, Austria, and in 11 different schools and 52 classrooms in Izmir, Turkey, between December 2009 and June 2010. In both countries, the 12-year-olds were recruited in secondary schools and the 15-year-olds in high schools. Questionnaires were individually completed in classes during regular teaching hours under the supervision of two trained research assistants. Because schools in Vienna are very diverse regarding the ethnic backgrounds of students, only students with Turkish or native Austrian origin were invited to take part in the study. In Austria, bilingual research assistants offered German and Turkish versions of the questionnaire to the students. Students were able to ask the research assistants at any time if they had any questions during data collection.

Categorisation of migration experiences and sample description

In Austria, adolescents who were born in Vienna with at least one parent also born in Vienna were classified as non-migrant Austrians (NA). Those whose mother and father were born in Turkey, and who were born in Turkey, were classified as first generation international migrants (FG). The adolescents whose mother and/or father were born in Turkey, but who were born in Austria, were classified as second generation international migrations (SG). In Turkey, adolescents who were born in Izmir with at least one parent also born in Izmir were categorised as non-migrant Turks (NT); those who were born in a city other than Izmir, with at least one parent also born in a city other than Izmir, were categorised as national migrants (NM).

With this procedure, out of 2174 adolescents who participated, 2154 could be categorised (the remaining 20 comprised third generation Turks in Austria; those with at least one parent born in a country other than Turkey or Austria; and 11 with missing migration status data). The final sample comprised 1112 preadolescents (583 girls) with a mean age of 11.84 (SD = 0.81) years and 1042 adolescents (598 girls) with a mean age of 14.73 (SD = 0.85) years. There were 82 first generation youth (FG), 202 second generation youth (SG), 379 native Austrians (NA), 501 national migrants (NM) and 990 native Turks (NT). While 92% of the SG Turks were born in Vienna, the most common cities of origin of the FG Turks were located in the central part of Turkey, e.g. Yozgat (34%), Ankara (6%), Kayseri (4%) and Kirsehir (4%). The NM in Turkey had moved from cities all over Turkey, e.g. Erzurum (11%), Van (8%), Manisa (7%), Agri (7%), Batman (5%), Kars (5%), Ankara (4%), Balikesir (4%) and Istanbul (4%).

Table 1 compares the five groups on demographic information. Girls were slightly underrepresented in the FG group and slightly overrepresented in the NM group. Preadolescents were slightly underrepresented in the NA group. Regarding marital status, parents of NA were less likely to be married compared with the four Turkish groups; a high percentage of parents of NA adolescents were divorced (31%) or separated (14%, numbers not shown in Table 1). Fathers of FG and SG were more likely to be uneducated compared with fathers of NM, NA and NT. Mothers of NM, FG and SG youth were more likely to be uneducated compared with mothers of NA and NT. Fathers of NA were least likely to be unemployed, while fathers of NM were most likely to be unemployed. These differences were even greater for mothers. Only 16% of the mothers from NA but 84% of the mothers from FG did not have a job.

For all three migrant groups, the most common reason for migration was work, followed by education. Half of the FG and NM migrated before the age of seven. No differences in years passed since migration between the two groups were found.

Regarding new media access, more than 90% of the NA and SG, but less than 50% of the NM had their own mobile phone, a computer and Internet access at home.

Results

To test for differences between the five groups, multivariate analyses of variance (ANOVAs) with migrant group as an independent variable and the five victimisation items as dependent variables were conducted, controlling for gender and age.

Levels of different forms of victimisation

The means and standard deviations are presented in Table 2. Application of a multivariate test using Pillai's criterion revealed a significant effect, $F(20,8580) = 3.05$, $p < 0.01$, $\eta^2 = 0.01$. Follow-up univariate analyses revealed differences between the five migrant groups regarding global, verbal and social victimisation. NT scored lower than NA on these three items. An additional univariate ANOVA confirmed these results for the overall victimisation score (mean of the five items), $F(4,2143) = 11.56$, $p < 0.01$, $\eta^2 = 0.02$.

Levels of different forms of emotional problems

The means and standard deviations are presented in Table 3. Application of a multivariate test using Pillai's criterion revealed a significant effect, $F(16,8584) = 7.70$, $p < 0.01$,

Table 1. Demographic information and media access.

Variable	Native Turks (NT) ($n = 990$)	Native Austrians (NA) ($n = 379$)	National migrants (NM) ($n = 501$)	First generation international migrants (FG) ($n = 82$)	Second generation international migrants (SG) ($n = 202$)	p
Girls (%)	58	51	55	44	53	<0.01
Preadolescents (%)	56	40	54	56	47	<0.01
Married parents (%)	92	45	92	92	86	<0.01
Uneducated father (%)	1	4	9	14	17	<0.01
Uneducated mother (%)	7	4	30	25	23	<0.01
Unemployed father (%)	15	10	24	18	16	<0.01
Unemployed mother (%)	71	16	78	84	51	<0.01
Work as reason for migration (%)			66	75	67	ns
Education as reason for migration (%)			17	20	22	ns
Asylum as reason for migration (%)			0	1	7	<0.01
Migrated before age 7 (%)			53	50		ns
Years passed since migration, mean (SD)			6.63 (4.18)	6.72 (3.43)		ns
Own mobile phone (%)	66	98	49	87	96	<0.01
Computer at home (%)	76	98	48	85	96	<0.01
Internet at home (%)	64	97	34	78	93	<0.01

Note: ns: not significant.

Table 2. Levels of different forms of victimisation.

	Native Turks (NT) ($n = 988$)	Native Austrians (NA) ($n = 378$)	National Migrants (NM) ($n = 501$)	First generation international migrants (FG) ($n = 82$)	Second generation international migrants (SG) ($n = 202$)	$F(4,2146)$
Global	1.96^{b} (1.17)	2.20^{a} (1.23)	1.98 (1.21)	2.02 (1.21)	1.82^{b} (1.07)	4.10**
Verbal	1.93^{b} (1.21)	2.16^{a} (1.24)	2.02 (1.23)	2.00 (1.19)	1.92 (1.27)	2.60*
Social	1.32^{b} (0.81)	1.59^{a} (0.99)	1.45 (0.97)	1.63^{a} (0.97)	1.44 (0.86)	8.00**
Physical	1.48 (0.94)	1.51 (0.97)	1.57 (1.05)	1.57 (0.96)	1.47 (0.93)	0.97
Cyber	1.13 (0.51)	1.11 (0.46)	1.17 (0.68)	1.23 (0.74)	1.09 (0.49)	1.54
Victimisation score	1.56^{b} (0.67)	1.71^{a} (0.76)	1.63 (0.76)	1.69 (0.77)	1.54 (0.70)	11.56**

Notes: $^{**}p < 0.01$, $^{*}p < 0.05$. Means with different superscript letters differ at the $p < 0.05$ level.

Table 3. Levels of different forms of emotional problems.

	Native Turks (NT) ($n = 990$)	Native Austrians (NA) ($n = 378$)	National migrants (NM) ($n = 500$)	First generation international migrants (FG) ($n = 82$)	Second generation international migrants (SG) ($n = 201$)	$F(4,2146)$
Depression	1.40^{b} (0.24)	1.42 (0.25)	1.46^{a} (0.28)	1.50^{a} (0.21)	1.44 (0.25)	6.74**
Self-esteem	3.14^{b} (0.48)	3.17^{b} (0.56)	3.04^{a} (0.51)	2.94^{a} (0.47)	3.12 (0.46)	6.83**
Social anxiety	2.34^{b} (0.72)	2.16^{a} (0.70)	2.52^{c} (0.79)	2.39 (0.80)	2.20^{a} (0.71)	15.45**
Loneliness	1.62^{b} (0.55)	1.74^{a} (0.56)	1.81^{a} (0.68)	1.80 (0.59)	1.70 (0.51)	9.39**

Notes: $^{**}p < 0.01$. Means with different superscript letters differ at the $p < 0.05$ level.

$\eta^2 = 0.01$. Follow-up univariate analyses revealed differences between the five migration groups regarding all four scales (see Table 3). NM and FG scored higher in depression compared with NT. NM and FG also scored lower in self-esteem compared with NT and NA. NM scored highest in social anxiety compared with NT, NA and SG. NM also scored higher in loneliness compared with NT.

Migration experiences and emotional problems as risk factors for victimisation: testing the hypothesised model

The associations between migration experiences, emotional problems, and victimisation were investigated with a concurrent structural equation model. The modelling was done using Mplus 5.0 (Muthen and Muthen 2007). We implemented maximum likelihood estimation using the MLR estimator of Mplus, which provides standard errors and test statistics that are robust to non-normality of the data and to non-independence of observations. In addition, we controlled for the nested data structure on a class level. Three criteria were used in evaluating the model fit: the chi-squared test, Comparative Fit Index (CFI) (Bentler 1990) and the root mean squared error of approximation (RMSEA) (Steiger 1990).

Measurement model

In the first step, two latent variables were constructed: victimisation and social anxiety (see Figure 1). The latent factor 'victimisation' was built using the five items as indicators. The latent factor 'social anxiety' was constructed using the three subscales (sadg, sadn, fne) as indicators. In the confirmatory factor analysis, the two latent factors were allowed to correlate. The model fit was excellent, $\chi^2(19) = 109.58, p < 0.01$, CFI = 0.97, RMSEA 0.047.

Structural model

In the second step, the hypothesised model was constructed (see Figure 1). The model had a good fit, $\chi^2(73) = 534.96, p < 0.01$, CFI = 0.93, RMSEA = 0.05, and it explained a substantial amount of variance in victimisation ($R^2 = 0.31$). The mediators were all allowed to correlate to avoid a seriously mis-specified model. Statistically significant paths (standardised coefficients) are shown in Table 4. All four Turkish groups were less likely to be victimised compared to the non-migrant Austrian reference group. The four different forms of emotional problems significantly predicted victimisation. Boys, and 12-year-olds, were more likely to be victimised compared to girls, and 15-year-olds. NM and FG had higher levels of depression and social anxiety and lower levels of self-esteem compared to NM, while no differences were found for SG. NT scored lower than NA regarding loneliness. The residuals of the different forms of emotion substantially correlated with each other (not shown in Table 4).

Testing indirect effects

The hypothesised model suggests that high levels of emotional problems help to explain victimisation in NM and FG. We found some evidence of such indirect effects, and we next tested their statistical significance using the Sobel test. Total indirect, specific indirect and total effects were specified using Mplus (Muthen and Muthen 2007, 68). Total effects

Table 4. Migration experiences and emotional problems as risk factors for victimisation: final model results.

	Victimisation		Depression		Self-esteem		Social anxiety		Loneliness	
	B	SE	*B*	SE	*B*	SE	*B*	SE	*B*	SE
Native Turks	−0.35**	0.07	−0.07	0.06	−0.05	0.07	0.20**	0.06	−0.23**	0.06
National migrants	−0.39**	0.08	0.16*	0.07	−0.25**	0.08	0.50**	0.08	0.09	0.07
1st generation migrants	−0.28*	0.12	0.36**	0.12	−0.41**	0.12	0.32*	0.15	0.13	0.13
2nd generation migrants	−0.30**	0.09	0.09	0.09	−0.07	0.09	0.05	0.10	−0.09	0.08
Age cohort (1 = young, 2= old)	−0.51**	0.06	0.05	0.05	0.02	0.06	−0.43**	0.05	−0.17**	0.05
Gender (1 = boy, 2 = girl)	−0.14**	0.05	0.13**	0.05	−0.08	0.05	0.20**	0.05	0.08*	0.04
Depression	0.13**	0.03								
Self-esteem	0.08*	0.04								
Social anxiety	0.32**	0.05								
Loneliness	0.16**	0.04								

Notes: Standardised regression coefficients are reported. Reference group is native Austrians. $^{*}p < 0.05$, $^{**}p < 0.01$.

included all indirect effects and the direct effect. The total indirect effect from being a national migrant to victimisation was substantial ($\beta = 0.16, p < 0.001$). Looking at the specific indirect effects travelling through the four forms of emotional problems, we found that social anxiety ($\beta = 0.15, p < 0.01$) and depression ($\beta = 0.02, p < 0.01$) were statistically significant. In addition, there was a total indirect effect from being a first generation international migrant to victimisation ($\beta = 0.12, p = 0.04$). Again, social anxiety ($\beta = 0.09, p = 0.04$) and depression ($\beta = 0.04, p < 0.01$) were the significant specific indirect effects. For the remaining three groups, no significant indirect effects were found.

Discussion

The main goal of this study was to investigate victimisation experiences and emotional problems of nationally and internationally migrated youth. Expanding the designs of previous studies (e.g. Aksel et al. 2007; Beirens and Fontaine 2011; Gün and Bayraktar 2008; Sam et al. 2008), migration experiences of youth were examined both within and between countries. First, we compared the levels of emotional problems and victimisation experiences of five groups of youth differing in terms of their migration experiences. Youth without any migration experience in Turkey and Austria, youth who had migrated nationally within Turkey and youth who had migrated internationally (both first and second generation) were compared. Second, the associations between victimisation experiences and emotional problems were examined.

We predicted that both nationally and first generation internationally migrated youth would report higher levels of peer victimisation compared to non-migrant and second generation international migrants. Contrary to our expectations, all Turkish youth, irrespective of their migration experiences, reported lower levels of victimisation than non-migrant Austrians. Because we utilised a five-group design, it is possible to attribute these results to cultural values (Hofstede 2001) and to disentangle them from acculturation (Beirens and Fontaine 2011).

Previous studies in Austria have found that being an international migrant from Turkey was a protective factor against peer victimisation (Stefanek et al. 2011). Turkey is rated high on a collectivistic value index indicating interdependence, in-group loyalties and cohesive social networks; whereas Austria is ranked high on the index of individualism indicating independence, assertiveness and competitiveness. These cultural values make it likely that Turkish youth generally have more cohesive social networks and protective friendships compared with non-migrant Austrians or international migrants stemming from more individualistic countries (e.g. the former Yugoslavia). These strong friendship networks and in-group loyalties might act as protective factors against peer victimisation. It is likely that in the Turkish group a victim is defended more readily by friends because it might be a natural act to interfere in social situations in a collectivistic society. In Austria, however, victimisation might be interpreted as an individual issue that should be solved individually by the victim. Therefore, future studies should closely focus on peer networks of immigrant youth stemming from different countries.

Regarding emotional problems, we predicted that nationally and first generation internationally migrated youth would exhibit higher levels of emotional problems such as depression, social anxiety, loneliness and lower self-esteem compared to the natives and the second generation internationally migrated youth. The results showed that nationally migrated youth and first generation internationally migrated youth reported higher levels of depression and social anxiety and lower levels of self-esteem compared to natives and second generation internationally migrated youth. However, no differences were found regarding the loneliness scores of these two groups. These results point out the manifold challenges associated with resettlement (Berry 1997; Strohmeier and Schmitt-Rodermund 2008). Children and youth have to cope with major life changes such as a new school environment, family relations and social networks when the family moves. As our results indicate, these major life changes are associated with emotional problems when youth migrate both nationally and internationally. In line with our prediction and the existing literature (Sam et al. 2008), second generation internationally migrated youth did not differ regarding emotional problems from native Austrian youth. In contrast to the first generation, second generation youth had been born in Austria and never experienced the major life event of resettlement.

Contrary to our expectations, native Turks reported lower levels of loneliness and higher levels of social anxiety than their Austrian peers. These differences might be explained in terms of collectivism and individualism (Hofstede 2001; Markus and Kitayama 1991; Triandis 1995). In a collectivistic culture, social networks are generally more cohesive and loneliness is a comparatively rare experience. On the other hand, because friends and being accepted by peers are very important issues in a collectivistic culture, youth are more likely to worry about the lack of these factors. These findings are also supported by studies showing that Turkish children and youth were found to be more anxious than their western European peers (Bengi-Arslan et al. 2007; Darwish Murad et al. 2003).

In addition, we investigated whether national and first generation international migration experiences predict individual variation in emotional problems such as depression, anxiety, loneliness and low self-esteem, and whether each type of problem further increases the risk for victimisation. The analyses revealed that high levels of depression and social anxiety were indeed associated with high levels of victimisation among national and first generation international migrants. In line with the acculturative stress perspective, youth who have experienced resettlement are at higher risk for manifold challenges leading to poor psychological health. In line with our prediction, these emotional problems heightened their risk of being victimised by their peers. This mechanism was not present for second generation internationally migrated youth and non-migrant youth.

Strengths and limitations

The large number of youth who were recruited from an exceptionally wide range of schools and classes is a strength of the study. This approach allows generalisation of the present results. Another major strength is the five-group design. While previous studies mostly compared internationally migrated youth with natives, this study differentiated between nationally and internationally migrated youth. In addition, international migration was further distinguished according to generational status, and non-migrant youth stemming from both the receiving and the sending country were examined. The unique design of this study allowed us to shed light on the underlying mechanisms associated with peer victimisation among youth with migration experiences.

We examined a wide variety of emotional problems such as depression, anxiety, loneliness and self-esteem, and different forms of victimisation including cybervictimisation. These constructs were measured using well-established and culturally validated instruments. The questionnaire was provided in both the German and Turkish languages in Austria to prevent the exclusion of recently arrived Turkish youth with very poor German language proficiency. This strategy further increased the validity of the present findings.

Despite these strengths, some limitations should be noted. We relied exclusively on self-reports. A multi-informant approach would provide a fuller picture and is recommended in future studies. In addition, the design of this study was cross-sectional. Therefore, it is not possible to understand the causal relationships between the study variables.

Recommendations for future research

This study demonstrated the complexity of migration experiences of youth. More studies are needed on youth experiencing different forms of migrations. Ideally, these studies should focus on youth who have experienced voluntary and forced migration. An increasing number of children and youth migrate both nationally and internationally as a result of civil wars, natural disasters, human trafficking or international adoption. Studies examining emotional and behavioural problems in these youth are lacking. It is recommended that future studies focus on these issues.

Acknowledgements

The present study was supported by a Jacobs Foundation Young Researcher Grant awarded to the first and second authors during 2009 and 2011. In addition, parts of the study were supported by a grant from EBİLTEM, Ege University, to the second author in 2010. Moreover, the second author was awarded with a travel grant to Linz, Austria, in 2011 within the programme 'Innovatives OÖ 2010plus'. We thank all schools and students who participated in this study. We are very grateful for being able to work with excellent research assistants in both Austria and Turkey. Without Marie Therese Schultes, Burcu Uysal, Elisabeth Ziebland, Sophie Theres Schmid and Gülcan Keklik (in Austria), and Duygu Ertan, Bilge Kaplan, Ezgi Mehmetoğlu, Ayça Çavuşoğlu, Servet Kaçar and Pınar Kurban (in Turkey), this research could never have been realised.

References

Aksel, S., Z. Gün, T. Yılmaz-Irmak, and B. Cengelci. 2007. Migration and psychological status of adolescents in Turkey. *Adolescence* 42: 589–602.

Asher, S., S. Hymel, and P. Renshaw. 1984. Loneliness in children. *Child Development* 55: 1456–64.

Asher, S., and V. Wheeler. 1985. Children's loneliness: A comparison of rejected and neglected peer status. *Journal of Consulting and Clinical Psychology* 53: 500–5.

Aydin, A., and S. Tekinsav-Sutcu. 2007. Ergenler için sosyal kaygı ölçeğinin (ESKÖ) geçerlik ve güvenirliğinin incelenmesi. *Çocuk ve Gençlik Ruh Sağlığı Dergisi* 14, no. 2: 79–89.

Beirens, K., and J.R.J. Fontaine. 2011. Somatic and emotional well-being among Turkish immigrants in Belgium: Acculturation or culture? *Journal of Cross Cultural Psychology* 42: 56–74.

Bengi-Arslan, L., F.C. Verhulst, J. Van der Ende, and N. Erol. 2007. Understanding childhood (problem) behaviors from a cultural perspective: comparison of problem behaviours and competencies in Turkish immigrant, Turkish and Dutch children. *Social Psychiatry and Psychiatric Epidemiology* 32: 477–84.

Bentler, P. 1990. Comparative fit indexes in structural models. *Psychological Bulletin* 107: 238–46.

Bergmüller, S., and C. Wiesner. 2009. Schulische Gewalt- und Aggressionserfahrungen 15-/16-Jähriger. In *PISA 2006. Österreichischer Expertenbericht zum Naturwissenschafts-Schwerpunkt*, ed. C. Schreiner and U. Schwandtner, 314–20. Graz: Leykam.

Berry, J.W. 1997. Immigration, acculturation and adaptation. *Applied Psychology: An International Review* 46: 5–68.

Berry, J.W. 2006. Stress perspectives on acculturation. In *Acculturation psychology*, ed. D.L. Sam and J.W. Berry, 43–57. Cambridge: Cambridge University Press.

Berry, J.W., J.S. Phinney, D.L. Sam, and P. Vedder. 2006. Immigrant youth: Acculturation, identity, and adaptation. *Applied Psychology: An International Review* 55: 303–32.

Card, N.A., and E. Hodges. 2008. Peer victimization among schoolchildren: Correlations, causes, consequences, and considerations in assessment and intervention. *School Psychology Quarterly* 23: 451–61.

Çuhadaroğlu, F. 1986. Adolesanlarda benlik saygısı [Self-esteem among adolescents]. Unpublished master's thesis, Hacettepe University, Ankara.

Darwish Murad, S., I.M.A. Joung, F.J. van Lenthe, L. Bengi-Arslan, and A.A.M. Crijnen. 2003. Predictors of self-reported problem behaviours in Turkish immigrant and Dutch adolescents in the Netherlands. *Journal of Child Psychology and Psychiatry* 44: 412–23.

Fandrem, H., D.L. Sam, and E. Roland. 2009. Depressive symptoms among native and immigrant adolescents in Norway: The role of gender and urbanization. *Social Indicator Research* 92: 91–109.

Fandrem, H., D. Strohmeier, and E. Roland. 2009. Bullying and victimization among Norwegian and immigrant adolescents in Norway: The role of proactive and reactive aggressiveness. *Journal of Early Adolescence* 29: 898–923.

Ferring, D., and S.-H. Filipp. 1996. Messung des Selbstwertgefuehls: Befunde zu Reliabilitaet, Validitaet und Stabilitaet der Rosenberg-Skala. *Diagnostica* 42: 284–92.

Graham, S., and J. Juvonen. 2002. Ethnicity, peer harassment, and adjustment in middle school: An exploratory study. *Journal of Early Adolescence* 22: 173–99.

von Grünigen, R., S. Perren, C. Nägele, and F. Alsaker. 2009. Immigrant children's peer acceptance and victimization in kindergarten: The role of local language competence. *British Journal of Developmental Psychology* 28: 679–97.

Gün, Z. and F. Bayraktar. 2008. Türkiye'de iç göçün ergenlerin uyumundaki rolü [The role of migration on the adjustment of adolescents in Turkey]. *Turkish Psychiatry Journal* 19: 167–76.

Hawker, D., and M.J. Boulton. 2000. Twenty years' research on peer victimization and psychosocial maladjustment: A meta-analytic review of cross-sectional studies. *Journal of Child Psychology and Psychiatry* 41: 441–55.

Hodges, E., and D.G. Perry. 1999. Personal and interpersonal antecedents and consequences of victimization by peers. *Journal of Personality and Social Psychology* 76: 677–85.

Hofstede, G. 2001. *Culture's consequences: Comparing values, behaviours, institutions, and organizations across nations*. Thousand Oaks, CA: Sage.

Icduygu, A. and İ. Sirkeci. 1999. Cumhuriyet dönemi Türkiye'sinde göç hareketleri. In *75 yılda Köylerden Şehirlere*, 249–68. İstanbul: Tarih Vakfı Yayınları.

International Organization for Migration. 2010. *World migration report 2010. The future of migration: Building capacities for change*. Geneva: International Organization for Migration.

Kovacs, M. 1981. The Children's Depression Inventory (CDI). *Psychopharmacological Bulletin* 21: 995–8.

La Greca, A., and N. Lopez. 1998. Social anxiety among adolescents: Linkages with peer relations and friendships. *Journal of Abnormal Child Psychology* 26: 83–94.

Markus, H.R., and S. Kitayama. 1991. Culture and self: Implications for cognition, emotion, and motivation. *Psychological Review* 98: 224–53.

McKenney, K.S., D. Pepler, W.M. Craig, and J. Connolly. 2006. Peer victimization and psychosocial adjustment: The experiences of Canadian immigrant youth. *Electronic Journal of Research in Educational Psychology* 9: 230–64.

Melfsen, S. 1998. Die deutsche Fassung der Social Anxiety Scale for Children Revised (SARC-R-D): Psychometrische Eigenschaften und Normierung. *Diagnostica* 44: 153–63.

Melfsen, S., and I. Florin. 1997. Ein Fragebogen zur Erfassung sozialer Angst bei Kindern (SASC-R-D). *Kindheit und Entwicklung* 6: 224–9.

Monks, C., R. Ortega-Ruiz, and A.J. Rodriguez-Hidalgo. 2008. Peer victimization in multicultural schools in Spain and England. *European Journal of Developmental Psychology* 5: 507–35.

Muthen, L.K., and B.O. Muthen. 2007. *Mplus User's guide*. 5th ed. Los Angeles, CA: Muthen & Muthen.

Oppedal, B., and E. Roysamb. 2004. Mental health, life stress, and social support among young Norwegian adolescents with immigrant and host national background. *Scandinavian Journal of Psychology* 45: 131–44.

Öy, B. 1991. Cocuklar icin depresyon ölcegi: Gecerlik ve güvenirlik calismasi. *Türk Psikiyatri Dergisi* 2: 132–37.

Özen, Ş., S. Antar, Ö. Özbulut, A. Altındağ, and R. Oto. 2001. İç göç yaşayan bir grup lise öğrencisinde ruhsal belirti şiddetinin cinsiyet ile ilişkisi. *Çocuk ve Ergen Ruh Sağlığı Dergisi* 8: 156–62.

Özgür, E.M. 2003. XXI yüzyılın başında Türkiye nüfusu. *Coğrafi Bilimler Dergisi*, 1, no. 1: 43–53.

Pazarlıoğlu, M.V. 2007. İzmir örneğinde iç göçün ekonometrik analizi. *Yönetim ve. Ekonomi* 14, no. 1: 121–35.

Rigby, K. 2002. *New perspectives on bullying*. London: Jessica Kingsley Publishers.

Rosenberg, M. 1965. *Society and the adolescent self image*. Princeton, NJ: Princeton University Press.

Sağlam, S. 2006. Türkiye'de iç göç olgusu ve kentleşme. *Türkiyat Araştırmaları* 5: 33–44.

Sam, D.L., P. Vedder, K. Liebkind, F. Neto, and E. Virta. 2008. Immigration, acculturation and the paradox of adaptation in Europe. *European Journal of Developmental Psychology* 5: 138–58.

Smith, P.K., H. Cowie, R.F. Olafsson, and A.P.D. Liefooghe. 2002. Definitions of bullying: A comparison of terms used, and age and gender differences, in a fourteen-country international comparison. *Child Development* 73: 1119–33.

Statistik Austria. 2010. *Migration and integration. Zahlen. Daten. Indikatoren 2010*. Wien: Statistik Austria.

Stefanek, E., D. Strohmeier, H. Fandrem, and C. Spiel. 2012. Depressive symptoms in native and immigrant adolescents: The role of critical life events and daily hassles. *Anxiety, Stress and Coping* 25: 201–17.

Stefanek, E., D. Strohmeier, R. van de Schoot, and C. Spiel. 2011. Bullying and victimization in ethnically diverse schools: Risk and protective factors on the individual and class level. *International Journal of Developmental Science* 5: 73–84.

Steiger, J. 1990. Structural model evaluation and modification: An interval estimation approach. *Multivariate Behavioral Research* 25: 173–80.

Stiensmeier-Pelster, J., M. Schürmann, and K. Duda. 2000. *DIKJ. Depressions-Inventar für Kinder und Jugendliche*. Göttingen: Hogrefe Verlag für Psychologie.

Strohmeier, D., I. Aoyama, P. Gradinger, and Y. Toda. 2012, in press. Cybervictimization and cyberaggression in eastern and western countries: challenges of constructing a cross culturally appropriate scale. In *Principles of cyberbullying research: Definition, methods, and measures*, ed. S. Bauman, J. Walker and D. Cross. New York: Guilford Press.

Strohmeier, D., M. Atria, and C. Spiel. 2005. Bullying und Viktimisierung in multikulturellen Schulklassen. Wer ist betroffen? Wie begründen Opfer ihre Erfahrungen? In *Lästern, Lügen, Leiden: Aggression bei Kindern und Jugendlichen*, ed. A. Ittel and M. v Salisch, 204–19. Stuttgart: Kohlhammer.

Strohmeier, D., A. Kärnä, and C. Salmivalli. 2011. Interpersonal and interpersonal risk factors for peer victimization in immigrant youth in Finland. *Developmental Psychology* 47: 248–58.
Strohmeier, D., D. Nestler, and C. Spiel. 2006. Freundschaftsmuster, Freundschaftsqualität und aggressives Verhalten von Immigrantenkindern in der Grundschule. *Diskurs Kindheits- und Jugendforschung* 1: 21–37.
Strohmeier, D., and E. Schmitt-Rodermund. 2008. Immigrant youth in European countries: The manifold challenges of adaptation. *European Journal of Developmental Psychology* 8: 129–37.
Strohmeier, D., and C. Spiel. 2003. Immigrant children in Austria: Aggressive behavior and friendship patterns in multicultural school classes. *Journal of Applied School Psychology* 19: 99–116.
Strohmeier, D., C. Spiel, and P. Gradinger. 2008. Social relationships in multicultural schools: Bullying and victimization. *European Journal of Developmental Psychology* 5: 262–85.
Sweeting, H., R. Young, P. West, and G. Der. 2006. Peer victimization and depression in early–mid adolescence: A longitudinal study. *British Journal of Educational Psychology* 76: 577–94.
Tarhan, N. 1996. Relationships sociometric status, sex, academic achievement, school type and grade level with loneliness levels of secondary school students. Unpublished Master's thesis, Middle East Technical University, Ankara.
Triandis, H.C. 1995. *Individualism and collectivism*. Boulder, CO: Westview Press.
Türkiye İstatistik Kurumu. 2009. *Türkiye nüfus sayımı verileri*. Ankara: Türkiye İstatistik Kurumu.
Ucanok, Z., P.K. Smith, and D. Sertkaya Karasoy. 2011. Definitions of bullying: Age and sex differences in a Turkish sample. *Asian Journal of Social Psychology*, 14: 75–83.
Uslu, S., and G. Cassina. 1999. *Türkiye'den Avrupa'ya Göç*. Ankara: Türkiye Hak İşçi Sendikaları Konfederasyonu.
Verkuyten, M., and J. Thijs. 2006. Ethnic discrimination and global self-worth in early adolescents: The mediating role of ethnic self esteem. *International Journal of Behavioral Development* 30: 107–16.

From cyberbullying to electronic aggression: typology of the phenomenon

Jacek Pyżalski

Nofer Institute of Occupational Medicine, Lodz, Poland

Cyberbullying is usually operationalised as a kind of bullying understood as peer aggression that is intentional and continuous, and involves an aspect of imbalance of power between a victim and a perpetrator or perpetrators. Despite the tool used (new media), cyberbullying often takes place within a traditional group (e.g. school class). However, cyberspace gives Internet users the opportunity to attack other individuals: people known only from the Internet, celebrities, teachers, totally unknown individuals or whole groups of people. Involvement in such actions brings suffering to those victimised as well as potential negative consequences for the perpetrators. This article presents a typology of electronic aggression based on qualitative research data (interviews with teachers and students). The typology was validated in a large quantitative survey on a representative sample of Polish 15-year-olds. The survey gives the prevalence of perpetration of different kinds of electronic aggression, as well as some influencing factors (e.g. gender) and risk and protective factors (attitudes towards school, peer norms, negative relations in the family, norms concerning online behaviour at school/home, pro-aggressive beliefs, level of self-esteem). The need to broaden prevention and intervention measures, and not restrict them to the issue of electronic peer aggression, is discussed.

Introduction: new media as tools for aggression in young people

Modern communication technologies (the Internet and mobile phones) can be used as tools to conduct aggressive acts against other people. For those acts one can use an umbrella term 'electronic aggression', understood as any type of harassment or bullying, including teasing, telling lies, making fun of, making rude or mean comments, spreading rumours, or making threatening or aggressive comments, that occurs through email, a chatroom, instant messaging, a website or text messaging (David-Ferdon and Feldman Hertz 2007).

Young people in all developed and developing countries are among the most frequent users of new media (Calmaestra et al. 2010; Domitrek and Raby 2008; Smith 2012; Tokunaga 2010; Ybarra, Mitchell, and Lenhart 2010) and some of them will engage in conducting aggressive acts against other people online. Indeed, bullying and harassment are listed spontaneously by young people when asked about their unpleasant online experiences (Larsen and Ryberg 2011). Thus, it is not surprising that most research conducted so far has focused on young people, mostly adolescents (e.g. Steffgen et al. 2011; Twyman et al. 2010) and less often on primary school students (e.g. Tangen and Campbell 2010).

Looking more closely at the phenomenon of electronic aggression, researchers have tried to distinguish different kinds. This can be done from different perspectives and by adopting various criteria. Some researchers have focused on different technologies or tools used to conduct aggressive acts through new media (Katzer, Fetchenhauer, and Belschak 2009; Nocentini et al. 2010; Slonje and Smith 2008). Some technologies take the form of one-to-one communication that can be synchronous (e.g. chat) or asynchronous (e.g. email). Users may also publish multimedia content that is available to wider audiences (e.g. websites). Aggressive acts via some kinds of electronic media are more harmful than others, e.g. those including visual material that pictures a victim (Slonje and Smith 2008). This calls for measurement instruments that acknowledge the variety of media or technologies used. General scales that do not take this into account are often criticised in the literature (e.g. Calvete et al. 2010). On the other hand, electronic aggression is a dynamic phenomenon with new media developing rapidly, forcing a need to frequently update research instruments.

Some researchers have focused on the way the aggressive acts are conducted, using the presence of criteria relevant to school bullying to label a particular set of electronic aggression acts as cyberbullying (Cassidy, Brown, and Jackson 2011). Adopting this paradigm means shifting electronic aggression research into cyberbullying research, and three key features of bullying – repetition, imbalance of power and intentionality on the side of a perpetrator – should be explicitly considered (Monks et al. 2009). These three features are generally accepted, although discussed critically in the literature in terms of the new features that occur with cyberaggression (Dooley, Pyżalski, and Cross 2009; Menesini and Nocentini 2009; Nocentini et al. 2010). For instance, repetition in cyberspace may be caused not by a perpetrator but by the features of new media (Boyd 2007).

However, this school bullying conceptualisation brings another assumption: that all the aggressive acts are conducted within a peer group, and that both victims and perpetrators are young people. Although not explicitly stated in the definition, the school bullying research maintains this kind of understanding. Most widely used scales operationalise bullying with the use of terms such as ‘a student’ or ‘a pupil’ where victimisation or perpetration is concerned. These instruments often focus on a class or school setting where peer aggression occurs (Monks et al. 2009; Smith 2010, 2012).

Only a few researchers have examined the variety of targets that may be attacked by a young perpetrator or include other age groups as perpetrators (Pyżalski 2011; Ševčíková and Šmahel 2009). Even when analysis is restricted to the situation when a perpetrator is a young person, one should remember that the growth of the Internet allows the possibility of harassing different types of individuals, of various age and status, as well as those having a different or no relationship with an adolescent perpetrator. Dowell, Burgess, and Cavanaugh (2009) have shown that a significant percentage of young people use the Internet to attack people who are strangers to them. That means that when exploring electronic aggression perpetrated by young people, it is reasonable to extend the context to focus on kinds of aggression that go beyond a peer group.

However, this broader concept is very general and may simply define a victim of electronic aggression as ‘someone’, while not specifying the character and context of aggression in connection with a victim’s identity (Ybarra, Mitchell, and Lenhart 2010). In Poland, a typology of electronic aggression acts based on the identity of the victim has been elaborated, based on qualitative analysis of interviews with students and teachers conducted within an initial phase of the quantitative study presented here (Pyżalski 2011). The categories were defined based on similar cases frequently described by the students as well as theoretical assumptions concerning the potential different psychosocial mechanisms and

Table 1. Typology of electronic aggression based on identity of the victim.

Type of electronic aggression	Description
Electronic peer aggression (possible cyberbullying)	Both the perpetrator and the victim are young people, usually from the same offline/online group. In some cases, when the relevant characteristics are present, electronic peer aggression may become cyberbullying
Electronic aggression against school staff	Aggressive acts are targeted against teachers or other school staff
Electronic aggression against the vulnerable	The victims of electronic aggression are 'weaker' people, particularly homeless, alcoholics, etc., who are usually unaware of the victimisation they experience. Aggression often has a form of visual material presenting the victims in embarrassing situations
Aggression against random victims (random electronic aggression)	The victim is to great extent anonymous to the perpetrator and an aggressive act is usually an impulse, e.g. when someone attacks an unknown person in the chatroom or Internet forum
Electronic aggression against groups	The victim is not an individual but a group of people. An example of such electronic aggression is making vulgar comments about an ethnic or religious group on the Internet. Although it is not against a particular person, everyone affiliated to the group may feel offended
Electronic aggression against celebrities	The victims are well-known people, e.g. singers or sport stars. This kind of aggression is usually indirect, e.g. the young Internet users make harsh comments on the so-called gossip portals

consequences that are involved in each electronic aggression type (Pyżalski 2011). This typology is presented in Table 1.

In summary, much of the research has been carried out in terms of electronic aggression typologies based on the technical means (Internet, mobile phones) or the measures used to conduct electronic aggression (understood as behavioural character of acts, e.g. impersonation, happy slapping). A substantial amount of research and theory has been elaborated in the field of comparison between traditional bullying and cyberbullying (Smith 2012). However, much less is known empirically with respect to the exploration of electronic aggression acts that go beyond the peer group.

The potential negative consequences of involvement in different kinds of electronic aggression based on the identity of the victim can vary substantially (Pyzalski 2011). As regards the main body of research on cyberbullying and cyberaggression to date, various risk and protective factors have been investigated. Findings regarding gender are far from consistent, with some showing that boys are more involved, some that girls are more involved, and some showing no gender differences (Gradinger, Strohmeier, and Spiel 2009; Juvonen and Gross 2008; Kowalski and Limber 2007). However, a meta-analysis by Patchin and Hinduja (2012) suggests that a majority of studies point to boys as more frequent perpetrators.

With regard to traditional risk behaviours such as legal and illegal substance use, traditional peer aggression/bullying, youth delinquency and risky sexual behaviour (Dunn et al. 2011), the data seem to be quite consistent, showing that those young people who engage in one risk behaviour have a tendency to be involved in others at the same time.

The research on cyberbullying suggests that cyberbullying should be added to the 'risk behaviours basket'. Many studies have shown a substantial overlap between bullying and cyberbullying, particularly so far as perpetration is concerned; it is rather rare for young people to perpetrate cyberbullying when they are not involved in face-to-face bullying (Gradinger, Strohmeier, and Spiel 2009; Juvonen and Gross 2008; Kowalski and Limber 2007). Young perpetrators of cyberbullying more often use psychoactive substances and are less engaged in school activities compared to those who are not involved (Ybarra, Mitchell, and Lenhart 2010). Cyberbullying victimisation is also connected to offline problems; youth harassed online more often report detentions or suspensions and skipping school, and are eight times more likely than all other youth to carry a weapon to school (Ybarra and Mitchell 2008).

The most frequently explored areas concerning risk and protective factors cover issues connected to traditional socialisation environments such as family, school and peer group. All these environments may provide both risk and protective factors (Kapadia et al. 2012; Ostaszewski et al. 2009; Schinke, Fang, and Cole 2008). For example, strong family communication, positive role models in the family, high parental expectation and firm social norms against risk behaviours protect adolescents from involvement in alcohol or marijuana use (Schinke, Fang, and Cole 2008); this has also proved true to some extent in cyberbullying research (Mesch 2009). On the other hand, young people from families with low social support, where less time is spent together with children and with frequent conflict situations, tend to engage more often in risk behaviours.

Regarding the school setting, young people perceiving the school environment as safe and the school staff as supportive are less likely to be involved in risk behaviours (Ostaszewski et al. 2009).

As for the peer group, those young people who perceive their peers as supporting and respecting risk behaviours often engage in such behaviours themselves (Wolman et al. 2010). Some research data have shown this association for both bullying and cyberbullying perpetration (Ang, Tan, and Mansor 2011). More general norms concerning prosocial behaviour (not only those concerning aggression in the peer group) may act as protective factors for bullying and cyberbullying perpetration.

Another factor is self-esteem. Findings are varied, but Peets, Hodges, and Salmivalli (2011) found that high self-esteem may have a reinforcing effect on traditional bullying perpetration.

The aim of this study is to explore electronic aggression by adolescents, adopting a typology based on victims' identity as a framework for a new electronic aggression typology that covers perpetrations against different types of victim. Besides prevalence, some influencing factors and risk and protective factors are examined in connection to involvement in the perpetration of electronic aggression.

Method

Sample

The material was gathered within the activities of a research project that aimed to explore the phenomenology, determinants and consequences of electronic aggression received and perpetrated by adolescents. The data come from a survey on a representative sample of Polish grade 9 students (third class of gymnasium), with a self-report questionnaire. It was collected in November and December 2010. Passive consent of the respondents' parents was obtained, as well as active consent of the participants. The research was carried out in randomly chosen secondary schools from eight voivodships (regions) of Poland. There were 2143 respondents: 1027 boys (48.72%), 1081 girls (51.28%) and 35 (1.66%) respondents who did not indicate their gender. Most of the respondents (about 94%) were 15 years old.

Instruments

The questionnaire consisted of scales measuring electronic aggression and cyberbullying as well as determinants and consequences of those phenomena. Only those relevant to this article are described here.

Electronic aggression

This was measured with the Lodz Electronic Aggression Prevalence Questionnaire (Pyżalski 2009). Respondents were asked whether during the last 12 months they had been perpetrators of 20 technical kinds of electronic aggression (regardless of who was their victim). Sample items are: 'I have made up a false profile on a social networking site in order to make fun of someone else' and 'I have revealed someone's else talks/photos on the Internet against the will of that person'. All items were formulated to indicate intention to harm a victim. For each item the respondents had six response options: never, before one year ago, and (within the previous year) once or a few times a year, once or a few times a month, once or a few times a week, or once or a few times a day. Cronbach's alpha was 0.91.

Identity of victims

A question listed the identity of potential victims (e.g. known peers, random people, vulnerable people). Those who were perpetrators were asked to provide information on their victim. The list was based on the typology shown in Table 1, but more detailed (see Table 2), providing four types of peers in cyberbullying and adding an item beyond the proposed typology (i.e. other known adults). Respondents who had attacked someone electronically within the previous year were asked to indicate as many types of victim as were relevant from the list.

Cyberbullying

In the electronic aggression scales, only intention as a traditional bullying characteristic was operationalised. The two other characteristics of bullying (repetition, imbalance of power) were included in one additional item on cyberbullying. This was defined as electronic aggression that takes place within a peer group (traditional or online) and is conducted intentionally for a longer period in a way that makes a victim helpless. Respondents were asked to indicate whether they had cyberbullied another student within the last year: 'Have you within the last year harassed for a longer period (individually or with a group) another student from your school/class or the group on the Internet or by a mobile phone in a way that was difficult for him/her to defend?' (no, once, 2–3 times, 4 times or more).

Risk and protective factors

The scales measuring protecting and risk factors are mostly the Polish validated versions of the scales in the Flynt Adolescents Study (Zimmerman and Schmeelk-Cone 2003;

Table 2. Different kinds of victim attacked by the respondents during 12 months, with percentages of overall perpetrators, and separately by gender.

Type of victim [a]	% of 1 year perpetrators	Boys (%)	Girls (%)	χ^2
People known only from the Internet (in some cases could be electronic peer aggression)	42.5	50.6	34.1	48.4***
Young people known offline (from school, place of living) but not close friends (Cyberbullying/electronic peer aggression)	39.0	36.5	41.6	4.8*
Close friends (Cyberbullying/electronic peer aggression)	26.8	30.5	22.2	51.6***
Random persons/totally unknown (Random electronic aggression)	24.2	28.2	19.1	20.2***
Former girlfriend/boyfriend (Cyberbullying/ electronic peer aggression)	16.9	12.7	20.2	17.9***
Not individuals but groups (e.g. fans of a certain band or football team) (Electronic aggression against groups)	15.9	21.1	10.0	41.6***
Celebrities, e.g. actors, singers (Electronic aggression against celebrities)	11.1	12.4	9.1	5.9*
People like the homeless, alcoholics, etc. (Electronic aggression against the vulnerable)	10.8	14.7	6.1	35.4***
Teachers (Electronic aggression against school staff)	9.0	10.4	6.9	6.9**
Other known adults	8.9	11.3	6.0	16.1***

Note: [a] Type of electronic aggression (see Table 1) is given in parentheses.
$*p < 0.05$, $**p < 0.01$, $***p < 0.001$.

Ostaszewski et al. 2009; Ostaszewski 2010). The exception is the norms concerning online activities at school and at home scale.

Positive and negative norms in peer group

This measures how the respondent perceives norms as present in his or her peer group. These may be positive (three items) or negative (five items). Sample items are: 'What would your friends think if you were a member of a school club or took part in other activities organised by your school?' (positive norm) and 'What would your friends think if you smoked cigarettes?' (negative norm). There were five response options, ranging from 'They would think it is totally wrong' to 'They would think it is totally fine'. Cronbach's alphas were 0.74 for positive norms and 0.84 for negative norms.

Conflicts in the family

This five-item scale measures the extent to which a respondent perceives relationships within a family as hostile and aggressive (mostly in the sense of verbal aggression). Sample items are: 'In our family we often lose our temper' and 'In our family we maliciously comment on each other'. There are four response options, from 'never' to 'very often'. Cronbach's alpha was 0.86.

Attitude towards school

This five-item scale measures the extent to which a student likes his or her school, and the activities at school in which he or she is involved. Sample items are: 'I like my school' and

'I like the teachers who teach me this year'. There are four response options, from 'totally untrue' to 'totally true'. Cronbach's alpha was 0.74.

Norms concerning online activities at school and at home

This was a new scale designed for the present study, measuring whether there are established and imposed rules concerning online behaviour of young people, at school and at home. Sample items are: 'Your parents establish and impose rules concerning your online behaviour' and 'Your school establishes and imposes the rules concerning the Internet and mobile phones usage on its premises' (altogether five items). There are four response options, from 'totally untrue' to 'totally true'. Cronbach's alphas were 0.67 for home norms and 0.84 for school norms.

Acceptance of violence as a method to solve conflict

This five-item scale measures the extent to which respondents think it is right to conduct violent behaviour in order to solve conflicts and achieve goals (both offline and online). Sample items are: 'Fighting is OK' and 'To attack someone on the Internet is funny'. There are four response options, from 'I totally disagree' to 'I totally agree'. Cronbach's alpha was 0.74.

Level of self-esteem

This four-item scale measures whether a student accepts and values him- or herself highly and likes him- or herself. Sample items are: 'I am a happy person' and 'I am disappointed with myself'. There are five response options, from total disagreement to total agreement. Cronbach's alpha was 0.86.

Results

Different types of electronic aggression

During the past 12 months, almost 66% of the students had conducted at least one of the 20 electronic aggression acts listed. That should by no means be interpreted as involvement in cyberbullying, since in many cases those acts would have been single, non-repeated situations with no imbalance of power present.

Adolescent perpetrators targeted many different types of victim (Table 2). However, these young people more often attacked those people they knew only on the Internet, and less often those belonging to their traditional social environments, namely school classes or groups functioning in the place where they live. Sometimes those individuals known only from the Internet may be young people belonging to social groups online; these may be very similar to the traditional offline groups when the mechanisms of interpersonal relations and group development are taken into account (McKenna 2008). Slightly less often (39%), adolescents electronically attacked young people they meet in school or in the place where they live but who are not their close friends. A specific situation is present when a former romantic partner of a young person is attacked (16.9%), since the aggression appears in the context of the first serious romantic relationships of a young person, potentially amplifying the harmful consequences (Craig and Pepler 2003; Marshall and Stenner 2005).

Almost one in four young perpetrators attacked totally randomly chosen people on the Internet, an example of what is called random/impulsive electronic aggression. Also quite prevalent was electronic aggression against groups (15.9% of the respondents reported being perpetrators) as well as aggression against celebrities and against the homeless and alcoholics. Slightly less prevalent was electronic aggression specific to educational settings, i.e. aggression against teachers and electronic aggression against other known adults.

Different types of electronic aggression and gender

Involvement as a perpetrator in different types of electronic aggression is clearly associated with gender, as shown in Table 2. In general, boys more frequently attacked other people via new media. They were more frequent perpetrators in eight out of 10 categories. The biggest differences referred to aggression against people known only from the Internet, random aggression and aggression against groups/ideas. There are two exceptions: girls, compared to boys, more often attacked electronically young people known offline (but not close friends) and former romantic partners.

The number of different types of victim attacked was also examined. Only 23.2% of respondents attacked only one type of a victim during the previous year, and 32.5% attacked two or more types. One in five students attacked six or more types of target.

Cyberbullying

Separately, the young people were asked about perpetration of cyberbullying, understood as repeated actions, conducted for a longer period with negative intentions, and with an imbalance of power. In this study, 74.4% of young people had not been perpetrators of cyberbullying. Only 4.9% had been perpetrators four times or more during the past 12 months.

Frequency of involvement in cyberbullying was positively connected to the number of types of electronic aggression in which a respondent was involved ($\chi^2 = 333.35$, $p < 0.0001$). For example, 25% of those perpetrating cyberbullying four times or more during one year attacked six or more types of target, compared to less than 10% of those perpetrating cyberbullying only once in the previous year. Those young people who tended to seriously attack their peers (cyberbullying) also had a tendency to attack other targets who are available on the Internet.

Electronic aggression: risk and protective factors

Pearson correlations were calculated between the risk and protective factors examined, cyberbullying perpetration in a previous year as well as the number of electronic aggression types perpetrated by a respondent during the previous year (see Table 3).

All the correlations are significant. Those perpetrating cyberbullying more often and those involved in more types of electronic aggression have more negative attitudes toward school, and less often perceive peer norms as positive and much more frequently as negative. They also slightly less often acknowledge the existence of norms concerning online behaviour at school and at home. They have more pro-aggressive beliefs. The correlation with self-esteem is small but positive, so those who attack more types of victim tend to report higher self-esteem. The general tendency shows that correlations concerning cyberbullying are lower than those for electronic aggression.

Table 3. Correlation between risk and protective factors and cyberbullying/electronic aggression acts perpetrated during the previous year.

	Cyberbullying	Electronic aggression
Positive attitudes towards school	−0.15***	−0.22***
Positive peer norms	−0.08***	−0.13**
Negative peer norms	0.30***	0.37***
Negative relations in family	0.14***	0.16***
Norms concerning online activities at home	−0.11***	−0.08*
Norms concerning online activities at school	−0.06*	−0.07*
Pro-aggressive beliefs	0.32***	0.30***
Level of self-esteem	0.03	0.11**

Note: $^{*}p < 0.05$, $^{**}p < 0.01$, $^{***}p < 0.001$.

Discussion

This research suggests an extension to and re-formulation of a quite prevalent paradigm that restricts electronic aggression to cyberbullying and understands it as peer aggression. First, young people very often engage in electronic aggression with targets extending beyond their normal offline peer group. A significant proportion of young perpetrators attack other types of victim (Table 2). Secondly, an important finding is that although 66% of respondents had perpetrated some electronic aggression acts during the previous year, only 25% had been perpetrators of cyberbullying (understood as a repeated set of actions, with an imbalance of power and involving negative intentions towards a peer victim). Taking this into account does not mean, of course, that cyberbullying and electronic aggression research should not learn lessons from the traditional bullying research programme (Smith 2010).

Regarding the variety of victims who can be attacked electronically, some of these can be considered as peers (of similar age). These comprise at least four distinctive groups: close friends, young people known from offline environments but not labelled as close friends, young people known only from online groups, and former romantic partners (boyfriends/girlfriends). These distinctions may be of importance when discussing the potential seriousness of the consequences of electronic aggression (or, more narrowly, cyberbullying). For example, it is potentially easier to deal with cyberattacks perpetrated by someone known from an online group, compared to a situation when attacks are perpetrated by someone who a victim meets face-to-face in a place where attendance is obligatory (a school). Similarly, harm done by a former romantic partner may be more painful and may cause more serious mental health consequences on the victim's side owing to the impact that the first serious romantic relationships have in adolescence.

However, adolescents also attacked at least five other types of victim, namely school staff, vulnerable people, celebrities, groups of people and random/unknown others. All these types of victim or target are qualitatively distinctive, and aggression against them may involve different psychological and social mechanisms. It is interesting that a significant proportion of the respondents electronically attacked many types of victim, clearly extending beyond a peer context; for instance, 8.6% of respondents had electronically attacked more than five types of victim during the previous year.

The analysis of gender differences in the context of perpetrating different kinds of electronic aggression produced interesting findings (Table 2). Although the prevalence is higher in boys for eight types of victim, girls score higher on electronic aggression against young people known offline (but not close friends) and against a former romantic partner. It is possible that measuring perpetration against different types of victim is a key issue in understanding the inconsistency in research data concerning gender differences in cyberbullying (Kowalski, Limber, and Agatson 2008; Tokunaga, 2010). A greater perpetration rate observed in girls in some electronic aggression types may be related to their relative preference for indirect aggression in traditional aggression and bullying research (Patchin and Hinduja 2012). This may also be caused by a specific attitude of girls concerning a romantic relationship and jealousy concerning a former partner.

Lastly, the findings revealed a kind of cumulative effect of electronic aggression which could be treated as a kind of 'layer cake' with many pieces representing different electronic aggression types. The correlational analysis (Table 3) showed that those who engaged in more types of electronic aggression during the previous year had significantly worse attitudes towards school, were less likely to perceive peer norms as positive, more often assessed relations within a family as hostile, were less likely to acknowledge the existence of norms concerning online behaviour in a school and in a family, and more often held generalised pro-aggressive beliefs. These findings are generally in line with previous research on traditional risky behaviours (Kapadia et al. 2012; Ostaszewski et al. 2009; Schinke, Fang, and Cole 2008). Such correlations were lower when cyberbullying alone was considered.

The self-esteem of those conducting more electronic aggression types was higher; this finding contrasts with most research data concerning involvement in risky behaviours and self-esteem, which shows an inverse correlation (Geckil and Dunbar 2011; Veselska et al. 2009). It might be explained by a lack of sense of guilt that electronic perpetrators may feel, making educational work with young perpetrators quite a serious challenge. These findings are in line with those of Peets, Hodges, and Salmivalli (2011) on self-esteem and traditional bullying perpetration; these authors call for more in-depth investigation to take account of different kinds of self-esteem.

Some limitations of the present study should be noted. It was conducted in a particular cultural environment, and it is possible that the typology and patterns of electronic aggression are culturally specific. This clearly needs verification in other countries in order to confirm, adjust or elaborate a new typology. The data are all based on self-report; so, for example, verification of risk and protective factors would be enhanced by data from parents or teachers. In addition, the analysis of risk and protective factors was correlational, so any causative associations concerning determinants of electronic aggression are of a speculative nature and should be confirmed in a longitudinal research model (Jaffee, Strait, and Odgers 2012).

Implications

The finding that adolescents on the Internet attack a whole 'palette' of victims seems to be a robust result of this study. These data suggest that instruments measuring cyberbullying should acknowledge these different kinds of victim, and not only ask about attacking 'another student'. In addition, professionals intervening in cyberbullying situations should be aware of these differences and sensitive to those situations that can potentially be most harmful for a victim.

It also seems that for some cyberbullying situations we should seek new prevention and intervention methods, particularly regarding a situation when online-only friends could be attacked. As all the communication processes and relationships take place in cyberspace, the introduction of any traditional methods based on face-to-face contacts is rather limited.

Some of the activities should be designed in such a way that educators can implement them in online environments. For example, that could refer to using online games or online help (advice, therapy), although in all cases this requires further research, particularly concerning effectiveness and tailoring such measures to different groups' needs.

Acknowledgements

This research was financed by a habilitation grant to the author, funded from sources for scientific research by the Ministry of Science and Higher Education (grant no. 106 067735, year 2008); grant affiliated in Wyższa Szkoła Pedagogiczna w Łodzi.

References

Ang, R. P., K.-A. Tan, and A.T. Mansor. 2011. Normative beliefs about aggression as a mediator of narcissistic exploitativeness and cyberbullying. *Journal of Interpersonal Violence* 26: 2619–34.

Boyd, D. 2007. Why youth (heart) social network sites: The role of networked publics in teenage social life. In *MacArthur Foundation Series on Digital Learning: Youth, identity, and digital media*, ed. D. Buckingham, 119–42. Cambridge, MA: MIT Press.

Calmaestra, J., R. Ortega, A. Maldonado, and J.A. Mora-Merchán. 2010. Exploring cyberbullying in Spain. In *Cyberbullying: A cross-national comparison*, ed. J.A. Mora-Merchán and T. Jäger, 146–62. Landau: Verlag Empirische Pädagogik.

Calvete, E., I. Orue, A. Estévez, L. Villardón, and P. Padilla. 2010. Cyberbullying in adolescents: Modalities and aggressors' profile. *Computers in Human Behavior* 5: 1128–35.

Cassidy, W., K. Brown, and M. Jackson, 2011. Moving from cyber-bullying to cyber-kindness: What do students, educators and parents say? In *Youth culture and net culture: Online social practices*, ed. C. Hällgren, E. Dunkels and G.-M. Frånberg, 256–77. Hershey, PA: IGI Global.

Craig, W.M., and D.J. Pepler. 2003. Identifying and targeting risk for involvement in bullying and victimization. *Canadian Journal of Psychiatry* 48: 577–82.

David-Ferdon, C.M., and M. Feldman Hertz. 2007. Electronic media, violence, and adolescents: An emerging public health problem. *Journal of Adolescent Health* 41: S1–5.

Domitrek, J., and R. Raby. 2008. Are you listening to me? Space, context and perspective in the regulation of Mp3 players and cell phones in secondary school. *Canadian Journal of Educational Administration and Policy* 81: 1–33.

Dooley, J.J., J. Pyżalski, and D. Cross. 2009. Cyberbullying versus face-to-face bullying: A theoretical and conceptual review. *Zeitschrift für Psychologie/Journal of Psychology* 217: 182–8.

Dowell, E.B., A.W. Burgess, and D.J. Cavanaugh. 2009. Clustering of internet risk behaviors in a middle school student population. *Journal of School Health* 11: 547–53.

Dunn, M.S., C. Kitts, S. Lewis, B. Goodrow, and G.D. Scherzer. 2011. Effects of youth assets on adolescent alcohol, tobacco, marijuana use, and sexual behavior. *Journal of Alcohol & Drug Education* 3: 23–40.

Geckil, E., and O. Dundar. 2011. Turkish adolescent health risk behaviors and self-esteem. *Social Behavior & Personality* 39: 219–27.

Gradinger, P., D. Strohmeier, and C. Spiel. 2009. Traditional bullying and cyberbullying. Identification of risk groups for adjustment problems. *Zeitschrift für Psychologie/Journal of Psychology* 214: 205–13.

Jaffee, S.R., L.B. Strait, and C.L. Odgers. 2012. From correlates to causes: Can quasi-experimental studies and statistical innovations bring us closer to identifying the causes of antisocial behavior? *Psychological Bulletin* 138: 272–95.

Juvonen, J. and E.F. Gross. 2008. Extending the school grounds? Bullying experiences in cyberspace. *Journal of School Health* 78: 496–505.

Kapadia, F., V. Frye, S. Bonner, P.J. Emmanuel, C.L. Samples, and M.H. Latka. 2012. Perceived peer safer sex norms and sexual risk behaviors among substance-using Latino adolescents. *AIDS Education & Prevention* 24: 27–40.

Katzer, C., D. Fetchenhauer, and F. Belschak. 2009. Cyberbullying: Who are the victims? A comparison of victimization in internet chatrooms and victimization in school. *Journal of Media Psychology* 21: 25–36.

Kowalski, R.M., and S.P. Limber. 2007. Electronic bullying among middle school students. *Journal of Adolescent Health* 41: S22–30.

Kowalski, R.M., S.P. Limber, and P.W. Agatson. 2008. *Cyberbullying. Bullying in the digital age*. Malden, MA: Blackwell.

Larsen, M.C., and T. Ryberg. 2011. Youth and online social networking: from local experiences to public discourses. In *Youth culture and net culture: Online social practices*, ed. C. Hällgren, E. Dunkels and G.-M. Frånberg, 17–40. Hershey, PA: IGI Global.

Marshall, H., and P. Stenner. 2005. Friends and lovers. In *Youth in society. Contemporary theory, policy and practice*, ed. J. Roche, S. Tucker, R. Thomson and R. Flynn, 168–76. London: Sage.

McKenna, K.Y.A. 2008. Influences on the nature and functioning of online groups. In *Psychology of cyberspace. Theory, research, applications*, ed. A. Barak, 228–42. New York: Cambridge University Press.

Menesini, E., and A. Nocentini. 2009. Cyberbullying definition and measurement: Some critical considerations. *Zeitschrift für Psychologie/Journal of Psychology* 217: 230–232.

Mesch, G.S. 2009. Parental mediation, online activities, and cyberbullying. *Cyberpsychology & Behavior* 12: 387–93.

Monks, C.P., P.K. Smith, P. Naylor, C. Barter, J.L. Ireland, and I. Coyne. 2009. Bullying in different contexts: Commonalities, differences and the role of theory. *Aggression and Violent Behavior* 14: 146–56.

Nocentini, A., J. Calmaestra, A. Schultze-Krumbholz, H. Scheithauer, R. Ortega, and E. Menesini. 2010. Cyberbullying: Labels, behaviours and definition in three European countries. *Australian Journal of Guidance & Counselling* 20: 129–42.

Ostaszewski, K. 2010. Badania zachowań ryzykownych warszawskich gimnazjalistów. Koncepcja i metoda. In *Promocja zdrowia psychicznego. Badania i działania w Polsce*, ed. K. Okulicz-Kozaryn and K. Ostaszewski. Warszawa: Instytut Psychiatrii i Neurologii.

Ostaszewski, K., K. Bobrowski, A. Borucka, M. Cybulska, K. Kocoń, K. Okulicz-Kozaryn, and A. Pisarska 2009. *Raport techniczny realizacji projektu badawczego p.n. Monitorowanie zachowań ryzykownych młodzieży. Badania mokotowskie*. Warszawa: Instytut Psychiatrii i Neurologii w Warszawie, Zakład Psychologii i Promocji Zdrowia Psychicznego, Pracownia Profilaktyki Młodzieżowej 'Pro-M'.

Patchin, J.W., and S. Hinduja. 2012. Cyberbullying: An update and synthesis of the research. In *Cyberbullying prevention and response: Expert perspective*, ed. J. W. Patchin and S. Hinduja, 13–36. New York: Routledge.

Peets, K., E.V.E. Hodges, and C. Salmivalli. 2011. Relationship specificity of aggressogenic thought-behavior processes. *Journal of Personality and Social Psychology* 101: 386–400.

Pyżalski, J. 2009. Lodz Electronic Aggression Questionnaire – a tool for measuring cyberbullying. In *The good the bad and the challenging. The user and the future of information and communication technologies*, ed. B. Sapio, L. Haddon, E. Mante-Meijer, L. Fortunati, T. Turk and E. Loos, 1018–24. Copenhagen: COST.

Pyżalski, J. 2011. Electronic aggression among adolescents: An old house with a new facade (or even a number of houses). In *Youth culture and net culture: Online social practices*, ed. C. Hällgren, E. Dunkels and G.-M. Frånberg, 278–95. Hershey, PA: IGI Global.

Schinke, S.P., L. Fang, and K. Cole. 2008. Substance use among adolescent girls: Risk and protective factors. *Journal of Adolescent Health* 43: 191–4.

Ševčíková, A., and D. Šmahel. 2009. Online harassment and cyberbullying in the Czech Republic: Comparison across age groups. *Zeitschrift für Psychologie/Journal of Psychology* 217: 227–9.

Slonje, R., and P.K. Smith. 2008. Cyberbullying: Another main type of bullying? *Scandinavian Journal of Psychology* 49: 147–54.

Smith, P.K. 2010. Cyberbullying: The European perspective. In *Cyberbullying: A cross-national comparison*, ed. J.A. Mora-Merchán and T. Jäger, 7–19. Landau: Verlag Empirische Pädagogik.

Smith, P.K. 2012. Cyberbullying and cyber aggression. In *Handbook of school violence and school safety: International research and practice*, ed. S.R. Jimerson, A.B. Nickerson, M.J. Mayer and M.J. Furlong, 93–103. New York: Routledge.

Steffgen, G., A.König, J. Pfetsch, and A. Melzer. 2011. Are cyberbullies less empathic? Adolescents' cyberbullying behavior and empathic responsiveness. *Cyberpsychology, Behavior, and Social Networking* 14: 643–8.

Tangen, D., and M. Campbell. 2010. Cyberbullying prevention: One primary school's approach. *Australian Journal of Guidance & Counselling* 20: 225–34.

Tokunaga, R.S. 2010. Following you home from school: A critical review and synthesis of research on cyberbullying victimization. *Computers in Human Behavior* 26: 277–87.

Twyman, K., C. Saylor, L.A. Taylor, and C. Comeaux. 2010. Comparing children and adolescents engaged in cyberbullying to matched peers. *Cyberpsychology, Behavior, and Social Networking* 13: 195–9.

Veselska, Z., A. Madarasova Geckova, O. Orosova, B. Gajdosova, J.P. van Dijk, and S.A. Reijneveld. 2009. Self-esteem and resilience: The connection with risky behavior among adolescents. *Addictive Behaviors* 34: 287–91.

Wolman, M.B., M. Sandoval, P.L. Flom, P.M. Gelabert, and S.R. Friedman. 2010. Drug use and peer norms among youth in a high-risk drug use neighbourhood in Buenos Aires. *Drugs: Education, Prevention & Policy* 17: 544–59.

Ybarra, M.L., and K.J. Mitchell. 2008. How risky are social networking sites? A comparison of places online where youth sexual solicitation and harassment occurs. *Pediatrics* 121: 350–7.

Ybarra, M.L., K.J. Mitchell, and A. Lenhart. 2010. Cyberbullying research in the United States. In *Cyberbullying: A cross-national comparison*, ed. J.A. Mora-Merchán and T. Jäger, 256–68. Landau: Verlag Empirische Pädagogik.

Zimmerman M., and K. Schmeelk-Cone. 2003. A longitudinal analysis of adolescent substance use and school motivation among African American youth. *Journal of Research on Adolescence* 13: 185–210.

The perception of cyberbullying in adolescent victims

Anna Ševčíková, David Šmahel and Mlada Otavová

Institute for Research on Children, Youth and Family, Masaryk University, Brno, Czech Republic

The goal of this study was to explore how victims of cyberbullying perceive online aggressive attacks and when they see them as harmful. Interviews were carried out with 16 cybervictimised participants aged 15–17 years. The findings showed differences in the perception of online victimisation when perpetrated by an anonymous Internet user versus by a known person from the real world. The tendency of unknown online aggressors to threaten to hurt their victims offline increased the victims' feelings of harm. Where cyberbullying interconnected with the school environment, the feeling of harm was intensified by collective perpetration, and by onlookers being personally identifiable. Where cyberbullying was a part of traditional bullying, online victimisation being discussed at school reproduced the bullying and thus the trauma. The results showed that the link between cyberbullying and the physical environment is significant with respect to the victim's perception of its severity.

Introduction

With the development of new information technology, the significance of the use of media and the Internet in adolescence has increased. Roughly 93% of Czech adolescents aged 12–18 years have Internet access (Lupač and Sládek 2008). As previous studies indicate, the Internet has become an inseparable part of everyday life for today's youth (Subrahmanyam and Šmahel 2011), bringing with it both positives and negatives. One of the negative phenomena that young people may face is cyberbullying. In the Czech Republic Ševčíková and Šmahel (2009) found that 7.6% of adolescents aged 12–19 years had experienced some kind of pestering or slandering on the Internet, and 3.4% had faced online victimisation which occurred several times a month.

Although cyberbullying appears to affect only a small percentage of young Internet users, it is connected with negative effects (Livingstone et al. 2011) such as depression and suicidal intention (Hinduja and Patchin 2010; Mitchell, Ybarra, and Finkelhor 2007; Perren et al. 2010). However, studies also point out that for a significant portion of adolescents victimised online, attacks have only short-term or no negative effects (Livingstone et al. 2011; Ortega et al. 2009). Therefore, this study is focused on the experiences of those adolescents who have been victimised on the Internet or via cell phones. It looks at what causes the adolescent harm in this kind of attack, and when, and under which circumstances, the online attack is connected with negative effects.

Cyberbullying and its characteristics

Cyberbullying is one of the forms of online aggression; its characteristics are derived from Olweus' (1993) definition of traditional bullying. It is the intentional aggressive behaviour of an individual which has a repetitive character, conducted individually or by a group using electronic media towards a person who is not able to defend themselves (Smith et al. 2008). This concept and criteria are problematic owing to the uniqueness of the Internet, and to a certain degree the mobile phone, environment (Dooley, Pyzalski, and Cross 2009).

Repetition is important in distinguishing between bullying and random or isolated attacks (Olweus 1993). Identification of repeated attacks is relatively easy in the offline world as the frequency of incidents can be counted. A similar approach is used here for attacks via mobile phone or email to find out how many times the victim was sent aggressive messages or calls (Dooley, Pyzalski, and Cross 2009; Slonje and Smith 2007). Nevertheless, previous studies have shown that a single harmful act can have similar effects for the victim as repetitive aggressive attacks (Vandebosch and Van Cleemput 2008; Ybarra, Diener-West, and Leaf 2007). One upload of humiliating photos, videos and other visual material to the Internet has the character of repetition as the content is permanent and at the same time available to a wide audience (Heirman and Walrave 2008). The aggressor also often controls when the content is withdrawn from the server (Dooley, Pyzalski, and Cross 2009).

An *imbalance of power* on the Internet can be represented by (1) technological knowledge, (2) anonymity and (3) limited escape options (Heirman and Walrave 2008; Slonje and Smith 2007; Smith et al. 2008; Vandebosch and Van Cleemput 2008). In the first scenario, the aggressor has superior technological knowledge to the victim (Smith et al. 2008). In the second, the aggressor's anonymity can have psychological significance, with the offender often knowing their victim better than the victim knows their aggressor (Kowalski and Limber 2007; Ševčíková and Šmahel 2009; Ybarra and Mitchell 2004). This often prevents the victim from defending themselves effectively (Vandebosch and Van Cleemput 2008). Finally, the Internet's constant presence means that online victimisation is not limited in time and space (Heirman and Walrave 2008; Smith et al. 2008).

Cyberbullying's diversity is shown through the attempts made to understand it. This diversity may also produce the variability in victims' experiences of online attacks. The impact of cyberbullying differs according to its form. For example, visual imagery of the victim, i.e. abuse including the use of videos and photos, was considered the most harmful (Smith et al. 2008). How the victim responds may also be affected by whether the online victimisation occurs as part of an offline abusive peer relationship. Previous studies have revealed that some incidents of cyberbullying are closely interconnected with traditional bullying (Tokunaga 2010; Smith et al. 2008). If an adolescent is a victim both at school and online then the impact may be aggravated.

Goals

Online victimisation has a wide variety of manifestations, which may explain why certain adolescents consider the online attacks harmful while others do not (Livingstone et al. 2011). However, there is a lack of research studying adolescents' perception of harmful experiences. Previously published qualitative work dedicated to online victimisation has only in part reflected the perspective of the victim (Smith et al. 2008; Spears et al. 2009; Vandebosch and Van Cleemput 2008). Therefore, this study's goal was to describe how the victims of cyberbullying perceived different forms of online attack and in what context they considered them harmful.

Method

Research sample and choice of participants

The research sample was made up of 16 secondary school participants, nine boys and seven girls, aged 15–17 years, who had all been victims of some form of cyberbullying. The adolescents were addressed via a message on a Czech server www.lide.cz, which was widely used by adolescents in the Czech Republic and included a social network, email account and blogging capabilities. This server was chosen as it was the most broadly used social network in the Czech Republic which allowed its users to be addressed via a message; at the time, the server did not allow private profiles so all users could be contacted in this way. The message was sent to all active users aged 15–18 years who were registered on the server in 2009. This age group was chosen on the basis of previous empirical studies that documented the increased occurrence of online victimisation in this age group (Juvonen and Gross 2008; Ševčíková and Šmahel 2009).

The initial message sent to participants clarified the research focus on victims of cyberbullying, described what was meant by cyberbullying (behaviour where the aggressor(s) abuses the Internet to carry out intentional, repetitive and hostile harm to others) and the basic forms of cyberbullying. It explained that two interviews were to be conducted, with the second being a shorter supplementary interview. In total, 6935 adolescents (4740 girls and 2195 boys) were sent a message (the gender imbalance was caused by the respective number of profiles on the server). Sixteen participants (seven girls and nine boys) agreed to participate in the interviews, stating that they had experienced some form of cyberbullying. With the exception of three cases, the cyberbullying had finished. On average, the online victimisation continued for 9 months, while the shortest lasted for only 2 weeks and the longest went on for 2.5 years (Table 1). Participants' names have been replaced by P1–P16 to ensure anonymity. All statements have been translated from Czech to English by the authors.

Table 1. Participants in the study.

Participants	Gender	Age/Age at cybervictimisation	Length of cybervictimisation	Relationship to an aggressor
P1	M	16/15	6 months	Known/totality
P2	F	15/13	1 year	Unknown
P3	M	16/16	4 months	Known
P4	F	17/17	1 month	Known
P5	F	16/15	3 months	Known/totality
P6	M	16/15	1 year	Unknown
P7	M	18/16	2.5 years	Known/totality
P8	M	15/13	1 month	Known/totality
P9	F	17/15	1 month	Known
P10	M	17/16	1 year	Known/totality
P11	F	16/15	1 year	Unknown
P12	M	17/15	2 years	Unknown
P13	F	17/17	1 year	Unknown
P14	F	17/13	3 months	Unknown
P15	M	15/15	14 days	Known
P16	M	17/16	1 year	Known/totality

Note: Totality = online aggression both online and offline.

Interviews

The interviews were conducted by the third author online via ICQ instant messenger. This allowed simultaneous text communication. ICQ was the most widely used application of this kind at the time. The immediate advantage of online interviews is anonymity, which helps the adolescent to feel safe, increasing their willingness to talk about their experiences (Schouten, Valkenburg, and Peter 2009). The basic structure of the interview touched on several topics: descriptions of the online attacks, where they took place, how often, how long they lasted, and their content; the relationship between the victim and the aggressor, who they were, whether they were pure victims or whether they also bullied someone else, whether they were known to the victim, whether they were from school; the connection between online and traditional bullying; the role of onlookers; and the response to the online attacks, how the adolescent experienced them, for how long, and how they responded. Each participant was interviewed twice within 2 weeks. The first comprehensive interview took approximately 90 minutes, the second approximately 45 minutes, serving to verify and deepen the understanding of the information acquired from the first interview.

Analysis of data

As this was a qualitative study, the grounded theory method was used. This is based on the inductive creation of theoretical concepts from the phenomenon that is examined (Strauss and Corbin 1990) and on constant comparison, which helps to specify investigated topics (Charmaz 2008). First, notes were assigned to the data. Then, in the framework of 'open coding', the content of answers was classified and ordered into subcategories according to semantic interconnections.

For example, the subcategory 'who was the aggressor' summarises all statements that defined the offender:

> First I thought of him as an average friend from school . . . when he behaved how he behaved; I tried not to communicate with him (referred to a schoolmate).
>
> I sent a photo to a boy who I met online . . . he made a photo montage where I was naked and uploaded it onto the Internet (referred to an unknown online contact).

In the next phase, these subcategories were reorganised and merged into higher categories on the basis of similarities or interconnections. In this phase, referred to as 'axial coding' by Strauss and Corbin (1990), the first drafts of concepts were created. For example, the category 'relationships of people involved' captured the dynamics of the relationship between the victim, aggressors and bystanders. Furthermore, the category of anonymity versus being known summarised knowledge of the borders between the online and offline world. These higher categories were repeatedly compared to the interviews and integrated into three contexts of online aggressive attacks characterised by different processes used to harm the victims. These contexts are described in the results of the research.

Ethics of the research

This research was carried out with respect to ethical principles (Miovský 2006) and therefore with awareness that the participants shared their personal experiences under the condition that their anonymity was maintained (choice of a nickname), that their privacy was maintained, and that they could choose to end their participation or not to answer some questions. Involvement in the research was by informed consent. Participants were informed in advance about the form of the qualitative research and expected duration of the interview, and this could be adjusted to their time needs. At the end of the interview the adolescents could ask for whatever information they were interested in. Attention was paid to ensuring that the participants did not feel uncomfortable after the interview. The concluding questions directed participants towards social help and possible solutions. At the end of the interview those who were interested were given links to websites and other institutions that offer help to adolescents who face online aggression.

Results

Three basic contexts in which cyberbullying occurred were identified: (1) online attacks perpetrated by an unknown aggressor (six participants); (2) online attacks perpetrated by a known aggressor (four participants); and (3) bullying with elements of totality (i.e. online aggression both online and offline) (six participants) (see Table 1 for further details). These contexts also differed in the extent of harm that the victim experienced.

Online attacks by an unknown aggressor

Relationships between aggressors and victims were differentiated on a continuum from anonymous online communication, through previous online friendship, to relationships within an age group both inside and outside the school environment. The degree of anonymity and the overlap of cyberbullying to offline life appeared to be the crucial element in the degree of harm felt by the victim. The results showed that in anonymous contact, the greater the connection between the online aggression and the real world the greater the victim's perceived harm.

P2: I used to chat with a guy on lide.cz and then suddenly this girl started to message me saying I shouldn't chat with him, that he sleeps with her and stuff. But we only chatted. And when I removed him from my friends, she wrote to me for maybe a year afterwards and threatened to find me. She wrote many insults to my friends too.

P14: I sent a photo to a boy [whom she did not know offline] . . . he made a photo montage where I was naked and uploaded it onto the Internet . . . then he blackmailed me that if I didn't meet him or sleep with him or whatever, he'd send the link to my parents, people at school would know and whatever.

I: What were you afraid of?

P14: Of what would happen . . . of how it could be solved, who could help me out of it, what that guy could do.

These excerpts document that the impact of online attacks by anonymous people was increased when the aggressors connected their virtual threats with the real world, e.g. in the form of attacking the victim offline or humiliation in front of people who were part of their real lives. Lack of acquaintance with the offender also played a role in that the victim could not be sure whether the offender would be able to carry out their threats.

Online attacks by a known aggressor

Victims of online bullying were encountered who knew their aggressor or connected them with a person from their real lives. In many cases they were a person from school. This was a repetitive form of aggression from a known person with whom the victim was often in everyday contact. Although the attacks happened only in the online world, some aggressors used online applications that allowed others to watch the victimisation.

> P15: I have experienced cyberbullying in the sense that a girl uploaded my photo to her profile on a social network and wrote a comment which humiliated and offended me.

In this situation the victim could not defend himself as the photo was published on the Internet and the aggressor had control of when the photo and comments were deleted. The participant also considered it distressing that the aggressor chose a social network to carry out this cyberbullying, as in so doing they allowed the content to be made publicly available. In this case it meant that the victim was humiliated in front of a wide circle of people who knew both him and the offender.

Another form of cyberbullying in which the aggressors came from the victim's real world was victimisation carried out by multiple people. The following example is from an interview with a girl whose classmates pretended to be an unknown boy during online communication. It illustrates a case where the victim was bothered by the fact that she became the target of a plot by several people who she knew offline.

> I: How did you learn that multiple people were pretending to be that boy? How did you discover their true identity?
>
> P9: From the beginning, I knew that it was probably them from the way they wrote . . . and I was told by a friend who knew.

Similarly, in the next excerpt the dynamics of collective participation in attacks can be seen on a victim who was attacked because of the race of his mother's boyfriend.

> P15: I've come across cyberbullying at school on the spoluzaci.cz server where there were swearwords about the nationality of my mum's boyfriend, further pics and texts, also verbal suggestions, so I deleted them. There were several people (aggressors) . . . they were friends, one of them is sort of my best friend, another is sort of a leader, but also the punk of the class if you see, they started it and the others followed.

In the online environment adolescents seem to succumb more easily to collective participation in bullying. As this excerpt suggests, even those peers who the victim considers friends can be drawn in. This exacerbates the victim's feelings of powerlessness and therefore also the negative experience connected with the attacks.

Bullying with elements of totality

The participants' experiences with cyberbullying also served to demonstrate that the extent of the harm perceived was influenced by the victimisation spreading from one environment to another, from school to the Internet. As opposed to the previous form of online attack committed by a known person, the third context of cyberbullying was distinctive in that it represented a direct extension of traditional bullying. Metaphorically speaking, the Internet replaced the school playground, where the bullying would move after classes. Through the story of one victimised participant it was clear how the victim had to face bullying both on the Internet and at school. The excerpt also demonstrates how the imbalance of power was established in the online environment. The offline aggressor, who was seen as a star of the class, mastered the Internet environment by becoming an administrator of the class site at the Czech social networking site www.spoluzaci.cz (a web server which is widely used by primary school children and secondary school students for networking).

> P16: He comes up with everything and the others join, he rules over the weaker and if they don't conform, he bullies them . . . . for example they always talk about what admin wrote like that I'm gay and stuff which isn't true.

The aggressor from school thus used the Internet to increase the victimisation by abusing a social network that connected classmates in the online environment. It can also be seen here that the mechanism by which the offline aggressor strengthened his position on the Internet was built on the interconnection between the online and offline lives of today's adolescents. Through the social network site the offline relationships of the class were extended to the online environment and thus the class dynamics were reproduced online.

The following excerpt shows that the content of the online victimisation was discussed in the offline environment (at school), which leads to further victimisation and thus a deepening of the trauma.

> P1: The others mocked me about being bullied, etc., he then took a photo of me and someone mutilated the photo totally and uploaded it to classmates server (www.spoluzaci.cz). I haven't dared to look there yet and it's been a year . . . The next day a classmate told me that he'd seen the photo at a classmates and that it's really cool but I was so down that I haven't dared to look at it yet because many people have told me that they've seen it and that it's cool.

It is worth noting that the excerpt comes from an interview with a participant who was continuously bullied at school for two-and-a-half years. The traditional bullying had reached the state where members of the group, including the victim himself, had accepted the standards of the aggressor. As this interview demonstrates, the Internet intensified the bullying in the sense that classmates who had not before witnessed the bullying became part of the bullying owing to the easy spread of victimising materials (deformation of photos). It contributed to widening the circle of people in front of whom the victimisation was realised, and thus to deepening the victim's trauma.

Discussion

The goal of this study was to examine how adolescent victims perceive online attacks and when they consider them harmful. The character of aggressive online attacks was differentiated according to the relationships between the people involved, on a scale from online perpetration by unknown aggressors, through known and close attackers from the offline world, to cyberbullying carried out by members of existing social groups (school classes). Although the distinction between anonymous online attackers and offline aggressors from their offline world may seem schematic at first glance, the findings document the importance of this distinction.

Perpetration that took place only in the online environment was less bothering for the adolescents if it was not transferred offline or if it did not interfere with the victim's offline relationships. Partially, the different perceptions can be explained by online dissociation effects, i.e. Internet users in general tend to dissociate experiences in the online world from their offline lives (Suler 2004). Therefore, it can be assumed that to strengthen the impact of online threats the aggressor points their aggressive behaviour to the offline life of the victim, which increases the victim's fear of whether the aggressor can cross the border between online and offline worlds and thus fulfil online threats.

Online victimisation was also harmful when the offender was connected with the offline world and when online victimisation was collective in the sense that others joined the main aggressor in the role of bystanders or co-aggressors. It may be that an ability to blend with the group contributes to the deregulation of social behaviour, which then conforms to the standards of the group. In addition, according to de-individualisation theory, aggressive forms can occur relatively easily because online interaction is characterised by a loss of direct feedback and physical contact, and thus a loss of awareness that someone is being hurt (Spears et al. 2002). Therefore, bystanders who would not tend to behave aggressively face to face may easily join the primary aggressor's side without thinking through the consequences of their behaviour (Lüders, Brandtzaeg, and Dunkels 2009).

This study showed that adolescents who were bullied both at school and on the Internet had greater feelings of harm when online victimisation served to reproduce bullying at school. In this context the harm of online victimisation seems to originate from school bullying as the mechanism of hurting was primarily based on abusive peer (school) relationships being extended to the online environment. Therefore, it is assumed that cyberbullying characterised by abuse of school-based peer relationships is a subtype of traditional bullying rather than a new isolated phenomenon.

Although, according to Slonje and Smith (2008), the perception of online attacks depends on their manner of perpetration (i.e. abuse via photos or spread of defamation), our study shows that it is not only this that is important, but also the context of the aggression itself. Feelings of trauma and danger appeared mainly in connection with the offline world. It can be assumed that compared with anonymous forms of aggression, cyberbullying connected with the offline world defines significantly better the context of victimisation, providing a social space where the victim is humiliated in front of known onlookers. Further research could look at bystanders and their role in the process of victimisation.

There are certain limitations to the results of this study. It is important to mention that the sample included only those who considered their experience to be within the invitation message's definition of cyberbullying. The narrowness of this definition or its interpretation by certain recipients may mean that the sample excluded some whose participation could have facilitated a more diverse perspective of the phenomenon of harming via the Internet. Furthermore, the findings are overwhelmingly based on pure victims; however, in the Czech environment online perpetration and cyberbullying occur most commonly in the context of sharing the role of aggressor and victim (Ševčíková and Šmahel 2009). Including those who have experienced both roles might provide a greater understanding of the contexts in which online victimisation is harmful.

Conclusion

This study has shown differences in perception of online aggression committed by an unknown person, and by a person with whom the victim connects in the real world. As a result, specific differences contribute to the variability in perceptions of online attacks. In relation to perpetration by an unknown aggressor, the perception of victimisation is influenced to a degree by the attacker's tendency to focus the aggression towards the victim's real life. In cases of connection between cyberbullying and the real world, most precisely the school environment, collective participation in victimisation becomes significantly more important, as well as the identification of bystanders. If cyberbullying follows school bullying, then the online victimisation can deepen the impact of bullying in the physical world in that the content of online victimisation discussed offline (at school) reproduces the bullying and thus the trauma itself.

These findings also have practical implications. The fact that cyberbullying occurred in the context of existing peer relationships shows the importance of remembering that school bullying can spread into the online world. Specifically, offline bullying intervention should be expanded to cover the online world. Furthermore, cyberbullying preventive education should be extended to teach pupils that even online aggressive behaviour may have serious negative impacts on the targeted peers. Finally, adolescents should be made more aware that the Internet and its features can easily provoke dissociative behaviours, including aggressive conduct towards peers.

Acknowledgements

The authors acknowledge the support of the Czech Ministry of Education, Youth and Sports (LD11008), the Czech Science Foundation (GAP407/11/0585) and the Faculty of Social Studies, Masaryk University.

References

Charmaz, K. 2008. Grounded theory. In *Qualitative psychology: A practical guide to methods*, ed. J.A. Smith, 81–110. London: Sage.

Dooley, J.J., J. Pyzalski, and D. Cross. 2009. Cyberbullying versus face-to-face bullying: A theoretical and conceptual review. *Zeitschrift für Psychologie/Journal of Psychology* 217: 182–8.

Heirman, W., and M. Walrave. 2008. Assessing concerns and issues about the mediation of technology in cyberbullying. *Cyberpsychology: Journal of Psychosocial Research on Cyberspace* 2, no. 2. http://cyberpsychology.eu/view.php?cisloclanku=2008111401&article=1

Hinduja, S., and J.W. Patchin. 2010. Bullying, cyberbullying, and suicide. *Archives of Suicide Research* 14: 206–21.

Juvonen, J., and E.F. Gross. 2008. Extending the school grounds? Bullying experiences in cyberspace. *The Journal of School Health* 78: 496–505.

Kowalski, R.M., and S.P. Limber. 2007. Electronic bullying among middle school students. *Journal of Adolescent Health* 41, 6 Suppl. no. 1: S22–30.

Livingstone, S., L. Haddon, A. Görzig, and K. Ólafsson. 2011. *Risks and safety on the internet: The perspective of European children. Full findings*. London: EU Kids Online, LSE.

Lüders, M.H., P.B. Brandtzaeg, and E. Dunkels. 2009. Risky contacts. In *Kids online: Opportunities risks for children*, eds. S. Livingstone and L. Haddon, 123–35. Bristol: Policy Press.

Lupač, P., and J. Sládek. 2008. The deepening of the digital divide in the Czech Republic. *Cyberpsychology: Journal of Psychosocial Research on Cyberspace* 2, no. 1. http://cyberpsychology.eu/view.php?cisloclanku=2008060203&article=2

Miovský, M. 2006. *Kvalitativní přístup a metody v psychologickém výzkumu* [Qualitative approach and methods in psychological research]. Praha: Grada.

Mitchell, K.J., M. Ybarra, and D. Finkelhor. 2007. The relative importance of online victimization in understanding depression, delinquency, and substance use. *Child Maltreatment* 12, no. 12: 314–324.

Olweus, D. 1993. *Bullying at school: What we know and what we can do*. Oxford: Blackwell.

Ortega, R., P. Elipe, J.A. Mora-Merchán, J. Calmaestra, and E. Vega. 2009. The emotional impact on victims of traditional bullying and cyberbullying. A study of Spanish adolescents. *Zeitschrift für Psychologie/Journal of Psychology* 217: 197–204.

Perren, S., J. Dooley, T. Shaw, and D. Cross. 2010. Bullying in school and cyberspace: Associations with depressive symptoms in Swiss and Australian adolescents. *Child and Adolescent Psychiatry and Mental Health* 4, no. 28: 4–28.

Schouten, A. P., P.M. Valkenburg, and J. Peter. 2009. An experimental test of processes underlying self-disclosure in computer-mediated communication. *Cyberpsychology: Journal of Psychosocial Research on Cyberspace* 3, no. 2. http://cyberpsychology.eu/view.php?cisloclanku=2009111601&article=1

Ševčíková, A., and D. Šmahel. 2009. Online harassment and cyberbullying in the Czech Republic: Comparison across age. *Zeitschrift für Psychologie/Journal of Psychology* 217: 227–9.

Slonje, R., and P.K. Smith. 2008. Cyberbullying: Another main type of bullying? *Scandinavian Journal of Psychology* 49: 147–54.

Smith, P.K., J. Mahdavi, M. Carvalho, S. Fisher, S. Russell, and N. Tippett. 2008. Cyberbullying: Its nature and impact in secondary school pupils. *Journal of Child Psychology and Psychiatry* 49: 376–85.

Spears, B., P. Slee, L. Owens, and B. Johnson. 2009. Behind the scenes and screens: Insights into the human dimension of covert and cyber bullying. *Zeitschrift für Psychologie/Journal of Psychology* 217: 189–96.

Spears, R, T. Postmest, M. Leam, and A. Wolbert. 2002. When are net effects gross products? The power of influence and the influence of power in computer-mediated communication. *Journal of Social Issues* 58: 91–107.

Strauss, A., and J. Corbin. 1990. *Basics of qualitative research: Grounded theory procedures and techniques*. Thousand Oaks, CA: Sage.

Subrahmanyam, K., and D. Šmahel. 2011. *Digital youth: The role of media in development*. New York: Springer.

Suler, J. 2004. The online disinhibition effect. *CyberPsychology & Behavior* 7: 321–6.

Tokunaga, R.S. 2010. Following you home from school: A critical review and synthesis of research on cyberbullying victimization. *Computers in Human Behavior* 26: 277–87.

Vandebosch, H., and K. Van Cleemput. 2008. Defining cyberbullying: A qualitative research into the perceptions of youngsters. *Cyberpsychology and Behavior* 11: 499–503.

Ybarra, M.L., M. Diener-West, and P.J. Leaf. 2007. Examining the overlap in internet-harassment and school bullying: Implications for school intervention. *Journal of Adolescent Health* 41, 6 Suppl. no. 1: S42–50.

Ybarra, M.L., and K.J. Mitchell. 2004. Online aggressor/targets, aggressors, and targets: A comparison of associated youth characteristics. *Journal of Child Psychology and Psychiatry* 45: 1308–16.

Emotional and behavioural problems in the context of cyberbullying: a longitudinal study among German adolescents

Anja Schultze-Krumbholz, Anne Jäkel, Martin Schultze and Herbert Scheithauer

Department of Educational Science and Psychology, Freie Universität Berlin, Germany

Although many studies have reported on internalising and externalising problems related to cyberbullying roles, there is a lack of longitudinal research in this area. This study reports (1) cross-sectional data from 412 German middle-school students to examine differences between cyberbullies, cybervictims and cyberbully–victims compared to non-involved students in regard to internalising (depressiveness and loneliness) and externalising (instrumental and reactive aggression) problems; and (2) longitudinal data from 223 students about links of cyberbullying and cybervictimisation with internalising and externalising problems across two measurement occasions, analysed using path analysis (separately by gender). Self-report measures were used. The results revealed no significant differences between groups in internalising problems, but all three cyberbullying groups differed significantly from the non-involved group in externalising problems. Female victims showed increases in externalising problems while male victims did not show changes across time in either internalising or externalising problems. Male bullies reported decreases in internalising problems across time. For boys, scoring high in both cyberbullying and cybervictimisation led to increases in loneliness, while for girls this predicted decreases in reactive aggression.

Introduction

Cyberbullying has become a growing concern in Germany since the first media reports in 2004 (Jäger, Arbinger, and Lissmann 2010). In 2011, public awareness reached a peak when a website encouraged students throughout Germany to spread gossip and rumours about each other, following the model of a popular American teen television series. It guaranteed students complete anonymity and that the operators would not share identity information with the authorities. The website was very popular with adolescents. Apart from online threats and insults there also were offline consequences such as physical attacks between perpetrators and victims (Lischka, Stöcker, and Ternieden 2011). These incidents put pressure on schools and policy makers to adequately address the problem of cyberbullying.

Internationally, most early studies used their own definition of cyberbullying while later studies relied on previous and widely accepted definitions, such as the one by Smith et al. (2008), which is used in many European studies. To provide an integrative definition of a number of generally accepted, but partly inconsistent definitions, Tokunaga

(2010, 278) proposes this synthesis: 'Cyberbullying is any behavior performed through electronic or digital media by individuals or groups that repeatedly communicates hostile or aggressive messages intended to inflict harm or discomfort on others'. We used this definition in the present study, not regarding the additional criteria of anonymity and publicity which have also been examined in some studies focusing on the definition and, for example, adolescents' understanding of it (Menesini et al. in press; Nocentini et al. 2010).

Research on cyberbullying in Germany dates from 2007 (Jäger, Arbinger, and Lissmann 2010). The prevalence rates of cyberbullying in Germany range from 7.6% to 32.8% for cyberbullies and from 3.3% to 43.1% for cybervictims (Schultze-Krumbholz and Scheithauer 2010). The overlap between cyberbullies and cyber-victims has been little documented, but Schultze-Krumbholz and Scheithauer (2009a) found a prevalence of 6.8% for so-called bully–victims in a small, non-representative sample. As cyberbully–victims have been shown to be impacted most seriously by cyberbullying (Gradinger, Strohmeier, and Spiel 2009), this group should be taken into account in studies on cyberbullying.

Many studies have documented adverse effects of participation in traditional bullying. Also, many studies have shown substantial overlap between participation in traditional and cyberbullying (Tokunaga 2010). However, differing definitions and unique characteristics support the view that both should be treated as different although not independent phenomena. For example, in our own studies, 8.8–14.1% of participating students were involved solely in cyberbullying, 7.0–14.2% were involved only in traditional bullying and the overlap ranged from 8.5% to 9.8% (Schultze-Krumbholz and Scheithauer 2009a). The focus of the present study is on the impact of cyberbullying on all involved adolescents, so we do not review the research on traditional bullying further.

Emotional and behavioural difficulties associated with cyberbullying

Several cross-sectional studies, mainly correlational or regression studies, have examined the co-occurrence of internalising and/or externalising difficulties with involvement in cyberbullying (as bully, victim or bully–victim) among adolescents. Most of the reported studies – unless indicated otherwise – used student samples.

Internalising problems and cyberbullying

Many studies have focused on internalising problems, especially depression or depressive symptoms, and emotional problems in general. Studies from the USA, Spain and Germany report that large proportions of cybervictims experience a range of negative emotions such as sadness, anxiety, embarrassment and helplessness (Finkelhor, Mitchell, and Wolak 2000; Ortega et al. 2009; Raskauskas and Stoltz 2007; Techniker Krankenkasse 2011). Cybervictims feel more negatively affected if they are victimised frequently (Ortega et al. 2009). Also, cybervictims felt more suspicious of their environment when the perpetrator was anonymous (Raskauskas and Stoltz 2007). In a population-based study with Finnish adolescents, Sourander et al. (2010) found cybervictimisation to be associated with emotional problems generally and physical health indicators. In Germany, cybervictims reported psychosomatic symptoms such as trouble sleeping, headaches and abdominal pain (Techniker Krankenkasse 2011). In a US study, somatisation symptoms were also significantly correlated with cybervictimisation (Carter 2011), although the depression scale was not. Dempsey et al. (2009) found cybervictimisation to be associated with social anxiety, but not depression, in a US sample.

In regression analyses of a Swiss and an Australian student sample, Perren et al. (2010) found that cybervictimisation predicted depressive symptoms even when controlling for traditional victimisation. This effect was culturally independent and not moderated by country. Depressive symptoms were also predicted by cybervictimisation in Turkey (Erdur Baker, and Tanrikulu 2010).

Analyses of other involvement groups in the USA also showed bullies and bully–victims to be highly depressed (Ybarra and Mitchell 2004a, 2004b) Sontag et al. (2011) found that both cyberbullies and cybervictims showed higher levels of anxiety and depression. In Austria, differentiated patterns for involvement groups emerged, with victims showing more internalising problems (depressive and somatic symptoms) and bully–victims showing both internalising and externalising behaviour (Gradinger, Strohmeier, and Spiel 2009).

Externalising problems and cyberbullying

Cyberbullying and cybervictimisation have also been linked to externalising problems. In Austria, Gradinger, Strohmeier, and Spiel (2009) reported more externalising problems (instrumental and reactive aggression) only for cyberbullies and cyberbully–victims. Ybarra and Mitchell (2004a, 2004b) found more online harassers in the USA to be delinquent, and many bully–victims to exhibit problem behaviours. But some studies also found externalising problems associated with cybervictimisation. In Finland, Sourander et al. (2010) found that cyberbullies reported hyperactivity, conduct problems and other externalising behaviours, but cybervictimisation was linked to behaviour problems with peers. Sontag et al. (2011) found high scores on proactive and reactive aggression scales for both cyberbullies and cybervictims in a US sample. In Germany, Schultze-Krumbholz and Scheithauer (2009b) found that both cybervictims and bullies were more relationally aggressive than non-involved students. Katzer, Fetchenhauer, and Belschak (2009a, 2009b) identified antisocial online behaviour and delinquency, among others, as predictors of chat bullying and antisocial online behaviour, among others, as a predictor of chat victimisation in Germany. Cybervictims can also demonstrate externalising emotional reactions. Ortega et al. (2009) found a group of Spanish cybervictims who reacted angrily to the experience; in a German sample two-thirds of cybervictims reported feeling angry (the most frequent answer) when asked what being cyberbullied made them feel like (Techniker Krankenkasse 2011), and in a US sample cybervictims felt angry and annoyed (Carter 2011).

Gender differences in cyberbullying and internalising and externalising problems

When examining internalising and externalising problems associated with cyberbullying, gender differences need to be taken into account. So far, no clear patterns have emerged in previous research regarding the gender distribution in cyberbullying and cybervictimisation (Tokunaga 2010). In Germany, studies either report no significant differences or report boys to be involved more often (Schultze-Krumbholz and Scheithauer 2010).

There are clear gender differences in internalising and externalising problems. During adolescence, girls tend to show more internalising problems such as depression and anxiety, while boys exhibit more externalising problems such as conduct disorders or aggression (Crick and Zahn-Waxler 2003). This may interact with involvement in cyberbullying. Ortega et al. (2009) found girls to be more emotionally impacted by cybervictimisation than boys. More girls than boys belonged to a cluster of students showing a range of negative emotions, while more boys were 'not bothered' by the experience.

Summary

Many studies have found cybervictimisation to be associated with internalising problems, while cyberbullies showed higher levels of externalising problems. However, some studies also showed negative emotional effects on cyberbullies, such as depression. In addition, aggression levels were higher in victims than with non-involved students. There is a clear picture of the detrimental effects of cyberbullying on all the involved individuals. Gender may also be a factor but it has been little investigated in this context. Despite a range of cross-sectional studies, little is known with regard to the longitudinal impact of cyberbullying, although Williams and Guerra (2007) analysed school context variables and normative orientation as predictors of cyberbullying. Thus, previous research results only allow conclusions to be drawn about the co-occurrence of cyberbullying and cybervictimisation with emotional and behavioural problems, but do not provide insight into whether these problems are actually caused by cyberbullying and cybervictimisation. However, knowledge about the long-term impact of cyberbullying involvement on internalising and externalising problems is crucial for the development of prevention and intervention strategies.

Research objectives

Given the lack of longitudinal research on cyberbullying with regard to emotional and behavioural outcomes, the main aim of this study was to gain insight into consequences of cyberbullying and cybervictimisation and to find clear indications of the sequence using longitudinal data. We operationalised internalising (or emotional problems) as depressiveness and loneliness, and externalising (or behavioural problems) as instrumental and reactive aggression. Therefore, the research questions were:

(1) Do the conventional groups (cyberbullies, cybervictims and cyberbully–victims) differ in internalising and externalising problems?
We hypothesised that cybervictims should show higher levels of depressiveness and loneliness than cyberbullies. Cyberbullies are expected to show higher levels of instrumental and reactive aggression than victims. Cyberbully–victims should show higher scores on all problem variables than non-involved students and cybervictims.

(2) Does the extent of involvement in cyberbullying as perpetrator or victim predict increases in internalising and/or externalising problems at a later time-point?
As previous research shows gender differences in internalising and externalising problems, both types of problems were included in the model so as not to confound results about the consequences of cyberbullying with actual gender differences. We hypothesised that boys and girls will show different paths regarding the impact of cyberbullying and cybervictimisation, with girls showing more internalising and boys showing more externalising problems.

Method

Design

Data were collected as part of a comprehensive evaluation study of a cyberbullying prevention programme ('Medienhelden') (Schultze-Krumbholz et al. 2012). The analyses are based on the pre-measurement (t1, in January/February 2011) and post-measurement (t2, in April to June 2011) of the control group participants. The control group did not receive any kind of intervention.

Participants

Participants were 452 secondary school students from 16 classes from five different schools in Berlin, Germany. In total, 412 students took part in the study at t1, and 307 at t2. A total of 267 students participated at both measurement points (attrition rate about 35%). Besides normal attrition (students sick on the assessment day, leaving the class/school, etc.), there were organisational problems with one school and the long-term absence of one of the coordinating teachers. Hence, whole classes did not take part at t2 (the school was still represented by classes which did take part at t2 and therefore the attrition was not selective regarding whole schools). The attrition was not systematic as regards involvement in cyberbullying. For the longitudinal analyses 44 students were excluded owing to missing values on any of the study variables, leaving 223 to be included in the analyses. Almost all students (97%) were born in Germany.

Cross-sectional sample

The cross-sectional sample of 412 students consisted of 237 girls (52.4%) and 212 boys (46.9%) (three did not indicate gender). Students were on average aged 13.35 years (SD = 1.04), and attended grade 7 (32.3%), grade 8 (49.3%), grade 9 (13.1%) and grade 10 (5.3%). Distribution across schools was School A 31.1%, School B 11.2%, School C 18.2%, School D 22.6% and School E 16.7%.

Longitudinal sample

The longitudinal sample had 223 students, consisting of 109 girls (48.9%) and 114 boys (51.1%). The mean age was 13.14 years (SD = 0.87), with students in grade 7 (37.7%), grade 8 (51.6%), grade 9 (7.6%) and grade 10 (3.1%). The high attrition at one school led to a changed distribution across schools: School A 14.7%, School B 10.3%, School C 18.8%, School D 35.0% and School E 21.1%.

Procedure

Schools were contacted by phone and informed about the study. If they expressed interest they were sent further information along with a consent form, which was to be returned by fax as this was needed for the permission of the Senate Department in Berlin. Parents were sent letters with information about the study and asking for their consent via the students at every measurement point. Parents' and students' informed, active consent was collected by the classroom teachers. Owing to missing parental consent or active refusal to take part, 3.1% of students were not allowed to participate.

A standardised paper questionnaire was administered during ethics school lessons by trained researchers. Students were assured of voluntariness and anonymity before the questionnaires were distributed. Ethics education was chosen as the framework for the implementation of this project as the study topic fits well into the predefined curriculum. All students were in grades 7–10, which receive compulsory ethics education in Berlin schools.

Measures

All of the measures used are self-report instruments. Reported reliabilities are Cronbach's alpha and are always reported for both measurement occasions (t1 and t2). Except for the depressiveness scale, which was originally in German, all the measures were translated by the research team.

Cyberbullying and cybervictimisation

Cyberbullying and cybervictimisation were assessed with the DAPHNE III questionnaire (Brighi et al. 2012), developed within the framework of the project 'Cyberbullying in Adolescence: Investigation and Intervention in Six European Countries' (bullyingand-cyber.net). Twelve multiple-choice self-report items listed specific behaviours for both cyberbullying and cybervictimisation. Students were asked to indicate how often they had experienced or taken part in the specific behaviour (e.g. name-calling, threatening, hacking personal accounts, embarrassing pictures) online or through a mobile phone during the previous two months, on a five-point Likert scale (0 = never to 4 = more than once a week). The reliabilities for the cyberbullying scale were $\alpha_{t1} = 0.90$ and $\alpha_{t2} = 0.94$, and for the cybervictimisation scale $\alpha_{t1} = 0.62$ and $\alpha_{t2} = 0.86$.

Students with total scores of 0–2 were categorised as not involved. Students with scores above 2 were categorised as cybervictims or cyberbullies. Participants with scores above 2 on both cyberbullying and cybervictimisation were labelled as cyberbully–victims. The four types of involvement are mutually exclusive. A score of 2 corresponds to showing or experiencing two specific behaviours 'once or twice' or showing or experiencing one specific behaviour 'once or twice a month'.

Depressiveness

On a six-item scale (Schwarzer and Bäßler 1999), students rated their depressive thoughts (e.g. 'I often feel sad without a reason') in depressive emotional and motivational situations by utilising a four-point Likert scale (1 = not true to 4 = completely true). Reliabilities were $\alpha_{t1} = 0.70$ and $\alpha_{t2} = 0.80$. The measure was somewhat stable across time ($r = 0.48$, $p < 0.001$).

Loneliness

Using the UCLA Loneliness Scale-8 (ULS-8) (Hays and DiMatteo 1987), students indicated their feeling of being separated from others on eight items (e.g. 'There is no one I can turn to') using a Likert scale (1 = never to 4 = always). Reliabilities were $\alpha_{t1} = 0.75$ and $\alpha_{t2} = 0.77$. The measure was stable across time ($r = 0.55, p < 0.001$).

Instrumental aggression

An instrumental overt aggression scale by Little et al. (2003; extended by Gradinger, Strohmeier, and Spiel 2009) was used. This has six original items, and one additional item within the cyber context ('To get what I want I often use the mobile phone or the computer to send mean text messages, e-mails, videos, or photos to others'). These were answered on a Likert scale (1 = not true to 4 = completely true). Reliabilities were $\alpha_{t1} = 0.92$ and $\alpha_{t2} = 0.95$. The measure was somewhat stable across time ($r = 0.46$, $p < 0.001$).

Reactive aggression

A corresponding reactive aggression scale (Little et al. 2003; extended by Gradinger, Strohmeier, and Spiel 2009) similarly had six original and one cyber-specific item ('If others have angered me, I often use the mobile phone or the computer to send them mean text messages, e-mails, videos, or photos'). These were answered on a Likert scale (1 = not true to 4 = completely true). Reliabilities were $\alpha_{t1} = 0.87$ and $\alpha_{t2} = 0.89$. The measure was stable across time ($r = 0.66, p < 0.001$).

Data analysis

The basis for comparisons between subgroups for research question (1) was the complete t1 sample ($N = 412$). Using a threshold on a summative scale covering different bullying episodes (see Method), cybervictimisation and cyberbullying were dichotomised to analyse for finding differences between distinct groups.

For research question (2), the longitudinal subsample of 223 students was used. Continuous variables were used, computed through mean scores. This approach was chosen because it was of interest to identify potential consequences within the general student population and not just within extreme groups. To take into account the skewness of the data, the robust estimator MLR was used during statistical analyses as suggested by Finney and DiStefano (2006). As school survey data are naturally clustered within classes, a priori analyses were conducted to test the necessity of multilevel modelling. Intraclass correlations were very low (0.01–0.06) and there were no significant group effects on any of the variables examined here. We proceeded without explicitly accounting for nested structures (cf. Snijders and Bosker 1999, 21–2). Statistical analyses were conducted using the statistics programs SPSS 20.0 (SPSS 2011) and Mplus 6.11 (Muthén and Muthén 1998–2010).

Results

Descriptive results for the study variables are presented in Table 1. We found no significant gender difference regarding cybervictimisation and cyberbullying. Girls showed higher levels of depressiveness and loneliness at t1, supporting the assumption of gender differences

Table 1. Mean values, standard deviations and gender differences of study variables.

	Overall *M* (SD)	Girls *M* (SD)	Boys *M* (SD)	T	df	*p*
Cyberbullying t1	0.11 (0.35)	0.09 (0.30)	0.13 (0.40)	−1.175	405	0.24
Cybervictimisation t1	0.09 (0.19)	0.09 (0.20)	0.09 (0.18)	0.332	409	0.74
Internalising problems						
Depressiveness t1	1.50 (0.47)	1.58 (0.50)	1.43 (0.46)	2.576	253	< 0.05*
Depressiveness t2	1.49 (0.54)	1.53 (0.48)	1.48 (0.61)	0.184	253	0.85
Loneliness t1	1.85 (0.47)	2.00 (0.49)	1.79 (0.44)	3.319	248	< 0.01**
Loneliness t2	1.89 (0.51)	1.96 (0.49)	1.85 (0.53)	1.554	248	0.12
Externalising problems						
Instrumental aggression t1	1.28 (0.48)	1.19 (0.37)	1.37 (0.57)	−2.300	217	< 0.05*
Instrumental aggression t2	1.36 (0.63)	1.23 (0.46)	1.53 (0.75)	−3.231	217	< 0.05*
Reactive aggression t1	1.71 (0.61)	1.49 (0.50)	1.95 (0.65)	−5.397	217	< 0.001***
Reactive aggression t2	1.71 (0.71)	1.44 (0.54)	1.99 (0.77)	−5.561	217	< 0.001***

Note: All participants with valid scores for both measurement points of the respective study variable (i.e. longitudinal sample, $N = 223$) were included.

in internalising problems, but these were not statistically significant at t2. Boys persistently reported significantly higher levels of instrumental and reactive aggression than girls at both measurement occasions.

Cross-sectional results: differences between groups at t1 (research question 1)

At the first measurement point, 22 students (5.3%) were scored as cyberbullies, 29 (7.0%) as victims and 18 (4.4%) as both (cyberbully–victims). Multivariate analyses of variance (MANOVAs) were conducted for comparisons of the three involved groups and the non-involved group regarding the internalising (depressiveness and loneliness) and externalising (instrumental and reactive aggression) variables. Gender was not included as a covariate owing to small subgroups.

For internalising variables, the multivariate test revealed a significant effect: Pillai criterion $F(2{,}786) = 4.17$, $p < 0.001$, $\eta^2 = 0.03$. However, Scheffé post-hoc tests did not show any significant differences between cybervictims, cyberbullies, cyberbully–victims and non-involved students in either depressiveness or loneliness at t1.

For externalising variables, the MANOVA revealed a significant multivariate effect: Pillai Criterion $F(2{,}710) = 11.83$, $p < 0.001$, $\eta^2 = 0.09$. Scheffé post-hoc tests showed that all groups involved in cyberbullying scored significantly higher on instrumental aggression than students not involved in cyberbullying (Table 2). For reactive aggression the results for Scheffé post-hoc tests presented in Table 2 show that cyberbullies and cyberbully–victims scored significantly higher than non-involved students (and cyberbullies higher than cybervictims).

Longitudinal results: impact of cyberbullying on internalising/externalising problems at t2 (research question 2)

A longitudinal path analysis was conducted and continuous variables for cybervictimisation and cyberbullying were used. A comparison of models showed separate models for girls and boys to be more adequate than one general model for the whole sample (AIC = 995.8 vs. AIC = 1033.5). As cyberbully–victims showed the worst psychosocial profiles in previous research (Gradinger, Strohmeier, and Spiel 2009) an interaction term was included in the model. This model separating by gender fits the data well on all of the conventional goodness-of-fit indices: $\chi^2(16) = 17.898$, $p = 0.275$, RMSEA = 0.03, CFI = 1.00, TLI = 0.99, SRMR = 0.03.

Table 2. Mean scores (SD in parentheses) and results of Scheffé post-hoc tests of the MANOVA for differences between all involvement groups regarding externalising problems at t1.

Group	Instrumental aggression M (SD)	Reactive aggression M (SD)
(a) Not involved	1.21 (0.36)^{b,c,d}	1.63 (0.55)^{b,d}
(b) Cyberbully	1.81 (1.01)^{a}	2.57 (0.84)^{a,c}
(c) Cybervictim	1.56 (0.67)^{a}	1.87 (0.50)^{b}
(d) Cyberbully–victim	1.79 (0.79)^{a}	2.30 (0.87)^{a}

Note: Mean values with superscript letters are significantly different by at least $p < 0.05$ from the respective group (a: not involved; b: cyberbully; c: cybervictim; d: cyberbully–victim).

One of the questions of major interest is whether cyberbullying and cybervictimisation lead to detrimental outcomes. The results show different paths for girls and boys.

For girls, higher levels of cybervictimisation predict increases in depressiveness, but not loneliness, over time (Table 3). However, increases in loneliness were predicted by higher depressiveness, indicating the need for more complex analyses such as mediator analyses to investigate whether depressiveness is a mediator between victimisation and loneliness.

Cybervictimisation in girls led to increased levels of reactive and instrumental aggression. However, the interaction term indicates that showing higher levels of both cyberbullying and cybervictimisation at the same time predicted decreases in reactive aggression, while pure cyberbullying again predicted increases in reactive aggression.

Taking into account autoregression, the model for girls explains 46% of the variance in depressiveness, 40% of the variance in loneliness, 66% of the variance in instrumental aggression and 82% of the variance in reactive aggression across time (Table 3). The only exception from the stability of the internalising and externalising problems across time is presented by instrumental aggression. The level of instrumental aggression at t1 is not predictive of instrumental aggression three months later.

Table 3. Path coefficients for the prediction of internalising and externalising problems by cyberbullying, cybervictimisation and an interaction term for girls.

	Estimate	Standardised estimate	Standard error	p
Depressiveness t2				
Depressiveness t1	0.561	0.571	0.094	< 0.001***
Loneliness t1	0.104	0.104	0.090	0.25
Cybervictimisation t1	0.388	0.147	0.162	< 0.05*
Interaction t1	−1.373	−0.059	1.888	0.47
Cyberbullying t1	0.039	0.033	0.030	0.19
$N = 109, R^2 = 0.46$				
Loneliness t2				
Loneliness t1	0.512	0.474	0.097	< 0.001***
Depressiveness t1	0.242	0.228	0.099	< 0.05*
Cybervictimisation t1	0.045	0.016	0.189	0.81
Interaction t1	−0.645	−0.026	1.782	0.72
Cyberbullying t1	0.024	0.019	0.755	0.45
$N = 109, R^2 = 0.40$				
Instrumental aggression t2				
Instrumental aggression t1	0.423	0.275	0.323	0.19
Reactive aggression t1	0.252	0.188	0.125	< 0.05*
Cybervictimisation t1	0.964	0.249	0.425	< 0.05*
Interaction t1	−7.272	−0.215	3.767	0.05
Cyberbullying t1	0.799	0.461	0.548	0.14
$N = 109, R^2 = 0.66$				
Reactive aggression t2				
Reactive aggression t1	0.757	0.446	0.131	< 0.001***
Instrumental aggression t1	0.110	0.056	0.161	0.493
Cybervictimisation t1	0.932	0.190	0.379	< 0.05*
Interaction t1	−7.986	−0.186	3.437	< 0.05*
Cyberbullying t1	1.217	0.552	0.581	< 0.05*
$N = 109, R^2 = 0.82$				

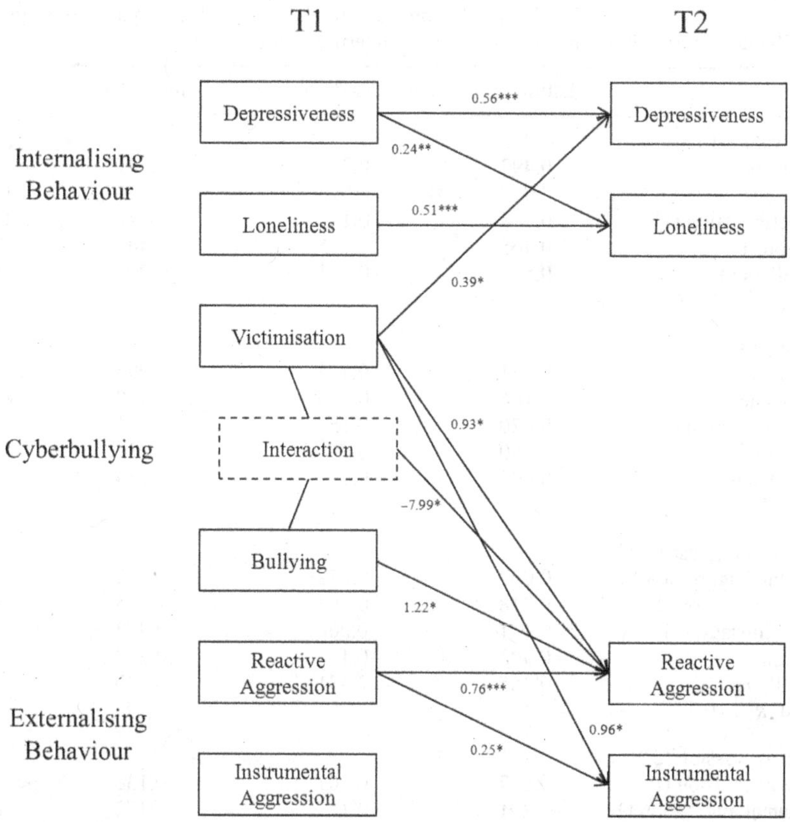

Figure 1. The final model displaying significant paths and path coefficients for predicting direct outcomes of cyberbullying for girls.

Summarising, for girls, cybervictimisation predicted increases in internalising as well as externalising problems. Simultaneous cybervictimisation and cyberbullying predicted decreases in parts of externalising behaviour while pure cyberbullying predicted increases in parts of externalising problems. Figure 1 gives an overview of the significant regression paths.

For boys, pure cybervictimisation did not predict any of the emotional or behavioural difficulties (Table 4). Cyberbullying significantly predicted decreases in both depressiveness and loneliness. However, cyberbullying did not predict any changes over time in externalising behaviour, and neither did cybervictimisation, but the interaction term indicated that boys felt lonelier at t2 if they showed high levels of both cyberbullying and cybervictimisation at t1.

The model for boys explains 18% of the variance in depressiveness and 36% of variance in loneliness at t2. The autoregression of reactive aggression accounts for 34% of explained variance, while 22% of the variance of instrumental aggression at t2 was explained by a marginally significant path between reactive aggression at t1 and instrumental aggression at t2 and a number of non-significant predictors (Table 4). As for girls, the level of instrumental aggression at t1 is not predictive of instrumental aggression three months later. When comparing the proportions of explained variance, the model evidently has more explanatory power for girls than for boys.

Table 4. Path coefficients for the prediction of internalising and externalising problems by cyberbullying, cybervictimisation and an interaction term for boys.

	Estimate	Standardised estimate	Standard error	p
Depressiveness t2				
Depressiveness t1	0.493	0.361	0.147	$< 0.01^{**}$
Loneliness t1	−0.020	−0.015	0.136	0.89
Cybervictimisation t1	0.758	0.160	0.742	0.31
Interaction t1	0.465	0.115	0.461	0.31
Cyberbullying t1	−0.559	−0.241	0.208	$< 0.01^{**}$
$N = 114$, $R^2 = 0.18$				
Loneliness t2				
Loneliness t1	0.461	0.413	0.093	$< 0.001^{***}$
Depressiveness t1	0.166	0.146	0.100	0.10
Cybervictimisation t1	0.620	0.157	0.501	0.22
Interaction t1	0.880	0.261	0.334	$< 0.01^{**}$
Cyberbullying t1	−0.493	−0.255	0.164	$< 0.01^{**}$
$N = 114$, $\mathrm{R}^2 = 0.36$				
Instrumental aggression t2				
Instrumental aggression t1	0.067	0.052	0.192	0.73
Reactive aggression t1	0.318	0.294	0.163	0.05
Cybervictimisation t1	0.031	0.006	0.422	0.94
Interaction t1	−0.903	−0.198	0.809	0.26
Cyberbullying t1	0.865	0.331	0.570	0.13
$N = 114$, $R^2 = 0.22$				
Reactive aggression t2				
Reactive aggression t1	0.697	0.607	0.133	$< 0.001^{***}$
Instrumental aggression t1	−0.201	−0.147	0.172	0.24
Cybervictimisation t1	−0.107	−0.019	0.443	0.81
Interaction t1	−0.990	−0.205	0.692	0.15
Cyberbullying t1	0.758	0.274	0.495	0.13
$N = 114$, $R^2 = 0.34$				

Summarising, for boys, decreases in internalising problems were predicted by the involvement in cyberbullying, while increases in parts of internalising behaviour were predicted by simultaneous cybervictimisation and cyberbullying. Externalising behaviour was not predicted by any of the cyberbullying variables and pure cybervictimisation did not predict any internalising or externalising problems. Figure 2 illustrates the significant regression paths.

Discussion

The aim of this study was to explore differences among groups involved in cyberbullying, and the longitudinal impact of cyberbullying and cybervictimisation on internalising and externalising problems, analysed using a longitudinal path analysis. Cross-sectionally, we found significant differences in externalising behaviour between the groups. No significant differences in internalising behaviour were found. Unfortunately, gender differences could not be considered in this first analysis.

Investigating longitudinal links from cyberbullying to internalising and externalising behaviour, the path analysis revealed different patterns for girls and boys. For girls,

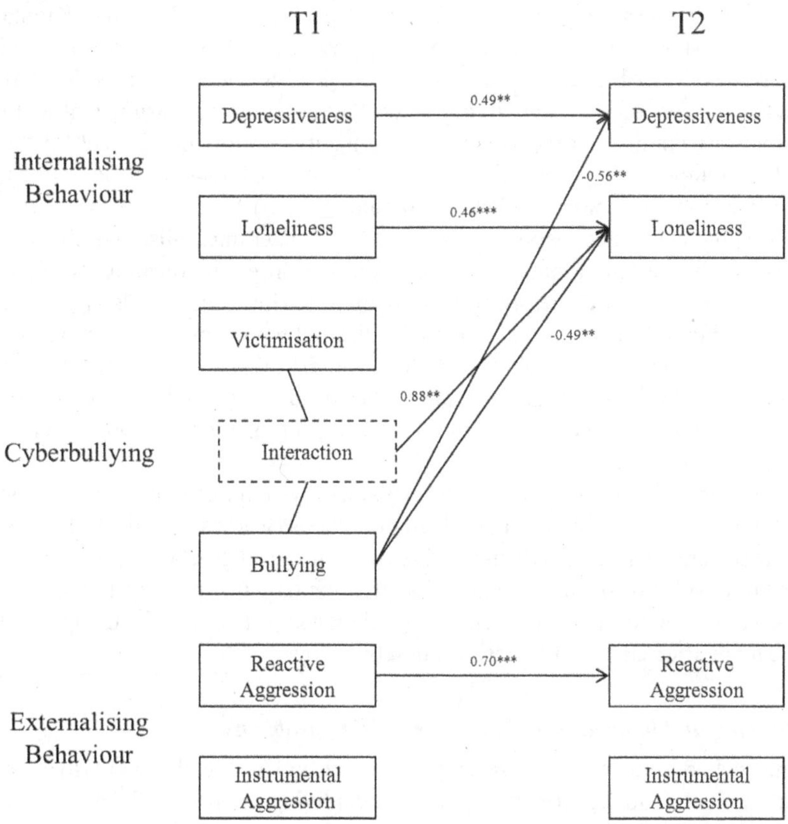

Figure 2. The final model displaying significant paths and path coefficients for predicting direct outcomes of cyberbullying for boys.

increases in externalising behaviour and in parts of internalising behaviour were predicted by cybervictimisation. Higher scores on the cyberbullying perpetration scale predicted more reactive aggression. Higher levels of cybervictimisation combined with higher scores of cyberbullying perpetration at the same time led to a reduction in reactive aggression. Victimised boys did not show any increases in internalising or externalising problems. However, at higher levels of cyberbullying perpetration victimised boys showed increases in loneliness. In contrast, boys with higher cyberbullying scores showed decreases in internalising behaviour.

Cybervictimisation and internalising and externalising problems

We found a significant difference between non-involved students and cybervictims regarding instrumental aggression, with cybervictims reporting higher levels. They did not differ significantly from cyberbullies or cyberbully–victims. Instrumental aggression as understood in the present study describes aggressive behaviours used to achieve self-serving goals (Little et al. 2003). This difference cannot be explained by the overlap between cyberbullying and cybervictimisation as a bully–victim group was explicitly included in the analysis. However, in previous research, cybervictimisation has also been linked to externalising problems. Previous research results suggest that victims who show anger as a result of their victimisation (e.g. Carter 2011; Ortega et al. 2009; Techniker Krankenkasse 2011) will also show higher levels of reactive aggression. Indeed, for girls the longitudinal analysis revealed that higher victimisation scores lead to increases in both instrumental and reactive aggression. Possibly, in our study the measures of instrumental and reactive aggression were not distinct from each other or the items were too abstract for the participants. They might have conceived reactive aggressive behaviours to be instrumental (e.g. using aggression to get someone to stop harassing oneself).

We had predicted that cybervictims would show greater internalising problems. In fact, cross-sectionally, we found that cybervictims did not differ significantly from any of the other groups in regard to depressiveness or loneliness. However, in girls higher victimisation scores led to increased depressiveness. Victimised boys showed no increased in either internalising or externalising problems. At least for girls, this result is in line with previous findings which show that girls are generally more strongly affected by cybervictimisation, including feelings of anger as well as internalising problems (e.g. Dooley et al. 2010; Ortega et al. 2009).

This greater effect on girls might be explained by findings that relational victimisation contributes considerably to internalising problems, whereas physical victimisation is strongly associated with externalising problems (Prinstein et al. 2001). Cybervictimisation can also be considered a form of relational aggression targeting peer relationships. As girls are more vulnerable to threats to their social relationships (Rose and Rudolph 2006) they might be more affected by cybervictimisation than boys.

Cyberbullying and internalising and externalising problems

We found cyberbullies to be more instrumentally and reactively aggressive than non-involved students and cybervictims. As cyberbullying is also a form of aggression, this cross-sectional finding may indicate a general antisocial behaviour pattern. Katzer, Fetchenhauer, and Belschak (2009a) found cyberbullies to show other forms of antisocial behaviour such as delinquency, school truancy and negative chatroom behaviour. The co-occurrence of cyberbullying and reactive aggression may indicate that cyberbullying can be an act of retaliation, as postulated by Ybarra and Mitchell (2004a).

In girls, higher scores of cyberbullying perpetration led to increases in reactive aggression. Female cyberbullies might have learned to defend themselves by reacting aggressively to relational threats. A lack of consequences or perhaps even positive feedback (e.g. through 'likes' on an offensive post) in the online environment may reinforce their use of reactive aggressive behaviour. Boys showing higher cyberbullying scores reported decreases in depressiveness and loneliness. 'Acting out' online may subjectively make boys feel better, for example by feeling more powerful. Future analyses should also include measures of social status or popularity, as being a cyberbully may make boys more popular among peers and therefore may make them feel less lonely. Findings from previous research that cyberbullies, too, showed increased internalising problems (Sontag et al. 2011; Ybarra and Mitchell 2004b) were only replicated in part for girls and even revealed contrary directions for boys. Also contrary to previous research findings, male cyberbullies did not show any associations with changes in externalising problems.

Simultaneous cybervictimisation and cyberbullying and the associations with internalising and externalising problems

This study is one of few to explicitly take into account the interaction between cybervictimisation and cyberbullying. This seems justified as the analyses revealed differentiated effects. Cyberbully–victims showed more externalising problems on a cross-sectional basis. However, these did not exceed those of pure cyberbullies, in contrast to findings by Gradinger, Strohmeier, and Spiel (2009). There were also differentiated results for male and female cyberbully–victims. Girls who scored high on both cybervictimisation and cyberbullying reported decreases in reactive aggression over time, while both pure cyberbullies and pure cybervictims showed increases in internalising and externalising problems. Possibly, 'acting out' may improve the situation for girls over time and resolve problems when 'fighting back' by perpetrating cyberbullying themselves. Another possible explanation is that by being cybervictimised themselves and possibly taking the perspective of other victims, female cyberbullies may reduce their aggressive behaviour. This needs to be investigated in future analyses, including mediator variables such as empathy and perspective-taking, and by including more measurement occasions to analyse the chronology of being a cyberbully–victim (e.g. are cyberbully–victims victimised first and then become perpetrators themselves, or the other way around?). The transition from being involved in cyberbullying to becoming uninvolved should also be examined.

In boys, scoring high on cyberbullying perpetration and victimisation at the same time led to increases in depressiveness. This is the only detrimental outcome for boys in the present model as the only other significant paths show 'improvements' for male cyberbullies. Possibly, male cyberbully–victims are especially affected by their status through feeling shame and guilt. Schoffstall and Cohen (2011) found cyberbullies to be less popular. In addition to being less popular when being a victim, this may increase the impact of being a cyberbully–victim.

Conclusions

In the present study we could not find confirmation of our expectation of clear internalising patterns for cybervictims and externalising patterns for cyberbullies, or internalising patterns for girls and externalising patterns for boys. Rather, female victims also showed externalising behaviour. This may seem surprising. However, previous studies have shown the same pattern, albeit separate from each other and not within one analysis. Dempsey et al. (2009) and Carter (2011) could not replicate the results of victims showing more depression. We also found that boys involved in cyberbullying did not show any longitudinal links to externalising problems. Moreover, there were no significant differences for the involvement groups on a cross-sectional basis for internalising problems.

As loneliness is predicted by depressiveness, which in turn is predicted by cybervictimisation in girls, depressiveness may be a mediator of the association between loneliness and cybervictimisation. To investigate this, more longitudinal research with greater intervals and across a longer timespan is needed. Reactive aggression being predicted by cybervictimisation, cyberbullying and the interaction term may indicate a vicious circle of victimisation and retaliation. Further and more complex studies should be conducted to analyse potential moderator and/or mediator effects on the outcomes of cyberbullying and cybervictimisation.

Furthermore, if boys do not cyberbully anonymously, but are known in their social environment to be cyberbullies, peers may avoid them, leading to feelings of loneliness and isolation.

In the present analyses, girls were clearly more affected by cyberbullying involvement. This might be ascribed to the importance of social relationships for adolescent girls.

On the other hand, boys might have experienced less severe incidents or perceived them as less severe. As during adolescence, cyberbullying incidents increasingly gain a sexual connotation (Spears et al. 2009), this may also be harder for girls to cope with or may make girls easier or more frequent targets. For boys, the amount of explained variance shows that internalising and externalising problems are not sufficiently explained by cyberbullying involvement. At the same time, cyberbullying involvement may have consequences other than those included in this study and which were not covered by the variables of the present study.

Limitations

Limitations of the present study are the exclusive reliance on self-reports and the limited number of variables operationalising internalising and externalising behaviour. The proportion of explained variances in some analyses indicates the need to include further variables to reach a satisfactory result. In addition, some repeatedly documented results from previous research could not be replicated, which may be due to methodological issues such as a lack of power of the measures used, a suboptimal selection of instruments, or the use of different cut-off scores or continuous variables. Further reasons might be the use of prospective longitudinal analyses or specific cultural effects. The high attrition rate and the lack of representation of the longitudinal subsample versus the total sample and also the large sample reduction might have distorted the results. The sample was selective and the participating schools might have had larger or smaller problems with cyberbullying compared to the general school population.

Furthermore, moderator and mediator effects should be analysed. For example, as seen in one of the findings, the impact of cyberbullying involvement on one of the internalising variables may be influenced by the presence or level of the other.

Implications

We focused on internalising (emotional) and externalising (behavioural) problems as we were especially interested in investigating the detrimental effects of cyberbullying to underscore the importance of prevention and intervention efforts. Future studies should also include students' resources in dealing with cyberbullying such as social support and coping strategies. The opposite direction of effects should also be examined to determine whether adolescents already showing internalising or externalising problems are more likely to be involved in cyberbullying. This kind of result may also be an indication for vicious cycles (e.g. depressed girls being cybervictims more often, which further increases their depressiveness).

However, the present study is one of the first to use longitudinal data and the results present a starting point for future research and provide information for prevention and intervention efforts.

Acknowledgements

This research was funded by the DAPHNE III programme to combat violence against children, young persons and women of the European Commission (Action Number: JLS/2008/DAP3/AG/1211-30-CE-0311025/00-69; Cyberbullying in Adolescence: Investigation and Intervention in Six European Countries). This work was also supported by the International Max Planck Research School 'The Life Course: Evolutionary and Ontogenetic Dynamics (LIFE)' (www.imprs-life.mpg.de).

References

Brighi, A., R. Ortega, J. Pyzalski, H. Scheithauer, P.K. Smith, H. Tsormpatzoudis, V. Barkoukis, et al. 2012. *European Cyberbullying Intervention Project Questionnaire – ECIPQ*.

Carter, J.M. 2011. Examining the relationship among physical and psychological health, parent and peer attachment, and cyberbullying in adolescents in urban and suburban environments. PhD dissertation, Wayne State University.

Crick, N.R., and C. Zahn-Waxler. 2003. The development of psychopathology in females and males: Current progress and future challenges. *Development and Psychopathology* 15: 719–42.

Dempsey, A.G., M.L. Sulkowski, R. Nichols, and E.A. Storch. 2009. Differences between peer victimization in cyber and physical settings and associated psychosocial adjustment in early adolescence. *Psychology in the Schools* 46: 962–72.

Dooley, J., P. Gradinger, D. Strohmeier, D. Cross, and C. Spiel. 2010. Cyber-victimisation: The association between help-seeking behaviours and self-reported emotional symptoms in Australia and Austria. *Australian Journal of Guidance and Counselling* 20: 194–209.

Erdur Baker, Ö., and I. Tanrikulu. 2010. Psychological consequences of cyber bullying experiences among Turkish secondary school children. *Procedia – Social and Behavioral Sciences* 2: 2771–6.

Finkelhor, D., K.J. Mitchell, and J. Wolak. 2000. Online victimization: A report on the nation's youth. Alexandria, VA: National Center for Missing & Exploited Children.

Finney, S.J., and C. DiStefano. 2006. Non-normal and categorical data in structural equation modeling. In *Structural equation modeling: A second course*, ed. G. Hancock and R.O. Mueller. Greenwich: Information Age Publishing.

Gradinger, P., D. Strohmeier, and C. Spiel. 2009. Traditional bullying and cyberbullying – Identification of risk groups for adjustment problems. *Zeitschrift für Psychologie/Journal of Psychology* 217: 205–13.

Hays, R.D., and M.R. DiMatteo. 1987. A short-form measure of loneliness. *Journal of Personality Assessment* 51: 69–81.

Jäger, T., R. Arbinger, and U. Lissmann. 2010. Cyberbullying: The situation in Germany. In *Cyberbullying: A cross-national comparison*, ed. J.A. Mora-Merchán and T. Jäger, 69–86. Landau: Verlag Empirische Pädagogik.

Katzer, C., D. Fetchenhauer, and F. Belschak. 2009a. Cyberbullying in Internet-Chatrooms – Wer sind die Täter? *Zeitschrift für Entwicklungspsychologie und Pädagogische Psychologie* 41: 33–44.

Katzer, C., D. Fetchenhauer, and F. Belschak. 2009b. Cyberbullying: Who are the victims? A comparison of victimization in internet chatrooms and victimization in school. *Journal of Media Psychology: Theories, Methods, and Applications* 21: 25–36.

Lischka, K., C. Stöcker, and H. Ternieden. 2011. Mobbing-Plattform isharegossip – Pöbeln als Gesellschaftsmodell. Spiegel Online, http://www.spiegel.de/netzwelt/web/0,1518,752748,00.html (accessed January 3, 2012).

Little, T.D., S.M. Jones, C.C. Henrich, and P.H. Hawley. 2003. Disentangling the 'Whys' from the 'Whats' of aggressive behaviour. *International Journal of Behavioral Development* 27: 122–33.

Menesini, E., A. Nocentini, B.E. Palladino, A. Frisen, S. Berne, R. Ortega, J. Calmaestra, et al. in press. Cyberbullying definition among adolescents: A comparison across six European countries. *Cyberpsychology, Behavior, and Social Networking*.

Muthén, L.K., and B.O. Muthén. 1998–2010. *Mplus user's guide*. 6th edition. Los Angeles, CA: Muthén & Muthén.

Nocentini, A., J. Calmaestra, A. Schultze-Krumbholz, H. Scheithauer, R. Ortega, and E. Menesini. 2010. Cyberbullying: Labels, behaviours and definition in three European countries. *Australian Journal of Guidance and Counselling* 20: 129–42.

Ortega, R., P. Elipe, J.A. Mora-Merchán, J. Calmaestra, and E. Vega. 2009. The emotional impact on victims of traditional bullying and cyberbullying – A study of Spanish adolescents. *Zeitschrift für Psychologie/Journal of Psychology* 217: 197–204.

Perren, S., J. Dooley, T. Shaw, and D. Cross. 2010. Bullying in school and cyberspace: Associations with depressive symptoms in Swiss and Australian adolescents. *Child and Adolescent Psychiatry and Mental Health* 4, no. 28.

Prinstein, M.J., J. Boergers, and E.M. Vernberg. 2001. Overt and relational aggression in adolescents: Social–psychological adjustment of aggressors and victims. *Journal of Clinical Child Psychology* 30: 479–91.

Raskauskas, J., and A.D. Stoltz. 2007. Involvement in traditional and electronic bullying among adolescents. *Developmental Psychology* 43: 564–75.

Rose, A.R., and K.D. Rudolph. 2006. A review of sex differences in peer relationship processes: Potential trade-offs for the emotional and behavioral development of girls and boys. *Psychological Bulletin* 132: 98–131.

Schoffstall, C.L., and R. Cohen. 2011. Cyber aggression: The relation between online offenders and offline social competence. *Social Development* 20: 587–604.

Schultze-Krumbholz, A., and H. Scheithauer. 2009a. Cyberbullying unter Schülern – Erste Ergebnisse einer Studie an Berliner und Bremer Schulen. In *IX Workshop on aggression*, November 6–8, Berlin.

Schultze-Krumbholz, A., and H. Scheithauer. 2009b. Social–behavioural correlates of cyberbullying in a German student sample. *Zeitschrift für Psychologie/Journal of Psychology* 217: 224–6.

Schultze-Krumbholz, A., and H. Scheithauer. 2010. Cyberbullying unter Kindern und Jugendlichen – ein Forschungsüberblick. *Psychosozial* 122: 79–91.

Schultze-Krumbholz, A., P. Zagorscak, A. Siebenbrock, and H. Scheithauer. 2012. *Medienhelden – Unterrichtsmanual zur Förderung von Medienkompetenz und Prävention von Cybermobbing.* München: Reinhardt Verlag.

Schwarzer, R., and J. Bäßler. 1999. Depressivität (depres). In *Skalen zur Erfassung von Lehrer- und Schülermerkmalen: Dokumentation der psychometrischen Verfahren im Rahmen der wissenschaftlichen Begleitung des Modellversuchs Selbstwirksame Schulen*, ed. R. Schwarzer and M. Jerusalem, 42–9. Berlin: Freie Universität Berlin.

Smith, P.K., J. Mahdavi, M. Carvalho, S. Fisher, S. Russell, and N. Tippett. 2008. Cyberbullying: Its nature and impact in secondary school pupils. *Journal of Child Psychology and Psychiatry* 49: 376–85.

Snijders, T.A.B., and R.J. Bosker. 1999. *Multilevel analysis – An introduction to basic and advanced multilevel modeling*. London: Sage.

Sontag, L.M., K.H. Clemans, J.A. Graber, and S.T. Lyndon. 2011. Traditional and cyber aggressors and victims: A comparison of psychosocial characteristics. *Journal of Youth and Adolescence* 40: 392–404.

Sourander, A., A. Brunstein Klomek, M. Ikonen, J. Lindroos, T. Luntamo, M. Koskelainen, T. Ristkari, and H. Helenius. 2010. Psychosocial risk factors associated with cyberbullying among adolescents – A population-based study. *Archives of General Psychiatry* 67: 720–28.

Spears, B., P. Slee, L. Owens, and B. Johnson. 2009. Behind the scenes and screens – Insights into the human dimension of covert and cyberbullying. *Zeitschrift für Psychologie/Journal of Psychology* 217: 189–96.

SPSS. 2011. *IBM SPSS statistics for Windows*, release 20.0.0. Chicago, IL: SPSS.

Techniker Krankenkasse (Landesvertretung NRW). 2011. *TK Meinungspuls Gesundheit 2011 – Erhebung 'Cyberbullying'*. http://www.tk.de/tk/kinder-jugendliche-undfamilie/gewalt-gegen-kinder/cybermobbing/343730 (accessed April 6, 2012).

Tokunaga, R.S. 2010. Following you home from school: A critical review and synthesis of research on cyberbullying victimization. *Computers in Human Behavior* 26: 277–87.

Williams, K.R., and N.G. Guerra. 2007. Prevalence and predictors of internet bullying. *Journal of Adolescent Health* 41: S14–21.

Ybarra, M.L., and K.J. Mitchell. 2004a. Online aggressor/targets, aggressors, and targets: A comparison of associated youth characteristics. *Journal of Child Psychology and Psychiatry* 45: 1308–16.

Ybarra, M.L., and K.J. Mitchell. 2004b. Youth engaging in online harassment: Associations with caregiver–child relationships, internet use, and personal characteristics. *Journal of Adolescence* 27: 319–36.

Moral disengagement and emotional and social difficulties in bullying and cyberbullying: differences by participant role

Sebastian Wachs

Department of Educational Studies, University of Bremen, Bremen, Germany

Participant roles in traditional bullying have been well researched, and the social and emotional characteristics identified with each role are clearly documented. However, little is known about the participant roles in cyberbullying and the degree to which these correspond to traditional bullying roles. This study aims to investigate similarities and differences between participant roles in traditional bullying and cyberbullying, in terms of moral disengagement and social and emotional characteristics. In total, 517 German students in grades 5–10 were assessed for bullying involvement using the Computer Assisted Personal Interview (CAPI) method. Cyberbullying was slightly less frequent than traditional bullying, although there was considerable overlap, with many students involved in cyberbullying also participating in traditional bullying. More cyberbullies had a bad conscience compared to traditional bullies, hence students involved in cyberbullying showed greater moral disengagement. High school satisfaction emerged as a protective factor for nearly all roles, while feeling lonely, feeling unpopular and being friendless appeared as risk factors for (cyber)victimisation. The enhancement of empathy by (cyber)bullies and (cyber)assistants for their targets, and the development of a positive school culture, are proposed as key aspects for both anti-bullying and anti-cyberbullying prevention and intervention.

Introduction

According to Olweus (1999), bullying can be defined through four behavioural characteristics: attacks must be carried out repeatedly and over a period of time; the offender must intend to deliberately hurt the victim; the victim must feel helplessly exposed to the offender; and finally, there is an imbalance of power between the offender(s) and the victim. Cyberbullying is a recently identified form of bullying that includes the use of information and communication technologies (ICTs) (Smith et al. 2008).

Within Germany, research shows the prevalence of cyberbullying to be slightly less than traditional forms of bullying. Among over 2000 5th to 10th grade students, 12.1% reported being traditional bullies and 11.1% traditional victims (Scheithauer et al. 2006). Using a similar sample size (N = 1997, aged 6–18), Jäger, Fischer, and Riebel (2007) found that 5.5% of participants reported being cybervictims and 3.9% cyberbullies. Repeating this study two years later yielded almost identical results (Jäger, Fischer, and Riebel 2009).

A representative telephone study of 14–20-year-olds living throughout Germany showed a slightly higher prevalence rate, with 8% of adolescents identified as cybervictims and 6% as cyberbullies (Techniker Krankenkasse 2011). There were notable regional differences among the sample, with adolescents in northern Germany showing the greatest involvement in cyberbullying as both bullies and victims.

More recently, Wachs and Wolf (2011) compared traditional and cyber forms of bullying among a class-based sample of adolescents ($N = 837$, aged 11–17) in northern Germany. Imposing a strict criterion for bullying (of once a week or more often), they found that 8.3% of students were traditional victims and 2.9% cybervictims; also, 10.7% were traditional bullies and 4.7% cyberbullies. However, these studies all use differing samples and criteria for bullying involvement, so direct comparisons cannot be made. In a review, Tokunaga (2010) argued that adolescents at the age of 13–15 years were most involved in cyberbullying. The role that gender plays in cyberbullying varied considerably between studies.

Understanding how cyberbullying relates to traditional bullying, and the similarities and differences between these two types of aggressive behaviours, is an important consideration of contemporary research. Previous research shows a strong association between traditional and cyberbullying: the majority of adolescents who cyberbully others also engage in traditional methods of bullying, and similarly, victims of cyberbullying are often victims of other forms of bullying (Riebel 2008; Ortega et al. 2009; Wachs and Wolf 2011).

Involvement in traditional bullying, as either bully, victim or bully–victim, can have severe consequences on psychological well-being and health (Olweus 1999). In addition, a range of risk factors has been identified for involvement in traditional bullying, including parenting style, home environment and psychosocial characteristics, such as social and behavioural difficulties (Marini, Dane, and Bosacki 2006).

Although bullying is often considered in terms of the dyadic relationship between the bully and the victim, there is a variety of roles involved, ranging from assistants and reinforcers who provide support to the bully, to defenders who often try to help the victim, and outsiders, who take no direct action, but through this may passively provide support for the bullying (Salmivalli et al. 1996). As with traditional bullying, primary roles in cyberbullying (cyberbully, cybervictim, cyberbully–cybervictim) have been identified and continue to be investigated, but more recently the role of cyberbystanders has attracted research attention (Slonje, Smith, and Frisén 2012).

The emotional and social characteristics of adolescents differ greatly between these roles, and in understanding the relationship between cyberbullying and bullying it is important to identify whether differing roles are also present in cyberbullying, and whether they share the same social and emotional characteristics found in traditional bullying.

Associations with emotional and/or social difficulties

Previous research has shown how bullying can have a negative impact on the psychosocial well-being of the victim, which leads to emotional difficulties, and more recently, research has found similar effects among victims of cyberbullying. In the short term, the majority of victims of both bullying and cyberbullying show a variety of negative feelings (stress, embarrassment, anxiousness) (Ortega et al. 2009), display depressive symptoms (Perren et al. 2010), and have lower life satisfaction and greater feelings of loneliness (Kroon 2011) as well as a higher risk of suicide and suicidal ideation (Hinduja and Patchin 2010). If victims of (cyber)bullying are unable to cope with these persistent traumatic experiences, this can manifest in post-traumatic stress disorder, and the effects on the mental health of victims can become extremely destructive (Aluede et al. 2008). Traditional victims can also deal with victimisation by showing aggressive behaviour against peers

(Hodges et al. 1999), i.e. as bully–victims, while both defenders and bystanders tend to be less aggressive and are more able to cope with peer problems by themselves (Camodeca and Goossens 2005). Olweus (1999) recognises that there are also harmful consequences for the bullies (e.g. drug abuse, high perceived feelings of loneliness, mental diseases, suicidal ideation). But research also suggests that some bullies possess certain social skills that help them to manipulate others in order to achieve their personal goals (Sutton, Smith, and Swettenham 1999). Finally, simply observing bullying in school as a bystander seems to predict risk for mental health problems (Rivers et al. 2009).

School satisfaction is a critical aspect of quality of life in young people. The level of school satisfaction is important because it affects psychological well-being, school engagement, absenteeism and dropout rates (Ainley 1991). Spriggs et al. (2007) found that school satisfaction is negatively associated with involvement in bullying. Rigby (1996, 1999) posited that low school satisfaction could have negative effects for bullies, victims and bully–victims on educational development owing to higher than normal absentee and dropout rates.

Aside from emotional difficulties, research has found that victims of traditional bullying exhibit significant social difficulties, such as social withdrawal and peer rejection (Hodges, Malone, and Perry 1997), which damages their ability to form friendships (Ladd and Troop-Gordon 2003; Rigby 1996). The ability to establish and maintain good relationships with peers and friendships is critical for healthy development (Salmivalli and Isaacs 2005; Ladd and Troop-Gordon 2003), and acts as a key protective factor against victimisation. Among adolescents, peers take on increasing importance because interaction with peers aids in developing social understanding, and helps to build social, emotional and communicative competence and moral attitudes (Rohlfs, Harring, and Palentien 2008). However, victimised adolescents are more likely to be rejected by peers (Nansel et al. 2004; Hodges, Malone, and Perry 1997) and often lack friendships (Ladd and Troop-Gordon 2003; Rigby 1996). The chronic friendlessness associated with victimisation can have a negative impact on both social self-concept and generalised peer beliefs (Ladd and Troop-Gordon 2003), while adolescents whose friendships have a positive quality display higher levels of prosocial behaviour (Ladd, Kochenderfer, and Coleman 1996). Friends can help to break up this victimisation schema or even protect against it. But friends only seem to be an effective buffer against victimisation if they exhibit certain qualities, such as being able and willing to defend the other in critical situations, having a warm, trust-based relationship built on reciprocity, and the general popularity of the friend (Salmivalli and Isaacs 2005).

Research suggests that in particular bully–victims have fewer friends and become more rejected compared to traditional bullies, their assistants or victims (Wolke and Stanford 1999). In addition, bully–victims seem to provoke negative peer interactions which may lead to further peer problems (Nansel et al. 2004; Andreou 2001). Students who act as defenders seem to be the most popular group with participant roles with good peer relationships (Salmivalli and Isaacs 2005).

Moral disengagement

An additional characteristic that is especially pertinent for bullies and assistants is moral disengagement. Bandura (1999) argued that humans sometimes disengage from their moral responsibilities. Moral disengagement is the socio-cognitive process through which humans are able to harm others without having a bad conscience. Research shows a clear relationship between moral disengagement and bullying, providing a theoretical framework through which bullying can be better understood (Hymel et al. 2005, 2010). Bullies show, or are associated with, a higher level of moral disengagement compared to victims and outsiders (Menesini et al. 2003), while the role of defender is associated with lower levels of moral disengagement (Almeida, Correia, and Marinho 2010).

In terms of cyberbullying, cyberbullies exhibit less of a bad conscience, hence greater moral disengagement than traditional bullies (Slonje, Smith, and Frisén 2012). The lack of face-to-face contact in most ICTs not only promotes playful teasing but also reduces social responsibility, thus making it easier for users to engage in cyberaggression without feeling guilt or remorse (Willard 2006). One explanation for this may be that when communicating online, individuals feel that they are part of an anonymous mass and therefore do not sense that they have to take responsibility for their actions (Döring 2003). The lack of face-to-face contact can also reduce the likelihood of having a bad conscience following the act since the perpetrator is not directly confronted with the harm that he or she causes (Hymel et al. 2010). In addition, perpetrators of aggressive acts mediated by ICTs may not feel that their actions are particularly harmful because these are not perceived as 'real'.

Overall, it can be assumed that emotional and social difficulties are intertwined. Victims and bully–victims have difficulties in social situations and establishing friendships, which may then cause the negative emotional consequences they experience. Bullies and their assistants, on the other hand, exhibit a higher social status among peers, but lack emotion that allows them to harm and manipulate others without having a bad conscience; hence, they show higher moral disengagement. In contrast, defenders exhibit a higher level of popularity as bullies, and show much higher levels of emotion and empathy which may encourage them to prevent harmful behaviours.

Emotional and social difficulties with regard to traditional bullying have been well researched, but the same is not true in the case of cyberbullying. Whether moral disengagement is the same for bullies and cyberbullies, and whether the social and emotional characteristics of victims, defenders, etc., are the same in traditional and cyberbullying needs further consideration.

Aims of the study

Building on the findings of previous research, this study aimed to investigate the similarities and differences between traditional bullying and cyberbullying. It focuses on participant roles (as bully, victim, bully–victim, defender and bystander) across bullying and cyberbullying, with particular attention paid to how these roles differ between types of bullying in relation to moral disengagement, and social and emotional characteristics.

Method

Participants

A total of 518 students from four secondary schools in northern Germany was recruited as a convenience sample. This region had a high proportion of immigrant families and a relatively poor urban economic situation. The gender distribution was 254 males (49.0%) and 263 females (50.8%) (one respondent did not record their gender). Students were from grades 5 to 10 (approximately 11–17 years of age): 14 students (2.7%) in 5th grade, 120 (23.4%) in 6th grade, 162 (31.3%) in 7th grade, 100 (19.3%) in 8th grade, 78 (15.1%) in 9th grade and 43 (8.3%) in 10th grade.

Measures

The Mobbing Questionnaire for Students by Jäger, Fischer, and Riebel (2007) was used to measure bullying involvement. This starts with a definition of traditional bullying which includes the four central characteristics mentioned by Olweus (1999). Cyberbullying was explained in the same way but concerning the use of ICTs.

Roles in bullying

Using a reference period of within the last 12 months, traditional and cybervictimisation were first assessed by asking two questions: 'How often have you been bullied?' and 'How often have you been cyberbullied?' Corresponding questions were asked to assess bullying others: 'How often have you bullied others/How often have you cyberbullied others?'; being an assistant: 'How often have you helped to bully others?/How often have you helped to cyberbully others?'; being a defender: 'How often did you defend someone who was being bullied by others?/How often did you defend someone who was being cyberbullied by others?'; and being a bystander: 'How often did you observe someone being bullied without helping the victim or the bully?/How often did you observe someone being cyberbullied without helping the victim or the bully?' The role of bully–victim was obtained by cross-tabulating the variables of traditional bully/traditional victim and cyberbully/cybervictim.

Each question was responded to using a five-point ordinal scale, with options of never; once or twice; twice or three times; about once a week; or several times a week. A strict criterion was used to determine prevalence rates (Riebel 2008; Scheithauer, Hayer, and Petermann 2003), so only students who answered 'about once a week' or more often were classified as being involved in bullying. Using this strict criterion identifies adolescents who engage in bullying frequently, and thus would be expected to exhibit the typical social and emotional characteristics associated with each bullying role. Students who responded to any of the above questions by stating 'never', 'once or twice' or 'twice or three times' were classified as non-involved.

Emotional difficulties

Individual items were used to determine whether students felt popular, felt lonely, or were satisfied with their school. For popularity, students were asked: 'How popular do you feel?', with response options of 'Not popular at all', 'Mostly unpopular' (these two combined as not popular), 'A little popular' and 'Very popular' (these two combined as popular). For loneliness, students were asked: 'Do you feel lonely at school?', with response options 'Yes, always', 'Yes, often' (these two combined as high feelings of loneliness), 'Yes, occasionally', 'Yes, rarely' (these two combined as average feelings of loneliness), 'Almost never' and 'No, never' (these two combined as low feelings of loneliness). For school satisfaction, students were asked: 'How do you like school at present?', with response options of 'A lot' 'Quite a lot' (these two combined as high school satisfaction), 'Satisfactory' (coded as moderate school satisfaction), 'Not much' and 'Not at all' (these two combined as low school satisfaction).

Social difficulties

Social difficulties were measured by asking: 'How many friends do you have in school?', with response options 'I have 6 or more good friends in school', 'I have 4 or 5 good friends in school', 'I have 2 or 3 good friends in school', 'I have 1 good friend in school' and 'I have no friends in school'.

Moral disengagement

Moral disengagement was measured on the basis of whether students felt they had a bad conscience after engaging in bullying others, either traditionally or through cyberbullying. Only students who had reported that they were involved in traditional bullying or cyberbullying as a bully or assistant at least once or twice were asked: 'Did you have a bad conscience after bullying?' and 'Did you have a bad conscience after cyberbullying?', with response options of 'Yes I did', 'A little bit' (these two combined as having a bad conscience), 'Almost never' and 'Not at all' (these two combined as no bad conscience).

Procedure

A pilot study was carried out as a free online survey with 78 adolescents in order to determine the effectiveness, strengths and weaknesses of the survey concerning question format, wording and order. The main study was then conducted in the summer of 2011 in school computer rooms, during normal school time. For the main study the Computer Assisted Personal Interview (CAPI) method was applied. CAPI is a data collection method that takes place in person. The participants sit at a PC in school computer room and enter the answers while the interviewer is present. The data are collected by an online survey that transcribes the results into a file that can be exported to SPSS. The CAPI method proved to be particularly suitable because, through the participation of whole classes, the results are not subject to distortion due to self-selection. The possibility of asking questions if a respondent has problems understanding items can be seen as another advantage of the CAPI method compared to pure online surveys. The data protection officer of the federal state and the parents' association of the participating schools approved this procedure. As the students were under the age of 18, parents had to sign a written consent form entitling them to participate.

Students were told that participation in the study was optional, questions could be skipped and participation in the survey could be stopped at any time, without the need for giving a reason. Students were then told why this study was being conducted and how they could participate. The average time needed to complete the questionnaire was about 30 minutes.

Results

Participant roles in traditional bullying and cyberbullying

Table 1 shows the distribution of prevalence rates by participant roles, for traditional and cyberbullying. Using dichotomised variables (Yes/No) based on a strict criterion (once a week or more often), overall, 44 students (8.5%) could be identified as traditional bullies, while 51 (9.8%) were traditional victims; 26 (5.0%) of all students could be identified as bully–victims. In addition, 41 (7.9%) of participants were assistants and 44 (8.5%) traditional defenders. A substantial number of students, 143 (27.6%), were bystanders.

With respect to cyberbullying, overall, 32 (6.2%) could be identified as cyberbullies, 26 (5.0%) were cybervictims and 22 (4.2%) were both cyberbully and cybervictim. Furthermore, 22 (4.2%) were cyberassistants, 26 (5.0%) cyberdefenders and 58 (11.2%) were classed as cyberbystanders.

Table 1. Frequencies (% over past 12 months) of traditional and cyberbullying roles ($N = 518$).

Role	Never	Once or twice	Twice or three times	About once a week	Several times a week
Traditional bully	61.8	22.4	7.3	3.3	5.2
Cyberbully	80.1	9.8	3.9	3.3	2.9
Traditional victim	67.0	18.0	5.2	4.4	5.4
Cybervictim	78.0	12.5	4.4	2.5	2.5
Traditional assistant	65.6	20.1	6.4	4.8	3.1
Cyberassistant	85.9	7.7	2.1	2.1	2.1
Traditional defender	51.7	30.1	9.7	4.1	4.4
Cyberdefender	75.5	16.0	3.5	2.5	2.5
Traditional bystander	30.7	29.0	12.7	14.7	12.9
Cyberbystander	68.1	14.5	6.2	5.0	6.2

Overlaps among cyber and traditional roles

For the following contingency analyses, binary variables for roles in traditional and cyberbullying were used. A comparison between traditional roles and cyber roles showed that 59.4% of cyberbullies were also traditional bullies [$\chi^2(1, N = 518) = 113.6$, $p < 0.001$; $\varphi = 0.468$], 63.6% of cyberassistants were also traditional assistants [$\chi^2(1, N = 518) = 97.9, p < 0.001$; $\varphi = 0.435$], 66.2% of cybervictims were traditional victims [$\chi^2(1, N = 518) = 40.7, p < 0.001$; $\varphi = 0.280$], and 59.2% of cyberdefenders were traditional defenders [$\chi^2(1, N = 518) = 49.9, p < 0.001$; $\varphi = 0.311$]. In addition, 63.4% of all cyberbystanders were at the same time traditional bystanders [$\chi^2(1, N = 518) = 21.8$, $p < 0.001$; $\phi = 0.205$]. Furthermore, 59.1% of all cyberbully–victims turned out to be traditional bully–victims [$\chi^2(1, N = 518) = 62.1$, $p < 0.001$; $\varphi = 0.327$]. Finally, only 21.9% of all cyberbullies are traditional victims [$\chi^2(1, N = 518) = 5.5, p < 0.02$; $\varphi = 0.104$].

Associations between emotional and social difficulties, and roles

A simple binary logistic regression was applied for each role by using dichotomous dependent variables based on the strict criterion (e.g. victims vs. non-victims; assistants vs. non-assistants). Table 2 shows the results of the multivariate analyses between the dependent variables (traditional and cyber roles) and the predictor variables: number of friendships; feeling popular; feeling lonely and school satisfaction, grade and gender. Regression coefficients, Wald statistics, significance, odds ratio (OR > 1 = risk factor; OR < 1 = protective factor with 95% confidence interval) and identified significant associations are given in Table 2. Significant associations with emotional and social difficulties were found for every role except traditional and cyberdefenders.

Age and gender

Students in the 8th grade showed nearly 3 times higher odds of being a traditional victim and 4.5 higher risk of being cybervictims compared to all other grades. Compared to girls, boys were at approximately 3 times higher odds of being traditional assistants, 3 times higher risk of being traditional bullies and 3.5 higher risk of being cyberbullies.

Table 2. Significant results of logistic regression analysis.

	B	SE	Wald	Sig.	Odds ratio
Bully					
Gender (male)	1.046	0.353	8.770	0.003	2.84
School satisfaction (high)	−1.250	0.416	9.016	0.003	0.286
Cyberbully					
Gender (male)	1.264	0.423	8.935	0.003	3.54
School satisfaction (high)	−1.121	0.415	7.286	0.007	0.326
Assistant					
Gender (male)	1.009	0.373	7.320	0.007	2.74
School satisfaction (high)	−2.223	0.626	12.622	0.001	0.108
Cyberassistant					
School satisfaction (high)	−1.386	0.432	10.319	0.001	0.250
Victim					
Grade (8th)	1.081	0.509	4.515	0.034	2.94
Feeling unpopular	1.184	0.358	10.944	0.001	4.43
School satisfaction (high)	−2.219	0.516	18.521	0.001	0.109
Loneliness (high)	1.556	0.500	9.676	0.002	4.74
Friends in class (one)	2.171	0.634	11.722	0.001	8.76
Friends in class (zero)	3.110	0.770	16.314	0.001	22.41
Cybervictim					
Grade (8th)	1.471	0.698	4.446	0.035	4.35
School satisfaction (high)	−0.956	0.422	5.645	0.018	0.216
Feeling unpopular	1.489	0.641	5.396	0.020	3.26
Friends in class (zero)	2.392	0.701	11.638	0.001	10.93
Loneliness (high)	1.117	0.545	4.196	0.041	3.05
Bully–victim					
Feeling unpopular	1.480	0.680	4.752	0.029	4.394
School satisfaction (high)	−1.148	0.358	10.29	0.001	0.317
Cyberbully–cybervictim					
School satisfaction (high)	−1.198	0.478	6.278	0.012	0.314
Bystander					
Feeling unpopular	1.142	0.522	4.791	0.029	3.13
School satisfaction (high)	−0.687	0.279	6.067	0.014	0.503
Cyberbystander					
School satisfaction (high)	−1.083	0.422	5.627	0.01	0.339

Emotional difficulties

Students who reported that they often felt lonely at school had 4.5 times higher odds of being traditional victims and 3 times higher risk of being cybervictims than students who reported moderate or low feelings of loneliness. Students who perceived themselves as unpopular had 3 times higher odds of being cybervictims and traditional bystanders, and 4 times higher odds of being bully–victims and victims than students who reported feeling popular. High reported school satisfaction appeared to be a protective factor: students who were highly satisfied with school were approximately 3 times less likely to be traditional bullies, cyberbullies, bully–victims, cyberbully–cybervictims and cyberbystanders, and 4 times less likely to be cyberassistants and cybervictims, and they had around 10 times lower odds of being traditional victims or traditional assistants compared to students who had moderate or low satisfaction with school.

Social difficulties

Students who had no friends at school had 22.5 times higher odds of being traditional victims, and 11 times higher risk of being cybervictims.

Moral disengagement after cyberbullying and traditional bullying

Only students who had reported that they were involved at least once or twice in traditional bullying or cyberbullying as a bully or assistant were asked whether they had a bad conscience after participating in bullying (n = 199) or cyberbullying (n = 103).

As Table 3 shows, more traditional bullies (based on strict criteria) than cyberbullies reported having a bad conscience (38.6% vs. 21.9%), and a higher percentage of traditional assistants than cyberassistants also stated that they had a bad conscience after bullying (21.5% vs. 14.3%).

For traditional bullying no gender differences were found; however, for cyberbullying, boys were less likely to have a bad conscience than girls (71.4% vs. 46.3%) [$\chi^2(1, N = 103) = 6.7; p < 0.05; \phi = 0.255$].

A one-way analysis of variance (ANOVA) was performed to investigate the possible effect of age (independent variable) on the extent of bad conscience after traditional and cyberbullying (dependent variable) using the original scale. No statistically significant differences emerged among the different grades.

Further analysis was conducted to examine whether moral disengagement differed between students who were involved in bullying or cyberbullying frequently, and those who participated occasionally. Frequent traditional and cyberbullies, and frequent traditional and cyberassistants were classified as those who bullied others at least once a week and more often (strict criterion). Occasional traditional/cyberbullies and assistants were those who had bullied others either once or twice, or two or three times. Comparing these groups, frequent traditional bullies (38.6% vs. 62.6%) [$\chi^2(1, N = 199) = 8.0, p < 0.05; \varphi = 0.201$] and frequent traditional assistants (21.1% vs. 56.8%) [$\chi^2(1, N = 199) = 25.2, p < 0.001; \varphi = 0.356$] were less likely to have a bad conscience than occasional bullies and assistants. Similarly, with cyberbullying, frequent cyberbullies (21.9% vs. 50.7%) [$\chi^2(1, N = 103) = 7.5, p < 0.05; \varphi = 0.271$] and frequent cyberassistants (14.3% vs. 48.8%) [$\chi^2(1, N = 103) = 8.1, p < 0.004; \varphi = 0.282$] were less likely to have a bad conscience than occasional cyberbullies and cyberassistants.

A final analysis examined whether students who both traditionally and cyberbullied others had a bad conscience after each type of bullying. In order to analyse this overlap, binary variables were formed (see Method). A chi-squared test showed a significant

Table 3. Bad conscience after traditional and cyberbullying.

	Bad conscience after bullying		Bad conscience after cyberbullying	
	Bullies	Assistants	Cyberbullies	Cyberassistants
Yes I did	6 (13.6%)	4 (10.5%)	0 (0%)	0 (0%)
A little bit	11 (25.0%)	4 (10.5%)	7 (21.9%)	3 (14.3%)
Almost never	7 (15.9%)	9 (23.7%)	7 (21.9%)	6 (28.6%)
Not at all	20 (45.5%)	12 (55.3%)	18 (56.3%)	12 (57.1%)

overlap: 24 of the 36 students (66.7%) who had a bad conscience after traditionally bullying also reported a bad conscience after cyberbullying others [$\chi^2(1, N = 76) = 21.1$, $p < 0.001$; $\varphi = 0.528$].

Discussion

This study examined bullying and cyberbullying roles in a sample of German students. It identified participant roles in bullying and cyberbullying, and the extent to which they overlap between these two forms. The main aim was to examine how moral disengagement, and emotional and social characteristics differed by participant roles across forms of bullying.

The findings showed that both cyberbullying and traditional bullying were not infrequent (Table 1). The substantial prevalence rates for the main roles (approximately 5% for cyberbullying and 10% for traditional bullying) may be explained by the socio-economic circumstances of the area where the study was conducted; this area is characterised by high youth unemployment, pessimistic future aspirations and low school satisfaction. However, the results found in this study are in line with those of other studies with German samples (Techniker Krankenkasse 2011; Jäger, Fischer, and Riebel 2007, 2009; Scheithauer et al. 2006). Although regional differences within Germany concerning the extent of (cyber)bullying may exist, more representative studies are urgently needed. Nevertheless, owing to the non-representative nature of this sample, the prevalence rates must be interpreted carefully.

Cybervictimisation was less common than traditional victimisation, which is in accordance with other studies (Wachs and Wolf 2011; Tokunaga 2010). The differing roles in bullying (victim, bully, bully–victim, assistant, defender and outsider) showed a similar distribution according to both traditional and cyber forms of bullying, with the exception that there were fewer bullies and more victims for traditional bullying than cyberbullying. This may be because aggression mediated by ICTs can be easier to carry out, owing to the possibility of anonymity. The majority of adolescents involved in bullying were bystanders, in both cyber and traditional contexts. For traditional bullying, this is in line with Salmivalli et al. (1996), highlighting the importance of enhancing awareness of the role played by bystanders in the bullying process. In a comparison between cyber and traditional roles it is apparent that there are substantially fewer cyberbystanders than traditional bystanders.

Analysing the overlap between the different types of bullying revealed not only that traditional bullies and victims carry over their status into cyberbullying, but also that other roles, such as assistants and defenders, reprise their school role within a cyber-environment.

The findings indicate that participant roles in both traditional and cyberbullying are associated with specific social and emotional characteristics. In terms of traditional bullying this is broadly in line with the findings of other studies (Livingstone et al. 2011; Perren et al. 2010; Ortega et al. 2009). In particular, victims and cybervictims are more likely to have multiple social and emotional difficulties. The number of friendships in school is not a buffer against victimisation on its own; however, having no friends seems to be a strong risk factor. This may relate to the quality of peer contacts in school; however, this information was not gathered in the present study. In addition, students who reported that they feel unpopular have a higher risk of being a bystander, while high school satisfaction reduces the likelihood of being a bystander. This means that students who feel less popular and more dissatisfied with school are less likely to intervene (i.e. act as a defender) when they see bullying happening. The empowerment of the bystander could be effected by improvement of the class climate and measures that enhance civic courage.

A comparison between emotional and social associations and participant roles in traditional bullying and cyberbullying (Table 2) shows that students who were highly satisfied with school seemed to be better protected against traditional bullying than cyberbullying. The issue of school satisfaction needs to be considered in prevention and intervention programmes. It may be that bullying and cyberbullying can act as a compensatory response to low school satisfaction, and vice versa. It seems to be important to create a more empathetic school culture where differences are supported rather than attacked, since the incidence of bullying in schools has a negative impact on students' need to learn in an environment that is safe and secure (Rigby 1996, 1999).

In terms of moral disengagement, students who participated in traditionally bullying others were more likely to have a bad conscience than students who cyberbullied others (Table 3). Overall, this is consistent with Slonje, Smith, and Frisén (2012); however, they found that boys had less of a bad conscience than girls after both traditional and cyberbullying, whereas in this study boys had less of a bad conscience than girls only after cyberbullying. In both studies no significant differences were found for age.

One idea that has not been investigated before relates to the overlap between having a bad conscience after either form of bullying. This study found that two-thirds of students who had a bad conscience after traditional bullying also had a bad conscience after cyberbullying, which suggests that in both cases, many bullies know that what they are doing is intended to cause harm, and thus are likely to experience feelings of guilt or remorse. This overlap between forms of bullying also suggests that interventions which aim to enhance empathy and reduce moral disengagement may be effective for both traditional and cyberbullying. Further studies should investigate differences between students who have a bad conscience after taking part in only one type of bullying, and those who have a bad conscience after participating in both. The form of (cyber)bullying (i.e. direct vs. indirect or anonymous vs. named) should also be considered as this may impact on students' moral disengagement.

Students who bullied others or assisted in bullying frequently, both traditionally and through cyberbullying, were less likely to have a bad conscience than students who participated in bullying only occasionally. This is in line with previous studies (Hymel et al. 2010; Kochanska et al. 1994), which show that the development of moral engagement is associated with lower impulsiveness and an increased level of behavioural control.

This study builds on previous research by exploring the consistency of participant roles between traditional and cyberbullying, while also exploring moral disengagement, and social and emotional characteristics between participant roles. Although the results are largely consistent with those of earlier studies, certain methodological limitations should be taken into account in considering the findings. First, the results are based on self-assessments. A validation of the results through independent assessment (e.g. peer nominations) was not undertaken. For example, number of friendships could be assessed with reciprocal self- and peer-nominations, which would improve the validity of the data (Salmivalli and Isaacs 2005; Hymel et al. 2010). Secondly, feeling lonely, number of friends and feeling popular were assessed only with single items; future studies could include validated scales to investigate these variables in more depth. Thirdly, the study design was cross-sectional. No interpretation of direction of causality between cyberbullying and emotional or social difficulties can be drawn.

Practical implications

The structure of inhibition of aggression is an essential task in adolescents' development and may be important for prevention and intervention work with bullies and their assistants. In terms of prevention and intervention, the issue of moral disengagement among participant roles may also be of importance. The KiVa programme in Finland is an example of a successful anti-bullying programme that takes into account the different participant roles and acknowledges the importance of feeling empathy for the victim, based on the principle that a positive change in the behaviour of classmates can reduce both bullying and cyberbullying (Salmivalli, Kärna, and Poskiparta 2011).

However, boys not only exhibit less of a bad conscience after cyberbullying but also appear to have a higher risk of being cyberbullies. Therefore, the enhancement of empathy by boys seems to be particularly important to prevent cyberbullying.

References

Ainley, J. 1991. High school factors that influence students to remain in school. *Journal of Educational Research* 85: 69–80.

Almeida, A., I. Correia, and S. Marinho. 2010. Moral disengagement, normative beliefs of peer groups, and attitudes regarding roles in bullying. *Journal of School Violence* 9: 23–36.

Aluede, O., F. Adeleke, D. Omoike, and J. Afen-Akpaida. 2008. A review of the extent, nature, characteristics and effects of bullying behaviour in school. *Journal of Instructional Psychology* 35: 151–8.

Andreou, E. 2001. Bully/victim problems and their association with coping behaviour in conflictual peer interactions among school-aged children. *Educational Psychology* 21: 59–66.

Bandura, A. 1999. Moral disengagement in the perpetration of inhumanities. *Personality and Social Psychology Review* 3: 193–209.

Camodeca, M., and A. Goossens. 2005. Aggression, social cognitions, anger and sadness in bullies and victims. *Journal of Child Psychology and Psychiatry* 46: 186–97.

Döring, N. 2003. *Sozialpsychologie des Internet. Die Bedeutung des Internet für Kommunikationsprozesse, Identitäten, soziale Beziehungen und Gruppen*. 2nd ed. Göttingen: Hogrefe.

Hinduja, S., and J.W. Patchin. 2010. Bullying, cyberbullying, and suicide. *Archives of Suicide Research* 14: 206–21.

Hodges, E., M. Boivin, F. Vitaro, and W.M. Bukowski. 1999. The power of friendship: Protection against an escalating cycle of peer victimization. *Developmental Psychology* 35: 94–101.

Hodges E., M.J. Malone, and D.G. Perry. 1997. Individual risk and social risk as interacting determinants of victimization in the peer group. *Developmental Psychology* 33: 1032–9.

Hymel, S., N. Rocke Henderson, and R. Bonanno. 2005. Moral disengagement: A framework for understanding bullying among adolescents. In *Peer victimization in schools: An international perspective*, ed. O. Aluede, A.G. McEachern and M.C. Kenny. *Journal of Social Sciences*, Special Issue 8: 1–11.

Hymel, S., K.A. Schonert-Reichl, R.A. Bonanno, T. Vaillancourt, and N.R. Henderson. 2010. Bullying and morality: Understanding how good kids can behave badly. In *Handbook of bullying in schools: An international perspective*, ed. S.R. Jimerson, S.M. Swearer and D.L. Espelage, 101–18. New York: Routledge.

Jäger, R.S., U. Fischer, and J. Riebel. 2007. *Mobbing bei Schülerinnen und Schülern in der Bundesrepublik Deutschland*. Landau: Zentrum für empirisch pädagogische Forschung.

Jäger, R.S., U. Fischer, and J. Riebel. 2009. *Mobbing bei Schülerinnen und Schülern in der Bundesrepublik Deutschland*. Landau: Zentrum für empirisch pädagogische Forschung.

Kochanska, G., K. DeVet, M. Goldman, K. Murray, and S.P. Putnam. 1994. Maternal reports of conscience development and temperament in young children. *Child Development* 65: 852–68.

Kroon, W. 2011. Bullying and cyberbullying in adolescence and its relations with life satisfaction, loneliness, depressive symptoms and reputation. Unpublished Master's thesis, Arizona State University.

Ladd, G.W., B.J. Kochenderfer, and C.C. Coleman. 1996. Friendship quality as a predictor of young children's early school adjustment. *Child Development* 67: 1103–18.

Ladd, G.W., and W. Troop-Gordon. 2003. The role of chronic peer difficulties in the development of children's psychological adjustment problems. *Child Development* 74: 1344–67.

Livingstone, S., L. Haddon, A. Görzig, and K. Ólafsson. 2011. Risks and safety on the internet: The perspective of European children. Full findings. London: LSE, EU Kids Online.

Marini, Z.A., A.V. Dane, and S.L. Bosacki. 2006. Direct and indirect bully–victims: differential psychosocial risk factors associated with adolescents involved in bullying and victimization. *Aggressive Behavior* 32: 551–69.

Menesini, E., V. Sanchez, A. Fonzi, R. Ortega, A. Costabile, and G. Lo Feudo. 2003. Moral emotions and bullying: A cross-national comparison of differences between bullies, victims and outsiders. *Aggressive Behavior* 29: 515–30.

Nansel, T.R., W. Craig, M.D. Overpeck, G. Saluja, W.J. Ruan, and the Health Behaviour in School-aged Children Bullying Analyses Working Group. 2004. Cross-national consistency in the relationship between bullying behaviors and psychosocial adjustment. *Journal of the American Medical Association* 158: 730–6.

Olweus, D. 1999. Sweden. In P. K. Smith, Catalano, R., Junger-Tas, J., Morita, Y. Olweus, D., and Slee, P., eds. *The nature of school bullying: A cross-national perspective*, 7–27. London: Routledge.

Ortega, R., P. Elipe, J.A. Mora-Merchan, J. Calmaestra, and E. Vega. 2009. The emotional impact on victims of traditional bullying and cyberbullying: A study of Spanish adolescents. *Zeitschrift für Psychologie/Journal of Psychology* 217: 197–204.

Perren, S., J. Dooley, T. Shaw, and D. Cross. 2010. Bullying in school and cyberspace: Associations with depressive symptoms in Swiss and Australian adolescents. *Child and Adolescent Psychiatry and Mental Health* 4, no. 28: 1–10.

Riebel, J. 2008. *Spotten, Schimpfen, Schlagen . . . Gewalt unter Schülern – Bullying und Cyberbullying*. Landau: Verlag Empirische Pädagogik.

Rigby, K. 1996. *Bullying in schools: And what to do about it*. London: Jessica Kingsley.

Rigby, K. 1999. Peer victimisation at school and the health of secondary students. *British Journal of Educational Psychology* 22, no. 2: 28–34.

Rivers, I., V.P. Poteat, N. Noret, and N. Ashurst. 2009. Observing bullying at school: The mental health implications of witness status. *School Psychology Quarterly* 24, no. 4: 211–223.

Rohlfs, C., M. Harring, and C. Palentien. 2008. Bildung, Kompetenz, Kompetenz-Bildung – eine Einleitung in die Thematik. In *Kompetenz-Bildung. Soziale, emotionale und kommunikative Kompetenzen von Kindern und Jugendlichen*, ed. C. Rohlfs, M. Harring and C. Palentien, 9–18. Wiesbaden: VS Verlag für Sozialwissenschaften.

Salmivalli, C., and J. Isaacs. 2005. Prospective relations among victimization, rejection, friendlessness, and children's self- and peer-perceptions. *Child Development* 76, 1161–71.

Salmivalli, C., A. Kärna, and E. Poskiparta. 2011. Counteracting bullying in Finland: The KiVA Program and its effects on different forms of being bullied. *International Journal of Behavioural Development* 35: 405–11.

Salmivalli, C., K.M.J. Lagerspetz, K. Bjorkqvist, K. Osterman, and A. Kaukiainen. 1996. Bullying as a group process: Participant roles and their relations to social status within the group. *Aggressive Behavior* 22: 1–15.

Scheithauer, H., T. Hayer, and F. Petermann. 2003. *Bullying unter Schülern: Erschei-nungsformen, Risikobedingungen und Interventionskonzepte*. Göttingen: Hogrefe.

Scheithauer, H., T. Hayer, F. Petermann, and G. Jugert. 2006. Physical, verbal and relational forms of bullying among German students: Age trends, gender differences, and correlates. *Aggressive Behavior* 32: 261–75.

Slonje, R., P.K. Smith, and A. Frisén. 2012. Processes of cyberbullying, and feelings of remorse by bullies: A pilot study. *European Journal of Developmental Psychology* 9: 244–59.

Smith, P.K., J. Mahdavi, M. Carvalho, S. Fisher, S. Russell, and N. Tippett. 2008. Cyberbullying, it forms and impact in secondary school pupils. *Journal of Child Psychology and Psychiatry* 49: 376–85.

Spriggs, A.L., R.J. Iannotti, T.R. Nansel, and D.L. Haynie. 2007. Adolescent bullying involvement and perceived family, peer and school relations: Commonalities and differences across race/ethnicity. *Journal of Adolescent Health* 41: 283–93.

Sutton, J., P.K. Smith, and J. Swettenham. 1999. Social cognition and bullying: Social inadequacy or skilled manipulation? *British Journal of Developmental Psychology* 17: 435–50.

Techniker Krankenkasse. 2011. Forsa-Umfrage: Jeder dritte Schüler in NRW bereits Opfer von Cybermobbing. Pressemitteilung. http://www.tk.de/tk/pressemitteilungen/regionalepressemitteilungen/pressemitteilung-en-regional-anwendung/309240?newsroomPressemitteilung=343466 (accessed November 20, 2011).

Tokunaga, R.S. 2010. Following you home from school: A critical review and synthesis of research on cyberbullying victimization. *Computers in Human Behavior* 26: 277–87.

Wachs, S., and K. Wolf. 2011. Über den Zusammenhang von Bullying und Cyberbullying. Erste Ergebnisse einer Selbstberichtsstudie. *Praxis der Kinderpsychologie und Kinderpsychiatrie* 60: 735–44.

Willard, N.E. 2006. *Cyberbullying and cyberthreats: Responding to the challenge of online social cruelty, threats, and distress*. Eugene, OR: Center for Safe and Responsible Internet Use.

Wolke, D., and K. Stanford. 1999. Bullying in school children. In *Developmental psychology*, ed. D. Messer and S. Millar, 341–60. London: Arnold.

Cyberbullying victimisation in adolescence: relationships with loneliness and depressive mood

Dorit Olenik-Shemesh[a] , Tali Heiman[a] and Sigal Eden[b]

[a]Department of Education and Psychology, The Open University of Israel, Raanana, Israel;
[b]Department of Education, Bar Ilan University, Ramat-Gan, Israel

Cyberbullying is deliberate, aggressive activity carried out through digital means. Cybervictimisation in adolescence may be related to negative psychosocial variables such as loneliness and depressive mood. The purpose of the present study, the first of its kind in Israel, was to examine the association between adolescent cybervictimisation and two socio-emotional variables: loneliness and depressive mood. The sample consisted of 242 Israeli adolescents, aged 13–16 years, who completed questionnaires regarding Internet use, cyberbullying, traditional bullying, loneliness and depressive mood. In total, 16.5% of the participants reported being cybervictims and 32.5% reported knowing someone who was cybervictimised. The results revealed a relationship between cybervictimisation and loneliness (social, emotional and general) as well as depressive mood. A logistic hierarchical regression found that loneliness, gender and depressive mood each explained some variance in cybervictimisation in adolescents. As an anchor for comparison, and in order to shed light on the findings, results are presented in comparison to traditional bullying. The results make a contribution to national and international cyberbullying research and broaden the knowledge about potential risk factors for cybervictimisation.

Introduction

The phenomenon of cyberbullying among children and adolescents has been on the rise in recent years. Studies in Europe, the USA and Canada indicate that approximately 20% of teenagers aged 7–18 who used the Internet reported repeated experiences of cyberbullying (Ybarra and Mitchell 2004; CyberTraining 2008; Vandebosch and Van Cleemput 2009; Cyberbullying Research Center 2010; Mishna et al. 2012). In Israel, the use of social networks is very high (75% of 16–18-year-olds, 50% of 10–12-year-olds and 25% of 7-year-olds) (Knesset–Israeli Parliament 2011). However, only a few studies (Mesch 2009; Tarablus, Heiman, and Olenik Shemesh 2011) have examined cyberbullying in Israel, its rates, patterns and associations with socio-emotional variables. The current study, the first of its kind in Israel, aims at studying cybervictimisation in Israeli adolescents, focusing on the link between cybervictimisation and two socio-emotional variables: loneliness and depressive mood.

In episodes of cyberbullying, three kinds of participants take part: the *perpetrators*, who deliberately send verbal or visual messages (photos, video clips) in order to threaten, intimidate, hurt or humiliate another person; the *victims*, who suffer the harm, insult and/or injury; and the *bystanders* (Levine and Crowther 2008), who see the hurtful messages and occasionally take an active part in cyberbullying, such as forwarding the messages to others (Slonje, Smith, and Frisén 2012) or responding behind the scenes.

The *cybervictims* receive hurtful, offensive or threatening verbal messages, photos and/or video clips, and are influenced intensively by cyberbullying. Most cybervictimisation occurs during adolescence (11–17 years) (Tokunaga 2010). Studies have found a close relationship between cybervictimisation and traditional victimisation (Ybarra and Mitchell 2004; Vandebosch and Van Cleemput 2008); for example, Li (2007) found that one-third of the victims of traditional bullying are victims of cyberbullying.

Until recently, victims of traditional bullying could find sanctuary in the privacy of their home, but cyberbullying has left victims nowhere to escape to. Cybervictims may have their social network account broken into; they may fall victim to various activities such as impersonation and spreading of rumours about them (Druck and Kaplowitz 2005). Most of them feel helpless towards the hurt and do not know how to stop the attacks through the net, but do not tend to share their concerns with surrounding adults (parents, teachers). Price and Dalgleish (2010) noted that adolescents who are cybervictims believe that adults are less familiar with the cyberworld and afraid that if they involve their parents, they will not allow them to use the computer.

Loneliness, depressive mood and adolescents' cybervictimisation

Aside from specific types of social difficulties (e.g. low social status, low level of social integration), the literature regarding social and emotional links with cybervictimisation points to a sense of loneliness and depressive mood as affecting the risk of being victimised (Ybarra et al. 2006; Didden et al. 2009).

A sense of *loneliness* reflects a discrepancy between an individual's expectations of interpersonal relations and his or her social situation in reality (Peplau and Perlman 1982); it arises when the universal and fundamental need for belongingness and establishing stable social bonds with caring others is not adequately satisfied (Cacioppo and Patrick 2008). The experience of loneliness may be manifested by difficulty in establishing close intimate relationships, having few friends, and experiencing frustration and dissatisfaction with existing relationships (Asher et al. 1990), less interest in developing social relationships and reduced active involvement in friendships (Nurmi and Salmela-Aro 1997). The sense of loneliness contains characteristics that may interfere with an adolescent's ability to initiate contacts with others, e.g. low social risk-taking, low perceived likability, high social anxiety and high public self-consciousness, in a period in life when all these variables are most important. As Rappoport (1972) noted, the social role of adolescents is in a sort of 'limbo', in which they are deprived of a clear sense of belonging, attachments, avenues of participation and a socially affirmed role in the society. Lonely adolescents experience this social limbo most directly through the sense of emptiness, isolation and boredom, while their main developmental task at this age is to facilitate attachments, commitments and new modes of social participation.

The distinction between *social loneliness* and *emotional loneliness* was first presented by Weiss (1973), but remained largely ignored by many studies (Clinton and Anderson 1999). *Social loneliness* is defined by an absence of companionship or a failure of social integration. *Emotional loneliness* is defined as an unsatisfied 'need for intimacy' (Weiss 1989, 8–11), an absence of psychological intimacy. It is the failure of a relationship to move beyond companionship and into a realm where private and deeply personal hopes, confusions and failures are both shared and clarified. The absence of such intense emotional support and attachment signals loneliness that is close to the pathology of chronic anxiety and complete psychological isolation (Clinton and Anderson 1999). Emotional loneliness may be satisfied, especially in adolescence, through a best-friend relationship that becomes sufficiently unwavering to mollify these needs for intimacy and attachment.

Moods are generally defined as diffuse and long-lasting emotional states that influence rather than interrupt behaviour. *Depressive mood* is assessed through mood states of anger, confusion, depression, fatigue and tension (Russell 2003; Terry, Lane, and Fogarty 2003). Loneliness and depressive mood are usually intercorrelated. It appears that adolescents with depressive mood symptoms may have difficulties identifying social cues and interacting successfully with peers. Feelings of loneliness would be accompanied by a sense of negative mood, which may develop into depression (Kazdin and Marciano 1998).

In research on traditional bullying, loneliness and depressive mood have been found to show a strong positive correlation with victimisation. In adolescence, when social status and peer relations have great importance (Steinberg and Morris 2001), the social avoidance, lack of close peer relationships and sense of loneliness become even more crucial than in other periods of life.

It seems that these two socio-emotional variables are also associated with cybervictimisation. The research literature regarding cybervictimisation suggests that being a cybervictim might be associated with strong negative feelings, sometimes higher than those experienced in traditional victimisation (Mitchell, Ybarra, and Finkelhor 2007). Studies imply that adolescents who tend to be lonely and relatively isolated as well as suffer bad mood and sadness sometimes seek to compensate for their lack of social contacts by finding refuge on the Internet, where they do manage to develop relationships but become more prone and vulnerable to cybervictimisation (Peter, Valkenburg, and Schouten 2005; Van den Eijnden et al. 2006). Hodges, Malone, and Perry (1999) describe a vicious cycle in which lonely teenagers become targets for bullies, and as they experience more victimisation are more likely to become socially withdrawn, which in turn creates further victimisation, followed by further loneliness. Sahin (2012) claims that loneliness plus Internet use creates an ideal environment for cybervictimisation in children. However, only a few studies have focused on this specific relationship between loneliness, depressive mood and cybervictimisation in teenagers. Some studies have found a link between cybervictimisation, depressive symptoms and suicidal thoughts (Wang, Iannotti, and Nansel 2009; NIH 2010; Brighi et al. 2012), particularly for boys (Ybarra 2004). McGilvray (2009) found that cybervictimisation is more associated with suicidal thoughts than any other type of bullying.

Research objectives

This study focuses on the relationship between cybervictimisation, loneliness and depressive mood in adolescents. It investigates the role of loneliness and depressive mood in the experience of being a cybervictim. We hypothesised that cybervictimisation would be associated with loneliness and depressive mood. We first studied cybervictimisation, its prevalence and patterns in an Israeli sample, and then we studied the relationship between cybervictimisation, loneliness and depressive mood. While examining the relationship between cybervictimisation and loneliness, the study addresses general sense of loneliness as well as the two constituent components: social loneliness and emotional loneliness. As an anchor for comparison, and in order to shed light on and study the uniqueness of cybervictimisation, results are presented in comparison to traditional victimisation.

Method

Participants

The sample consisted of 242 Jewish Israeli adolescents (117 boys, 125 girls) aged 13–16 years (mean = 14.40, SD = 1.14) who completed questionnaires regarding Internet use, cyberbullying, traditional bullying, loneliness and depressive mood. Three schools took part; in each school, three or four classes participated. Data were collected between March and June 2010.

School characteristics

The three schools represented different parts of the country: the north area, the central part and near the coast. The northern and central schools were from 7th to 12th grade (junior high and high school) with 1500–2000 students each; these schools were regional schools that served the surrounding villages and towns in the area. The near-coast school was from 10th to 12th grade with 1200 students; it served a main city.

Within all schools, the student population was heterogeneous and the classes were integrative; schools offered the students a flexible schedule with various combinations of majors (subjects which the students choose to study on an advanced level); parents were involved in school life and the students were expected to carry out service for the community.

The socio-economic level of the students was reported by the school principal. According to the school criteria based on the parents' education and salary, the distribution was: 10% low, 35% low–medium, 40% medium–high and 15% high socio-economic level.

Procedure

After receiving approval from the research ethics board and the local school principal, letters were sent to parents via the class teachers, and returned to school by students. The letters explained the nature of cyberbullying and the intended study, and parents could object to their child's participation. The questionnaires were distributed to the students during one study period in their classrooms, under the supervision of one of the researchers. Students completed the questionnaires anonymously. The participation rate was high, with 95% of eligible students participating in the study.

Measures

Cyberbullying Questionnaire (Smith et al. 2008)

This 28-item self-report questionnaire examines children's and adolescents' experiences of cyberbullying and is divided into four subsections: (1) general information on Internet usage (i.e. email, ICQ/Messenger, schoolwork, games, etc.).; the respondent is requested to report the location of the 'Internet usage'; (2) the participant's personal experience of being exposed to traditional bullying and cyberbullying; the questionnaire presents a definition of bullying and cyberbullying followed by questions regarding involvement in traditional bullying and cyberbullying as a victim, as a perpetrator and as a bystander; the prevalence of cybervictimisation and traditional victimisation was examined through a series of questions regarding the hurt: 'Have you ever been cyberbullied/bullied?' (yes/no), 'Do you know of anyone who has been cyberbullied/bullied?' (yes/no), 'What was the frequency of harassment?' (often, sometimes, a few times); the types of cybervictimisation (verbal abuse, offensive ICQ, offensive text messages, rude and offensive emails, offensive pictures and video clips); (3) involvement as a bystander in a bullied setting; and (4) information about the participant's opinions and perceptions regarding cyberbullying and traditional bullying.

Evidence for construct validity has been shown in previous studies (Smith et al. 2008; Steffgen et al. 2011; Brighi et al. 2012). The questionnaire was translated from English into Hebrew and then translated back into English (back-translation) by three judges to check the accuracy of the translation.

Loneliness Questionnaire (Asher et al. 1990)

This questionnaire rates 17 primary items and eight filler items on a five-point Likert scale ranging from 'never feel like this' (1) to 'always feel like this' (5). Higher scores reflect greater loneliness, or stronger feelings of loneliness. The 16 primary school-based items (e.g. 'It's easy for me to make new friends at school' or 'I feel left out of things at school') comprised the general loneliness measure (Cronbach's alpha = 0.86). The general scale was divided into two subscales: Social loneliness (four items, Cronbach's alpha = 0.83) and Emotional loneliness (10 items, Cronbach's alpha = 0.82).

Children's Depression Inventory (CDI) (Kovacs and Beck 1977)

In this questionnaire, 27 statements (e.g. 'No one really loves me', 'All the bad things are my own fault' or 'I am sad all the time') are scored on a three-point Likert scale, never (0), sometimes (1), always (2), as the best description of the respondent's feelings for the past two weeks. A higher score represents greater depressive mood (Cronbach's alpha = 0.80).

Data analysis

SPSS 18 was used to analyse the data. In the first phase, we studied the descriptive data related to cybervictimisation (prevalence, frequency, patterns and gender differences). In the second phase, we studied the associations between cybervictimisation and loneliness and depressive mood, by conducting two-way multivariate analyses of variance (MANOVAs) with gender and cybervictimisation, in the form of a comparison between the two groups (cybervictims and non-victims), in terms of emotional loneliness, social loneliness, general loneliness and depressive mood. In addition, a hierarchical logistic regression was performed to explain the variance and predict cybervictimisation by the independent variables: gender, loneliness and depressive mood.

Results

Prevalence of cybervictimisation and gender differences

Table 1 presents descriptive statistics regarding cybervictimisation: the prevalence of cybervictimisation, traditional victimisation and of knowing someone who was a victim, and a breakdown by gender. Altogether, 40 participants reported that they have been cybervictims; of these, none reported it 'often', but seven reported 'sometimes' and 33 as

Table 1. Prevalence and frequency of cybervictimisation compared to traditional victimisation.

		Cybervictimisation				Traditional victimisation			
		n	Frequency	% within gender	% within victims	*n*	Frequency	% within gender	% within victims
Victim prevalence	Total	242	40	16.5	100	242	66	27.3	100
	Boys	113	14	12.4	35.0	112	30	26.8	45.5
	Girls	121	26	21.5	65.0	118	36	30.5	54.5
	χ^2		3.47*				0.39 *ns*		
Knows someone who was victim	Total	242	77	31.8	100	242	125	51.7	100
	Boys	114	28	24.6	36.4	116	57	46.3	49.1
	Girls	123	49	39.8	63.6	124	66	53.2	53.7
	χ^2		6.36**				0.40 *ns*		

Note: The distribution within gender includes only participants who reported their gender ($n = 240$) and answered each question. *$p < 0.05$, **$p < 0.01$; ns: not significant.

'a few times'. More participants, 66, had been traditional victims. Of these, one reported it 'often', but 10 reported 'sometimes' and 55 as 'a few times'. Rather more participants reported that they knew someone who was a cybervictim (77) or a traditional victim (125). For both experiencing and knowing a victim, figures were lower for cybervictimisation than for traditional victimisation, but were still appreciable.

Regarding gender differences, two-thirds of the cybervictim samples were girls, a larger proportion than for traditional victims. A chi-squared test showed that significantly more girls than boys were cybervictims ($\chi^2 = 3.47$, $df = 1$, $p < 0.05$). A similar pattern, but not statistically significant ($\chi^2 = 0.39$, $df = 1$, p ns), was found for traditional victimisation. Similarly, a significantly higher rate of girls reported that they knew someone who was a cybervictim ($\chi^2 = 6.36$, $df = 1$, $p < 0.01$), whereas for knowing traditional victims this was not significant ($\chi^2 = 0.40$, $df = 1$, p ns). The types of cybervictimisation reported were also examined: verbal abuse constituted 11.2%, offensive ICQ 5.8%, offensive text messages 1.7%, rude and offensive emails 1.2%, and offensive pictures and video clips 0.8%.

Relationship between cybervictimisation, loneliness and depressive mood

A key aim was to examine the relationship between cybervictimisation and two socio-emotional factors: loneliness and depressive mood. A two-way MANOVA was run, by gender (boys, girls) and cybervictimisation (online victims and non-victims). The dependent variables were general loneliness (with two dimensions: emotional and social) and depressive mood. Table 2 shows significant differences in each variable between cybervictims ($n = 40$) and those who were not cybervictims ($n = 202$). Cybervictims reported significantly more general loneliness (and both emotional and social loneliness) than those who were not cybervictims; they also reported higher depressive mood levels. No significant differences were found by gender, nor interactions between gender, cybervictimisation, loneliness and depressive mood.

Table 3 shows corresponding analyses comparing traditional victims ($n = 66$) with those who were not traditional victims ($n = 176$). There is a similar pattern in traditional victimisation as for cybervictimisation, but not identical. Significant differences were found in general loneliness (and both emotional and social loneliness) between traditional victims and those who were not traditional victims, but not for depressive mood. No significant differences were found by gender, nor interactions between gender, traditional victimisation, loneliness and depressive mood.

Finally, a hierarchical logistic regression model was run to explain the variance and predict cybervictimisation. The question posed was to what extent can the independent variables of gender, general loneliness and depressive mood explain the variance in the dependent variable of cybervictimisation (victim/non-victim), and the unique contribution of each variable in the regression model? Because the same pattern of differences was found for general loneliness and the subscales of emotional and social loneliness, and these two forms of loneliness correlated highly ($r = 0.76$, $p < 0.01$), in the following analysis, we just used general loneliness in the hierarchical logistic regression. We put gender in at the first step and the two psychological variables at the second step in order to see the impact of psychological variables adjusted for the effect of gender. The results are presented in Table 4. The model was significant, and explains about 8% of the total variance in cybervictimisation. The most significant predicting variables were loneliness (first) followed by gender (second) and finally depressive mood.

Table 2. MANOVA of loneliness and depressive mood by cybervictimisation and gender.

	Cybervictim			Not a cybervictim			
Variable	Total ($n = 40$)	Boys ($n = 14$)	Girls ($n = 26$)	Total ($n = 202$)	Boys ($n = 103$)	Girls ($n = 99$)	F (df = 1,23)
General loneliness	30.45 (10.54)	33.50 (10.90)	28.81 (10.17)	26.66 (9.84)	26.44 (9.84)	26.89 (8.42)	26.97*
Emotional loneliness	17.9 (7.5)	19.57 (9.24)	17.00 (6.52)	15.76 (6.54)	15.76 (7.54)	15.76 (5.37)	14.29*
Social loneliness	12.55 (5.03)	13.93 (5.82)	11.81 (4.50)	10.90 (4.12)	10.68 (4.31)	11.13 (3.92)	26.41*
Depressive mood	1.74 (0.27)	1.73 (0.45)	1.79 (0.32)	1.36 (0.92)	1.32 (0.95)	1.38 (0.88)	9.67*

Note: Data are shown as mean (SD). *$p < 0.05$.

Table 3. MANOVA of loneliness and depressive mood by traditional victimisation and gender.

	Traditional victim			Not a traditional victim			
Variable	Total ($n = 66$)	Boys ($n = 30$)	Girls ($n = 36$)	Total ($n = 176$)	Boys ($n = 89$)	Girls ($n = 87$)	F (df = 1,224)
General loneliness	29.88 (10.00)	30.03 (10.27)	27.95 (9.92)	26.42 (9.20)	26.41 (10.04)	26.40 (8.34)	6.21*
Emotional loneliness	17.61 (6.48)	17.90 (6.83)	17.36 (6.26)	16.65 (6.89)	15.75 (8.10)	15.55 (5.46)	3.95*
Social loneliness	12.27 (4.51)	12.13 (4.54)	12.39 (4.57)	10.78 (4.17)	10.67 (4.58)	10.89 (3.74)	5.55*
Depressive mood	1.78 (0.25)	1.79 (0.19)	1.83 (0.23)	1.64 (0.41)	1.63 (0.94)	1.67 (0.31)	25.69 *ns*

Note: Data are shown as mean (SD). *$p < 0.05$; ns: not significant.

Table 4. Hierarchical logistic regression analysis explaining the variance of cybervictimisation.

	B	*SE*	Wald (df = 1)	Exp*(B)*
Gender	0.66	0.36	3.28	1.96*
Loneliness (general)	0.030	0.010	3.61	1.03**
Depressive mood	−0.20	0.20	0.95	0.82*

*$p < 0.05$, **$p < 0.01$.

Discussion

The current study presents results regarding the prevalence of cybervictimisation in Israeli adolescents, but mainly focuses on the associations of cybervictimisation with loneliness and depressive mood. Altogether, 16.5% of participants reported that they had been cybervictims (at least a few times) and 31.8% reported that they knew someone who was a cybervictim. It seems that the scope of the phenomenon in Israel is similar to that in other countries, as referred to in the Introduction. The results suggest that more teenagers suffer traditional victimisation (27.3%) than cybervictimisation (16.5%); however, a significant proportion of teenagers are cybervictims. Other studies have also indicated lower rates of cybervictimisation compared to traditional victimisation (Smith et al. 2008; Ybarra 2004). One explanation could be that in cyberbullying, the perpetrator's strength stems mostly from an ability to handle and control electronic media (Patchin and Hinduja 2006), and occurs only in digital media, whereas traditional bullying occurs everywhere and includes all means. Future longitudinal research is needed to follow this direction along time, as well as studying the overlap of these two kinds of victimisation.

As for gender differences, more girls than boys were cybervictims, similar to the pattern of traditional bullying. These findings correspond to those of Agatston, Kowalski, and Limber (2007); however, the literature is not unequivocal on this issue. There are studies stating that girls are more likely to be victims on the net (Smith et al. 2008; Li 2006), while other studies (Hinduja and Patchin 2008) show that in cyberbullying, more boys are victims compared to girls and compared to traditional bullying. Agatston, Kowalski, and Limber (2007) interviewed middle-school and high-school students in a focus group format and found that girls, more than boys, viewed cyberbullying as a serious problem. The fact that girls view cyberbullying as more serious may influence their answers and may explain the higher rates of girls reporting cybervictimisation. We recommend that future studies investigate boys and girls separately to broaden the understanding of the role of gender in cybervictimisation.

The main goal of this study was to study the relationship between adolescent cybervictimisation and socio-emotional variables. As expected, an association between cybervictimisation, loneliness and depressive mood was found. Depressive mood and more loneliness were found to be associated with cybervictimisation, as compared with non-victimisation. Adolescents who were cybervictims expressed a higher sense of loneliness and higher feelings of depressive mood than those who were not cybervictims. Findings indicate that this is true for both dimensions of loneliness: the emotional facet – the feelings of loneliness as a result of a of a lack of intimate friend; and also the social facet – the distress feelings of loneliness experienced as a result of the lack of a wider social network, when youngsters feel that they do not belong to any community, or that they do not have friends or allies that they can rely on.

A logistic hierarchical regression analysis found that loneliness, gender and depressive mood may explain the variance and predict cybervictimisation in adolescents. The results of the study are consistent with previous studies that suggest that cybervictimisation may be associated with depression symptoms and depressive mood aside from other socio-emotional difficulties (Patchin and Hinduja 2006; Ybarra 2004; Ybarra and Mitchell 2004). These findings may be explained in one of two ways. The first is that adolescents with a more intense sense of loneliness (emotional as well as social) and depressive mood may have difficulties in developing useful social networks, have limited social experiences and seek more for social connections on the Internet, and may become more vulnerable to cybervictimisation. The second is that low peer acceptance may be an indication of limited social skills, resulting in the lack of friends, which then adversely affects and intensifies students' sense of loneliness.

The study raises the question of cause and effect in the relationship between cybervictimisation, loneliness and depressive mood. The social isolation and depressive mood may be the reasons for increased Internet use. It is possible that it is particularly the depressive mood and solitude that lead teenagers to look for anonymous relationships on the Internet, which then may trigger the vulnerability to cybervictimisation. Adolescents who are cybervictims experience increased solitude and depression and suffer from low self-esteem, loneliness and depression (Van den Eijnden et al. 2006), which in turn create a vicious circle. A similar question is raised by Ybarra (2004) regarding the link between depressive symptomatology and Internet harassment. Ybarra suggests that future studies should focus on establishing the temporality of events, 'that is, whether depressive symptoms confer risks for later negative online incidents or whether young people report depressive symptoms in response to the negative internet experiences' (Ybarra 2004, 247).

Longitudinal research is required to examine cause and effect issues. In addition, the possibility that a mutually underlying factor is confounding the relationship between cybervictimisation and depressive mood, such as lack of social support or lower social skills, should be considered. Moreover, in order to gain a better understanding of these associations between cybervictimisation, loneliness and depressive mood, we propose that further research should examine a mediation model that will consider Internet use as a mediating variable in the relationship between loneliness/depressive mood and cybervictimisation, and also other variables such as lack of social support (peers, family) and low self-esteem.

Since many studies report a high positive correlation between cybervictimisation and traditional victimisation (Ybarra and Mitchell 2004; Vandebosch and Van Cleemput 2009), we compared the associations with traditional victimisation and found a similar pattern with a slight difference for depressive mood. While research regarding traditional victimisation indicates strong associations with socio-emotional maladjustment, it was not known whether a similar association is also applicable to cybervictimisation. The present study has shown association between cybervictimisation and two specific socio-emotional difficulties: loneliness and depressive mood. Further research is needed to enlarge the scope of associations of cybervictimisation with other variables that manifest socio-emotional maladjustment and give a more complete picture regarding the uniqueness and distinctiveness of cybervictimisation. It should be noted that the research literature has yet to come to a definitive answer to the question as to whether cyberbullying is 'old wine in a new bottle' or an entirely new phenomenon (Li 2007).

Some limitations of this study should be noted. Regarding prevalence rates, it should be borne in mind that the sample was not very large. The measures used were self-reported, and some of the observed relationships may be accounted for by common method variance.

Adding external information sources that are not based only on self-reporting to the data could validate the results. Further research should draw on more external measures to further our understanding of the links of cybervictimisation to socio-emotional aspects. Although the data support the hypothesised relationship between loneliness, depressive mood and cybervictimisation, this relationship should be explored on a broader spectrum, taking into account more emotional and social variables and examining the relative contribution of diverse socio-emotional variables, preferably in a large-sample longitudinal study, in order to gain a deeper understanding of the sources of cyberbullying in adolescents.

In summary, the present study contributes to the field of cyberbullying research and practice in detecting two socio-emotional variables that are associated with cybervictimisation and, more speculatively, have a causal role. Detecting these variables is of great importance when planning and conducting programmes for cyberbullying prevention and intervention. The results suggest that such programmes for adolescents should focus on strengthening social networks, social skills and peer support, in order to prevent a sense of loneliness and depressive mood, and to help build a 'social protection layer' against becoming cybervictims. Programmes of this kind should focus on developing adolescents' ability to establish close, intimate relationships, and promote abilities to gain one or two good friends, in order to diminish the frustration and dissatisfaction of being lonely and becoming more vulnerable to cyberbullying. Since loneliness, in both dimensions (social and emotional) was found to be significantly associated with cybervictimisation, it is important to ensure that such programmes address the need to develop both the ability for social integration and the ability to generate close relationships and psychological intimacy.

References

Agatston, P.W., R. Kowalski, and S. Limber. 2007. Students' perspectives of cyberbullying. Brief report. *Journal of Adolescent Health* 41: 59–60.

Asher, S.R., J.T. Parkhurst, S. Hymel, and G.A. Williams. 1990. Peer rejection and loneliness in childhood. In *Peer rejection in childhood*, ed. S.R. Asher and J.D. Coie, 253–73. New York: Cambridge University Press.

Brighi, A., G. Melotti, A. Guarini, M.L. Genta, R. Ortega, J. Mora-Merchan, P.K. Smith, and F. Thompson. 2012. Self esteem and loneliness in relation to cyberbullying in three European countries. In *Cyberbullying in the global playground: Research from international perspectives*, ed. Q. Li, D. Cross and P. K. Smith, 32–56. Chichester: Wiley-Blackwell.

Cacioppo, J.T., and B. Patrick. 2008. *Loneliness: Human nature and the need for social connection*. New York: W.W. Norton & Co.

Clinton, M., and L. Anderson. 1999. Social and emotional loneliness: Gender differences and relationships with self-monitoring and perceived control. *Journal of Black Psychology* 25: 61–77.

Cyberbullying Research Center – USA. 2010. http://webcache.googleusercontent.com/search?client=gmail&rls=gm&hl=iw&q=cache:_x2D35DhB_4J:http://www.cyberbullying.us/research.php+cyberbullying+in+USA+percentage&ct=clnk (accessed August 31, 2011).

CyberTraining – A research-based training manual on cyberbullying. 2008. Project 142237-LLP-1-2008-1-DE-LEONARDO-LMP. http://www.adam-europe.eu/adam/project/view.htm?prj=4306 (accessed August 31, 2011).

Didden, R., R. Scholte, H. Korzilius, M.H. Jan, A. Vermeulen, M. O'Reilly, R. Lang, and G.E. Lancioni. 2009. Cyberbullying among students with intellectual and developmental disability in special education settings. *Developmental Neurorehabilitation* 12: 146–51.

Druck, K., and M. Kaplowitz. 2005. Setting up a no-bully zone. *Virginia Journal of Education* 98: 11–13.

Hinduja, S., and J.W. Patchin. 2008. Cyberbullying: An exploratory analysis of factors related to offending and victimization. *Deviant Behavior* 29: 129–56.

Hodges, E., M.J. Malone, and D.G. Perry. 1999. Individual risk and social risk as interacting determinant of victimization in the peer group. *Developmental Psychology* 33: 1032–9.

Kazdin, A.E., and P.L. Marciano. 1998. Childhood and adolescent depression. In *Treatment of childhood disorders*. 2nd ed., ed. R.A. Barkley and E. J. Mash, 211–48. New York: Guilford Press.

Knesset–Israeli Parliament. 2011. *Children in social nets on the internet* (written by E. Weisbali). The Knesset, Center for Research and Information. (In Hebrew.)

Kovacs, M., and A. Beck. 1977. An empirical clinical approach toward a definition of childhood depression. In *Depression in childhood: Diagnosis, treatment and conceptual models*, ed. J. Schlterbrant and A. Raskin, 1–25. New York: Raven Press.

Kowalski, R.M., and S.P. Limber. 2007. Electronic bullying among middle school students. *Journal of Adolescent Health* 41: 22–30.

Levine, M., and S. Crowther. 2008. The responsive bystander: How social group membership and group size can encourage as well as inhibit bystander intervention. *Journal of Personality and Social Psychology* 95: 1429–39.

Li, Q. 2006. Cyberbullying in schools: A research of gender differences. *Schools Psychology International* 27: 157–70.

Li, Q. 2007. Bullying in the new playground: Research into cyberbullying and cyber victimization. *Australasian Journal of Educational Technology* 23: 435–54.

McGilvray, A. 2009. *Cyberbullying: A challenge in the digital age*. ABC Health News, ABC Health & Wellbeing. http://www.abc.net.au/health/thepulse/stories/2009/09/17/2679508.htm

Mesch, G.S. 2009. Parental mediation, online activities, and cyberbullying. *CyberPsychology & Behavior* 12: 387–93.

Mishna, F., M. Khoury-Kassabri, T. Gadalla, and J. Daciuk. 2012. Risk factors for involvement in cyber bullying: Victims, bullies and bully–victims. *Children and Youth Services Review* 34: 63–70.

Mitchell, K.J., M. Ybarra, and D. Finkelhor. 2007. The relative importance of online victimization in understanding depression, delinquency and substance use. *Child Maltreatment* 12: 314–24.

NIH. 2010. *Depression high among youth victims of school cyber bullying*. NIH researchers' report. Washington, DC: National Institutes of Health, US Department of Health and Human Services.

Nurmi, J., and K. Salmela-Aro. 1997. Social strategies and loneliness: A prospective study. *Personal and Individual Differences* 23: 205–15.

Patchin, J.W., and S. Hinduja. 2006. Bullies move beyond the schoolyard. A preliminary look at cyberbullying. *Youth Violence and Juvenile Justice* 4: 148–69.

Peplau, L.A., and D. Perlman. 1982. Perspectives on loneliness. In *Loneliness: A sourcebook of current theory, research and therapy*, ed. L.A. Peplau and D. Perlman, 1–18. New York: Wiley.

Peter, J., P. Valkenburg, and A. Schouten. 2005. Developing a model of adolescent friendship formation on the internet. *Cyber Psychology & Behavior* 8: 423–30.

Price, M., and J. Dalgleish. 2010. Cyberbullying experiences, impacts and coping strategies as describes by Australian young people. *Youth Studies Australia*, 29, no. 2: 51–9.

Rappoport, L. 1972. *Personality development: The chronology of experience*. Glenview, IL: Scott & Foresman.

Russell, J.A. 2003. Core affect and the psychological instruction of emotion. *Psychological Review* 110: 145–72.

Sahin, M. 2012. The relationship between cyberbullying/cybervictimization and loneliness. *Children and Youth Services Review* 34: 834–7.

Slonje, R., P.K. Smith, and A. Frisén. 2012. Processes of cyberbullying, and feelings of remorse by bullies: A pilot study. *European Journal of Developmental Psychology* 9: 244–59.

Smith, P.K., J. Mahdavi, M. Carvalho, S. Fisher, S. Russell, and N. Tippett. 2008. Cyberbullying: Its nature and impact in secondary school pupils. *Journal of Child Psychology and Psychiatry* 49: 376–85.

Steffgen, G., A. Kowing, J. Pfetsch, and A. Melzer. 2011. Are cyberbullies less empathic? Adolescents' cyberbullying behavior and empathic responsiveness. *Cyberpsychology, Behavior, and Social Networking* 14: 643–48.

Steinberg, L., and A. Morris. 2001. Adolescent development. *Annual Review of Psychology* 52: 111–39.

Tarablus, T., T. Heiman, and D. Olenik Shemesh. 2011. *Cyber-bullying vs. face to face bullying among adolescents*. Research Center for Innovation in Learning Technologies Proceedings, Open University of Israel, 287.

Terry, P., A. Lane, and G. Fogarty. 2003. Construct validity of the Profile of Mood States–A for use with adults. *Psychology of Sport and Exercise* 4: 125–39.

Tokunaga, R.S. 2010. Following you home from school: A critical review and synthesis of research on cyberbullying victimization. *Computers in Human Behavior* 26: 277–87.

Van den Eijnden, E.R., A. Vermulst, T. Van Rooy, and G. Meerkerk. 2006. *Bullying on internet and psychosocial well-being of youth*. Rotterdam: IVO.

Vandebosch, H., and K. Van Cleemput. 2009. Cyberbullying among youngsters: Profiles of bullies and victims. *New Media & Society* 11: 1349–71.

Wang, J., R.J. Iannotti, and T.R. Nansel. 2009. School bullying among adolescents in the United States: Physical, verbal, relational and cyber. *Journal of Adolescent Health* 45: 368–75.

Weiss, R.S. 1973. *Loneliness: The experience of emotional and social isolation*. Cambridge, MA: MIT Press.

Weiss, R.S. 1989. Reflections on the present state of loneliness research. In *Loneliness: Theory, research, and applications*, ed. M. Hojat and R. Crandall, 1–16. Newbury Park, CA: Sage.

Ybarra, M.L. 2004. Linkage between depressive symptomatology and Internet harassment among young regular Internet users. *Cyberpsychology and Behavior* 7: 247–57.

Ybarra, M.L., and K.J. Mitchell. 2004. Youth engaging in online harassment: Associations with caregiver–child relationships, Internet use, and personal characteristics. *Journal of Adolescence* 27: 319–36.

Ybarra, M.L., K.J. Mitchell, J. Wolak, and D. Finkelhor. 2006. Examining characteristics and associated distress related to Internet harassment: Findings from second youth Internet safety survey. *Pediatrics* 118: 1169–77.

Predictors of victimisation across direct bullying, indirect bullying and cyberbullying

Antonella Brighi[a], Annalisa Guarini[a], Giannino Melotti[a], Silvia Galli[b] and Maria Luisa Genta[a]

[a]*Department of Psychology, University of Bologna, Bologna, Italy;* [b]*Department of Psychology University of Florence, Florence, Italy*

Cyberbullying may sometimes be an extension of traditional bullying. However, some particular features of cyberbullying suggest that it may have a distinct causal pathway, due to the social context of a virtual environment within which peer social processes occur. Moreover, boys and girls may perceive and respond differentially to their social context, which may heighten the risk for victimisation. This study aimed to describe how the perceived relational context (school, peers and family) may influence the probability of becoming a victim, in both offline and virtual contexts, among boys and girls. A questionnaire, measuring school climate; global, family and peer self-esteem; loneliness in relationship with parents and peers; and victimisation in traditional direct, traditional indirect and cyberbullying, was completed by 2326 Italian adolescents (mean age 13.9 years). For traditional victimisation, significant predictors were loneliness in relations with peers and a negative perception of school climate, in both males and females, while younger age (for direct victimisation) and lower global self-esteem (for indirect victimisation) were predictors for males only. For cybervictimisation, involvement as either a direct or an indirect victim was a very strong predictor for both males and females, but with an element of distinction compared to traditional victimisation, as lower self-esteem in family relationships was a predictor of cybervictimisation for males, while parent loneliness was a predictor for females. Implications for understanding the continuity/discontinuity between traditional bullying and cyberbullying, and for the development of intervention strategies, taking into account some differences by gender, are discussed.

Introduction

For many young people being part of both offline and online or virtual communities can foster feelings of inclusiveness and support self-esteem. Chatrooms or Facebook can represent an ideal environment in which to start relationships and friendships, and exchange information with people who share similar ideas and interests. The Internet creates new scenarios for communication, offering very different processes from what takes place via direct face-to-face communication. Online communication affects relationships in the offline world: young people regularly communicate online with their existing friends, but they also regularly establish relationships that originate online and then develop offline

(Valkenburg and Peter 2007). This latter type of relationship has been referred to as a 'mixed-mode friendship' (Walther and Parks 2002).

However, new communication technologies may also represent a forum for aggressive dynamics and/or other dysfunctional behaviours, including Internet abuse (Melotti, Biolcati, and Passini 2009) and cyberbullying. These raise new questions about the continuity between processes of social exclusion and victimisation offline and online, and the possible effect on self-evaluations such as self-esteem and loneliness from peers.

Cyberbullying can be described as an aggressive and intentional act conducted by an individual or a group of individuals using various forms of electronic contact, repeatedly over time against a victim (Smith et al. 2008). Analysing the contextual differences between traditional bullying and cyberbullying, Wolak, Mitchell, and Finkelhor (2007) point out the need for distinguishing between them. Traditional bullying has been widely studied, and the day-to-day, face-to-face interactions involved can lead to a high level of stress for the victims. Cyberbullying involves relations with a wider network of people, some of them unknown or known only in the virtual context, and with few limits of time and space (Slonje and Smith 2008; Law et al. 2012). Anonymity of the aggressor, moreover, may foster feelings of insecurity in the victim (Willard 2007). Law et al. (2012), examining whether cyberaggression can be measured using items similar to those used for measuring traditional bullying, showed that students clearly distinguished between bullies and victims for traditional bullying, but not for the cyberaggression items, underscoring that cyberaggression can be more reciprocal in nature than traditional bullying.

Nevertheless, much research has emphasised the continuity between traditional bullying and cyberbullying, in terms of correlations between the roles of bully or victim in the two contexts (McGuckin, Cumming, and Lewis 2010; Sourander et al. 2010; Brighi 2009; Raskauskas and Stoltz 2007); this suggests that besides differences, traditional bullying and cyberbullying may share common risk factors. Recent findings (Tokunaga 2010; Law et al. 2012) concur that it is important to explore the discontinuity as well as continuity embedded in context-specific risk factors between processes of victimisation online and offline, in order to devise tailored intervention plans.

A large body of research on traditional bullying has shown that being victimised by peers is associated with psychosocial problems, as summarised by some reviews and meta-analyses. A review of cross-sectional associations between peer victimisation and psychosocial maladjustment showed that victimisation was strongly related to depression, and less so to anxiety (Hawker and Boulton 2000). In another meta-analysis, Gini and Pozzoli (2009) found that victims of traditional bullying more frequently experienced poor emotional adjustment, poor relationships with classmates and psychosomatic problems than peers not involved in bullying. Cook et al. (2010), in another meta-analytical review, showed a positive relation between and victimisation and internalising problems in traditional bullying during adolescence.

Although the research on cybervictimisation and its consequences on psychological adjustment is more limited, some evidence suggests that this experience too may be frequently associated with internalising problems, psychosomatic symptoms, social maladjustment and low self-esteem (Perren et al. 2010; Cross et al. 2009; Campfield 2008; Kowalski, Limber, and Agatston 2012). A large-scale investigation on Australian adolescents also demonstrated that cybervictimisation is associated with higher levels of stress symptoms (Cross et al. 2009). Exploring the associations among victimisation in cyberbullying, loneliness and self-esteem, Campfield (2008) reported that cybervictims scored significantly lower on peer self-esteem than the cyber control group. A similar result was reported by Patchin and Hinduja (2010), who showed that cyberbullying victims, as well as offenders, had significantly lower scores in a global measure of self-esteem than those who had not been cyberbullying victims or offenders. This persisted even while controlling for gender, race and age, although males, non-whites and older middle schoolers tended to have lower levels of self-esteem than their peers. Concerning the associations between cybervictimisation and loneliness, Sahin (2012) reported that loneliness was not a meaningful predictor of cyberbullying perpetration, although it predicted cybervictimisation.

Beside interindividual factors, some studies focused on contextual characteristics such as the perception of the school climate and the quality of family relationships as predictors of cybervictimisation. Sourander et al. (2010) reported that cybervictim status was associated with living in a family with other than two biological parents, perceived difficulties, emotional and peer problems, psychosomatic symptoms and not feeling safe at school.

A few studies have examined the characteristics of the victimisation experience, comparing traditional and cyberbullying. Perren et al. (2010) found that cybervictims reported significantly higher levels of depressive symptoms, even when controlling for the involvement in traditional bullying/victimisation. Fredstrom, Adam, and Gilman (2011) found that the experience of school and electronic victimisation was associated with lower self-esteem and self-efficacy, higher stress, anxiety, depressive symptoms and locus of control. Moreover, even after controlling for school-based victimisation, cybervictimisation remained a significant predictor for all outcomes. Different profiles of traditional victims, cybervictims and polyvictims were described in a cross-national European study, which found lower scores in self-esteem measures and higher perceptions of loneliness in polyvictims than in other types of victims (i.e. involved only in traditional or only in cyber-aggression), highlighting the high risk of psychological maladjustment in this subgroup of adolescents (Brighi et al. 2012).

Besides continuity factors, school climate was found to be more related to traditional bullying than to Internet bullying in a sample of preadolescents across three Italian regions, suggesting that the school context may play a different role in predicting specific types of victimisation (Brighi et al. 2011).

The findings discussed above suggest that it is important to distinguish between victimisation contexts in order to highlight specific adjustment outcomes, as well as targeting various social environments such as peer and family. However, little evidence is available in the literature on possible differential psychosocial risk factors as a function of gender across traditional and cyberbullying. Gender may well be important here, as there are well-established gender differences in types of bullying (Tokunaga 2010; Hawker and Boulton 2000), as well as in such risk factors as self-esteem and loneliness. Independently from the experience of victimisation, during adolescence, males generally score higher than females on many self-esteem dimensions (Falci 2011; Moksnes et al. 2010; McMullin and Cairney 2004; Melotti and Passini 2002; Dubois and Tevendale 1999). There is less evidence of gender differences in perceptions of loneliness, but Goossens and Marcoen (1999) and Melotti et al. (2006) have reported that females showed a higher feeling of loneliness in relationships with peers.

The present study aimed to make further a comparative analysis of risk factors in traditional (direct and indirect) and cybervictimisation, separately for adolescent males and females. We hypothesised that besides common features, traditional bullying and cyberbullying may be associated with different dimensions of self-esteem and loneliness in relationships with peers in males and females. We first provide a descriptive analysis of the prevalence of traditional victimisation (direct and indirect) and cyberbullying as a function of gender. Data concerning the perception of school climate, self-esteem (global, family and peers) and loneliness (parents and peers) are also given, taking into account gender differences. We then examine these as predictors of traditional and cybervictimisation, in order to identify common risk factors that may act in continuity across traditional bullying (direct and indirect) and cyberbullying, as well as any distinctive risk factors. The analysis was undertaken separately for males and females. Being a victim of traditional bullying (direct and indirect) was also analysed as a predictor of cybervictimisation.

Method

Participants

The study involved 2326 Italian students from 39 secondary schools in two central regions of Italy. Schools included all type of secondary education (lower secondary and upper secondary schools, such as lyceums, technical institutes and vocational schools) and they were located in different socio-economic areas. The mean age was 13.9 years (SD = 1.9, range = 11–21), with approximately equal numbers of boys (53%) and girls (47%). Regarding parents' education levels, 26% of mothers and 28% of fathers did not study beyond primary school, 47% of mothers and 46% of fathers completed secondary school, and 27% and 26% had university degrees. Students with disabilities represented around 3%. The main nationality was Italian (88%), with other European countries (6%), African (2%), Asian (3%), South American (1%). These figures are representative of the nationalities present in central Italy.

Questionnaire

The questionnaire was developed as part of a project 'An investigation into new forms of bullying among preadolescents and adolescents', funded by the EU Daphne II Programme (Genta, Brighi, and Guarini 2009c). It was based on previous questionnaires (Ortega, Calmaestra, and Mora-Merchán 2007; Smith et al. 2008) and consisted of three separate sections (Brighi et al. 2012; Guarini et al. 2010; Genta et al. 2012; the questionnaire is also available on www.bullyingandcyber.net).

First section

This covered demographic data, including gender, ethnicity, disability and parents' level of education.

Second section

This included scales about school climate, loneliness and self-esteem.

- *School climate*: Participants responded to eight items referring to their school and to relationships with teachers and schoolmates on a three-point Likert scale (Cronbach's $\alpha = 0.72$).
- *Self-esteem*: A reduced 24-item version of the Italian adaptation (Melotti and Passini 2002) of the Self-Esteem Questionnaire (SEQ; Dubois et al. 1996) was used. This measures six subscale dimensions on a four-point scale of agreement/disagreement (1 = totally disagree, 2 = disagree, 3 = agree, and 4 = totally agree). Three dimensions were analysed here as relevant predictors of victimisation: *global*

self-esteem (α = 0.74), *peer self-esteem* (α = 0.75) and *family self-esteem* ($\alpha = 0.86$).

- *Loneliness*: A reduced 16-item version of the Italian adaptation (Melotti et al. 2006) of the Louvain Loneliness Scale for Children and Adolescents (LLCA) (Marcoen, Goossens, and Caes 1987; Marcoen and Goossens 1993) was used. This has four subscales, each measured by four items on a four-point frequency scale (1 = never, 2 = seldom, 3 = sometimes, and 4 = often). We analysed two scales as most relevant here: *Loneliness in relationships with parents* (L-Parent): feelings of rejection, abandonment and desertion occurring within the relationships with parents ($\alpha = 0.83$); and *Loneliness in relationships with peers* (L-Peer): feelings of rejection, abandonment and desertion occurring within the relationships with peers ($\alpha = 0.83$).

Third section

This included questions regarding being a bully and/or a victim of bullying and cyberbullying. Brief definitions were given at the beginning of this section so that pupils had a clear understanding of the behaviours classified as traditional bullying and cyberbullying, and so they would not to confuse them with other aggressive behaviours (Genta et al. 2012). For the present study, we analysed four questions on students' experiences as a victim for each type of bullying: 'Have you been [directly bullied/indirectly bullied/bullied by mobile phone/bullied on the Internet] in the last 2 months?' Response options for each were on a five-point scale (scored from 1 to 5): 'I haven't been bullied', 'It has only happened once or twice', 'Two or three times a month', 'About once a week' and 'It happens several times a week'. For analysis, we distinguished between those not involved and victims (collapsing the last four response options). As only a low percentage of students were involved as victims in mobile and Internet cyberbullying, these two forms were collapsed into a new variable: victims of cyberbullying (all students who reported having been bullied via a mobile phone or the Internet at least once in one of the two forms of cyberbullying).

Procedure

The questionnaires were filled out by students during school hours during the academic year 2008/09. The researchers first explained the definitions of traditional bullying and cyberbullying, and clarified that the questionnaire was voluntary and anonymous. The researchers remained in the classroom while the questionnaires were filled in, to answer any queries and then collect the questionnaires. The pupils' parents and the school management board gave their consent.

Statistical analyses

Descriptive analyses are given, according to gender, with respect to school climate, self-esteem (global, family and peers), loneliness (relationship with parents and with peers) and prevalence of victimisation (direct bullying, indirect bullying, mobile cyberbullying, Internet cyberbullying). Chi-squared analyses and independent sample *t*-tests (after testing for normality) were run to investigate the association between gender and the above variables. Cohen's *d* was calculated as a measure of effect size.

Four logistic analyses (two for males and two for females) were run to investigate the predictive values of age, school climate, global self-esteem, peer self-esteem, family self-esteem, peer loneliness and parent loneliness on direct and indirect victimisation. For cybervictimisation, two logistic regressions were run (one for males and one for females), adding being a victim in direct and indirect bullying to the previous predictors. Statistical analyses were run using SPSS 17 software.

Results

Descriptive analyses

Means and standard deviations for school climate, self-esteem (global, family and peers) and loneliness (relationship with parents and with peers) are shown in Table 1, according to gender, together with significance of gender differences and effect size. With the exception of loneliness to parents, all variables showed significant gender differences, but with mostly small effect sizes. Females scored higher on school climate and peer loneliness, and males scored higher on the three self-esteem measures.

Table 2 shows the prevalence of traditional bullying (direct and indirect) and cyberbullying by gender. Males were more likely to be a target of direct bullying, while females were more likely to be a target of indirect bullying and cyberbullying.

Predictors of victimisation

Table 3 shows the results for the logistic regression analyses, separately for males and females. Looking first at predictors for direct victimisation, the logistic regression model was significant for both males and females. For males, peer loneliness was a strong predictor, followed by age (negatively) and school climate (negatively). Thus, the risk of being

Table 1. Numbers (*N*), means (*M*) and standard deviations (SD) for school climate, self-esteem (global, family and peers) and loneliness (parents and peers), in male and female adolescents.

	Males			Females			*t*-Test		Effect size
	N	*M*	SD	*N*	*M*	SD	*T*	*p*	*d*
School climate	998	18.53	3.33	930	19.67	2.93	−8.13	< 0.001	0.37
Global self-esteem	1187	12.76	1.83	1081	12.40	1.97	4.41	< 0.001	0.10
Family self-esteem	1184	13.41	2.24	1073	13.15	2.54	2.66	< 0.01	0.11
Peer self-esteem	1182	12.02	2.15	1065	11.08	2.28	4.80	< 0.001	0.18
Parent loneliness	1211	5.83	2.16	1079	5.94	2.44	−1.17	2.44	0.05
Peer loneliness	1185	6.07	2.57	1093	6.46	2.67	3.52	< 0.000	0.15

Table 2. Frequencies (percentages in parentheses) of students not involved, and who were victims in direct, indirect and cyberbullying, for males and females.

	Males, *n* (%)		Females, *n* (%)			
	Not involved	Victims	Not involved	Victims	χ^2	*p*
Direct victimisation	1003 (85)	205 (15)	967 (89)	125 (11)	14.04	< 0.001
Indirect victimisation	965 (80)	244 (20)	822 (75)	272 (25)	7.24	< 0.01
Cybervictimisation	1022 (90)	119 (10)	899 (85)	163 (15)	5.28	< 0.05

Table 3. Logistic regressions on direct, indirect and cyberbullying victimisation (not involved versus students who were victims) for males and females.

	Males						Females					
	Direct victimisation		Indirect victimisation		Cybervictimisation		Direct victimisation		Indirect victimisation		Cybervictimisation	
Predictor	B	e^B	B	e^B	B	e^B	B	e^B	B	e^B	B	e^B
Age	−0.117*	0.890	−0.024	−0.976	−0.036	0.965	−0.111	0.895	0.019	1.019	0.023	1.124
School climate	−0.084*	0.920	−0.085**	0.918	−0.051	0.950	−0.132**	0.876	−0.087**	0.917	−0.053	0.948
Global self-esteem	−0.124	0.883	−0.151*	0.860	−0.019	1.019	0.018	1.018	−0.042	0.959	0.060	1.062
Family self-esteem	0.039	1.040	−0.009	0.991	−0.149*	0.861	−0.042	0.959	0.000	0.999	−0.058	0.944
Peer self-esteem	0.059	1.061	0.088	1.092	0.075	1.077	0.076	1.079	0.047	1.048	0.074	1.077
Parent loneliness	−0.002	0.998	0.016	1.017	−0.096	0.892	0.086	1.089	0.044	1.045	0.137*	1.124
Peer loneliness	0.251***	1.286	0.213***	1.238	0.058	1.059	0.140**	1.150	0.122**	1.130	−0.024	0.976
Direct victim					0.878**	2.358					1.161***	3.143
Indirect victim					0.901***	2.464					1.117***	2.123

Note: B: standardised regression coefficient; e^B: exponentiated B; $^*p < 0.05$, $^{**}p < 0.01$, $^{***}p < 0.001$.
Males: Direct: $\chi^2(7, N = 917) = 81.75$, $p < 0.001$, R^2 Nagelkerke = 0.149; Indirect: $\chi^2(7, N = 916) = 77.28$, $p < 0.001$, R^2 Nagelkerke = 0.130; Cyber: $\chi^2(9, N = 863) = 60.22$, $p < 0.001$, R^2 Nagelkerke = 0.123.
Females: Direct: $\chi^2(7, N = 874) = 46.99$, $p < 0.001$, R^2 Nagelkerke = 0.106; Indirect: $\chi^2(7, N = 876) = 42.09$, $p < 0.001$, R^2 Nagelkerke = 0.069; Cyber: $\chi^2(9, N = 850) = 77.23$, $p < 0.001$, R^2 Nagelkerke = 0.177.

a victim of direct bullying was greater for males who had a high perception of loneliness in relationships with peers, were younger and had a negative perception of school climate. For females, peer loneliness and school climate (negatively) were predictors. The risk of being a direct victim was greater for females who had a high perception of loneliness in relationships with peers, and had a negative perception of school climate.

Looking at predictors for indirect victimisation, the logistic regression model was significant for both males and females. For males, peer loneliness was a strong predictor, followed by global self-esteem (negatively) and school climate (negatively). Thus, the risk of being a victim of indirect bullying was greater for males who had a high perception of loneliness in relationships with peers, had low global self-esteem and had a negative perception of school climate. For females, peer loneliness and school climate (negatively) were predictors. The risk of being an indirect victim was greater for females who had a high perception of loneliness in relationships with peers and had a negative perception of school climate. In general, predictors of direct and indirect victimisation were quite similar, although for males, younger age as a predictor for direct victimisation was replaced by lower global self-esteem for indirect victimisation.

Table 3 also shows the results of the logistic regression analyses for cybervictimisation. Here, being a victim in direct and being a victim in indirect victimisation were added as predictors. In fact, being a victim of direct or indirect bullying was a very strong predictor of being a victim of cyberbullying: students involved as victims in traditional bullying (direct or indirect) were about two to three times more likely to be cybervictims than those who had no involvement in traditional bullying (see e^B values in Table 3). In addition, for males, family self-esteem (negatively) was a significant predictor; a low perception of family self-esteem increased the risk for males to be cybervictimised. For females, parent loneliness was a significant predictor; females who experienced loneliness with parents were more likely to be cybervictimised.

Discussion

This study aimed to describe the phenomena of direct, indirect and cybervictimisation, assessing the role of the perceptions of school climate, aspects of self-esteem, and loneliness with parents and peers, as predictors for both males and females. We sought to identify common risk factors which act in continuity across traditional bullying and cyberbullying, as well as any specific risk factors.

Looking first at gender differences among the risk factors examined (Table 1), males reported in general a worse perception of their school environment, consistently with Wang and Dishion (2011), who found that girls reported better academic support, school behaviour management, teacher social support and peer social support than boys. Significant differences were also found in self-esteem and loneliness. Males had higher scores in global self-esteem, family self-esteem and peer self-esteem. This is consistent with previous literature on gender differences in self-esteem (Falci 2011; Moksnes et al. 2010; McMullin and Cairney 2004; Wild et al. 2004; Melotti and Passini 2002; Dubois and Tevendale 1999; Kling et al. 1999). Concerning loneliness, in the present study females had higher scores on peer loneliness, confirming the trend described by Prezza, Pacilli, and Dinelli (2004), although other authors did not find any gender difference in this measure (Vanhalst et al. 2012).

The descriptive findings on the prevalence of traditional victimisation in terms of gender (Table 2) confirm much previous research; males are more represented among victims of direct bullying and females more as victims of indirect bullying (Owens, Shute, and Slee

2000; Russell et al. 2003). Females were also more represented as victims of cyberbullying, in accordance with some other studies (e.g. Li 2007). However, as suggested by Tokunaga (2010), gender differences in cyberbullying are rather inconsistent between studies.

When the analysis moved to considering the predictors of different types of victimisation and as a function of gender, a somewhat complex picture emerged (Table 3). For traditional victimisation, peer loneliness, followed by negative perceptions of school climate, were significant predictors of both direct and indirect victimisation, for both genders. Those students who felt high loneliness in peer relationships had a higher probability of being involved as victims in traditional bullying, as reported also by Crick and Grotpeter (1996). Socialisation within the peer group is functional to the process of the adolescent's social identity building, in a period of experimentation and 'psychosocial moratorium' such as adolescence (Erikson 1950; Marcia 1980). Victimised adolescents may lack the social competencies that make one a valued member of the peer group, such as friendliness, cooperativeness, prosocial skills and low social anxiety (Egan and Perry 1998).

The relevance of school climate as a predictor has also been reported in other studies on victimised peers of traditional bullying, as indexed by lower levels of school satisfaction and higher levels of school avoidance (Kochenderfer and Ladd 1996). Being victimised may lead to students developing negative attitudes, feelings and perceptions towards school, which may in turn expose potential victims to increasing experiences of social exclusion. A poor school climate may also indicate that school personnel are less likely to respond effectively to bullying incidents.

We found that younger age was a significant predictor only for males' direct victimisation; boys' aggressive behaviour, in fact, often involves direct physical aggression, yelling, and assertions of status and dominance, where age is more likely to be a factor than in indirect victimisation (Bjorkqvist, Osterman, and Kaukiainen 1992; McMaster et al. 2002).

Our data showed that lower global self-esteem was a significant predictor only for males' indirect victimisation. Leary and Downs (1995) consider self-esteem to be an internal representation of social acceptance and rejection and a psychological gauge monitoring the degree to which a person is included versus excluded by others. The association between low global self-esteem and relational bullying can be explained considering the nature of indirect aggression, which is largely based on the ability of a perpetrator to utilise the social group to ostracise; this kind of relational aggression may be particularly harmful, especially for adolescent boys, who are relying on group social acceptance for their identity formation.

Looking at the predictors of cybervictimisation (Table 3), our findings suggested a strong continuity or comorbidity between being either a direct or an indirect victim of traditional bullying, and being a victim in cyberbullying. However, there is also an element of specificity represented by the role of the family context. Overall, experiences of traditional and cybervictimisation overlap strongly. This finding is consistent with many previous studies (e.g. Tokunaga 2010; Smith 2012). The prevalence of cybervictimisation is relatively low (Table 1), but many cybervictims appear to be polyvictims, who may be highly vulnerable adolescents for whom the victimisation becomes a 24/7 experience and goes beyond the school boundaries.

Nevertheless, a few specific risk factors for cyberbullying were found (Table 3). We identified two such factors, family self-esteem and parent loneliness, which act differently as a function of gender: low family self-esteem for males, and greater loneliness in the relationship with parents for females, independently predicted cybervictimisation beyond any effects of traditional victimisation. In discussing these results, consideration should be given to the different dimensions that the constructs of self-esteem and loneliness actually measured. Items for measuring self-esteem were focused on self evaluation in relationship with parents (e.g. 'I feel OK about how important I am for my family', 'I feel OK about how I get along well with my family') and on feelings of belonging to the family. Items concerning loneliness from parents, although focused on evaluating family relationships, required an evaluation of how parents behave according to the adolescent's expectations (e.g. 'My parents spend time to pay me attention', 'My parents are ready to listen to me or to help me'). These two different aspects of evaluations of family relations seem to reflect different perspectives by which males and females look to their family functioning. For adolescent males, the adoption of a more 'self-centred perspective' (as in the family self-esteem measure) may reflect an ongoing process of autonomisation from parental models (Cramer 2000; Gilligan 1982), where the family stands as a reference point for elaborating a self-image and self-evaluation. Self-esteem, in this case, may reflect a cognitive evaluation linked to the relation with the family. For adolescent females, their identity involves a sense of connectedness and attachment to others which may lead them to critically judge their parents' behaviour, as in the parent loneliness measure (Cramer 2000; Patterson, Sochting, and Marcia 1992), supporting the idea that loneliness may refer to emotional, rather than cognitive, evaluation.

Despite the differences discussed above, both males and females show poor family relationships as a risk factor for becoming a cybervictim. Both low family self-esteem and high perceived loneliness in family relationships could reflect low levels of reciprocal involvement among family members, which could also imply lower parental monitoring of adolescents' activity on the Internet and longer periods of time spent online by adolescents, thus increasing the possibility of receiving online attacks. An association between positive parenting styles and a 'healthy' use of the Internet in adolescence has been demonstrated; lack of emotional involvement, lack of parental monitoring, and an authoritative or neglectful parenting style is associated with online harassment (Law, Shapka, and Olson 2010; Ybarra and Mitchell 2004), and Li Lei and Wu (2007) found that a pathological use of the Internet was positively associated with alienation, and negatively with trust and communication in family relationships.

Our study has contributed to the literature in this area by identifying both common and specific predictors of direct, indirect and cybervictimisation, as a function of gender. Adopting several measures of self-esteem and of loneliness, specifically those referred to the self, to peers and to family was helpful to highlight how these psychosocial variables may vary according to context (traditional versus online victimisation) and across genders.

However, some limitations of the study need to be taken into account. First, the data were collected in 2008–2009, and changes over a even few years in information and communication technology (ICT) use may limit generalisation to present-day situations. Secondly, a lenient criterion for victimisation was used in the regression analyses (including 'only once or twice') to maximise numbers, even though most studies on bullying use a stricter criterion owing to the criterion of repetition. Thirdly, the findings are limited to our north–central Italian sample, although this is reasonably representative in an Italian context.

Our findings may have some relevance for devising interventions to prevent cyberbullying. Educators and parents need to be aware of the easy transfer between offline and online attacks that victims may suffer, and consider how the school network may be involved in carrying on cyberviolence against victims. Online relationships often reflect those offline (Valkenburg and Peter 2007). A 'whole school approach' for preventing traditional bullying may also be effective in preventing cyberbullying, promoting a school climate where aggressive dynamics are rejected (Kärnä et al. 2011). Such intervention programmes may improve their effect by working to develop high self-esteem in students, as our study suggests how this dimension can be involved in victimisation experiences, in both the online and offline contexts. Moreover, specifically for cyberbullying victimisation, our results highlight the crucial role of family involvement. Both self-esteem and loneliness constructs are internal representations of social acceptance and rejection expressed by individuals. Since in this study these dimensions appear strongly related to family context for cybervictims, we suggest that intervention strategies should tackle specifically this relational environment, in order to help parents not only to increase their active control of what their children are doing online, but also to enhance their parenting skills in engaging their children in caring and affective relations. This is in line with the findings of Kerr and Stattin (2000) and Kerr, Stattin, and Burk (2010) that open and caring parent–child relationships are associated with better protected and well-adjusted children and adolescents than those who are closely controlled by parents, whether on the Internet or not.

To sum up, this study described the complexity of predictors involved in both traditional and cybervictimisation, thus contributing to our understanding of the many bullying phenomena in adolescence. Moreover, it delineates continuity as well as some discontinuities among the different forms of victimisation and between genders, and points to possible insights for intervention, since it stresses the differential influence of peer and family contexts in traditional and in cybervictimisation.

Acknowledgements

This research was supported by the DAPHNE Program II 2004–2008 (Proposal No. 06-1/0, with the project entitled 'An investigation into forms of peer–peer bullying at school in preadolescent and adolescent groups') and by the DAPHNE Program III 2007–2013 (with the project entitled 'Cyberbullying in adolescence: investigation and intervention in six European Countries' JLS/2008/DAP3/AG1211-30-CE-0311025/00-69). We are also grateful to all the students, teachers and parents who agreed to participate in the study. Special thanks to Charlene Petersen for her precious help in checking the English style.

References

Bjorkqvist, K., K. Osterman, and A. Kaukiainen. 1992. The development of direct and indirect aggressive strategies in males and females. In *Of mice and women: Aspects of female aggression*, ed. K. Bjorkqvist and P. Niemela, 51–64. New York: Academic Press.

Brighi, A. 2009. Il bullismo tradizionale e il bullismo elettronico: Aggressività e nuovi media. In *Bullismo elettronico. Fattori di rischio connessi alle nuove tecnologie*, ed. M.L. Genta, A. Brighi and A. Guarini, 23–28. Rome: Carocci.

Brighi, A., A. Guarini, A. Palermiti, M.G. Bartolo, and M.L. Genta. 2011. Victimization in traditional bullying and cyberbullying among Italian preadolescents. An investigation in Emilia Romagna, Tuscany and Calabria. *Giornale di Psicologia dello Sviluppo/Journal of Developmental Psychology* 100: 38–48.

Brighi, A., G. Melotti, A. Guarini, M.L. Genta, R. Ortega, J. Mora-Merchan, P.K. Smith, and F. Thompson. 2012. Self-esteem and loneliness in relation to cyberbullying in three European countries. In *Cyberbullying in the global playground: Research from international perspectives*, ed. Q. Li, D. Cross and P.K. Smith, 32–56. Chichester: Wiley-Blackwell.

Campfield, D.C. 2008. Cyber bullying and victimization: Psychosocial characteristics of bullies, victims, and bully/victims. Unpublished doctoral dissertation, University of Montana Missoula, MT, USA.

Cook, C.R., K.R. Williams, N.G. Guerra, T.E. Kim, and S. Sadek. 2010. Predictors of bullying and victimization in childhood and adolescence: A meta-analytic investigation. *School Psychology Quarterly* 25: 65–83.

Cramer, P. 2000. Development of identity: Gender makes a difference. *Journal of Research in Personality* 34: 42–72.

Crick, N.R., and J.K. Grotpeter. 1996. Children's treatment by peers: Victims of relational and overt aggression. *Development and Psychopathology* 8: 367–80.

Cross, D., T. Shaw, L. Hearn, M. Epstein, H. Monks, L. Lester, and L. Thomas. 2009. *Australian Covert Bullying Prevalence Study (ACBPS)*. Perth: Child Health Promotion Research Centre, Edith Cowan University.

Dubois, D.L., N. Felner, S. Brand, R.S.C. Phillips, and A.M. Lease. 1996. Early adolescent self-esteem: A developmental–ecological framework and assessment strategy. *Journal of Research on Adolescence* 6: 543–79.

Dubois, D.L., and H.D. Tevendale. 1999. Self-esteem in childhood and adolescence: Vaccine or epiphenomenon? *Applied and Preventive Psychology* 8: 103–17.

Egan, S.K., and D.G. Perry. 1998. Does low self-regard invite victimization? *Developmental Psychology* 34: 299–309.

Erikson, E.H. 1950. *Childhood and society*. New York: Norton.

Falci, C.D. 2011. Self-esteem and mastery trajectories in high school by social class and gender. *Social Science Research* 40: 586–601.

Fredstrom B.K., R.E. Adams, and R. Gilman. 2011. Electronic and school-based victimization: Unique contexts for adjustment difficulties during adolescence. *Journal of Youth and Adolescence* 40, no. 4: 405–15.

Genta, M.L., A. Brighi, and A. Guarini. 2009. European project on bullying and cyberbullying granted by Daphne II Programme. *Zeitschrift für Psychologie/Journal of Psychology* 217: 233.

Genta, M.L., P.K. Smith, R. Ortega, A. Brighi, A. Guarini, F. Thompson, N. Tippett, J. Mora-Merchan, and J. Calmaestra. 2012. Comparative aspects of cyberbullying in Italy, England and Spain: Findings from a DAPHNE Project. In *Cyberbullying in the global playground: Research from international perspectives*, ed. Q. Li, D. Cross, and P.K Smith, 15–31. Chichester: Wiley-Blackwell.

Gilligan, C. 1982. *In a different voice*. Cambridge, MA: Harvard University Press.

Gini, G., and T. Pozzoli. 2009. Association between bullying and psychosomatic problems: A meta-analysis. *Pediatrics* 123: 1059–65.

Goossens, L., and A. Marcoen. 1999. Relationships during adolescence: Constructive vs. negative themes and relational dissatisfaction. *Journal of Adolescence* 22: 65–79.

Guarini, A., A. Brighi, and M.L. Genta. 2010. Cyberbullying among Italian adolescents. In *Cyberbullying: A cross-national comparison*, ed. J. Mora-Merchan and T. Jaeger, 114–30. Landau: Verlag Emprische Padagogik.

Hawker, D.S.J., and M.J. Boulton. 2000. Twenty years' research on peer victimization and psychosocial maladjustment. A meta-analytic review of cross-sectional studies. *Journal of Child Psychology and Psychiatry* 41: 441–55.

Kärnä, A., M. Voeten, T. Little, E. Poskiparta, A. Kaljonen, and C. Salmivalli. 2011. A large-scale evaluation of the KiVa antibullying program: Grades 4–6. *Child Development* 82: 311–30.

Kerr, M., and H. Stattin. 2000. What parents know, how they know it, and several forms of adolescent adjustment: Further support for a reinterpretation of monitoring. *Developmental Psychology* 36: 366–80.

Kerr, M., H. Stattin, and W.J. Burk. 2010. A reinterpretation of parental monitoring in longitudinal perspective. *Journal of Research on Adolescence* 20: 39–64.

Kling, K.C., J.S. Hyde, C.J. Showers, and B.N. Buswell. 1999. Gender differences in self-esteem: A meta-analysis. *Psychological Bulletin* 125: 470–500.

Kochenderfer, B.J., and G.W. Ladd. 1996. Peer victimization: Cause or consequence of school maladjustment? *Child Development* 67: 1305–17.

Kowalski, R.M., S.P. Limber and P.W. Agatston. 2012. *Cyberbullying: Bullying in the digital age* (2nd ed.). Chichester: Wiley-Blackwell.

Law, D.M., J.D. Shapka, and B.F. Olson. 2010. To control or not to control? Parenting behaviours and adolescent online aggression. *Computers in Human Behavior* 26: 1651–6.

Law, D.M., J.D. Shapka, S. Hymel, B.F. Olson, and T. Waterhouse. 2012. The changing face of bullying: An empirical comparison between traditional and internet bullying and victimization. *Computers in Human Behavior* 28: 226–32.

Leary, M.R., and D.L. Downs. 1995. Interpersonal functions of the self-esteem motive: The self-esteem system as a sociometer. In *Efficacy, agency, and self-esteem*, ed. M.H. Kernis, 123–44. New York: Plenum.

Li, Q. 2007. New bottle but old wine: A research of cyberbullying in schools. *Computers in Human Behavior* 23: 1–15.

Li Lei, Y., and M.A. Wu. 2007. Adolescents' paternal attachment and Internet use. *Cyberpsychology & Behavior* 10: 633–9.

Marcia, J.E. 1980. Identity in adolescence. In *Handbook of adolescent psychology*, ed. J. Adelson, 159–87. New York: Wiley.

Marcoen, A., and L. Goossens. 1993. Loneliness, attitude towards aloneness, and solitude: Age differences and developmental significance during adolescence. In *Adolescence and its social worlds*, ed. S. Jackson and H. Rodriguez-Tomé, 197–227. Hove: Lawrence Erlbaum.

Marcoen, A., L. Goossens, and P. Caes. 1987. Loneliness in pre- through late adolescence: Exploring the contributions of a multidimensional approach. *Journal of Youth and Adolescence* 16: 561–76.

McGuckin, C., P.K. Cummins, and C.A. Lewis. 2010. f2f and cyberbullying among children in Northern Ireland: Data from the Kids Life and Times Surveys. *Psychology, Society, & Education* 2: 83–96.

McMaster, L., J. Connolly, D.J. Pepler, and W.M. Craig. 2002. Peer to peer sexual harassment among early adolescents. *Developmental Psychopathology* 14: 91–105.

McMullin, J.A., and J. Cairney. 2004. Self-esteem and the intersection of age, class, and gender. *Journal of Aging Studies* 18: 75–90.

Melotti, G., R. Biolcati, and S. Passini. 2009. A psychosocial reading of cyberbullying. In *Bullying and cyberbullying in adolescence*, ed. M.L. Genta, A. Brighi and A. Guarini, 40–58. Rome: Carocci.

Melotti, G., P. Corsano, M. Majorano, and P. Scarpuzzi. 2006. An Italian application of the Louvain Loneliness Scale for Children and Adolescents (LLCA). *TPM-Testing, Psychometrics, Methodology in Applied Psychology* 13: 237–55.

Melotti, G., and S. Passini. 2002. L'applicazione ad un gruppo di adolescenti italiani del Self-esteem Questionnaire (SEQ). *Bollettino di Psicologia Applicata* 238: 59–70.

Moksnes, U.K., I.E.O. Moljord, G.A. Espnes, and D.G. Byrne. 2010. The association between stress and emotional states in adolescents: The role of gender and self-esteem. *Personality and Individual Differences* 49: 430–5.

Ortega, R., J. Calmaestra, and J. Mora-Merchán. 2007. Cyberbullying. *International Journal of Psychology and Psychological Therapy* 8: 183–92.

Owens, L., R. Shute, and R. Slee. 2000. 'I'm in and you're out': Explanations for teenage girls' indirect aggression. *Psychology, Evaluation and Gender* 2: 19–46.

Patchin, J.W., and S. Hinduja. 2010. Cyberbullying and self-esteem. *Journal of School Health* 80: 614–21.

Patterson, S., I. Sochting, and J. Marcia. 1992. The inner space and beyond: Women and identity. In *Adolescent identity formation*, ed. G. Adams, T. Gullotta and R. Montemayor, 9–24. Newbury Park: Sage.

Perren, S., J. Dooley, T. Shaw, and D. Cross. 2010. Bullying in school and cyberspace: Associations with depressive symptoms in Swiss and Australian adolescents. *Child and Adolescent Psychiatry and Mental Health* 4: 28.

Prezza, M., M.G. Pacilli, and S. Dinelli. 2004, Loneliness and new technologies in a group of Roman adolescents. *Computers in Human Behavior* 20: 691–709.

Raskauskas, J., and A.D. Stoltz. 2007. Involvement in traditional and electronic bullying among adolescents. *Developmental Psychology* 43: 564–75.

Russell, A., C.H. Hart, C.C. Robinson, and S.F. Olsen. 2003. Children's sociable and aggressive behaviour with peers: A comparison of the US and Australia, and contributions of temperament and parenting styles. *International Journal of Behavioral Development* 27: 74–86.

Sahin, M. 2012. The relationship between the cyberbullying/cybervictimization and loneliness among adolescents. *Children and Youth Services Review* 34: 834–7.

Slonje, R., and P.K. Smith. 2008. Cyberbullying: Another main type of bullying?. *Scandinavian Journal of Psychology* 49: 147–54.

Smith, P.K. 2012. Cyberbullying and cyber aggression. In *Handbook of school violence and school safety: International research and practice*, ed. S R. Jimerson, A B. Nickerson, M J. Mayer and M J. Furlong, 93–103. New York: Routledge.

Smith, P.K., J. Mahdavi, M. Carvalho, S. Fisher, S. Russell, and N. Tippett. 2008. Cyberbullying: Its nature and impact in secondary school pupils. *Journal of Child Psychology and Psychiatry* 49: 376–85.

Sourander, A., A. Brunstein Klomek, M. Ikonen, J. Lindroos, T. Luntamo, M. Koskelainen, T. Ristkari, and H. Helenius. 2010. Psychosocial risk factors associated with cyberbullying among adolescents. *Archives of General Psychiatry* 67: 720–8.

Tokunaga, R.S. 2010. Following you home from school: A critical review and synthesis of research on cyberbullying victimization. *Computers in Human Behavior* 26: 277–87.

Valkenburg, P.M., and J. Peter. 2007. Pre-adolescents' and adolescents' online communication and their closeness to friends. *Developmental Psychology* 43: 267–77.

Vanhalst J., L. Goossens, K. Luyckx, R.H. Scholte, and R.C. Engels. 2012. The development of loneliness from mid- to late adolescence: Trajectory classes, personality traits, and psychosocial functioning. *J. Adolesc*. PMID: 22560517.

Walther, J.B., and M.R. Parks. 2002. Cues filtered out, cues filtered in computer-mediated communication and relationships. In *Handbook of interpersonal communication*, ed. M.L. Knapp and J.A. Daly, 529–63. Thousand Oaks, CA: Sage.

Wang, M.T., and T.J. Dishion. 2012. The trajectories of adolescents' perceptions of school climate, deviant peer affiliation, and behavioral problems during the middle school years. *Journal of Research on Adolescence* 22: 40–53.

Wild, L.G., A.J. Flisher, A. Bhana, and C. Lombard. 2004. Associations among adolescent risk behaviours and self-esteem in six domains. *Journal of Child Psychology and Psychiatry* 45: 1454–67.

Willard, N.E. 2007. *Cyberbullying and cyberthreats: Responding to the challenge of online social aggression, threats, and distress*. Champaign, IL: Research Press.

Wolak, J., K. Mitchell, and D. Finkelhor. 2007. Unwanted and wanted exposure to online pornography in a national sample of youth internet users. *Pediatrics* 119: 247–57.

Ybarra, M.L., and K. Mitchell. 2004. Youth engaging in online harassment: Associations with caregiver–child relationships, Internet use, and personal characteristics. *Journal of Adolescence* 27: 319–36.

Victims' perceptions of traditional and cyberbullying, and the psychosocial correlates of their victimisation

Marilyn Campbell[a], Barbara Spears[b], Phillip Slee[c], Des Butler[d] and Sally Kift[d]

[a]*School of Learning and Professional Studies, Queensland University of Technology, Brisbane, Australia;* [b]*Centre for Research in Education, University of South Australia, Adelaide, Australia;* [c]*School of Education, Flinders University, Adelaide, Australia;* [d]*Faculty of Law, Queensland University of Technology, Brisbane, Australia*

It is well recognised that there are serious correlates for victims of traditional bullying. These have been shown to include increased levels of depression, anxiety and psychosomatic symptoms, in addition to often severe physical harm and even suicide. Bullied students also feel more socially ineffective and have greater interpersonal difficulties, together with higher absenteeism from school and lower academic competence. In the emerging field of cyberbullying many researchers have hypothesised a greater impact and more severe consequences for victims because of the 24/7 nature and the possibility of the wider audience with this form of bullying. However, to date there is scarce empirical evidence to support this. This study sought to compare victims' perceptions of the harshness and impact of bullying by traditional and cyber means. The major findings showed that although students who had been victimised by traditional bullying reported that they felt their bullying was harsher and crueller and had more impact on their lives than those students who had been cyberbullied, the correlates of their mental health revealed that cybervictims reported significantly more social difficulties, and higher levels of anxiety and depression than traditional victims. The implications for school counsellors and mental health workers are discussed.

Introduction

It is well established that traditional bullying has negative associations for both the students who are victims and those who bully. The correlates of traditional bullying for victims include increased levels of depression, anxiety and psychosomatic symptoms (Reijntjs et al. 2010). While the direction of causality is still not established, some longitudinal studies in the past decade have shown that students who have been victimised by bullies are at greater future risk for somatic symptoms, anxiety and depression (Fekkes et al. 2006; Kim et al. 2006) and that young children with internalising problems such as withdrawal and anxiety–depression show an increased risk of being bullied (Arseneault et al. 2006, 2008). It has also been found in one longitudinal study (Carbone-Lopez, Esbensen, and Brick 2010) that there were different detrimental associations for girls and boys who had been bullied; girls who had been indirectly bullied increased their drug use whereas boys did not, and while victimised girls showed lower self-esteem this did not occur for boys. In a meta-analysis of 18 longitudinal studies, Reijntjs et al. (2010) found that there were significant associations between peer victimisation and subsequent changes in internalising problems, as well as vice versa: between internalising problems and subsequent changes in peer victimisation. Thus, it was shown that internalising problems function as both antecedents and consequences of peer victimisation. Although these longitudinal studies are not proof of a causal relationship between bullying victimisation and mental health problems, they do suggest a cyclical pattern of influence.

As cyberbullying differs from traditional bullying owing to the characteristics of the medium used to bully, it has been hypothesised that its effects could be more severe than those of traditional bullying (Campbell 2005). Depending on the particular circumstances, reasons for this may include a wider audience, anonymity of the bully, the more enduring nature of the written word and images, and the ability to reach the target at any time and in any place, including the target's home. Furthermore, cyberbullies may feel emboldened because they cannot see their targets or their immediate responses and believe that, because of their anonymity, they will not be detected. It has been suggested that this anonymity may increase the intensity of the attacks and encourage them to continue for longer than they would otherwise do face-to-face (Conn 2004).

While it is true that cyberbullying can only threaten physical violence rather than inflict it, research has shown that verbal and psychological bullying may have more negative long-term effects for the victims (Reid, Monsen, and Rivers 2004). To date, cross-sectional studies of cyberbullying victimisation have measured the impact in terms of emotional correlates, the subjective perception of impact and the association with mental health through relatively simple measures, identifying that students who have been cyberbullied do report increased emotional stress, compared with those not bullied. This has been shown where students were asked to self-report which specific emotion they had experienced when cyberbullied. In an Australian study of 548 cyberbullying victims, it was reported that students said they felt sad, annoyed, embarrassed and afraid (Price and Dalgleish 2010). This reflects what is known about the emotions associated with the earliest studies of traditional bullying (e.g. Rigby and Slee 1993). Anxiety, feeling bad about oneself and not trusting people have also been reported by cybervictims (Raskauskas 2010). Anger was the most dominant emotion for both cyber and traditional victims in a Spanish sample of 12–17-year-olds (Ortega et al. 2009). More severe cyberbullying, however, was correlated with a profile of emotions labelled 'alone, defenceless and depressed' (Ortega et al. 2009, 202).

Cyberbullying can also have a subjective impact as measured by students' perceptions of the harshness and impact of the bullying on them. Student interview data recently collected in Australia showed that many young people feel that cyberbullying is far more harmful than traditional bullying. Some reasons for this include: the finding that nearly 50% of those bullied indicated they did not know who was doing the bullying, many finding it hard to get away from the bullying, which now followed them into their home; and more young people claiming that they would bully others more often using technology and that they could be nastier than they could be face-to-face (Cross et al. 2009). Spears et al. (2009), in their qualitative study of the impact and human dimension of covert and cyberbullying, found that cyberbullying in particular, evoked more than anger and sadness, i.e. strong, negative feelings and emotions and fear and concerns for safety; impacting on self; and dislocating and disrupting relationships (194). However, Smith et al. (2008) found that students qualified the impact of cyberbullying according to the medium employed; they felt that text messaging and email bullying had less of an impact than traditional bullying, but that bullying by pictures or video clips had a higher negative impact than traditional bullying, suggesting a continuum of subjective impact overlapping both forms of bullying.

However, the data from the three preceding studies were collected from all students and not only those who were victims of cyberbullying.

So far as victims are concerned, as well as the potential for impacting on well-being, cyberbullying has been found to impact on their mental health in the form of depression (Gradinger, Strohmeier, and Spiel 2009). Raskauskas (2010) found in a New Zealand study of secondary school students (11–18 years old) that cybervictims reported significantly more depressive symptoms than non-victims, with all victims reporting above the cut-off score of mild to moderate symptoms on the depression measure, and those experiencing cyberbullying more frequently having an increase in self-reported depressive symptoms. These findings were supported by an Australian and Swiss comparison of secondary school students where cybervictimisation was a significant predictor of depressive symptoms. In addition, this predictor was found to be over and above that of being victimised by traditional bullying (Perren et al. 2010). Students who have been cyberbullied have also been shown to have significantly lower self-esteem than those who were not cyberbullied (Patchin and Hinduja 2010).

This study aimed to ascertain the perceptions of students who had been cyberbullied and their mental health. We hypothesised that those students who had been cyberbullied would perceive this bullying as harsher and more impactful on their lives than students who had been traditionally bullied. We also examined the association of being bullied by any form with students' mental health, as measured by their symptoms of social difficulty, depression, anxiety and stress. We hypothesised that cyberbullied students would report more elevated scores on these measures than traditionally bullied students.

Method

Participants

Data came from a large-scale school-based survey of students' bullying experiences; 3112 students from grades 6–12 (1572 girls, 50.5%, and 1535 boys, 49.4%; five missing data) from 29 different schools, both government and non-government, in three Australian states participated. The age range was from 9 to 19 years ($M = 13.96$, $SD = 1.87$). Most students were able to access the Internet from their home (87.5%) and owned their own mobile (cell) phone (83.1%).

Procedure

Ethical clearance was obtained from the universities involved and the various educational systems as well as the participating schools. Participation was voluntary and only students who wished to participate and had written parental consent took part. Approximately 30% of eligible students undertook the survey, owing to the active parental consent required. No data were available from students who did not return the parental consent form and therefore the demographics of non-responders were not available. The surveys were administered to students in their classrooms during class time by a research assistant, and standardised instructions were read out loud to participants prior to survey administration. There were between 15 and 25 students per testing session and each session took 30–45 minutes. The anonymity of the survey responses was emphasised verbally and in writing to the students. The survey was conducted between August and September 2009 (term 3), when students had spent the previous 6–7 months of the school year together.

Measures

An anonymous, self-report paper-based survey was conducted, consisting of four sections. The first section asked for demographic information of gender, age and year of school, Internet access at home and ownership of a mobile (cell) phone.

The second section obtained information about cyberbullying experiences. The following definition of cyberbullying was provided, following the recommendations of Solberg and Olweus (2003) that definitions improve the validity of responses:

> Cyberbullying is when one person or a group of people repeatedly try to hurt or embarrass another person, *using their computer or mobile phone*, to use power over them. With cyberbullying, the person bullying usually has some advantage over the person targeted, and it is done on purpose to hurt them, not like an accident or when friends tease each other.

A filter question of 'Have you been cyberbullied this year?' (since January this year) was used to establish cybervictimisation, and a question 'Have you cyberbullied someone this year' to establish cyberbullies and cyberbully–victims. (The data on bullies will be published in another paper.) If the students answered 'no', they were directed to skip this section. If they answered 'yes,' they were asked three questions concerning feelings when cyberbullied: (1) how they felt, (2) how harsh or cruel the cyberbullying experienced was considered to be, and (3) how much of an impact the cyberbullying was thought to have had on their life. The first question used forced choice from a set of emotions previously found in the literature. The following two questions were answered on a five-point Likert scale from 'not at all harsh' to 'really harsh', and from 'no impact' to 'huge impact'.

The third section asked about traditional or face-to-face bullying experiences mirroring the cyberbullying questions. The following definition of face-to-face bullying was provided:

> There are lots of different ways to bully someone. A bully wants to hurt the other person (it's not an accident) and does it repeatedly and unfairly (the bully has some advantage over the victim). Sometimes a group of students will bully another student.

The fourth section of the survey used the Strengths and Difficulties Questionnaire (SDQ) to ascertain interpersonal difficulties, and the Depression Anxiety Stress Scale (DASS-21) to ascertain mental health symptoms.

The SDQ (Goodman 1997) is a self-report (11–17 years version) behavioural screening device that measures both positive and negative attributes. It has 25 items divided into five subscales: emotional symptoms, conduct problems, hyperactivity/inattention, peer relationship problems and prosocial behaviour; each subscale has five items. All subscales except for prosocial behaviour are summed to obtain a total 'difficulties' score. For each item, participants indicate, on a three-point scale, how things had been for them over the last six months. The reliabilities for the SDQ for the current study using Cronbach's alpha were: 0.75 for emotional symptoms, 0.61 for conduct problems, 0.66 for hyperactivity/inattention, 0.57 for peer relationship problems, 0.75 for prosocial behaviour and 0.82 for the total difficulties scale.

The Depression Anxiety Stress Scale (DASS-21) (Lovibond and Lovibond 1995) is a 42-item self-report measure. We used a short form of 21 items, with three seven-item subscales of depression, anxiety and stress. Participants rate the extent to which they experienced each state over the past week on a four-point Likert rating scale. Summed scores can be calculated for each subscale, and a total score obtained by summing all 21 items. The scores for all items were doubled to ensure consistency with the original 42-item version of the scale. The alpha coefficients obtained for the current study were 0.90 for depression, 0.85 for anxiety, 0.87 for stress and 0.95 for the total scale.

The survey ended with a list of counselling services available in the area for any students who became distressed or wanted more information on bullying.

Results

Students self-reported whether they had been traditionally or cyberbullied, and whether they had traditionally or cyberbullied others, by a filter question of yes or no during that school year. This resulted in six groups of victims: 16.1% ($n = 500$) classified as traditional victims only (group 1), 4.5% ($n = 139$) as cybervictims only (group 2), 4.5% ($n = 140$) as both cyber and traditional victims (group 3), 4.7% ($n = 147$) as traditional bully–victims (group 4), 1.5% ($n = 48$) as cyberbully–victims (group 5), and 5.4% ($n = 169$) as both cyber and traditional bully–victims (group 6) (Table 1).

Gender and age

There was no significant difference in gender in the traditional victim only group (group 1) or the traditional 'bully–victim' group (group 4). There was a significant difference in gender, with more girls than boys in the cybervictims only group (group 2)[($t(3105) = -2.65, p < 0.01$], the combined traditional and cybervictims group (group 3) [$t(3105) = -5.24, p < 0.001$] and the combined traditional and cyberbully–victims group (group 6) [$t(3105) = -2.14, p < 0.05$]. However, more boys than girls were classified as cyberbully–victims (group 5) [$t(3105) = 2.41, p < 0.05$].

Age differences found for the following groups: traditional victims ($r = -0.135$, $p < 0.001$), both traditional and cybervictims ($r = -0.080$, $p < 0.001$) and traditional bully–victims only ($r = -0.069$, $p < 0.001$) (all slightly less frequent at older ages). No other groups had any significant age differences.

Table 1. Number and gender of cyber and traditional victims and bully–victims.

	Gender		
	Male	Female	Total number
Cyberbullying			
Victims	53 (3.5%)*	85 (5.4%)*	139 (4.5%)
Bully–victims	32 (2.1%)*	16 (1%)*	48 (1.5%)
Traditional bullying			
Victims	230 (15%)	269 (17.1%)	500 (16.1%)
Bully–victims	74 (4.8%)	73 (4.6%)	147 (4.7%)
Cyber and traditional bullying			
Victims	39 (2.5%)*	101 (6.4%)*	140 (4.5%)
Bully–victims	70 (4.6%)*	99 (6.3%)*	169 (5.4%)
Uninvolved students	939 (61.2%)	871 (55.4%)	1813 (58.3%)

Note: *Significant difference between genders ($p < 0.001$).

Harshness

Of the traditional victims, 66% perceived this type of victimisation as being harsh or very harsh; the corresponding figures were 58.7% for victims of cyberbullying, 59% for traditional bully–victims and 50% for cyberbully–victims.

No gender differences were found in ratings of harshness for traditional victims only or for traditional bully–victims. However, female cybervictims rated the harshness of their cyberbullying ($M = 2.14$) more than male cybervictims ($M = 1.63$) [$t(130) = -2.23$, $p < 0.05$]. No age differences were found for ratings of the harshness of their experiences for three of the groups of victims: cybervictims, traditional victims or cyberbully–victims. There were, however, age differences in the perception of harshness of the bullying experienced for the traditional bully–victims ($r = -0.231, p < 0.01$), with younger age groups rating the bullying as harsher than older age groups.

Impact

Of the traditionally bullied victims, 36.8% believed that this bullying had a great impact on their lives; the corresponding figures were 29.6% for cybervictims, 30% for traditional bully–victims and 23% for cyberbully–victims.

There were gender differences. For those students who were traditional victims, females ($M = 1.41$) rated the bullying as more impactful than males ($M = 1.03$) [$t(486) = -3.70$, $p < 0.001$]. For those who were cybervictims, females ($M = 1.30$) rated the bullying as having more impact on their lives than males ($M = 0.67$) [$t(129) = -2.63$, $p < 0.05$]. Female traditional bully–victims ($M = 2.06$) also reported that the bullying had more of an impact on their lives than male traditional bully–victims ($M = 0.88$) [$t(142) = -2.47$, $p < 0.05$]. There were no age differences in the perception of impact for traditional victims, cybervictims or traditional bully–victims. However, there were age differences in the perception of impact for cyberbully–victims ($r = -0.292$, $p < 0.05$), with younger bully–victims rating the bullying as having more of an impact than older age groups.

Of those who reported that they were both traditional and cybervictims, and who completed the question regarding their perceptions of the severity of each form of bullying ($n = 96$), 59.4% ($n = 57$) indicated that traditional bullying was worse than cyberbullying, 12.5% ($n = 12$) felt that cyberbullying was worse, and 28.1% ($n = 27$) thought both forms were about the same. Of the 90 who reported being both traditional and cyberbully–victims and who completed the question, 47.7% ($n = 43$) reported that traditional bullying was worse, 16.7% ($n = 15$) felt that cyberbullying was worse, and 35.5% ($n = 32$) thought they were much the same.

The three highest reported feelings of cybervictims were being angry, feeling nothing and feeling sad. Cyberbully–victims, however, ranked feeling nothing as the highest response, followed by feeling angry and feeling sad. For traditional victims only and traditional bully–victims the three highest reported emotional responses were feeling angry, sad and embarrassed (Table 2).

Mental health

A multivariate analysis of variance (MANOVA) of victims (traditional, cyber, both cyber and traditional victims, traditional bully–victims, cyberbully–victims and both traditional and cyberbully–victims) by social difficulties and mental health (SDQ and DASS-21) showed significant differences [$F(10,2032) = 10.94$, $p < 0.001$; Hotelling's Trace $T = 0.011$, partial $\varepsilon^2 = 0.051$]. An examination of the univariate results showed

Table 2. Reported feelings of victims.

Feelings	Cybervictims	Cyberbully–victims	Traditional victims	Traditional bully–victims
Angry	48 (34%)	14 (29%)	243 (49%)	82 (56%)
Sad	34 (24%)	6 (13%)	173 (35%)	47 (32%)
Humiliated	12 (9%)	3 (6%)	86 (17%)	21 (14%)
Scared	22 (16%)	4 (8%)	45 (9%)	14 (9.5%)
Embarrassed	11 (8%)	4 (8%)	98 (20%)	33 (22%)
Felt nothing	42 (30%)	24 (50%)	68 (14%)	23 (18%)

there was a significant difference on the SDQ total difficulties scores [$F(5,1018) = 18.19$, $p < 0.001$] and the DASS total score [$F(5,1018) = 12.37$, $p < 0.001$], between cybervictims and traditional victims.

Strengths and Difficulties Questionnaire

A post-hoc analysis using Tukey's HSD showed significant differences on the SDQ total difficulties scores between *traditional victims* and both traditional and cybervictims, traditional bully–victims and combined cyber and traditional bully–victims. *Cybervictims* also differed significantly on the SDQ total difficulties scores from both traditional and cybervictims and combined cyber and traditional bully–victims. Those who identified as *both traditional and cybervictims* differed significantly from traditional victims and traditional bully–victims. *Traditional bully–victims* also differed from traditional victims, both traditional and cybervictims and combined cyber and traditional bully–victims. There were no significant differences on the SDQ total difficulties scores between *cyberbully–victims* and all the other categories. *Combined cyber and traditional bully–victims* differed from traditional victims, cybervictims and traditional bully–victims. A combination of forms of bullying, traditional and cyber, as well as roles in bullying, victim or bully–victim, correlated with the total difficulties scores on the SDQ, with bully–victims scoring higher than victims only.

Depression, Anxiety, Stress Scale

A post-hoc analysis using Tukey's HSD showed differences in DASS total scores for *traditional victims* and both traditional and cybervictims and combined cyber and traditional bully–victims. *Cybervictims* also differed significantly on the DASS total score from both traditional and cybervictims. Those who identified as *both traditional and cybervictims* differed from traditional victims, cybervictims, traditional bully–victims and cyberbully–victims on the total DASS score. *Traditional bully–victims* also differed from both traditional and cybervictims and combined cyber and traditional bully–victims. There were significant differences in DASS total scores for *cyberbully–victims* and both traditional and cybervictims. *Combined cyber and traditional bully victims* differed from traditional victims and traditional bully–victims on the total DASS score. The form of bullying, as well as the role, again influenced students' total DASS scores, with the form of bullying, traditional, increasing the score more than the role of victim or bully–victim.

Traditionally bullied students reported lower social difficulties than those who had been cyberbullied (Table 3). Regardless of the type of bullying, all students who reported having

Table 3. Mean scores for victims and bully–victims.

	Strengths and Difficulties Questionnaire (SDQ)						DASS-21			
	Emotional symptoms score	Conduct problem score	Hyperactivity score	Peer problem score	Total Difficulties score	Prosocial behaviour score	Depression	Anxiety	Stress	DASS total
Cyberbullying										
Victims	3.5 (2.74)	2.3 (2.20)	4.1 (2.29)	2.5 (2.10)	12.5 (7.06)	6.9 (2.38)	11.16 (11.91)	8.23 (9.83)	11.36 (9.94)	30.84 (29.71)
Bully–victims	2.5 (2.36)	3.0 (2.22)	4.7 (2.25)	3.2 (2.13)	13.5 (6.12)	5.7 (2.94)	8.05 (8.23)	7.22 (9.58)	9.56 (8.63)	24.83 (24.81)
Traditional bullying										
Victims	3.1 (2.55)	2.0 (1.61)	3.7 (2.31)	2.2 (1.80)	11.0 (5.94)	7.6 (1.93)	7.72 (9.17)	6.00 (7.10)	9.29 (8.60)	23.02 (22.53)
Bully–victims	3.1 (2.56)	2.8 (2.02)	4.6 (2.35)	2.1 (1.74)	12.7 (5.88)	6.7 (2.21)	8.13 (9.68)	6.57 (7.29)	10.61 (9.62)	25.31 (24.45)
Cyber and traditional bullying										
Victims	4.7 (2.82)	2.7 (1.89)	4.5 (2.22)	3.3 (2.15)	15.3 (6.48)	7.5 (2.05)	14.62 (12.00)	11.73 (10.00)	15.35 (10.92)	41.70 (29.83)
Bully–victims	4.0 (2.67)	3.6 (2.20)	5.1 (2.26)	2.9 (2.12)	15.6 (6.52)	6.4 (2.59)	12.09 (12.12)	9.41 (10.39)	14.13 (11.15)	35.63 (31.55)
Uninvolved students	2.5 (2.24)	1.8 (1.68)	3.7 (2.20)	1.7 (1.63)	9.7 (5.68)	7.1 (2.09)	5.92 (8.66)	4.75 (7.18)	6.9 (8.29)	17.57 (22.28)

Note: Data are shown as mean (SD). DASS-21: Depression Anxiety Stress Scale.

been victimised had significantly higher scores on mental health measures than those who had not been bullied. In addition, the students who had been cyberbullied were significantly more anxious and depressed than the students who had been traditionally bullied. Those who were bullied in both ways had similar anxiety and depression scores to cyberbullying victims.

Discussion

This current study adds to the literature on the harshness and impact of victimisation by comparing the perceptions of students who have been (1) cyberbullied, (2) traditionally bullied, or (3) bullied by both forms; and (4) traditional bully–victims, (5) cyberbully–victims, and (6) both traditional and cyberbully–victims. The study also examined the association of being bullied in the various forms with students' mental health, as measured by their symptoms of social difficulty, depression, anxiety and stress.

The major findings of this study showed that although students who had been victimised by traditional bullying reported that they felt their bullying was harsher and crueller and had more impact on their lives than those students who had been cyberbullied, the correlates of their mental health revealed that cybervictims reported significantly more social difficulties, and higher levels of anxiety and depression than traditional victims. Importantly, those who were bullied in both ways had similar anxiety and depression scores to cyberbullying victims, suggesting the power of cybervictimisation to impact over and above traditional victimisation. These findings are in line with researchers' hypotheses that cyberbullying would have greater effects on victims than traditional bullying.

In addition, victims' perceptions of the severity, harshness and impact of bullying were found to be a function of gender and type, with girls reporting more victimisation through traditional and cyber means than boys. This qualification of impact and severity is in line with Slonje and Smith's (2008) study, which reported that students in general tempered their views on the impact of cyberbullying according to the medium employed, suggesting a subjective continuum of impact in relation to cyber and traditional bullying. While their study reported that students perceived that text and email bullying were less impactful than traditional bullying, and that cyberbullying using static or video images was the most impacting, in the current study, victims' perceptions of impact differed according to their gender and victimisation experiences (traditional, cyber or both, and as victim or bully–victim).

Surprisingly, this study found that students who had been *traditionally* bullied rated their bullying experience as harsher than those who had been cyberbullied. This was further emphasised by those students who had been bullied by both forms: traditional bullying was still rated to be the harsher form of the two. This is in contrast to studies where students have expressed the opinion that cyberbullying is harsher than traditional bullying because of the possible anonymity of the bully, that it is hard to get away from the cyberbully and that cyberbullies can be nastier (Cross et al. 2009; Spears et al. 2009). These previous studies, however, asked all students about their perceptions of their experience and not only those students who had been bullied. As will be discussed below, perceptions of harshness and impact could be an artefact of the presence of a real, known audience, versus an unknown, cyber one. On the other hand, perhaps the immediacy of the physicality of traditional bullying seems harsher than text or pictures.

Students who were traditional victims also perceived that this form of bullying had more of an impact on their lives than those who had been cyberbullied. Again, this was surprising, given the hypotheses associated with the unique aspects linked with online bullying: the wider audience, the anonymity of the bully; the more enduring nature of the written word; and the ability to reach the target anytime and anywhere have led adults to consider that this form of bullying could be perceived as harsher and more impactful than traditional bullying.

Gender and age differences revealed that girls, who were victimised either by cyberbullying or by traditional bullying, reported that their bullying was harsher and had more impact on their lives than boys. This is perhaps because girls' bullying relies on covert manipulation of friendship structures within the peer group (Leckie 1996, 1997) and that they are more distressed by any kind of bullying owing to their emphasis on peer evaluation and the importance of maintaining relationships (Rudolph and Conley 2005).

Most students who reported being victimised also reported experiencing anger more than other emotions, as found in the study by Ortega et al. (2009); however, it was those being victimised through traditional means, rather than those being cyberbullied, who reported feeling more anger, humiliation and embarrassment overall. This could account for why these students felt that their bullying was harsher and crueller and had more impact on their lives than those students who had been cyberbullied.

The role of the audience and bystanders needs consideration here, particularly in terms of future research. Although it has been speculated that the wider audience online could potentially cause more harm to victims through extended humiliation and embarrassment, this does not seem to be so in this sample. The power of the known, actual peers may cause greater humiliation than an unknown, potential audience online. Bystanders who are physical witnesses to traditional bullying could cause students more anger, embarrassment and humiliation through their immediate, real, physical presence and their actual contribution to the power of the social dynamic. The *potential* audience may not be perceived to be comprised of peers known to them; rather, it is an anonymous ether, not visible or tangible in terms of those who matter most to them at this time: their at-school peers. The abstract nature of a *potential, largely unknown* audience may also mean that for young people in this study, online humiliation and embarrassment is not highly relevant, whereas the *actual* audience poses a more immediate threat to these concerns. Consideration of these cognitive elements related to being bullied on and offline is an area of future research and one which could shed further light on young people's perceptions of victimisation. By contrast, victims of cyberbullying, in reporting higher correlates of mental health, demonstrated severity of effect, not in terms of emotions or humiliation or embarrassment at the hands of their immediate peers, but in terms of the level of anxiety, depression and social difficulties experienced more generally.

The current study has demonstrated that the consequences for victims of bullying are not homogeneous and can be qualified by gender and type of bullying experienced. Differentiating between the consequences for those victimised traditionally, i.e. feelings of anger, humiliation and embarrassment, and the increased mental health concerns as reported by victims of cyberbullying and indeed both forms of bullying, would seem to be important not only in terms of developing tailored interventions for victims but also in terms of the mental health implications for this generation of cyber-active youth.

Limitations and strengths

A limitation of this study was that there was common method variance because the measures of all the variables came from the same rater. That is, both bullying experiences and mental health problems were self-reported by the children and therefore the correlations might be inflated. The study was also cross-sectional and not longitudinal, so it is not known whether these correlates are antecedents or consequences. Furthermore, only a single item assessed bullying.

There are quite a few methodological problems with existing research on cyberbullying correlates. The first of these is the extent to which the study has accurately identified those students who have been involved in cyberbullying. This is most commonly accomplished by self-reports, which are very commonly used in bullying research and are considered valid and reliable (Ladd and Kochenderfer-Ladd 2002). However, there is controversy over whether an accurate definition is included in surveys, which is a strength of this study. In addition, either surveys ask a global question as to whether a student has experienced cyberbullying, or students may be given discrete behavioural examples. These two measures give different results (Cross et al. 2009). This study provided both a global filtering question as well as specific sections related to each type of bullying, traditional, cyber and both, as well as victim/perpetrator and witness perspectives.

Secondly, many early case studies on the correlates of cyberbullying did not consider the overlap of traditional and cyberbullying, and failed to account for the considerable overlap of students who are involved in both traditional bullying and cyberbullying as well as the role in bullying of the victim or 'bully–victim' (see Tokunaga 2010 for a review). This was considered in the present study. Furthermore, well-validated and widely used questionnaires were used to assess mental health in a large, diverse sample of students.

Implications

Although it has been shown that cyberbullying is mainly conducted outside school hours and outside school grounds (Cross et al. 2009; Smith et al. 2008), it is a vexatious problem for schools as parents and the community are increasingly turning to schools to provide preventive strategies and to manage incidents of cyberbullying. As there is a considerable overlap between those students who traditionally bully and those who cyberbully, and victims of traditional bullying are 10 times more likely to be a cybervictim, it follows then that evidence-based strategies such as the KiVa programme (Salmivalli, Karna, and Poskiparta 2011) could be a starting point for schools dealing with cyberbullying. Research on a consensual definition of cyberbullying is needed so that the whole school community agrees on what cyberbullying is and when the incident is aggression rather than bullying. Further work is also needed on an agreed measure of determining cyberbullying incidence so that schools will have accurate baseline data upon which to determine whether the prevention and intervention strategies are effective. However, it needs to be acknowledged that as technology advances, there will always be a need to revisit definitions and behaviours in accordance with new developments. Clearly, those being targeted through cyber means are at greater risk than those being targeted traditionally, yet it must not be forgotten that *all* students reporting victimisation in this study had poorer mental health scores than those not targeted, indicating that bullying overall needs to be continually addressed in schools, but that cyberbullying requires greater focus and attention to support those being victimised in this way.

Acknowledgements

This study was funded by the Australian Research Council grant LP0882087. The authors wish to acknowledge the contribution of Robyn Garland as project manager.

References

Arseneault, L., B. Milne, A. Taylor, F. Adams, K. Delgado, A. Caspi, and T. Moffitt. 2008. Being bullied as an environmentally mediated contributing factor to children's internalizing problems. *Archives of Pediatrics and Adolescent Medicine* 162: 145–50.

Arseneault, L., E. Walsh, K. Trzesniewski, R. Newcombe, A. Caspi, and T. Moffitt. 2006. Bullying victimization uniquely contributes to adjustments problems in young children: A nationally representative cohort study. *Pediatrics* 118: 130–8.

Campbell, M.A. 2005. Cyber bullying: An old problem in a new guise? *Australian Journal of Guidance and Counselling* 15: 68–76.

Carbone-Lopez, K., F. Esbensen, and B. Brick. 2010. Correlates and consequences of peer victimization: Gender differences in direct and indirect forms of bullying. *Youth Violence and Juvenile Justice* 8: 332–50.

Conn, K. 2004. *Bullying and harassment: A legal guide for educators*. Alexandria: ASCD.

Cross, D., T. Shaw, L. Hearn, M. Epstein, H. Monks, L. Lester, and L. Thomas. 2009. *Australian Covert Bullying Prevalence Study (ACBPS)*. http://www.deewr.gov.au/Schooling/NationalSafeSchools/Pages/research.aspx

Fekkes, M., F. Pijpers, A. Fredriks, T. Vogels, and S. Verloove-Vanhorick. 2006. Do bullied children get ill, or do ill children get bullied? A prospective cohort study on the relationship between bullying and health-related symptoms. *Pediatrics* 117: 1568–74.

Goodman, R. 1997. The Strengths and Difficulties Questionnaire: A research note. *Journal of Child Psychology and Psychiatry* 38: 581–6.

Gradinger, P., D. Strohmeier, and C. Spiel. 2009. Traditional bullying and cyberbullying: Identification of risk groups for adjustment problems. *Journal of Psychology* 217: 205–13.

Kim, Y.S., B. Leventhal, Y. Koh, A. Hubbard, and A. Boyce. 2006. School bullying and youth violence: Causes or consequences of psychopathology? *Archives of General Psychiatry* 63: 1035–41.

Ladd, G.W., and B.J. Kochenderfer-Ladd. 2002. Identifying victims of peer aggression from early to middle childhood: Analysis of cross-informant data for concordance, estimation of relational adjustment, prevalence of victimization, and characteristics of identified victims. *Psychological Assessment* 14, no. 1: 74–96.

Leckie, B.A. 1996. Sugar and spice and all things not necessarily nice: Girls, peer relationships and bullying behaviours. In *School days: Past, present and future: Education of girls in 20th century Australia*, ed. J. Gill and M. Dyer, 115–30. Magill: Research Centre for Gender Studies.

Leckie, B.A. 1997. *Girls, bullying behaviours and peer relations: The double edged sword of exclusion and rejection*. Paper presented at the Australian Association for Research in Education conference, November 30–December 4, Brisbane, Queensland. http://www.aare.edu.au/97pap/leckb284.htm

Lovibond, S.H., and P. Lovibond. 1995. *Manual for the Depression Anxiety Stress Scales*. Sydney: Psychology Foundation.

Ortega, R., P. Elipe, J. Mora-Cercan, J. Calmaestra, and E. Vega. 2009. The emotional impact on victims of traditional bullying and cyberbullying: A study of Spanish adolescents. *Journal of Psychology* 217: 197–204.

Patchin, J.W., and S. Hinduja. 2010. Cyberbullying and self-esteem. *Journal of School Health* 80: 614–21.

Perren, S., J. Dooley, T. Shaw, and D. Cross. 2010. Bullying in school and cyberspace: Associations with depressive symptoms in Swiss and Australian adolescents. *Child and Adolescent Psychiatry and Mental Health* 4, no. 28: 1–10.

Price, M., and J. Dalgleish. 2010. Cyberbullying: Experiences, impacts and coping strategies as described by Australian young people. *Youth Studies Australia* 29, no. 2: 51–9.

Raskauskas, J. 2010. Text-bullying: Associations with traditional bullying and depression among New Zealand adolescents. *Journal of School Violence* 9: 74–97.

Reid, P., J. Monsen, and I. Rivers. 2004. Psychology's contribution to understanding and managing bullying within schools. *Educational Psychology in Practice* 20: 241–4.

Reijntjs, A., J. Kamphuis, P. Prinzie, and M. Telch. 2010. Peer victimization and internalizing problems in children: A meta-analysis of longitudinal studies. *Child Abuse and Neglect* 34: 244–52.

Rigby, K., and P.T. Slee. 1993. Dimensions of interpersonal relations among Australian children and implications for psychological well-being. *Journal of Social Psychology* 133: 33–42.

Rudolph, K.D., and C.S. Conley. 2005. The socio-emotional costs and benefits of social–evaluative concerns: Do girls care too much? *Journal of Personality* 73: 115–38.

Salmivalli, C., A. Karna, and E. Poskiparta. 2011. Counteracting bullying in Finland: The KiVa program and its effects on different forms of being bullied. *International Journal of Behavioral Development* 35: 405–11.

Slonje, R., and P.K. Smith. 2008. Cyberbullying: Another main type of bullying. *Scandinavian Journal of Psychology* 49: 147–54.

Smith, P.K., J. Mahdavi, M. Carvalho, S. Fisher, S. Russell, and N. Tippett. 2008. Cyberbullying: Its nature and impact in secondary school pupils. *Journal of Counselling Psychology and Psychiatry* 49: 376–85.

Solberg, M.E., and D. Olweus. 2003. Prevalence estimation of school bullying with the Olweus Bully/Victim Questionnaire. *Aggressive Behavior* 29: 239–68.

Spears, B.A., P. Slee, L. Owens, and B. Johnson. 2009. Behind the scenes and screens: Insights into the human dimension of covert and cyberbullying. *Zeitschrift für Psychologie/Journal of Psychology* 217: 189–96.

Tokunaga, R.S. 2010. Following you home from school: A critical review and synthesis of research on cyberbullying victimization. *Computers in Human Behavior* 26: 277–87.

Peer victimisation and depressive symptoms: can specific coping strategies buffer the negative impact of cybervictimisation?

Katja Machmutow[a], Sonja Perren[a], Fabio Sticca[a] and Françoise D. Alsaker[b]

[a]*Jacobs Center for Productive Youth Development, University of Zurich, Zurich, Switzerland;* [b]*Department of Psychology, University of Bern, Berne, Switzerland*

This longitudinal study investigated whether cybervictimisation is an additional risk factor for depressive symptoms over and beyond traditional victimisation in adolescents. Furthermore, it explored whether certain coping strategies moderate the impact of cybervictimisation on depressive symptoms. A total of 765 Swiss seventh graders (mean age at time-point 1 (*t*1) = 13.18 years) reported on the frequency of traditional and cybervictimisation, and of depressive symptoms twice in six months. At time-point 2 (*t*2) students also completed a questionnaire on coping strategies in response to a hypothetical cyberbullying scenario. Analyses showed that both traditional and cybervictimisation were associated with higher levels of depressive symptoms. Cybervictimisation also predicted increases in depressive symptoms over time. Regarding coping strategies, it was found that helpless reactions were positively associated with depressive symptoms. Moreover, support seeking from peers and family showed a significant buffering effect: cybervictims who recommended seeking close support showed lower levels of depressive symptoms at *t*2. In contrast, cybervictims recommending assertive coping strategies showed higher levels of depressive symptoms at *t*2.

Introduction

It is well established that peer victimisation has negative short- and long-term consequences for children's and adolescents' mental health. Depressive symptoms are amongst the most prominent negative consequences of peer victimisation (Desjardins and Leadbeater 2011; Pouwelse et al. 2011). Past research focused mainly on the influence of victimisation on emotional well-being, but during recent years the inverse relationship has also gained attention: depressive symptoms have also been considered as a vulnerability factor for victimisation (Sweeting et al. 2006). Therefore, a reciprocal relationship may exist between victimisation experiences and depressive symptoms.

Cross-sectional studies suggest that being victimised in cyberspace is also associated with psychological difficulties (Mason 2008), stronger negative feelings, fear and feelings of helplessness (Spears et al. 2009), and also with depression (Ybarra 2004). Owing to the conceptual and empirical overlap between traditional and cybervictimisation (e.g. Perren and Gutzwiller-Helfenfinger 2012), the question arises whether cybervictimisation leads to similar consequences as traditional victimisation, and whether it represents an additional risk factor when traditional victimisation is controlled for. Several cross-sectional studies have shown that cybervictimisation is an additional risk factor for depressive symptoms (Gradinger, Strohmeier, and Spiel 2009; Perren et al. 2010; Wang, Nansel, and Iannotti 2011). Mitchell, Ybarra, and Finkelhor (2007) reported even higher levels of depressive symptoms in cybervictims than in traditional victims.

Coping strategies in relation to cybervictimisation

Coping, defined as the ability to manage stress and related emotions, is relevant for the sustainment of emotional and psychological well-being in the presence of adversity (Lazarus 2006). Coping strategies may therefore buffer the negative impact of cybervictimisation on depressive symptoms. Several types of coping strategies have been investigated in relation to experiences of cybervictimisation: supportive strategies (e.g. seeking social support from adults, teachers, friends or external institutions), reactions towards cyberbullies (e.g. retaliation, confrontation), technical strategies (e.g. report abuse buttons, blocking the sender), and avoiding and emotion-focused strategies (e.g. doing nothing, ignoring, helplessness).

Support seeking

Many students recommend asking their parents for help in case of a cybervictimisation incident (Aricak et al. 2008; Bhat 2008; Slonje and Smith 2008; Smith et al. 2008; Stacey 2009; Topcu, Erdur-Baker, and Capa-Aydin 2008). Other adolescents recommend not consulting adults because they fear losing enjoyable privileges (e.g. having and using mobile phones and their own Internet access), and because they expect that their parents would simply recommend ignoring the situation or that they would not be able to help them as they are not that familiar with cyberspace (Hoff and Mitchell 2009; Kowalski, Limber and Agatston 2008; Mishna, Saini, and Solomon 2009; Smith et al. 2008; Stacey 2009). In fact, Slonje and Smith (2008) suppose that adults are less aware of cybervictimisation as a problem. Therefore, parents tend to underestimate the seriousness of the problem and may be unable to give adequate support to their child. Self-reliance is another reason not to report cybervictimisation experiences to adults. In a web-based survey of 12–17-year-olds, most of whom had experienced at least one cybervictimisation incident in the year preceding the survey, Juvonen and Gross (2008) found that 90% of the victims did not tell their parents about their experiences and 50% of them justified it with 'I need to learn to deal with it myself'.

Although cyberbullying also happens outside the school context, victims often know their perpetrators from school (Smith and Slonje 2010), and teachers and the school, as a functional system, should not overlook or belittle cybervictimisation. Therefore, assistance from teachers and principals is implicitly necessary. However, students have a more negative and critical attitude to teachers' support: a large percentage of them consider telling a teacher or the school principal to be rather ineffective (Aricak et al. 2008; DiBasilio 2008; Mishna, Saini, and Solomon 2009; Mitchell, Finkelhor, and Wolak 2003; Price and Dalgleish 2010). Hoff and Mitchell (2009) found that although 17% of students reported to a teacher after a cybervictimisation incident, in 70% of the cases the school did not react to it. Asking for help from peers is commonly used and recommended (Aricak et al. 2008; Bhat 2008; DiBasilio 2008; Stacey 2009; Topcu, Erdur-Baker, and Capa-Aydin 2008), although prevalence rates vary to a large extent. Slonje and Smith (2008) found that cybervictims were more likely to contact friends than other persons. At the same time, friends were less likely to consider cybervictimisation as relevant. Nonetheless, focusing on the perceived successfulness of coping strategies, Price and Dalgleish (2010) reported Australian cybervictims to consider 'telling a friend' as the most helpful strategy.

Reactions towards the bully

Confronting the bully is commonly reported by adolescents if the victim knows the bully or is able to contact her or him (Aricak et al. 2008; DiBasilio 2008; Stacey 2009). Although this strategy is often mentioned by those who experience victimisation, it has proved to be less helpful in retrospect (Price and Dalgleish 2010). Students consider retaliation as a less constructive way of contacting the perpetrator. When asking students what they had done to stop cybervictimisation, Hoff and Mitchell (2009) reported answers containing active and physically retaliatory behaviour, especially in boys. The assumption that bullying back through cyberspace is easier and therefore more often used than a face-to-face contact was not confirmed by Juvonen and Gross (2008): 60% of cybervictims defended against the bully in school using traditional means, whereas only 12% retaliated in cyberspace and 28% used both traditional and cyber retaliation.

Technical solutions

Cyberspace specific coping strategies such as deleting or blocking threatening messages are generally used and considered to be helpful (Aricak et al. 2008; Hinduja and Patchin 2007; Juvonen and Gross 2008; Kowalski, Limber, and Agatston 2008; Smith et al. 2008; Stacey 2009). Price and Dalgleish (2010) found that blocking was the most used technical strategy and was also considered the most helpful online action exerted by the self-identified cybervictims. Technical solutions are often reported along with preventive strategies used by parents, such as banning websites, and age-appropriate limits for the use of the computer and the Internet (Kowalski, Limber, and Agatston 2008).

Avoidant and emotion-focused strategies

According to coping theory (Roth and Cohen 1986), avoidance is a likely coping strategy in situations that are not under control of the affected person. Patchin and Hinduja (2006) reported 25% of victims doing nothing after a cybervictimisation incident. Dehue, Bolman, and Vollink (2008) found that 7.2% of students reported that with online victimisation they would usually pretend to ignore it, and 6.9% reported that they would ignore it. Chi and Frydenberg (2009) investigated the effects of a 10-week coping programme designed to reduce the negative impact of cybervictimisation. After completion of the programme the use of non-productive reactions, such as ignoring the problem, self-blaming or not coping, decreased and the level of emotional well-being increased. Tokunaga (2010) suggested that ignoring can be a very effective strategy following a single incident but that other (more active) coping strategies are more effective when the frequency and severity of episodes increase.

In sum, a range of coping strategies has been investigated in relation to cybervictimisation. However, most of the studies investigated the use (and not the success) of coping strategies in real cybervictims or in relation to hypothetical cybervictimisation. A few studies asked participants whether they think a certain coping strategy is successful (see also Perren et al. 2012). However, no study has yet investigated whether specific coping strategies buffer the negative impact of cybervictimisation on victims' emotional well-being.

Coping strategies and emotional well-being

Two main dimensions are commonly differentiated in coping theory: emotion- versus problem-oriented coping strategies (Eschenbeck 2010). Some researchers see a problem in this subdivision because some coping strategies could be defined as both problem and emotion focused (e.g. support seeking). Consequently, a categorisation of strategies is not an ideal methodological approach (Skinner et al. 2003; Tenenbaum et al. 2011). As outlined above, current research on coping with cyberbullying has adopted a more descriptive approach and differentiates between specific behavioural and emotional reactions.

From a theoretical perspective we expect strong relationships between the use of specific coping strategies and an individual's emotional well-being (Lazarus 2006). Empirical studies show that emotion-focused coping is associated with distressing emotions, whereas problem-focused strategies are seen in association with increased emotional regulation and positive affect (Hampel, Manhal, and Hayer 2009; Yamasaki and Uchida 2006). Avoidant coping strategies are negatively associated with emotional well-being (e.g. Seiffge-Krenke and Klessinger 2000).

In studies on traditional victimisation, it has been supposed that avoidance is linked to negative outcomes such as maladjustment, loneliness, anxiety (Kochenderfer-Ladd and Skinner 2002) and other mental health problems (Ebata and Moos 1991). Lodge and Feldman (2007) found that avoidant coping partially mediated the association between appearance-related bullying problems and self-esteem among young adolescents. Kochenderfer-Ladd (2004) showed that students ignoring the victimisation (cognitive distancing) showed an increased risk for later harassment and were therefore indirectly at risk for a higher level of internalising symptoms. By investigating the relationship between victimisation and depressive symptoms, Singh and Bussey (2010) found mediating effects of how students, when imagining a hypothetical cybervictimisation incident, would rate their self-efficacy to use different coping strategies. Students being more victimised showed decreased self-efficacy scores regarding the resistance to debilitating thoughts and the ability to engage in enabling thoughts. These lowered scores were related to a higher level of depressive symptoms.

If victimisation is seen as a stressor affecting psychological well-being, the question arises as to whether specific coping strategies can buffer the negative outcomes of this association. Some studies aimed to test the so-called 'buffering hypothesis of social support' (e.g. Jackson 1992): there is some evidence that different forms of support minimise the negative impact of victimisation on psychological well-being (Davidson and Demaray 2007; Flouri and Buchanan 2002; Holt and Espelage 2007; Kochenderfer-Ladd and Skinner 2002). In contrast, Rigby (2000) and Pouwelse and colleagues (2011) found no evidence for the buffering hypothesis of social support, and Dooley and colleagues (2010) could not find associations between help-seeking behaviour and emotional symptoms.

All of the studies mentioned above focused on traditional victimisation when investigating mediating or moderating effects of coping strategies on the association between victimisation and psychological well-being. Yet, empirical evidence of the role of coping strategies on the association between cybervictimisation and depressive symptoms is missing, especially in a longitudinal context. The present study fills this gap by investigating moderating effects of different coping strategies in the association between cybervictimisation and depressive symptoms, using a longitudinal approach.

Research questions

The first aim of this study was to investigate whether cybervictimisation is a longitudinal risk factor for depressive symptoms. We hypothesised that cybervictimisation predicts higher levels of depressive symptoms, even when controlling for traditional victimisation. The second aim was to explore the impact of specific coping strategies in relation to cybervictimisation on adolescents' depressive symptoms. We hypothesised that (1) support seeking (close support and distant advice) is associated with lower levels of depressive symptoms; and (2) avoidant and helpless reactions are associated with higher levels of depressive symptoms. Lastly, we explored whether specific coping strategies buffer the relationship between cybervictimisation and depressive symptoms. We hypothesised that support seeking buffers the negative impact of cybervictimisation.

Method

Procedure

Data are taken from the first (November/December 2010) and the second (May 2011) waves of data assessment in an ongoing longitudinal study carried out in Switzerland (netTEEN). Twelve randomly selected Swiss schools (43 classes) participated in the study. The assessments were conducted in three different cantons of Switzerland. The local languages of the schools were German (eight schools) and Italian (four schools). For the Italian-speaking schools questionnaires were translated from German into Italian by two bilingual native speakers.

All parents were informed about the study and invited to inform the respective teachers if they did not want their children to participate. A self-report questionnaire was administered in classrooms on netbooks. The questionnaire was administered by two research assistants. Students absent during the classroom assessment were asked to complete an online version of the questionnaire.

Sample

A total of 835 seventh graders participated in the first assessment ($t1$) and 820 students also participated in the second assessment ($t2$). Attrition was mainly due to adolescents no longer attending the school. Parents of four adolescents refused their children's participation. Because of time constraints, the coping measure was only completed by 765 students. Only these 765 students are included in the analysis (52.1% female, age at $t1$: mean = 13.18 years, SD = 0.63).

Instruments

Students reported on the frequency of cybervictimisation and traditional victimisation ($t1$ and $t2$) and depressive symptoms ($t1$ and $t2$). The coping questionnaire was only completed at $t2$.

Victimisation

Cybervictimisation was assessed with a self-developed six-item scale (Sticca et al. in press). Participants rated how often they had suffered from specific cyberbullying behaviours in the past four months. Possible responses ranged from 1 (never) to 5 (almost daily). The dimension of *publicity* (private, semi-public, public) was systematically varied in the items. The first two items (private) described an interaction involving only the bully and the victim (e.g. 'Did someone sent you nasty or threatening messages, i.e. text messages, MSN, Facebook, Netlog, etc.'). In the next two items (semi-public) the content (message, picture or video) would have been sent to groups of people (e.g. 'Are there adolescents sending nasty or embarrassing messages about you to other colleagues?'). In the last two items (public) the content would have been posted on the Internet (e.g. 'Are there adolescents publishing nasty or embarrassing pictures or videos on the internet?'). Item scores were averaged to gain an overall score of cybervictimisation ($\alpha\_t1/t2 = 0.62/0.78$), with higher scores indicating being more frequently victimised. Owing to its high skewness at the upper end of the scale, cybervictimisation was log transformed.

Involvement in traditional victimisation was assessed using an adapted version of a well-validated scale (Alsaker 2003; Alsaker and Brunner 1999). The items were introduced through a general definition of what bullying is. The scale consists of six items encompassing a set of different aggressive behaviours (e.g. being laughed at, insulted, excluded or hit by someone). Participants were asked how often they had suffered these behaviours in the past four months. Participants rated each item from 1 (never) to 5 (almost daily). Item scores were averaged to gain an overall score of traditional victimisation ($\alpha\_t1/t2 = 0.76/0.81$), with higher scores indicating being more frequently victimised. Owing to its high skewness at the upper end of the scale, traditional victimisation was log transformed.

Depressive symptoms

Students completed an eight-item scale addressing depressive symptoms at both assessment points. The scale has been validated in a longitudinal study (Alsaker 1992; Holsen, Kraft, and Vitterso 2000), and taps the following constructs: sad/depressed feelings (e.g. 'Sometimes I am just so depressed that I feel like staying in bed for the whole day'), lack of positive feeling, lack of motivation/energy, and worthlessness of life. Participants rated how much they agree with statements referring to the past four months. Possible responses ranged from 1 (not true) to 4 (true). Scores were averaged to obtain a single score for depressive symptoms ($\alpha\_t1/t2 = 0.86/0.88$). Higher scores indicate higher levels of depressive symptoms.

Coping strategies

Based on the results of a qualitative pilot study, a 14-item scale on coping strategies in relation to cybervictimisation was developed. The items were built based on adolescents' open answers regarding the perceived success of coping strategies in relation to cyberbullying (Machmutow and Perren 2011b). Students were given a hypothetical cyberbullying scenario (e.g. an embarrassing video was published on YouTube) and a list of 14 coping strategies was provided; they were asked what the hypothetical victim should do in this specific situation and rated each strategy on a scale ranging from 1 (definitely not) to 4 (definitely).

Each student was randomly given one cyberbullying scenario followed by the 14 items. The scenarios varied in publicity and severity of the incident as well as in the gender and victimisation experiences of the victim. The randomisation of the scenarios was applied to investigate the impact of situational variables on students' coping behaviour

(Machmutow and Perren 2011a). The analyses presented here were statistically controlled for the situational variations of the scenarios.

Running a factor analysis, three distinct subscales (distant advice, assertiveness, helplessness) were found, together with two further subscales (close support, retaliation), which were examined separately (items tapping close support correlated with all subscales and retaliation was measured only with one item). One item ('not to take something to heart') turned out to be understood ambiguously and was eliminated from the following analyses.

With regard to support seeking, we specified two subscales: distant advice, e.g. attending an advice centre ($\alpha = 0.67$), and close support, e.g. talking to friends ($\alpha = 0.65$). Whereas distant advice implies the more informational and instrumental aspects of relief, close support targets the more emotional way of getting help from people (Cohen and Wills 1985). The subscale 'assertiveness', e.g. finding and contacting the bully ($\alpha = 0.49$), includes different means to defend oneself without causing harm to others (confronting the bully and using technical means). In contrast, retaliation (single item) is understood as a reaction through counter-aggression and revenge (Camodeca and Goossens 2005). Avoidant and emotion-focused coping strategies were combined in the subscale 'helplessness', e.g. self-blaming for the incident ($\alpha = 0.36$). This scale consists of three items referring to the attributions one can use when confronted with problematic situations (Kelley and Michela 1980): internal causes (e.g. self-blame), global causes (withdrawing, e.g. because bullying is everywhere) and stable causes (ignoring, e.g. because bullying is uncontrollable and therefore there is nothing you can do against it). More information or a copy of the (currently revised) coping questionnaire is available from the authors.

Results

Descriptive statistics

Main effects of time, gender and age

Means and gender differences of all study variables are shown in Table 1. Regarding differences between the two time-points of assessment, participants showed a decrease in traditional victimisation ($t(726) = 3.79$, $p < 0.001$). The level of victimisation in cyberspace as well as the level of depressive symptoms did not differ between the two time-points. Cyber and traditional victimisation were moderately stable. Depressive symptoms showed rather high stability. Girls reported higher levels of cybervictimisation ($t1$) and higher levels of depressive symptoms (both time-points). Girls more frequently recommended assertiveness and close support, and less frequently recommended retaliation as a coping strategy than boys.

Victimisation, depressive symptoms and coping strategies

Bivariate associations between all study variables are shown in Table 2. Cyber- and traditional victimisation were positively associated with each other, as well as with depressive symptoms at $t1$ and $t2$. Higher levels of retaliation and helplessness and lower levels of close support were associated with a higher level of depressive symptoms ($t1$ and $t2$). Traditional victimisation ($t2$) was positively associated with higher levels of assertiveness and distant advice. Cybervictimisation ($t2$) was positively associated with retaliation and negatively with close support.

Table 1. Means (standard deviations in parentheses) of all study variables ($n = 345$–388).

	$t1$		$t2$		
	Female	Male	Female	Male	Gender differences
Traditional victimisation	1.33 (0.42)	1.37 (0.48)	1.28 (0.40)	1.31 (0.46)	ns
Cybervictimisation	1.10 (0.26)	1.06 (0.19)	1.08 (0.19)	1.06 (0.25)	$t1$: $F(1{,}729) = 6.05$; $p < 0.05$ $t2$: ns
Depressive symptoms	1.76 (0.69)	1.55 (0.62)	1.70 (0.66)	1.55 (0.67)	$t1$: $F(1{,}719) = 19.57$; $p < 0.001$ $t2$: $F(1{,}732) = 9.55$; $p < 0.01$
Distant advice	–	–	2.57 (0.77)	2.60 (0.85)	ns
Close support	–	–	3.23 (0.60)	2.97 (0.84)	$F(1{,}740) = 24.08$; $p < 0.001$
Assertiveness	–	–	3.05 (0.61)	2.95 (0.73)	$F(1{,}737) = 4.36$; $p < 0.05$
Helplessness	–	–	1.67 (0.58)	1.74 (0.65)	ns
Retaliation	–	–	2.03 (0.94)	2.42 (1.13)	$F(1{,}725) = 26.14$; $p < 0.001$

Note: ns: not significant.

Multivariate analyses

Cross-sectional and longitudinal generalised linear models (GLMs) were used to investigate the impact of traditional and cybervictimisation on depressive symptoms. In a last step, we analysed whether coping strategies moderate the effects of cybervictimisation (interactions). As the coping questionnaire contained cyber-specific scenarios, we were only interested in a possible moderating effect of coping strategies on the association between cybervictimisation and depressive symptoms; models with interactions concerning traditional victimisation were not calculated.

Predictors of depressive symptoms

Cross-sectional associations. In a first step, age, gender and both forms of victimisation ($t1$) were included in a model to investigate their predictive value for depressive symptoms at $t1$. Gender and both forms of victimisation yielded a significant effect. Being female (Wald $\chi^2(1{,}791) = 21.42$, $B = 0.20$, $p = 0.001$, $\omega = 0.16$), higher levels of traditional victimisation (Wald $\chi^2(1{,}791) = 39.35$, $B = 1.30$, $p = 0.001$, $\omega = 0.22$) and higher levels of cybervictimisation (Wald $\chi^2(1{,}791) = 24.39$, $B = 1.85$, $p = 0.001$, $\omega = 0.18$) predicted higher levels of depressive symptoms.

Longitudinal associations. For the longitudinal analyses, two models were computed: model 1 investigated the impact of victimisation at $t1$ on depressive symptoms at $t2$; in model 2 we controlled for depressive symptoms at $t1$ and thus investigated the impact of victimisation on changes in depressive symptoms over time (Table 3). Age, gender, traditional and cybervictimisation ($t1$ and $t2$), and coping strategies were used as independent variables. Gender and both types of victimisation at both time-points yielded significant main effects. Being female and higher frequency of victimisation were predictive of a

Table 2. Bivariate associations between all study variables ($n = 698–820$).

	2	3	4	5	6	7	8	9	10	11
1. Traditional victimisation (*t*1)	0.43**	0.27**	0.50**	0.22**	0.25**	−0.04	−0.03	−0.01	0.04	0.00
2. Cybervictimisation (*t*1)	1	0.26**	0.27**	0.22**	0.19**	0.01	−0.05	−0.01	−0.02	0.02
3. Depressive symptoms (*t*1)		1	0.22**	0.17**	0.56**	−0.06	−0.10**	−0.03	0.09*	0.09*
4. Traditional victimisation (*t*2)			1	0.35**	0.26**	0.09*	0.03	0.12**	0.04	0.02
5. Cybervictimisation (*t*2)				1	0.15**	0.01	−0.09*	−0.04	0.07	0.09*
6. Depressive symptoms (*t*2)					1	−0.02	−0.07	0.01	0.11**	0.08*
7. Distant advice						1	0.37**	0.43**	−0.04	−0.03
8. Close support							1	0.36**	−0.02	−0.22**
9. Assertiveness								1	−0.01	0.01
10. Helplessness									1	0.05
11. Retaliation										1

Notes: *$p < 0.05$; **$p < 0.01$.

Table 3. Results of the GLM analyses predicting depressive symptoms at *t*2 ($n_{M1} = 675$; $n_{M2} = 667$).

	Depressive symptoms *t*2			
	Model 1		Model 2	
	B	*p*	*B*	*p*
Intercept (constant)	0.320	0.576	−0.142	0.777
Depressive symptoms (*t*1)			0.499	0.000
Age	0.040	0.298	0.032	0.342
Gender (female)	0.189	0.000	0.054	0.231
Traditional victimisation (*t*1)	0.841	0.002	0.410	0.081
Cybervictimisation (*t*1)	0.975	0.026	0.205	0.609
Traditional victimisation (*t*2)	0.309	0.007	0.118	0.240
Cybervictimisation (*t*2)	0.460	0.029	0.462	0.012
Distant advice	0.014	0.701	0.012	0.704
Close support	−0.092	0.021	−0.038	0.278
Assertiveness	0.055	0.196	0.060	0.106
Helplessness	0.092	0.020	0.064	0.066
Retaliation	0.041	0.081	0.009	0.659

Notes: Analyses were controlled for the situational variability of the cyberbullying scenarios.

higher level of depressive symptoms at *t*2. In addition, the coping strategies helplessness and close support emerged as predictors of depressive symptoms at *t*2. Close support predicted a lower level of depressive symptoms, whereas feeling helpless predicted a higher level of depressive symptoms. When including depressive symptoms at *t*1 into model 2, cybervictimisation at *t*2 remained a significant predictor of depressive symptoms at *t*2. That is, higher levels of cybervictimisation at *t*2 predicted an increase in depressive symptoms over time.

Moderating effects of coping strategies

To test for possible moderating effects, interactions were included in the models. For the interaction analysis, variables were centred around the mean. In a first GLM analysis interaction effects between coping strategies and cybervictimisation at *t*1 were tested. These analyses yielded no significant interaction effects.

Next, interactions with cybervictimisation at *t*2 were calculated. The analysis yielded significant interaction effects for assertiveness and close support. To interpret the significant interaction effect, we used the procedures of Aiken and West (1991). The lines represent associations (slopes) between the independent and dependent variables for high and low levels (± SD) of the moderator (Figures 1 and 2).

The GLM analysis yielded significant effects of assertiveness × cybervictimisation on depressive symptoms at *t*2 (Wald $\chi^2(1,652) = 4.12$, $B = 0.68$, $p = 0.042$, $\omega = 0.08$). As can be seen in Figure 1, students with higher levels of cybervictimisation reported higher levels of depressive symptoms. This association was stronger when students recommended assertive coping strategies. When entering depressive symptoms at *t*1 as a control variable into the model this moderating effect remained significant (Wald $\chi^2(1,643) = 10.87$, $B = 0.96$, $p = 0.001$, $\omega = 0.13$). Moreover, the interaction between close support and cybervictimisation was significant regarding changes in depressive symptoms from

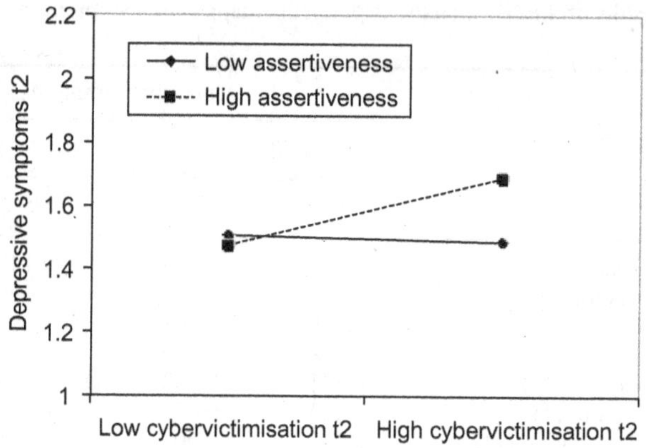

Figure 1. Interaction effect of cybervictimisation × assertiveness (on depressive symptoms at *t*2).

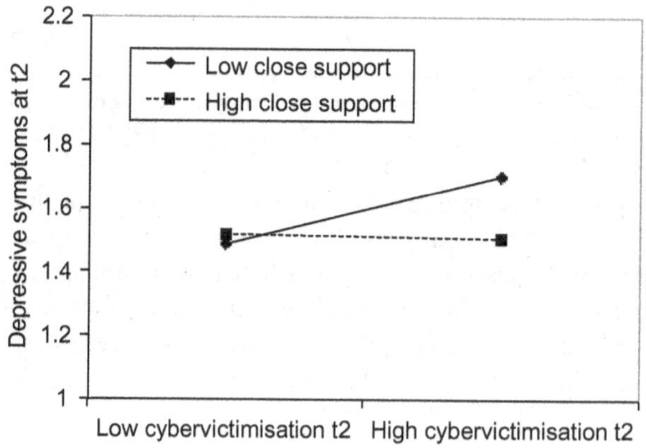

Figure 2. Interaction effect of cybervictimisation × close support (controlled for depressive symptoms at *t*1).

*t*1 to *t*2 (Wald $\chi^2(1{,}643) = 4.43$, $B = -0.61$, $p = 0.035$, $\omega = 0.08$). Figure 2 shows that cybervictimisation is more strongly associated with depressive symptoms at *t*2 when students report low levels of social support, i.e. higher levels of social support seem to buffer the negative impact of cybervictimisation.

Discussion

This study examined whether cybervictimisation is a longitudinal risk factor for depressive symptoms. Furthermore, the impact of recommending specific cybervictimisation coping strategies on the association between cybervictimisation and depressive symptoms was explored. The results show that cybervictimisation is a longitudinal risk factor for adolescents' depressive symptoms above and beyond traditional victimisation. The results also suggest that social support may buffer the negative impact of cybervictimisation, whereas assertive reaction may aggravate this negative impact.

Impact of victimisation on depressive symptoms

Results show that being victimised by traditional means and in cyberspace is a concurrent and longitudinal predictor of a higher level of depressive symptoms. These findings are in line with our expectations and with former cross-sectional studies (e.g. Baker and Tanrikulu 2010; Desjardins and Leadbeater 2011; Pouwelse et al. 2011; Ybarra 2004). The bivariate analyses also confirm that students who are victimised in one context (e.g. real world) are at a higher risk of becoming victimised in the other context, too (e.g. cyberspace). Despite this overlap, cybervictimisation emerges as an additional risk factor in regard to depressive symptoms. When analysing the effect of victimisation on changes in depressive symptoms over time, only cybervictimisation (and not traditional victimisation) at *t*2 emerges as a significant predictor. Therefore, being victimised online could be even more strongly related to depressive symptoms than traditional forms of victimisation. An additional and stronger negative impact of cybervictimisation on depressive symptoms could be explained by the larger audience provided in cyberspace (Kowalski and Limber 2007; Smith et al. 2008; Sticca et al. in press), which might increase feelings of helplessness and shame in the victim. The finding might also be related to the fact that cybervictimisation is not confined by time and place. If adolescents are victims of traditional victimisation they can withdraw from this harassment after school. Cybervictims never can rest because at home the victimisation goes on with text messages on their mobile phone, on Facebook, and in videos on YouTube and the like.

Coping strategies in cybervictimisation

Students indicated what coping strategies a hypothetical cybervictim should use in a specific cyberbullying situation. Close support and assertiveness were the most frequently recommended coping strategies, whereas helpless reactions and retaliation were less frequently recommended.

Talking to friends and/or parents might be one of the first ideas that come to mind when thinking about what to do when experiencing cybervictimisation, since the cost associated with asking significant others for support might be comparatively low. Moreover, students emphasise the importance that significant others have the resources to help, are trustworthy and take such incidents seriously (Hinduja and Patchin 2007; Smith et al. 2008). However, it is important to note that cybervictimisation was negatively associated with close support, possibly indicating that cybervictims more seldom use close support as a coping strategy, or that they have had unsuccessful experiences. As we only asked whether they would speak to friends or parents we do not know what kind of support they would ask for: they might ask for (and receive) consolation and comfort (emotional support), or they might expect instrumental help to cope with the cybervictimisation.

In contrast to close support, the coping strategy distant advice was not significantly associated with depressive symptoms or cybervictimisation. However, traditional victimisation was positively associated with distant advice. This might indicate that students who experienced traditional victimisation may be more willing to report the incident to consultants or the police. This might, in turn, be due to their own experiences with unsuccessful attempts to stop bullying and resulting feelings of helplessness.

Another way to cope with victimisation is fighting back. In the present sample, boys recommended retaliation more often than girls, although on a lower level than other more constructive coping strategies. Gender differences often appear regarding retaliation, but it seems that the observed/reported differences are based on the way girls (e.g. more verbal) and boys (e.g. more physical) fight back (Hoff and Mitchell 2009). In our coping scale we used only one item addressing revenge ('I would retaliate against this person') and we did not differentiate between forms of retaliation. Therefore, we were not able to test such a hypothesis. However, our results showed that boys recommended retaliation more often than girls. Cybervictimisation (*t*2) was positively associated with retaliation. This, again, might indicate that victims of cybervictimisation have used such strategies. As high correlations have been reported between cybervictimisation and cyberaggression in other studies (e.g. Perren et al. 2010; Sontag et al. 2011), it is possible that some of the cybervictims are themselves rather aggressive and use this kind of reaction when facing cybervictimisation. However, we did not investigate associations between own cyberbullying behaviour and the suggested coping strategies in this study.

In line with research into avoidant coping strategies (Seiffge-Krenke and Klessinger 2000), we found that helplessness reactions (ignoring, withdrawing and self-blame) are positively associated with depressive symptoms. This finding could be explained by the general failure to use adaptive coping strategies (Asarnow, Carlson, and Guthrie 1987). Also, feelings of uncontrollability of the situation (Roth and Cohen 1986) might be more relevant in cyberbullying incidents owing to the perpetrator's greater anonymity. Holahan and colleagues (2005) suggested that the use of avoidant coping strategies leads to more acute and/or chronic life stress which, in turn, predicts higher levels of depressive symptoms.

Buffering effects of coping strategies

As hypothesised and shown in other studies, seeking support from significant others predicted lower levels of depressive symptoms, whereas avoidant and emotion-focused coping (helplessness) predicted a higher level of depressive symptoms (Ebata and Moos 1991; Hay and Meldrum 2010; Seiffge-Krenke and Klessinger 2000). In addition, higher levels of retaliation were associated with higher levels of depressive symptoms.

One of the main research questions in the present study was whether recommended coping strategies regarding a hypothetical cyberbullying scenario buffer the negative impact of cybervictimisation on depressive symptoms. The analysis showed that two coping strategies (close support and assertiveness) moderate the association between cybervictimisation and depressive symptoms. Students suggesting close support as a coping strategy showed lower levels of depressive symptoms at *t*2. This finding is in line with the buffering hypothesis of social support (e.g. Jackson 1992) and indicates that support from significant others can reduce the negative effects of stress. However, cybervictims seem to use close support less frequently than others. That is, students recommending seeking close support are not necessarily victimised and might suggest this strategy on the basis of other situations in which they have used it successfully.

Assertiveness is commonly seen as a rather constructive and helpful way to cope with victimisation incidents (Camodeca and Goossens 2005). However, our study showed an unexpected result. For cybervictims, higher levels of assertiveness (contacting and showing own pain to the bully as well as taking technical precautions) were associated with higher levels of depressive symptoms. The moderating effect still remained when controlling for depressive symptoms at *t*1. This result suggests that any contact with the perpetrator, even a constructive one, is harmful and should be avoided to reduce negative emotions. Contacting the bully, telling him that his behaviour is bad and makes one angry could lead to the outcome the perpetrator wants to get: satisfaction. Therefore, as bullying is defined by a power differential between bully and victim, contacting a bully might not be a useful strategy. A logical conclusion would be to avoid any contact with the bully in the hope that he loses his motivation, and eventually stops bullying. Another interpretation of this finding might be associated with aggressive victims' behaviour and difficulties: traditional bully–victims show high levels of aggressive and assertive reactions and coping behaviour (Kristensen and Smith 2003; Perren and Alsaker 2006), and also the highest level of depressive symptoms (Perren et al. 2010). Maybe traditional bully–victims are overrepresented in the group of cybervictims who recommend assertive coping strategies. Studies regarding the role of assertive coping strategies in the relationship between victimisation and emotional well-being are needed.

Strengths and limitations

The present study has a number of strengths. One is the rather large sample with a very low percentage of attrition. Furthermore, to our knowledge, this was the first study to investigate moderating effects of coping strategies on the impact of cybervictimisation on depressive symptoms using a longitudinal design. Therefore, we not only assessed perceived success, but also measured the impact of recommended coping strategies on changes in depressive symptoms. Nevertheless, the study has limitations. The ability to generalise the results is limited because we had only two time-points with a six-month interval. Moreover, coping strategies were only measured at the second assessment. Furthermore, the study relied exclusively on self-report. Therefore, the strengths of associations might be biased through shared method variance.

The coping measure also has its strengths and limitations. We asked students which coping strategies they would recommend to a hypothetical cybervictim. On the one hand, this allowed us to generate data for the whole sample and not only from cybervictims. On the other hand, we do not know whether the recommended coping strategies are actually also used by the students in similar cybervictimisation experiences. The items of our coping instrument were developed from a qualitative pilot study. We used students' answers to generate the coping items. This is certainly a strength of the instrument, as we used students' own formulations of answers and did not imply theoretical subscales that might not be relevant to their everyday experiences (Parris et al. 2011). At the same time, this procedure is a major disadvantage because we were forced to build post-hoc subscales. Although we could identify some theoretically meaningful subscales, the internal consistencies were rather low to moderate. Furthermore, we had only one item in the retaliation scale.

Practical and research implications

The implications of these findings are important for intervention programmes and evince the extent of negative impact of cybervictimisation. Being victimised in cyberspace proved to be an additional longitudinal risk factor for depressive symptoms in young adolescents. However, it remains unclear whether cybervictimisation adds a unique and qualitatively different contribution to the harm caused by traditional victimisation or whether its effect on youngsters' health is just additive and qualitatively comparable to that of traditional victimisation. Further studies should address this issue.

Close support as a coping strategy was found to be able to buffer the negative impact of this association. Analyses concerning the other coping strategies provided unexpected or no significant results. Therefore, further investigation is needed to clarify the specific longitudinal effect of different coping strategies on the association between cybervictimisation and depressive symptoms. For example, clarification is needed on whether there are differences of a structural and functional nature between coping mechanisms in traditional and cybervictimisation, whether coping strategies are more universal and therefore independent of context, and whether there is an overlap between the perceived and real successfulness of coping strategies. Nonetheless, the results of this study raise important questions, as well as concerns, for those young people experiencing different forms of victimisation and suffering emotional problems.

In conclusion, close support emerges as a highly adaptive coping strategy in relation to cybervictimisation. In contrast to our expectations, assertive reactions seem to aggravate the negative impact of cybervictimisation. There exists a wide range of published guidelines and recommendations to cope with cyberbullying developed by governments, schools, and private or public initiatives. However, there is a severe lack of evidence regarding the success of these suggested coping strategies (Perren et al. 2012; Smith 2012). Further investigation of successful coping strategies in relation to cybervictimisation is necessary to eliminate recommendations that may be not useful for, or may even be detrimental to, cybervictims' adaptive coping and emotional well-being.

References

Aiken, L.S., and S.G. West. 1991. *Multiple regression: Testing and interpreting interactions.* Newbury Park, CA: Sage.

Alsaker, F.D. 1992. Pubertal timing, overweight, and psychological adjustment. *Journal of Early Adolescence* 12: 396–419.

Alsaker, F.D. 2003. *Quälgeister und ihre Opfer. Mobbing unter Kindern – und wie man damit umgeht.* Bern: Huber Verlag.

Alsaker, F.D., and A. Brunner. 1999. Switzerland. In *The nature of school bullying: A cross-national perspective*, ed. P.K. Smith, Y. Morita, J. Junger-Tas, D. Olweus, R. Catalano and P. Slee, 250–63. London: Routledge.

Aricak, T., S. Siyahhan, A. Uzunhasanoglu, S. Saribeyoglu, S. Ciplak, N. Yilmaz, and C. Memmedov. 2008. Cyberbullying among Turkish adolescents. *Cyberpsychology & Behavior* 11: 253–61.

Asarnow, J.R., G.A. Carlson, and D. Guthrie. 1987. Coping strategies, self-perceptions, hopelessness, and perceived family environments in depressed and suicidal children. *Journal of Consulting and Clinical Psychology* 55: 361–6.

Baker, O.E., and I. Tanrikulu. 2010. Psychological consequences of cyber bullying experiences among Turkish secondary school children. *Procedia Social and Behavioral Sciences* 2: 2771–2776.

Bhat, C.S. 2008. Cyber bullying: Overview and strategies for school counsellors, guidance officers, and all school personnel. *Australian Journal of Guidance and Counselling* 18: 53–66.

Camodeca, M., and F.A. Goossens. 2005. Children's opinions on effective strategies to cope with bullying: The importance of bullying role and perspective. *Educational Research* 47: 93–105.

Chi, C.W., and E. Frydenberg. 2009. Coping in the cyberworld: Program implementation and evaluation – a pilot project. *Australian Journal of Guidance and Counselling* 19: 196–215.

Cohen, S., and T.A. Wills. 1985. Stress, social support, and the buffering hypothesis. *Psychological Bulletin* 98: 310–57.

Davidson, L.M., and M.K. Demaray. 2007. Social support as a moderator between victimisation and internalizing–externalizing distress from bullying. *School Psychology Review* 36: 383–405.

Dehue, F., C. Bolman, and T. Vollink. 2008. Cyberbullying: Youngsters' experiences and parental perception. *Cyberpsychology & Behavior* 11: 217–23.

Desjardins, T.L., and B.J. Leadbeater. 2011. Relational victimisation and depressive symptoms in adolescence: Moderating effects of mother, father, and peer emotional support. *Journal of Youth and Adolescence* 40: 531–44.

DiBasilio, A. 2008. *Reducing bullying in middle school students through the use of student-leaders.* Saint Xavier University, Chicago.

Dooley, J.J., P. Gradinger, D. Strohmeier, D. Cross, and C. Spiel. 2010. Cyber-Victimisation: The association between help-seeking behaviours and self-reported emotional symptoms in Australia and Austria. *Australian Journal of Guidance & Counselling* 20: 194–209.

Ebata, A.T., and R.H. Moos. 1991. Coping and adjustment in distressed and healthy adolescents. *Journal of Applied Developmental Psychology* 12: 33–54.

Eschenbeck, H. 2010. Bewältigung alltäglicher Stresssituationen von Kindern und Jugendlichen. *Zeitschrift für Gesundheitspsychologie* 18: 103–18.

Flouri, E., and A. Buchanan. 2002. Life satisfaction in teenage boys: The moderating role of father involvement and bullying. *Aggressive Behavior* 28: 126–33.

Gradinger, P., D. Strohmeier, and C. Spiel. 2009. Traditional bullying and cyberbullying identification of risk groups for adjustment problems. *Zeitschrift für Psychologie/Journal of Psychology* 217: 205–13.

Hampel, P., S. Manhal, and T. Hayer. 2009. Direct and relational bullying among children and adolescents: Coping and psychological adjustment. *School Psychology International* 30: 474–90.

Hay, C., and R. Meldrum. 2010. Bullying victimisation and adolescent self-harm: Testing hypotheses from general strain theory. *Journal of Youth and Adolescence* 39: 446–59.

Hinduja, S., and J.W. Patchin. 2007. Offline consequences of online victimisation: School violence and delinquency. *Journal of School Violence* 6, no. 3: 89–112.

Hoff, D.L., and S.N. Mitchell. 2009. Cyberbullying: Causes, effects, and remedies. *Journal of Educational Administration* 47: 652–65.

Holahan, C.J., R.H. Moos, C.K. Holahan, P.L. Brennan, and K.K. Schutte. 2005. Stress generation, avoidance coping, and depressive symptoms: A 10-year model. *Journal of Consulting and Clinical Psychology* 73: 658–66.

Holsen, I., P. Kraft, and J. Vitterso. 2000. Stability in depressed mood in adolescence: Results from a 6-year longitudinal panel study. *Journal of Youth and Adolescence* 29: 61–78.

Holt, M.K., and D.L. Espelage. 2007. Perceived social support among bullies, victims, and bully–victims. *Journal of Youth and Adolescence* 36: 984–94.

Jackson, P.B. 1992. Specifying the buffering hypothesis – Support, strain, and depression. *Social Psychology Quarterly* 55: 363–78.

Juvonen, J., and E.F. Gross. 2008. Extending the school grounds? Bullying experiences in cyberspace. *Journal of School Health* 78: 496–505.

Kelley, H.H., and J.L. Michela. 1980. Attribution theory and research. *Annual Review of Psychology* 31: 457–501.

Kochenderfer-Ladd, B. 2004. Peer victimisation: The role of emotions in adaptive and maladaptive coping. *Social Development* 13: 329–49.

Kochenderfer-Ladd, B., and K. Skinner. 2002. Children's coping strategies: Moderators of the effects of peer victimisation? *Developmental Psychology* 38: 267–78.

Kowalski, R.M., and S.P. Limber. 2007. Electronic bullying among middle school students. *Journal of Adolescent Health* 41, 6 Suppl. no. 1: S22–30.

Kowalski, R.M., S.P. Limber, and P.W. Agatston. 2008. *Cyber bullying: Bullying in the digital age*. Malden, MA: Blackwell.

Kristensen, S.M., and P.K. Smith. 2003. The use of coping strategies by Danish children classed as bullies, victims, bully/victims, and not involved, in response to different (hypothetical) types of bullying. *Scandinavian Journal of Psychology* 44: 479–88.

Lazarus, R.S. 2006. Emotions and interpersonal relationships: Toward a person-centered conceptualization of emotions and coping. *Journal of Personality* 74: 9–46.

Lodge, J., and S.S. Feldman. 2007. Avoidant coping as a mediator between appearance-related victimisation and self-esteem in young Australian adolescents. *British Journal of Developmental Psychology* 25: 633–42.

Machmutow, K., and S. Perren. 2011a. Coping with cyberbullying: Successful and unsuccessful coping strategies. Poster presented at the 12th congress of the SGP, September 13, in Fribourg, Switzerland.

Machmutow, K., and S. Perren. 2011b. Coping with cyberbullying: Successful and unsuccessful coping strategies. Poster presented at the 3rd COST workshop on cyberbullying, May 13, in Turku, Finland.

Mason, K.L. 2008. Cyberbullying: A preliminary assessment for school personnel. *Psychology in the Schools* 45: 323–48.

Mishna, F., M. Saini, and S. Solomon. 2009. Ongoing and online: Children and youth's perceptions of cyber bullying. *Children and Youth Services Review* 31: 1222–8.

Mitchell, K.J., D. Finkelhor, and J. Wolak. 2003. The exposure of youth to unwanted sexual material on the internet – A national survey of risk, impact, and prevention. *Youth & Society* 34: 330–58.

Mitchell, K.J., M. Ybarra, and D. Finkelhor. 2007. The relative importance of online victimisation in understanding depression, delinquency, and substance use. *Child Maltreatment* 12: 314–24.

Parris, L., K. Varjas, J. Meyers, and H. Cutts. 2011. High school students' perceptions of coping with cyberbullying. *Youth & Society* 20, no. 10: 1–23.

Patchin, J.W., and S. Hinduja. 2006. Bullies move beyond the schoolyard: A preliminary look at cyberbullying. *Youth Violence and Juvenile Justice* 4: 148–69.

Perren, S., and F.D. Alsaker. 2006. Social behavior and peer relationships of victims, bully–victims, and bullies in kindergarten. *Journal of Child Psychology and Psychiatry* 47: 45–57.

Perren, S., L. Corcoran, H. Cowie, F. Dehue, D. Garcia, C. McGuckin, A. Sevcikova, P. Tsatsou, and T. Völlink. 2012. Coping with cyberbullying: Review of evidence regarding successful strategies. Manuscript submitted for publication.

Perren, S., J. Dooley, T. Shaw, and D. Cross. 2010. Bullying in school and cyberspace: Associations with depressive symptoms in Swiss and Australian adolescents. *Child and Adolescent Psychiatry and Mental Health* 4, no. 28: 1–10.

Perren, S., and E. Gutzwiller-Helfenfinger. 2012. Cyberbullying and traditional bullying in adolescence: Differential roles of moral disengagement, moral emotions, and moral values. *European Journal of Developmental Psychology* 9: 195–209.

Pouwelse, M., C. Bolman, H. Lodewijkx, and M. Spaa. 2011. Gender differences and social support: Mediators or moderators between peer victimisation and depressive feelings? *Psychology in the Schools* 48: 800–14.

Price, M., and J. Dalgleish. 2010. Cyberbullying: Experiences, impacts and coping strategies as described by Australian young people. *Youth Studies Australia* 29, no. 2: 51–9.

Rigby, K. 2000. Effects of peer victimisation in schools and perceived social support on adolescent well-being. *Journal of Adolescence* 23: 57–68.

Roth, S., and L.J. Cohen. 1986. Approach, avoidance, and coping with stress. *American Psychologist* 41: 813–19.

Seiffge-Krenke, I., and N. Klessinger. 2000. Long-term effects of avoidant coping on adolescents' depressive symptoms. *Journal of Youth and Adolescence* 29: 617–30.

Singh, P., and K. Bussey. 2010. Peer victimisation and psychological maladjustment: The mediating role of coping self-efficacy. *Journal of Research on Adolescence* 21: 420–33.

Skinner, E.A., K. Edge, J. Altman, and H. Sherwood. 2003. Searching for the structure of coping: A review and critique of category systems for classifying ways of coping. *Psychological Bulletin* 129: 216–69.

Slonje, R., and P.K. Smith. 2008. Cyberbullying: Another main type of bullying? *Scandinavian Journal of Psychology* 49: 147–54.

Smith, P.K. 2012. Cyberbullying and cyber aggression. In *Handbook of school violence and school safety: International research and practice*, ed. S.R. Jimerson, A.B. Nickerson, M.J. Mayer and M.J. Furlong, 93–103. New York: Routledge.

Smith, P.K., J. Mahdavi, M. Carvalho, S. Fisher, S. Russell, and N. Tippett. 2008. Cyberbullying: Its nature and impact in secondary school pupils. *Journal of Child Psychology and Psychiatry* 49: 376–85.

Smith, P.K., and R. Slonje. 2010. Cyberbullying: The nature and extent of a new kind of bullying, in and out of school. In *Handbook of bullying in schools: An international perspective*, ed. S.R. Jimerson, S.M. Swearer and D.L. Espelage, 249–62. New York: Routledge.

Sontag, L.M., K.H. Clemans, J.A. Graber, and S.T. Lyndon. 2011. Traditional and cyber aggressors and victims: A comparison of psychosocial characteristics. *Journal of Youth and Adolescence* 40: 392–404.

Spears, B., P. Slee, L. Owens, and B. Johnson. 2009. Behind the scenes and screens insights into the human dimension of covert and cyberbullying. *Zeitschrift für Psychologie/Journal of Psychology* 217: 189–96.

Stacey, E. 2009. Research into cyberbullying: Student perspectives on cybersafe learning environments. *Informatics in Education* 8: 115–30.

Sticca, F., S. Ruggieri, F.D. Alsaker, and S. Perren. In press. Longitudinal risk factors for cyberbullying in adolescence. *Journal of Community & Applied Social Psychology*.

Sweeting, H., R. Young, P. West, and G. Der. 2006. Peer victimisation and depression in early-mid adolescence: A longitudinal study. *British Journal of Educational Psychology* 76: 577–94.

Tenenbaum, L.S., K. Varjas, J. Meyers, and L. Parris. 2011. Coping strategies and perceived effectiveness in fourth through eighth grade victims of bullying. *School Psychology International* 32: 263–87.

Tokunaga, R.S. 2010. Following you home from school: A critical review and synthesis of research on cyberbullying victimisation. *Computers in Human Behavior* 26: 277–87.

Topcu, C., O. Erdur-Baker, and Y. Capa-Aydin. 2008. Examination of cyberbullying experiences among Turkish students from different school types. *Cyberpsychology & Behavior* 11: 643–8.

Wang, J., T.R. Nansel, and R.J. Iannotti. 2011. Cyber and traditional bullying: Differential association with depression. *Journal of Adolescent Health* 48: 415–7.

Yamasaki, K., and K. Uchida. 2006. Relation of positive effect with emotion-focused coping in Japanese undergraduates. *Psychological Reports* 98: 611–20.

Ybarra, M.L. 2004. Linkages between depressive symptomatology and internet harassment among young regular internet users. *Cyberpsychology & Behavior* 7: 247–57.

Does the association with psychosomatic health problems differ between cyberbullying and traditional bullying?

Linda Beckman, Curt Hagquist and Lisa Hellström

Karlstad University, Centre for Research on Child and Adolescent Mental Health, Karlstad, Sweden

The association between mental health problems and traditional bullying is well known, whereas the strength of the association in cyberbullying is less known. This study aimed to compare the association between mutually exclusive groups of bullying involvement and psychosomatic problems as measured by the PsychoSomatic Problems scale. The sample comprised 3820 students (13–16 years old) in Sweden. The results indicate an association between bullying and psychosomatic problems, regardless of type of bullying involvement. No statistically significant differences in psychosomatic problems were found between cyberbullying and traditional bullying, either for victims or for bullies. The results do not confirm the hypothesis that the association between bullying and mental health is stronger for cyberbullying than for traditional bullying. Another important finding is that cyberbullies seem as likely as cybervictims to be at risk for mental health problems.

Introduction

Bullying behaviour is considered a part of the wider concept of peer-victimisation. While peer-victimisation is defined as 'a form of peer abuse in which a child is frequently the target of peer-aggression' (Kochenderfer and Ladd 1996, 1305), three additional criteria are usually added to define bullying: there should be some kind of power imbalance between the bully and the victim, it is a negative and intentional act, and the behaviour is repeated over time (Olweus 1993). These are likely to be stressful aspects for the victim, and the negative health effects of victimisation exposure can be explained in a theoretical context of an individual's response to a stressful situation (Lazarus and Folkman 1984).

The source of stress can arise from people's various structural surroundings such as different stratifications, for example social class and ethnicity (Pearlin 1981, 1989). In relation to victimisation among children and adolescents, Turner, Finkelhor, and Ormrod (2006) argue that stressors rooted in structural contexts are likely to vary with age, gender, ethnicity, parental education and family structure. For example, Nordhagen et al. (2005) showed that children in single-parent families had an increased risk of being bullied compared with children in two-parent families. Other forms of adversity, such as parental mental illness, poverty, unemployment, parental alcohol or drug problems, are also likely to coexist along with victimisation experiences (Turner, Finkelhor, and Ormrod

2006). The association between ethnicity and victimisation is less consistent in the literature, and may vary with cultural origin, time lived in a new country, neighbourhood and other structural factors (Turner, Finkelhor, and Ormrod 2006). Exposure to multiple forms of victimisation in a child's life may account for a substantial source of mental health risk.

Repeated or chronic stress can lead to negative feelings, psychosomatic problems (Alfvén, Östberg, and Hjern 2008), depression, aggression (Turner, Finkelhor and Ormrod 2006) or even more adverse conditions such as mental disorders (Charmandari, Tsigos, and Chrousos 2004). Psychosomatic problems may lead to school absenteeism (Alfvén 1997) and may be regarded as an early indicator of later problems.

During the past few decades an extensive body of literature has shown the negative effects of involvement in traditional bullying on adolescent mental health (Gini and Pozzoli 2009; Hawker and Boulton 2000). Many studies have shown that victims generally report more internalising problems (e.g. anxiety, anguish, worry and depression) compared to bullies and bully–victims (i.e. individuals classified as both bullies and victims).

Furthermore, bullying may be regarded as a component of externalising behaviour, and bullies generally report more externalising behaviours, such as aggression, and frequent alcohol and drug use, compared to victims (Gini and Pozzoli 2009). However, some discrepancies are reported; for example, Kaltiala-Heino et al. (2000) found no differences in psychosomatic problems between bullies and victims (but most problems were found among bully–victims), and that bullies actually suffered from multiple mental health problems more frequently than victims did. Other studies have reported that bullies suffer from depressive symptoms just as much as, or more than victims (Forero et al. 1999; Kaltiala-Heino et al. 1999). Bully–victims are the most vulnerable group and usually show more behavioural, developmental and emotional problems (Nansel et al. 2004; Van Cleave and Davis 2006).

There are, however, fewer studies that have explored cyberbullying (bullying via the Internet or mobile phones) and its effect on mental health. It is still uncertain whether cyberbullying and traditional bullying affect mental health differently.

It is suggested that cybervictimisation could be experienced as even more stressful and thus more damaging to adolescents' health than traditional victimisation, owing to the possibility for cyberbullies to remain 'virtually' unknown by the victim and the feasibility of reaching a large audience in a short time via the Internet or mobile phones (Hinduja and Patchin 2007; Kiriakidis and Kavoura 2010; Campbell 2005). The victims' direct reaction is also obscured, which may diminish the bullies' empathy and aggravate the situation (Pornari and Wood 2010). In addition, cyberbullying acts can be both direct and indirect in form, but are most often operationalised as indirect, relational or social behaviours that disrupt relationships and inflict psychological harm (Spears et al. 2009). This may strengthen the argument that exposure to such acts may affect mental health more adversely than direct acts.

Most bullying studies have focused on comparisons between cyber- and traditional victimisation, but fewer have included bullies and/or bully–victims. In general, similar associations between cyberbullying and mental health as for traditional bullying and mental health problems have been reported. Hinduja and Patchin (2010) investigated victims and bullies within traditional bullying and cyberbullying and found that all groups, in similar ways, served as a predictor for suicidal thoughts. Others have focused only on cyberbullying, without comparisons with traditional involvement. For example, Hinduja and Patchin (2007) found that cybervictims experience anger, frustration and sadness. Sourander et al. (2010) reported that adolescents involved in cyberbullying as victims, bullies or bully–victims showed associations with psychiatric and psychosomatic problems, but that cybervictims were more likely to report emotional and peer problems while cyberbullies more often reported conduct problems, smoking and drinking. The bully–victims reported all of these problems. A Turkish study by Baker-Erdur (2010) reported that cybervictimisation was associated with depression.

Only a few studies have investigated traditional bullying, cyberbullying and mental health problems among adolescents, including victims, bullies and bully–victims simultaneously and using mutually exclusive groups (Perren et al. 2010; Gradinger, Strohmeier, and Speil 2009; Wang, Nansel, and Iannotti 2010). Since traditional bullying and cyberbullying often co-occur (Perren et al. 2010), it is important to use mutually exclusive groups when analysing the effect of specific bullying types. Gradinger, Strohmeier, and Speil (2009) and Perren et al. (2010) found that victims of both traditional and cyberbullying experienced more internalising problems compared to traditional victims or cybervictims alone, which suggests a strong argument for including this group in the analysis. The same may apply for combined groups of traditional bullies and cyberbullies. However, Gradinger and colleagues (2009) did not control for any background factors except gender in their study. Perren et al. (2010) did not control for background factors (e.g. family structure) other than age and gender, which might have affected the results. Wang, Nansel, and Iannotti (2010) compared levels of depression among bullies, victims and bully–victims of physical, verbal, relational and cyberbullying. They found depression to be associated with cybervictimisation, distinct from the traditional forms of bullying. Further, their results showed small differences in depression levels between cyberbullies and cybervictims at the occasional frequency level, but significant differences at the more frequent level. For traditional involvement, victims had significantly higher depression levels than bullies and bully–victims. Although they used mutually exclusive groups, no combined groups of traditional bullying and cyberbullying were included in the analysis. While they controlled for gender, grade, race/ethnicity and family affluence, family structure was not included as a control variable.

To summarise, there are still gaps in the literature regarding the association between cyberbullying and psychosomatic problems, and in particular studies analysing involvement in traditional bullying and cyberbullying simultaneously and studies taking into account background factors that may be regarded as stressful, such as family structure and ethnicity. Furthermore, it is crucial to use mutually exclusive groups of bullying (Gradinger, Strohmeier, and Speil 2009). The aim of this paper is to compare the association between psychosomatic problems and cyberbullying and traditional bullying with regard to involvement as victim, bully and bully–victim, taking into account family structure and ethnicity by using mutually exclusive groups of bullying involvement.

Method

Participants

Data were collected from grade 9 students (aged around 15–16 years) in 2009, and grade 7–9 students (aged around 13–16 years) in 2010, from 16 public schools in the county of Värmland in Sweden. The participation rate was 83.2% in 2009 and 90.3% in 2010. Following exclusion of 23 questionnaires (which had extremely one-sided response patterns, such as consistently filling in the extremes or with many questions unanswered), 3820 valid questionnaires was obtained.

The project was reviewed by the local ethics committee at Karlstad University and no objections were raised.

Procedure

Data collection took place in the late autumn term in the schools and was part of a community collaboration project, aiming at mental health promotion. The questionnaires were web based and included a broad set of questions regarding mental health and bullying. The parents of the students in grades 7 and 8 were informed about the study and encouraged to notify the school if they did not want their child to participate. Because of the 9th graders' age, no parental consent was requested. The students used the school computers to retrieve a link to the questionnaire from the Internet. A member of the project team was present to give information and organise the data collection. The questionnaire took approximately 30–40 minutes to complete.

Measurements

The questionnaire included different aspects of students' health and well-being and, for this study, background, bullying- and mental health questions were used. Descriptive statistics of socio-demographic characteristics of participants and study variables are shown in Table 1.

Background data

This included questions about gender, grade and country of birth for students ('In which country were you born?'), and about their parents ('In which country was your mother born?' and 'In which country was your father born?') and family structure. Two questions about family structure were asked. First, the participants were asked if they lived with both their parents. If so, they were asked whether they did so always ('Always together with my mother and father'; ' Mostly with my mother, sometimes with my father'; 'Mostly with my father, sometimes with my mother'; 'About the same with mother and father, for example, alternating weeks').

Bullying

Two global questions about traditional bullying were taken from the Olweus Bully/Victim Questionnaire (OBVQ) (Olweus 1996): 'How often have you been bullied at school in the past couple of months?' and 'How often have you taken part in bullying another student(s) at school in the past couple of months?', with five response alternatives ('I have not been bullied/bullied other students at school in the past couple of months', 'only once or twice', '2 or 3 times a month', 'about once a week' and 'several times a week'). The global questions were accompanied by a definition taken from the study Health Behavior in School-aged Children (HBSC) (Marklund 1997): 'We say a student is being bullied when another student, or a group of students, says or does nasty and unpleasant things to him or her. It is also bullying when a student is teased repeatedly in a way he or she does not like. But it is not bullying when two students of about the same strength quarrel or fight. It is also not bullying when the teasing is done in a friendly or playful way'.

The cyberbullying questions were adapted from Smith et al. (2008) and the Swedish translation by Slonje and Smith (2008). Two global questions ('How often have you been cyberbullied in the past couple of months?' and 'How often have you cyberbullied other student/s the past couple of months?') had the same five response alternatives. Cyberbullying was defined 'in the same way as traditional bullying above but involves

Table 1. Descriptive statistics of socio-demographic characteristics of participants and study variables based on the whole sample ($N = 3820$): frequency (F) and percentage (%).

$N = 3820$	F (%)
Gender	
Girl	1942 (51.1)
Boy	1858 (48.9)
Missing	20 (0.5)
Grade	
7	1018 (26.6)
8	1091 (28.6)
9	1701 (44.8)
Birth country – student	
Sweden	3640 (95.6)
Other country	167 (4.4)
Missing	13 (0.3)
Birth country – parents	
Both born in Sweden	3081 (80.9)
One born in another country	369 (9.7)
Both born in another country	360 (9.4)
Missing	10 (0.3)
Family structure	
With both parents	2407 (63.0)
Shared living[a]	821 (21.5)
Single parent	527 (13.8)
Other than parent/alone	63 (1.6)
Missing	2 (0.1)
Bullying involvement – once or twice or more	
Traditional victim	176 (4.6)
Boys	77 (2.0)
Girls	98 (2.6)
Cybervictim	74 (1.9)
Boys	22 (0.6)
Girls	54 (1.4)
Combined traditional + cybervictims	70 (1.8)
Boys	16 (0.4)
Girls	34 (1.0)
Traditional bully	309 (8.0)
Boys	195 (5.1)
Girls	113 (2.9)
Cyberbully	57 (1.5)
Boys	26 (0.7)
Girls	31 (0.8)
Combined traditional + cyberbully	59 (1.5)
Boys	38 (1.0)
Girls	21
Traditional bully–victim	74 (2.0)
Boys	62 (1.6)
Girls	12 (0.5)
Cyberbully–victim	22 (0.6)
Boys	8 (0.2)
Girls	14 (0.3)
Combined traditional + cyberbully–victim	144 (3.7)
Boys	69 (2.0)
Girls	72 (1.9)

(*Continued*)

Table 1. (Continued).

$N = 3820$	F (%)
Non-involved	2603 (67.7)
Not complete answers	273 (7.1)
Psychosomatic problems	
High percentile 75th	979 (25.6)
Boys	260 (6.8)
Girls	716 (18.7)
Mid percentile	1739 (45.6)
Boys	919 (24.0)
Girls	810 (21.2)
Low percentile 25th	1005 (26.3)
Boys	623 (16.3)
Girls	375 (9.9)
Total	3820 (100)

Note: [a] Shared living includes separated or divorced parents sharing care of the child/children.

bullying through for example mobile phones (calls or text messages), photo/video clips, E-mail, Chat-rooms, Web-pages, Instant Messaging (i.e. MSN)'. The recall period for all questions was the past couple of months. The student's frame of reference was the autumn term.

Students were classified as victims, bullies or bully–victims if they had answered that they had been bullied/bullied another student/other students once or twice or more frequently. Since the repetition criterion is not established in cyberbullying research (one cyber incident can be viewed by a large audience), we chose to use the lower cut-off for both traditional bullying and cyberbullying. To allow for comparisons a lower cut-off may be justified.

Psychosomatic problems

The PsychoSomatic Problems (PSP) scale was used to measure mental health (Hagquist 2008). This scale consists of eight single items: 'had difficulty in concentrating', 'had difficulty in sleeping', 'suffered from headaches', 'suffered from stomach aches', 'felt tense', 'had little appetite', 'felt sad' and 'felt giddy'. The response categories for all of these items were 'never', 'seldom', 'sometimes', 'often' and 'always', referring to the last school year. Psychometric analyses based on the Rasch model (Rasch 1960/1980) justified the summation of raw scores. The PSP scale has shown high reliability and invariant properties, making it useful for measuring psychosomatic health complaints in general populations of adolescents (Hagquist 2008). In the current data set, two items, felt sad and stomach ache, showed differential item functioning (DIF) across genders; this means that these two items worked differently for boys and girls. Given the same location on the PSP scale, girls tended to score higher than boys on these particular items. Since DIF violates measurement requirements of invariance, DIF was resolved by splitting both items into one item for boys (leaving girls a missing value) and one item for girls (leaving boys a missing value). Rasch analysis of the PSP scale was conducted using the software RUMM 2030.

A high value on the PSP scale indicates more psychosomatic problems. Using percentile values based on the entire sample as cut-off points, the linear PSP variable was categorised in two ways: adolescents located on or below the 25th percentile were compared with those located on or above the 75th percentile. The rationale behind this categorisation was to contrast individuals with no or relatively mild psychosomatic problems with those with relatively severe problems.

Analysis

ANOVA

Analysis of variance (ANOVA) was conducted to test for differences in mean values on the PSP scale for traditional victims and cybervictims (Table 2).

Multinomial logistic regression analysis

Multinomial logistic regression analysis was conducted to analyse associations between psychosomatic problems (PSP scale) and types and groups of bullying involvement. The mutually exclusive bullying types and groups were coded as traditional victims, traditional bullies, traditional bully–victims, cybervictims, cyberbullies, cyber bully–victims, combined traditional/cybervictims, combined traditional/cyberbullies and combined traditional/cyber bully–victims.

Two sets of regression analyses, both including three models with PSP scale as the dependent variable, were conducted. The first set of analysis included three models using (1) traditional, cyber and combined victims; (2) traditional, cyber and combined bullies; and (3) traditional, cyber and combined bully–victims. The second set of analyses also included three models, contrasting (1) traditional victims, bullies and bully–victims; (2) cybervictims, bullies and bully–victims; and (3) combined victims, bullies and bully–victims. All models used non-involved students as a reference category (Table 3).

In order to specifically contrast the extreme groups of the PSP scale distribution, individuals located on or above the 75th percentile were compared with individuals on or below the 25th percentile.

The multinomial regression analysis was performed using STATA 11.2 software. To take school clustering effects into account, robust standard errors were calculated.

Control variables

In all regression analyses, gender, grade, family structure and birth country (birth country for students and for parents) were included as control variables. Two dichotomous variables were included in the analysis: gender and children's country of birth (born in Sweden, or in another country). Grade was represented by 7, 8 or 9. Two variables were included to represent the students' family structure (living with one parent, living with both mother and father, shared living, or living with someone else) and parents' country of birth (one parent born in a country other than Sweden, both born in a country other than Sweden, or two parents born in Sweden).

Formal test of group differences

To formally test whether there was a significant difference in risk ratios between different groups, *Z*-scores was calculated: *Z*diff. = (log odds ratio 1 – log odds ratio 2)/($\surd$(SE1^2 + SE2^2 – 2 × Cov.).

Ordinary linear regression analysis

In addition, for tentative purposes, an ordinary linear regression was conducted (not reported in the tables) using the original PSP scale without any categorisation. Traditional victims and cybervictims, traditional bullies and cyberbullies, and control variables (gender, grade, family structure, country of birth) were constructed and analysed using dummy regression coding. The linear regression analysis was conducted using SPSS 19.0 software.

Results

ANOVA

The ANOVA test with one set of 2 (gender) × 4 (victimised groups) showed significant main effects for victimisation types ($F = 56.85, p < 0.000$) and a main effect for gender ($F = 28.82, p < 0.000$). No interaction effect (gender × victimisation) appeared.

Table 2 shows the mean PSP scores for victimisation by gender.

In accordance with the calculations of differences between risk ratios, the ANOVA showed no difference between traditional victims and cybervictims [mean difference −0.296, standard error 0.190, $p < 0.720$, confidence interval (CI) −0.798–0.206].

Multinomial regression analysis

This set of analyses is presented in the top half of Table 3 and includes three models (victims, bullies and bully–victims, contrasting traditional involvement, cyber involvement and combined groups).

Table 3 shows relative risk ratios for the association between type of bullying involvement and psychosomatic problems. These problems are significantly associated with all

Table 2. Mean scores on the PsychoSomatic Problems (PSP) scale, standard deviations (SD) and *n* by gender, for traditional victims (TV), cybervictims (CV), combined (both traditional and cybervictims) and non-involved groups.

		PSP score		
Victim group	Gender	Mean	SD	*n*
TV	Girl	−0.374	1.13	98
	Boy	−0.981	1.23	76
	Total	−0.639	1.21	174
CV	Girl	−0.101	1.02	50
	Boy	−0.663	0.91	21
	Total	−0.267	1.02	71
Combined	Girl	0.266	1.25	52
	Boy	−0.089	2.14	16
	Total	0.183	1.5	68
Non-involved	Girl	−1.117	1.24	1359
	Boy	−1.833	1.3	1172
	Total	−1.448	1.32	2531
Total	Girl	−0.991	1.26	1559
	Boy	−1.742	1.34	1285
	Total	−1.33	1.35	2844

Table 3. Multinomial regression analysis.

	Model 1 ($N = 2830$)				Model 2 ($N = 2929$)				Model 3 ($N = 2743$)			
	Victims	*B*	RR	95% CI	Bullies	*B*	RR	95% CI	b/v	*B*	RR	95% CI
75th vs 25th percentile groups/types of bullying	T victim	1.94	6.93	(4.9–9.8)[a]	T bully	1.28	3.58	(2.7–4.8)[a]	T b/v	2.7	15.67	(5.9–41.3)[a]
	C victim	2.70	14.91	(6.1–36.2)[a]	C bully	1.83	6.26	(3.0–13.0)[a]	C b/v	15.66	[b]	[b]
	Comb. victim	2.58	13.19	(4.5–38.7)[a]	Comb. bully	1.61	4.98	(3.2–7.7) [a]	Comb. b/v	2.66	14.29	(9.2–22.2)[a]
	Non-involved	0	1		Non-involved	0	1		Non-involved	0	1	

	Model 4 ($N = 3063$)				Model 5 ($N = 2664$)				Model 6 ($N = 2775$)			
	TB	*B*	RR	95% CI	CB	*B*	RR	95% CI	TB+CB (Comb)	*B*	RR	95% CI
75th vs 25th percentile groups/ types of bullying	T victim	1.95	6.97	(4.9–9.7)[a]	C victim	2.71	15.09	(6.3–36.3)[a]	Comb. victim	2.57	13.06	(4.5–38.4)[a]
	T bully	1.26	3.54	(2.6–4.7)[a]	C bully	1.81	6.14	(2.9–12.0)[a]	Comb. bully	1.52	4.56	(2.9–7.0) [a]
	T b/v	2.76	15.77	(5.9–41.9)[a]	C b/v	15.54	[b]	[b]	Comb. b/v	2.69	14.69	(9.5–22.5)[a]
	Non-involved	0	1		Non-involved	0	1		Non-involved	0	1	

Notes: Models 1–3: *B*, relative risk (RR) and 95% confidence intervals (95% CI) for psychosomatic problems (PSP scale) by (1) victims, (2) bullies and (3) bully–victims (b/v), contrasting T (traditional), C (cyber) and combined (Comb. = both traditional and cyber), with non-involved as reference category. Models 4–6: psychosomatic problems (PSP scale) by (1) T, (2) C and (3) combined, contrasting victims, bullies, and b/v with non-involved as reference category. Dependent variable comprised three categories, of which the first and the last are contrasted (25th percentile vs 75th percentile); coefficients of the mid category are not shown in the table. All analyses were adjusted for gender, grade, family structure, and country of birth for students and parents (coefficients not shown in the table).

[a]Significant at the 95% level.

[b]The confidence intervals are very wide owing to few observations. RR for CB bully–victim model 3 = 6,317,735, CI = 2,000,868 – 1.99+e07, and RR for CB bully–victim model 5 = 5,646,942, CI = 1786498 – 1.78e+07.

types and groups of bullying. The confidence intervals are overlapping, indicating that there may be no significant differences between cyberbullying and traditional bullying, either for victims or for bullies, with respect to psychosomatic problems.

The next set of regression analyses is presented in the bottom half of Table 3. The mutually exclusive groups remain the same as in models 1–3, but different groups are contrasted. These models (4–6) are complementary to models 1–3 in Table 3.

The results presented in models 4–6 are consistent with models 1–3, i.e. psychosomatic problems are significantly associated with all types and groups of bullying, but the confidence intervals for cyberbully–victims are difficult to interpret, probably owing to few observations in the cells.

All analyses were repeated at the 90th versus the 10th percentile. Since the observations in some cells were too small to estimate adequate risk ratios, only analyses using the 75th versus 25th percentiles are presented.

Formal test of group difference

Table 4 shows Z-scores for difference between the relative risk ratios of the two groups being compared. If the Z-score is above 1.96, the difference is statistically significant at the 95% level.

The Z-score tests showed no significant difference at the 95% level between traditional victimisation and cybervictimisation ($Z = 1.36$). Neither were there any differences between traditional victims and the combined groups ($Z = 1.3$), or between cybervictims and the combined groups ($Z = 0.15$).

The relative risk ratios did not differ significantly between traditional bullies and cyberbullies ($Z = 1.23$), between traditional bullies and the combined group ($Z = 1.15$), or between cyberbullies and the combined group ($Z = 0.48$). However, there were significant differences within the bully–victims groups: between traditional bully–victim

Table 4. Z-score differences between the groups and types of bullying at the 95% level.

Comparing groups from Table 3	Z-score
C victim–T victim	1.36
T victim–Comb. victim	1.3
C victim–Comb. victim	0.15
T bully–C bully	1.23
T bully–Comb. bully	1.15
C bully–Comb. bully	0.48
T b/v–C b/v	18.0*
C b/v–Comb. b/v	20.1*
T b/v–Comb. b/v	0.19
T victim–T bully	2.77*
T bully–T b/v	3.24*
T victim–T b/v	1.53
C victim–C bully	1.37
C victim–C b/v	20.15*
C bully–C b/v	14.55*
Comb. victim–Comb. bully	1.85
Comb. victim–Comb. b/v	3.08*
Comb. bully–Comb. b/v	0.2

Notes: C: cyber; T: traditional; Comb.: combined; b/v: bully–victim.
*Significant difference between groups at the 95% level ($p < 0.05$).

and cyberbully–victim ($Z = 18.0$) and between cyberbully–victim and the combined bully–victim group ($Z = 20.8$), but not between traditional bullies and the combined bully group ($Z = 0.19$).

There was a significant difference between the relative risk ratios at the 95% level between traditional victims and traditional bullies ($Z = 2.77$) and also between traditional bullies and bully–victims ($Z = 3.24$), meaning that victims and bully–victims are more likely to report psychosomatic problems than traditional bullies. No difference between traditional victims and bully–victims appeared ($Z = 1.53$), but there were differences between cybervictims and cyberbully–victims, and between cyberbullies and bully–victims ($Z = 14.55$ and $Z = 20.15$, respectively). Interestingly, there was no significant difference between cybervictims and cyberbullies ($Z = 1.37$). Among the combined groups there was a significant difference between the combined cyberbullies and the combined bully–victims, indicating more psychosomatic problems among combined bully–victims.

Linear regression analysis

The tentative analysis using ordinary linear regression (not reported in the tables) confirmed the general pattern from the logistic regression analyses: all groups involved in bullying showed significantly higher levels of psychosomatic problems than non-involved, even after adjustment for control variables.

Discussion

This study compares the associations between bullying involvement and psychosomatic problems. No difference between victims or between bullies of cyberbullying and traditional bullying were detected, but differences within traditional bullying (between bullies and victims) appeared. Bully–victims were significantly different from the bullies and victims in terms of experiencing more psychosomatic problems.

These results contradict the results of Wang, Nansel, and Iannotti (2010), as we found no significant differences in psychosomatic problems between cybervictims and traditional victims. Furthermore, the results did not indicate any differences for the combined victims groups (both traditional victims and cybervictims) compared to victims and bullies, as Gradinger, Strohmeier, and Speil (2009) and Perren et al. (2010) reported. The differences in results may in part be due to different ways of analysing the data, e.g. how the bullying groups are categorised or which control variables are used.

With regard to bullies, our results showed no significant difference between occasional cyberbullies and traditional bullies with regard to psychosomatic problems, which is in accordance with findings from Wang, Nansel, and Iannotti (2010). Although our results showed a significant difference between traditional bullies and traditional victims, there was no difference between cyberbullies and cybervictims. However, weak or no differences between victims and bullies with regard to psychosomatic problems have been shown earlier by Kaltiala-Heino et al. (2000, 670), who suggested that 'bullies are not simply straightforwardly aggressive and dominant. They also exhibit internalising disorders that associate with insecurity'.

In concordance with previous research (Nansel et al. 2004; Sourander et al. 2010), bully–victims were more likely to experience psychosomatic problems compared to bullies and victims. Bully–victims are considered a vulnerable group who generally experience a large amount of stressful situations and factors, such as behavioural, developmental and emotional problems (Van Cleave and Davis 2006).

Our results did not point to any obvious dose–response relationship of psychosomatic problems when being involved in both cyberbullying and traditional bullying. Although some researchers have investigated the cumulative effect of different types of bullying (Turner, Finkelhor, and Ormrod 2006; Gradinger, Strohmeier, and Speil 2009), the combined groups consisting of traditional bullying and cyberbullying have not yet been systematically investigated and further research is needed.

In conclusion, these results do not confirm the hypothesis that the association between bullying and mental health is stronger for cyberbullying than for traditional bullying. Another important finding is that cyberbullies seem as likely to be at risk of mental health problems as cybervictims. More research on the differences in individual characteristics is needed to understand the similarities and differences between cyberbullying and traditional bullying.

Methodological remarks

The analysis scheme applied in the present study enabled strict and proper distinctions to be made between different kinds of bullying involvement. The approach using mutually exclusive groups of bullying involvement enabled conceptually robust conclusions to be drawn about the association between different kinds of bullying involvement and psychosomatic problems. Regardless of sample group or type of bullying involvement, psychosomatic health problems are significantly more common among students involved in bullying than among non-involved students. The difference in results between some previous studies (e.g. Wang, Nansel, and Iannotti, 2010) and this study may in part be due to the use of different methodology. The absence of statistically significant differences in health effects between different forms of bullying may partly be due to the relatively low statistical power. In some cases this is manifested by wide confidence intervals. Hence, we cannot rule out the possibility that there are real differences between traditional bullying and cyberbullying with respect to the impact on psychosomatic health.

One problem in cyberbullying research is the lack of an established and agreed upon definition of cyberbullying. The repetition criterion for traditional bullying is not clearly applicable to cyberbullying, which was one reason why we applied the lower cut-off for bullying involvement. Furthermore, in this study we used a traditional definition for both types of bullying, and just added that cyberbullying included bullying via technology. The definition of bullying did not explicitly include indirect forms such as social exclusion or rumour spreading, which might have caused an underestimation of the bullying prevalence. Since the question on traditional bullying was given first, it is possible that students only exposed to cyberbullying also endorsed that question, implying that some overestimation among bully–victims and the combined groups might have occurred.

The cross-sectional design of this study does not permit definite inferences to be drawn about the directions of the relationships, i.e. whether bullying is affecting mental health or vice versa. In order to determine causal pathways longitudinal data for individuals are required.

References

Alfvén, G. 1997. Psychosomatic pain in children: A psychomuscular tension reaction? *European Journal of Pain* 1: 5–14.

Alfvén, G., V. Östberg, and A. Hjern. 2008. Stressor, perceived stress and recurrent pain in Swedish schoolchildren. *Journal of Psychosomatic Research* 65: 381–7.

Campbell, M. 2005. Cyber bullying: An old problem in a new guise? *Australian Journal of Guidance and Counselling* 15: 68–76.

Charmandari, E., C. Tsigos, and G. Chrousos. 2004. Endocrinology of the stress response 1. *Annual Review of Physiology* 67: 259–84.

Erdur-Baker, O. 2010. Cyberbullying and its correlation to traditional bullying, gender and frequent and risky usage of internet-mediated communication tools. *New Media & Society* 12: 109–125.

Forero, R., L. McLellan, C. Rissel, and A. Bauman. 1999. Bullying behaviour and psychosocial health among school students in New South Wales, Australia: Cross sectional survey. *British Medical Journal* 319, no. 7206: 344–8.

Gini, G., and T. Pozzoli. 2009. Association between bullying and psychosomatic problems: A meta-analysis. *Pediatrics* 123: 1059–65.

Gradinger, P., D. Strohmeier, and C. Spiel. 2009. Traditional bullying and cyberbullying. *Zeitschrift für Psychologie/Journal of Psychology* 217: 205–13.

Hagquist, C. 2008. Psychometric properties of the PsychoSomatic Problems scale: A Rasch analysis on adolescent data. *Social Indicators Research* 86: 511–23.

Hawker, D., and M. Boulton. 2000. Twenty years' research on peer victimization and psychosocial maladjustment: A meta-analytic review of cross-sectional studies. *Journal of Child Psychology and Psychiatry* 41: 441–55.

Hinduja, S., and J. Patchin. 2007. Offline consequences of online victimization. *Journal of School Violence* 6, no. 3: 89–112.

Hinduja, S., and J. Patchin. 2010. Bullying, cyberbullying, and suicide. *Archives of Suicide Research* 14: 206–21.

Kaltiala-Heino, R., M. Rimpelä, M. Marttunen, A. Rimpelä, and P. Rantanen. 1999. Bullying, depression, and suicidal ideation in Finnish adolescents: School survey. *British Medical Journal* 319: 348–51.

Kaltiala-Heino, R., M. Rimpelä, P. Rantanen, and A. Rimpelä. 2000. Bullying at school – an indicator of adolescents at risk for mental disorders. *Journal of Adolescence* 23: 661–74.

Kiriakidis, S., and A. Kavoura. 2010. Cyberbullying: A review of the literature on harassment through the internet and other electronic means. *Family & Community Health* 33: 82.

Kochenderfer, B.J., and G.W. Ladd. 1996. Peer victimization: Cause or consequence of school maladjustment? *Child Development* 67: 1305–17.

Lazarus, R.S., and S. Folkman. 1984. *Stress, appraisal, and coping*. Berlin: Springer.

Marklund, U. 1997. Skolbarns hälsovanor under ett decennium. *Tabell-Rapport. Health Behavior in School-Age Children. A WHO Collaborative Study*. Folkhälsoinstitutet: Stockholm.

Nansel, T., W. Craig, M. Overpeck, G. Saluja, and W. Ruan. 2004. Cross-national consistency in the relationship between bullying behaviors and psychosocial adjustment. *Archives of Pediatrics and Adolescent Medicine* 158: 730–6.

Nordhagen, R., A. Nielsen, H. Stigum, and L. Köhler. 2005. Parental reported bullying among Nordic children: A population-based study. *Child: Care, Health and Development* 31: 693–701.

Olweus, D. 1993. *Bullying at school: What we know and what we can do*. Cambridge, MA: Blackwell.

Olweus, D. 1996. *The revised Olweus bully/victim questionnaire*. University of Bergen: Mimeo HEMIL.

Pearlin, L.I. 1989. The sociological study of stress. *Journal of Health and Social Behavior* 30: 241–256.

Pearlin, L.I., E.G. Menaghan, M.A. Lieberman and J.T. Mullan. 1981. The stress process. *Journal of Health and Social Behavior* 22: 337–356.

Perren, S., J. Dooley, T. Shaw, and D. Cross. 2010. Bullying in school and cyberspace: Associations with depressive symptoms in Swiss and Australian adolescents. *Child and Adolescent Psychiatry and Mental Health* 4, no. 1: 1–10.

Pornari, C., and J. Wood. 2010. Peer and cyber aggression in secondary school students: The role of moral disengagement, hostile attribution bias, and outcome expectancies. *Aggressive Behavior* 36: 81–94.

Rasch, G. 1960/1980. *Probabilistic models for some intelligence and attainment tests (Copenhagen, Danish Institute for Educational Research). Expanded edition (1980) with foreword and afterword by Benjamin D. Wright*. Chicago, IL: University of Chicago Press.

Slonje, R., and P.K. Smith. 2008. Cyberbullying: Another main type of bullying? *Scandinavian Journal of Psychology* 49: 147–54.

Smith, P.K., J. Mahdavi, M. Carvalho, S. Fisher, S. Russel, and N. Tippett. 2008. Cyberbullying: Its nature and impact in secondary school. *Journal of Child Psychology and Psychiatry* 49: 376–85.

Sourander, A., A. Brunstein Klomek, M. Ikonen, J. Lindroos, T. Luntamo, M. Koskelainen, T. Ristkari, and H. Helenius. 2010. Psychosocial risk factors associated with cyberbullying among adolescents: A population-based study. *Archives of General Psychiatry* 67: 720–8.

Spears, B., P. Slee, L. Owens, and B. Johnson. 2009. Behind the scenes and screens. *Zeitschrift für Psychologie/Journal of Psychology* 217: 189–96.

Turner, H., Finkelhor, and R. Ormrod. 2006. The effect of lifetime victimization on the mental health of children and adolescents. *Social Science & Medicine* 62: 13–27.

Van Cleave, J., and M. Davis. 2006. Bullying and peer victimization among children with special health care needs. *Pediatrics* 118: e1212–19.

Wang, J., T. Nansel, and R. Iannotti. 2010. Cyber and traditional bullying: Differential association with depression. *Journal of Adolescent Health* 48: 415–17.

Problem behaviours, traditional bullying and cyberbullying among adolescents: longitudinal analyses

Leanne Lester, Donna Cross and Thérèse Shaw

Child Health Promotion Research Centre, Edith Cowan University, Mt Lawley, Australia

Problem Behaviour Theory suggests that young people's problem behaviours tend to cluster. This study examined the relationship between traditional bullying, cyberbullying and engagement in problem behaviours using longitudinal data from approximately 1500 students. Levels of traditional victimisation and perpetration at the beginning of secondary school (grade 8, age 12) predicted levels of engagement in problem behaviours at the end of grade 9 (age 14). Levels of victimisation and perpetration were found to moderate each other's associations with engagement in problem behaviours. Cyberbullying did not represent an independent risk factor over and above levels of traditional victimisation and perpetration for higher levels of engagement in problem behaviours. The findings suggest that to reduce the clustering of cyberbullying behaviours with other problem behaviours, it may be necessary to focus interventions on traditional bullying, specifically direct bullying.

Introduction

Relative to other age groups, adolescents have a disproportionately higher risk of engaging in problem behaviours that can have serious consequences for the individual, their family, friends and the community (Bartlett, Holditch-Davis, and Belyea 2007). Problem Behaviour Theory (Jessor and Jessor 1977) is a psychosocial model used to explain dysfunction and maladaptation in adolescence. It suggests that proneness to specific problem behaviours entails involvement in other problem behaviours and less participation in conventional behaviours. The theory has previously been employed to investigate a wide range of behaviours defined socially as a problem or undesirable, and which elicit a negative social response. The generality and robustness of the theory have been tested investigating behavioural outcomes such as substance use, deviancy, delinquency and risky sexual behaviours.

During adolescence, problem behaviours including antisocial behaviour, school failure, precocious sexual behaviour, drinking, cigarette smoking and substance use are intercorrelated (Petterson 1993) and tend to covary (Barrera et al. 2001). Jessor and Jessor (1977) suggest one reason young people's problem behaviours tend to cluster, is that society views each of them as unacceptable, deviant or rebellious. Social Cognitive Theory suggests that adolescents model their friends' behaviours, including bullying and other antisocial behaviours (Mouttapa et al. 2004). Consequently, adolescents who bully and/or cyberbully others may feel they have crossed the boundary of acceptable conduct, and become part of a 'deviant' subculture, where these behaviours are more prevalent and acceptable.

Traditionally, bullying behaviour is defined as a type of aggressive behaviour involving the systematic abuse of power through unjustified and repeated acts intended to inflict harm (Smith 2004), and includes both direct (overt) and indirect (covert) forms. Cyberbullying, or bullying using the Internet and mobile phones, appears to be a form of bullying including both direct and indirect aggressive components (Dooley, Pyżalski, and Cross 2009). Accordingly, problem behaviours associated with traditional bullying may also be associated with cyberbullying.

Cross-sectional research suggests that the perpetration of face-to-face bullying and cyberbullying is associated with problem behaviours such as poor academic achievement (Mitchell, Ybarra, and Finkelhor 2007), drinking alcohol (Mitchell, Ybarra, and Finkelhor 2007), smoking and other substance use problems (Niemelä et al. 2011), vandalism (Hay, Meldrum, and Mann 2010), stealing (Hay, Meldrum, and Mann 2010), intentionally hurting other people (Hay et al. 2010), weapon-carrying (Dukes, Stein, and Zane 2010) and other delinquent behaviours. Cyberbullying victimisation is significantly and positively related to school problems (such as absenteeism, cheating on an exam or being sent home for poor behaviour), shoplifting, carrying a weapon and running away from home (Hinduja and Patchin 2007, 2008). Both traditional and online victimisation are associated with stealing, vandalism, getting in trouble with the police, fighting and substance use (Hinduja and Patchin 2007, 2008; Mitchell, Ybarra, and Finkelhor 2007). This previous research measured either victimisation only or victimisation and perpetration separately, but did not take into account those who are bully–victims, which may explain the relationships found between victimisation (a non-problem behaviour) and problem behaviours.

Direct bullying perpetration has been found to be a stronger predictor than indirect bullying perpetration of violence, delinquency and other antisocial behaviours in adolescence (Bender and Lösel 2011; Hampela, Manhalb, and Hayera 2009), while indirect perpetration was a stronger predictor of weapon-carrying than direct perpetration (Dukes, Stein, and Zane 2010).

In a study of 7200 students in Australia, 7% of secondary school students (grades 8 and 9) reported being cyberbullied frequently (every few weeks or more often in the previous term), 4% reported cyberbullying others frequently and 2% reported frequent cybervictimisation perpetration. Frequent cybervictimisation was more prevalent for females and frequent cyberperpetration more prevalent for males (Cross et al. 2009).

Cyberbullying perpetration can be seen as a new manifestation of deviant behaviour that adolescents are adopting. Moreover, reviews show high correlations between traditional bullying and cyberbullying, with adolescents reporting traditional perpetration also reporting cyberperpetration and those reporting traditional victimisation also reporting cybervictimisation (Li, Cross, and Smith 2012; Tokunaga 2010).

To test the hypotheses of a relationship between traditional bullying and engagement in problem behaviours, we examined traditional victimisation and perpetration simultaneously to take into account victims, perpetrators and bully–victims to determine whether higher levels of traditional victimisation and perpetration predict higher levels of engagement in problem behaviours. As traditional bullying includes both direct and indirect forms and direct bullying has previously been linked with problem behaviours, we also examine the associations between these different forms of traditional victimisation and perpetration and levels of engagement in problem behaviours. Lastly, given that bullying at school has been found to be a gateway behaviour to other problem behaviours such as antisocial problems, delinquency, violence and aggression (Bender and Lösel 2011), we examined whether cyberbullying also has a significant influence on levels of engagement in problem behaviours.

The following three hypotheses will be examined: (1) higher levels of traditional victimisation and perpetration at the beginning of secondary school (grade 8) predict higher levels of engagement in problem behaviours at the end of grade 9; (2) higher levels of traditional *direct* victimisation and perpetration at the beginning of secondary school (grade 8) predict higher levels of engagement in problem behaviours at the end of grade 9; and (3) levels of cybervictimisation and perpetration represent independent risk factors over and above levels of traditional victimisation and perpetration for higher levels of engagement in problem behaviours.

Methods

Sample and procedure

Data were obtained from the Supportive Schools Project. This project aimed to enhance the capacity of secondary schools to implement a whole-school bullying intervention (including strategies to enhance student transition to secondary school) and compare this intervention to the standard behaviour management practices used in Western Australian secondary schools using a cluster randomised comparison trial. The longitudinal data collected included adolescents' experiences of bullying victimisation and perpetration during the transition from primary school to secondary school. Secondary schools affiliated with the Catholic Education Office (CEO) of Western Australia were approached to participate in the study; students in Australian Catholic schools are more likely than students attending schools in other sectors (e.g. government schools) to move in intact groups, so this reduced the rate of transition attrition as students moved from primary to secondary schools.

Schools were stratified according to the total number of students enrolled and each school's socio-economic status, and then were randomly assigned within each stratum to an intervention or a comparison group. Twenty-one of the 29 schools approached consented to participate; eight schools declined, citing reasons including other priorities within their school and demanding staff workloads. Following Edith Cowan University's Human Research Ethics Committee approval of the research protocol, a combination of active and passive consent was obtained from parents of the grade 8 students (13 years of age) enrolled in the schools in 2005. Parental consent was provided for 3462 of the 3769 (92%) students eligible to participate from 21 secondary schools in Perth, Western Australia. Data used in this paper were collected from 1782 students assigned to 11 comparison schools. Data from intervention students were not used, to ensure that the results were not confounded by the intervention programme.

Four waves of student data were collected from 2005 to 2007. Here, we analyse data from the second wave, after students' transition to secondary school, when the cohort completed questionnaires in April 2006 at the beginning of grade 8 (12 years old) ($n = 1745$, 98% of those eligible), and the fourth wave, in October/November 2007 at the end of grade 9 (14 years of age) ($n = 1616$, 95% of those eligible). Over the three-year study period, approximately 50% of the participants were males, and about 70% attended co-educational ($n = 8$) and 30% attended single-sex ($n = 3$) secondary schools.

Measures

Traditional victimisation and perpetration

Traditional victimisation was assessed using a seven-item categorical index adapted from Rigby and Slee (1998) and Olweus (1996): being hit, kicked or pushed around; someone deliberately broke their things or took money or other things away; were made to feel afraid they would get hurt; were made fun of and teased in a hurtful way; were called mean and hurtful names; other students ignored them, didn't let them join in, or left them out on purpose; and others told lies about them and tried to make other students not like them, over the previous school term. For each item students were asked how often they were bullied, rating each item on a five-point scale (1 = never, 2 = only once or twice, 3 = every few weeks, 4 = about once a week, 5 = most days). A victimisation score was calculated for each student by averaging the seven victimisation items, with a higher score indicating more victimisation experiences ($\alpha = 0.82$). Perpetration was assessed using a seven-item perpetration index, similar to the victimisation index, which asked students how often they bullied others in the different ways listed. A perpetration score was calculated for each student by averaging the perpetration items, with a higher score reflecting greater involvement in bullying perpetration ($\alpha = 0.79$). In addition, an indirect victimisation and perpetration score was calculated by combining the relational items ($n = 2$), and a direct victimisation and perpetration score was calculated by combining the verbal and physical items ($n = 5$).

Cybervictimisation and perpetration

Cybervictimisation was assessed using two items from the 2004 Youth Internet Survey (Ybarra and Mitchell 2004). The items assessed the frequency of receiving mean and hurtful text (SMS) messages (text messages, pictures or video clips) and mean and hurtful messages on the Internet (email; pictures, webcam or video clips; chat rooms; MSN messenger or another form of instant messenger; social networking sites like MySpace; Internet game; web log/blog or web page/website). Students rated each item on the same five-point scale as for traditional victimisation. A cybervictimisation score was calculated for each student by averaging the two items ($r = 0.46$), with a higher score indicating more cybervictimisation experiences. A cyberperpetration score was calculated in a corresponding way ($r = 0.40$).

Problem behaviours

Problem behaviours in the past month were assessed using six items adapted from Resnicow et al. (1995): stealing from a shop or person; being involved in a physical fight; breaking something of their own on purpose; damaging or destroying things that did not belong to them; not paying for something like sneaking onto a bus or train or into a movie; smoking cigarettes and drinking alcohol without parental knowledge. All items were measured on a five-point scale (1 = never, 2 = once, 3 = twice, 4 = three times, 5 = more than three times). Level of involvement in problem behaviours was calculated for each student by averaging all items, with a higher score reflecting a greater involvement (i.e. more behaviours, more frequently) (average $\alpha = 0.83$). Involvement in individual problem behaviours was also examined, with items recoded into binary variables of not being involved or being involved in the behaviour at least once in the past month.

Data collection

Grade 8 and grade 9 data collection was conducted by trained research staff who administered questionnaires to students during class time according to a strict procedural and verbal protocol. Students not participating were given alternative learning activities.

Statistical analysis

Analyses were conducted using STATA v10 and PASW v18. Multi-level Tobit regression models with random effects were used to determine predictors of the level of involvement in problem behaviours at the end of grade 9. Tobit regression models were used owing to the extreme skew of problem behaviours, with 47% at the minimum value. The level of involvement in problem behaviours at the beginning of grade 8, gender, victimisation, perpetration, the interaction of victimisation and perpetration, and clustering at the school level were taken into account in all models. Direct and indirect forms of bullying were tested separately. Cybervictimisation and perpetration were added to the models. Multi-level logistic regression models with random effects were used to determine the predictors of involvement in individual problem behaviours at the end of grade 9, taking into account clustering and the variables mentioned above.

Results

Table 1 lists the means and standard deviations for victimisation, perpetration and engagement in problem behaviours at the two time-points. On average, students did not report frequent victimisation or perpetration through traditional bullying or cyberbullying, and did not report engaging in many problem behaviours at either time-point. However, involvement in traditional bullying, cyberbullying and problem behaviours increased from the beginning of grade 8 to the end of grade 9. By the end of grade 9, at least one in four students had been involved in physically fighting and drinking alcohol without their parents' knowledge in the previous month, while one in five students had not paid for something, like sneaking onto a bus or train or into a movie, and had broken something of their own on purpose.

Table 2 shows that traditional bullying and cyberbullying were significantly correlated with each other and with the level of engagement in problem behaviours. Given the significant correlation between traditional and cyberbullying, the effects of traditional bullying were taken into account when estimating the effect of cyberbullying on the level of engagement in problem behaviours.

Level of engagement in problem behaviours, traditional victimisation and perpetration

Table 3 shows that gender, problem behaviours, victimisation and perpetration at the beginning of grade 8 were significant predictors of the level of engagement in problem behaviours at the end of grade 9. Boys were more engaged in problem behaviours than girls, and higher engagement in grade 8 was associated with higher engagement in grade 9.

Levels of victimisation and perpetration were also found to moderate each other's associations with engagement in problem behaviours (the interaction term of victimisation and perpetration was significant). These effects are illustrated in Figure 1. Non-involved students (neither perpetrated nor victimised) were least involved in problem behaviours.

Table 1. Descriptive statistics of sample and bullying involvement, and prevalence of problem behaviours.

	Beginning of grade 8	End of grade 9
Number of students	*n* (%)	*n* (%)
Total	1745	1616
Male	847 (48.6)	791 (49.0)
Female	896 (51.4)	823 (51.0)
Average age	12	14
Descriptive statistics [a]	Mean (SD)	Mean (SD)
Traditional victimisation (1–5)	1.30 (0.50)	1.49 (0.69)
Traditional perpetration (1–5)	1.13 (0.30)	1.28 (0.56)
Cyber victimisation (1–5)	1.06 (0.27)	1.17 (0.54)
Cyber perpetration (1–5)	1.02 (0.17)	1.12 (0.49)
Problem behaviours (1–5)	1.16 (0.39)	1.34 (0.62)
Problem behaviours	*n* (%)	*n* (%)
None in past month	1015 (56.1)	704 (39.5)
At least once in past month		
Stealing from a shop or person	159 (9.4)	255 (16.7)
In a physical fight	379 (22.5)	420 (27.6)
Breaking something of their own on purpose	250 (14.8)	297 (19.6)
Damaging or destroying things not belonging to them	92 (5.5)	161 (10.6)
Not paid for something like sneaking onto a bus, train or into a movie	177 (10.5)	342 (22.5)
Smoked cigarettes	51 (3.0)	111 (7.3)
Drunk alcohol without parents' knowledge	163 (9.7)	377 (24.9)

Note: [a] Higher scores correspond to greater victimisation, greater perpetration and greater involvement in problem behaviours.

Table 2. Bivariate correlations between bullying and problem behaviours.

	Traditional victimisation	Traditional perpetration	Cybervictimisation	Cyberperpetration
Traditional victimisation [a]	1			
Traditional perpetration [a]	0.333**	1		
Cybervictimisation [a]	0.366**	0.253**	1	
Cyberperpetration [a]	0.191**	0.507**	0.435**	1
Level of engagement in problem behaviours [b]	0.073**	0.216**	0.042	0.061*

Note: [a] Measured at beginning of grade 8, [b] measured at end of grade 9, *n* ranges from 1494 to 1704.
*Significant at 5% level, **significant at 1% level.

Frequent perpetrators (every few weeks or more often) had the highest average levels of engagement in problem behaviours; however, the level of engagement in problem behaviours decreased if they also experienced some victimisation (i.e. if they were bully–victims). In contrast, for those who did not bully others, their level of engagement in

Table 3. Tobit regression results for problem behaviours and victimisation and perpetration.

	β	SE	95% CI	p
Traditional bullying and cybervictimisation				
Problem behaviours grade 9 ($n = 1465$)				
Problem behaviours grade 8	0.40	0.04	(0.32, 0.48)	<0.001**
Gender – male	0.14	0.03	(0.08, 0.21)	<0.001**
Victimisation	0.28	0.07	(0.14, 0.42)	<0.001**
Perpetration	0.52	0.11	(0.31, 0.74)	<0.001**
Cybervictimisation	0.03	0.06	(−0.09, 0.15)	0.651
Victimisation × Perpetration	−0.22	0.05	(−0.32, −0.12)	<0.001**
Traditional bullying and cyberperpetration				
Problem behaviours grade 9 ($n = 1465$)				
Problem behaviours grade 8	0.39	0.04	(0.31, 0.48)	<0.001**
Gender – male	0.14	0.03	(0.08, 0.21)	<0.001**
Victimisation	0.28	0.07	(0.14, 0.43)	<0.001**
Perpetration	0.51	0.11	(0.30, 0.73)	<0.001**
Cyberperpetration	0.06	0.08	(−0.09, 0.22)	0.419
Victimisation × Perpetration	−0.21	0.05	(−0.31, −0.12)	0.007**

Note: Predictors measured at beginning of grade 8. CI: confidence interval.
*Significant at 5% level, **significant at 1% level.

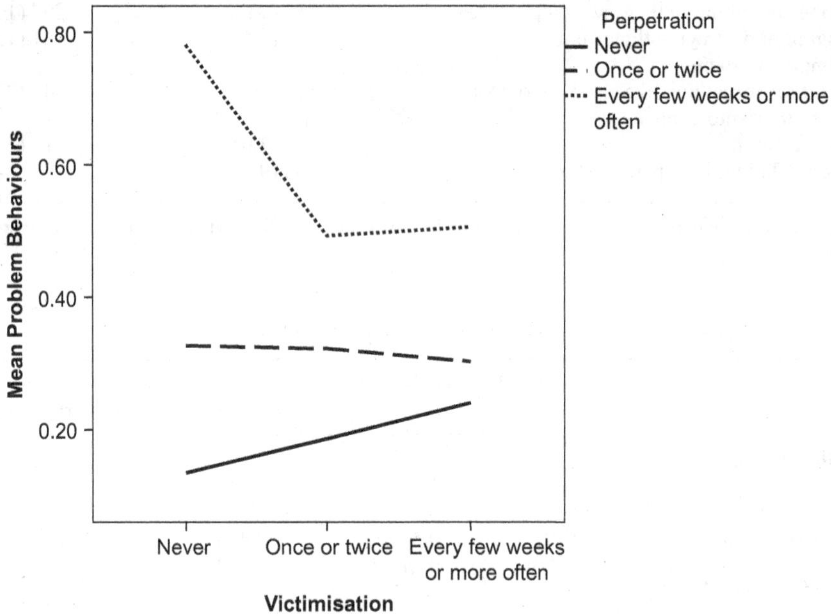

Figure 1. Interaction of victimisation with perpetration and average problem behaviours.

problem behaviours (although relatively low) increased as their level of victimisation increased. For those who bullied others once or twice, mean engagement in problem behaviours was similar for all levels of victimisation. No gender differences were found with regard to these moderation effects ($p = 0.684$).

Level of engagement in problem behaviours, traditional direct and indirect bullying

Table 4 shows results from the separate models testing direct and indirect forms of traditional bullying as predictors of level of engagement in problem behaviours, used to further examine the relationship between traditional bullying and level of involvement in problem behaviours. Gender, problem behaviours, traditional direct victimisation (verbal and physical) and traditional direct perpetration at the beginning of grade 8 were significant predictors of the level of engagement in problem behaviours at the end of grade 9. Levels of traditional direct victimisation and direct perpetration were also found to moderate each other's associations with engagement in problem behaviours. Traditional indirect victimisation and perpetration were not significant predictors of the level of engagement in problem behaviours at the end of grade 9.

Table 5 shows logistic regressions on individual problem behaviour involvement. Students with higher involvement in traditional victimisation and perpetration had

Table 4. Tobit regression results for problem behaviours and traditional direct and indirect bullying.

	β	SE	95% CI	p
Traditional direct bullying				
Problem behaviours grade 9 (n = 1465)				
Problem behaviours grade 8	0.42	0.04	(0.34, 0.50)	<0.001**
Gender – male	0.13	0.03	(0.10, 0.19)	<0.001**
Victimisation	0.23	0.06	(0.12, 0.35)	<0.001**
Perpetration	0.42	0.09	(0.25, 0.60)	<0.001**
Victimisation × Perpetration	−0.18	0.04	(−0.25, −0.10)	<0.001**
Traditional indirect bullying				
Problem behaviours grade 9 (n = 1465)				
Problem behaviours grade 8	0.43	0.04	(0.36, 0.51)	<0.001**
Gender – male	0.14	0.03	(0.09, 0.21)	<0.001**
Victimisation	−0.04	0.07	(−0.18, 0.10)	0.557
Perpetration	−0.001	0.10	(−0.20, 0.20)	0.990
Victimisation × Perpetration	0.05	0.06	(−0.06, 0.16)	0.373

Note: Predictors measured at beginning of grade 8. CI: confidence interval.
*Significant at 5% level, **significant at 1% level.

Table 5. Logistic regression results for involvement in individual problem behaviours and traditional victimisation and perpetration.

	OR (95% CI)	
	Victimisation	Perpetration
Stealing from a shop or person	1.3 (0.6, 3.0)	1.7 (0.5, 5.8)
In a physical fight	1.6 (0.7, 3.5)	2.9 (0.9, 9.6)
Breaking something of their own on purpose	2.4 (1.3, 4.4)**	4.0 (1.5, 10.3)**
Damaging or destroying things not belonging to them	1.9 (0.9, 3.9)	3.5 (1.1, 10.4)**
Not paid for something (i.e. sneaking onto a bus, train, into a movie)	3.3 (1.7, 6.6)**	9.6 (3.2, 28.6)**
Smoked cigarettes	1.6 (0.7, 3.9)	3.2 (0.9, 10.5)
Drunk alcohol without parents' knowledge	2.5 (1.2, 4.9)*	9.5 (3.2, 28.6)**

Notes: Models controlled for gender and level of involvement in problem behaviours at the beginning of grade 8. n ranges from 1451 to 1463.
*Significant at 5% level, **significant at 1% level.

increased odds of breaking something of their own on purpose, not paying for something like sneaking onto a bus or train or into a movie, and drinking alcohol without their parents' knowledge. In addition, traditional perpetration was a predictor of damaging and destroying things that did not belong to them.

Level of engagement in problem behaviours, cybervictimisation and perpetration

Cybervictimisation was added to the Tobit regression model to determine the independent effect of cybervictimisation over traditional victimisation and perpetration on engagement in problem behaviours. The same process was followed with cyberperpetration. After taking into account traditional victimisation and perpetration, neither cybervictimisation nor cyberperpetration was a significant independent predictor of the level of student engagement in problem behaviours (Table 3).

Discussion

The results of this study support the hypotheses that higher levels of traditional victimisation and perpetration at the beginning of secondary school (grade 8) predict higher levels of engagement in problem behaviours at the end of grade 9, and specifically, that traditional direct victimisation and perpetration are significant predictors of levels of engagement in problem behaviours. The hypothesis that cyberbullying represents an independent risk factor over and above levels of traditional bullying for higher levels of engagement in problem behaviours was not supported in this research.

The results for frequent perpetrators of traditional bullying provide further evidence of the clustering of some problem behaviours, as suggested by Problem Behaviour Theory (Jessor and Jessor 1977). It appears that engagement in problem behaviours over time was higher for students who also perpetrated bullying frequently; however, engagement in problem behaviours decreased as their level of victimisation increased. Adolescents' involvement in problem behaviours is more likely if supported by others, as peer influence and association with deviant peers is the most proximal social influence on engagement in problem behaviours (Ary et al. 1999). Students who use proactive bullying are more likely to be part of a highly structured social group and are adept at negotiating allegiances, jostling for power positions or coercing gang members to take orders (Sutton and Smith 1999), while adolescents who are victimised are more likely to be lonely, as other peers avoid them for fear of being bullied themselves or losing social status among their peers (Nansel et al. 2001), and perhaps therefore less likely to be involved in problem behaviours.

Social Cognitive Theory helps to explain a circular relationship between reprehensible behaviour and level of moral disengagement which allows one to engage in behaviours that are contrary to one's basic moral beliefs (Bandura 1991). The association/relationship between bullying and engagement in problem behaviours shown in this research and other bullying-related research (Bender and Lösel 2011) suggests that perpetrators can more easily deactivate moral controls to justify themselves and their negative behaviour, and that these cognitive mechanisms, in turn, can reinforce other negative behaviours (Menesini et al. 2003).

Further analysis of the relationship between traditional bullying and problem behaviours found that while direct forms of traditional bullying (both verbal and physical) were significantly associated with the level of engagement in problem behaviours, indirect bullying (relational) was not. Direct bullying, by its nature (involving direct physical harm, or associated threats or challenges towards the target) (Archer and Coyne 2005), may be more likely to be associated with problem behaviours intended to cause direct physical harm. Furthermore, Nansel et al. (2003) suggest that bullying others is consistently associated with violence-related behaviours (weapon-carrying, weapon-carrying in school, and physical fighting for boys and girls).

The Problem Behaviour Theory model is not supported in this study for cyberperpetration. This finding may be due to the largely indirect nature of cyberbullying afforded through opportunities for anonymity when a young person is bullying using technology. Recent studies have shown direct bullying to be a stronger predictor than indirect bullying of problem behaviours in adolescence (Bender and Lösel 2011; Hampela, Manhalb, and Hayera 2009). Problem Behaviour Theory suggests that motives for involvement in problem behaviours include overt repudiation of conventional norms which result in a form of social control response (Jessor and Jessor 1977). Respectively, the motives for perpetrating cyberbullying and traditional bullying include revenge (cyber) and domination (traditional) (Vandebosch and Van Cleemput 2009) resulting in harm or a reaction from the target person (Dooley, Pyżalski, and Cross 2009).

Consequently, it appears essential for schools to implement actions to stop or reduce the frequency of all forms of traditional bullying, but especially direct bullying (e.g. physical and verbal teasing), prior to transition and during the first few years of secondary school to reduce the likelihood of perpetrators engaging in other problem behaviours. These actions by schools may similarly help to reduce the number of victimised students who will potentially engage in other problem behaviours. Encouragement of prosocial behaviour (Jessor and Jessor 1977), high academic self-efficacy and involvement in extracurricular activities are also protective against involvement in problem behaviours (Chung and Elias 1996).

The correlations between traditional bullying, cyberbullying and problem behaviours were low, indicating that only a small proportion of variance in the problem behaviours measured is accounted for by victimisation and perpetration. Other confounders such as family structure, family functioning, socio-economic status and parental substance use may impact on involvement in problem behaviours (Hayatbakhsh et al. 2008). Separate models were used to examine the independent effect of cyberbullying over and above the effects of traditional bullying on problem behaviours. The relatively low prevalence of cyberbullying behaviours compared to traditional bullying behaviours may, however, have affected the results found in this study. As technology with online access becomes more readily available to adolescents, it is possible that increased time spent on the Internet combined with increasing technology expertise will increase the likelihood of cyberbullying behaviour (Walrave and Heirman 2011). Future research needs to continue to investigate the relationship between traditional bullying, cyberbullying and involvement with problem behaviours as relationships may change as accessibility to technology increases. Research also needs to involve students from a younger age, especially as the age of access to technology decreases, to identify opportunities for intervention.

The strengths of this study include the large sample size and the longitudinal nature of the research design enabling the examination of predictors as well as consequences of victimisation perpetration. The limitations include the reliance on student self-report of traditional and cyberbullying and involvement in problem behaviours during adolescence rather than peer, teacher or parent report. These self-report data may result in underreporting of involvement in bullying perpetration, victimisation and problem behaviours, and may inflate the estimates of the correlation between bullying behaviours and problem behaviours.

The use of mean scores for the traditional and cyberbullying scales provides the students' frequency of involvement in different forms of bullying behaviours, not the severity of the different acts in terms of impact on the targeted student. Impact as experienced by the victimised student, for example, could be assessed using separate questions asking students about the extent to which they were upset by the bullying. Similar limitations apply to the calculation of mean scores for involvement in problem behaviours. The equal weighting assigned to each of the different forms of bullying and problem behaviours may have impacted on the observed associations between these outcomes. The measurement of cyberbullying was also limited to only the number of nasty text messages or emails sent/received, which might also have resulted in the underreporting of involvement in these bullying behaviours.

Missing data from absentee students and students lost to attrition during transition may have led to fewer students who bully and engage in problem behaviours frequently being included in the analyses. To minimise this potential transition attrition the research was conducted with only Catholic secondary schools within the Perth metropolitan area. This does, however, limit the generalisability of the results, and further research which includes students from rural areas and government and non-government schools is needed.

The results suggest that bullying intervention programmes are critical prior to and at the beginning of secondary school as both direct victimisation and perpetration predict the level of engagement in problem behaviours. In their meta-analysis and review of anti-bullying programs, Ttofi and Farrington (2009) found that the anti-bullying intervention programme components which had the greatest effect in decreasing victimisation and perpetration included the use of videos, working with peers, group work, parent training and information for parents, playground supervision, classroom rules, and management and disciplinary methods. However, their conclusions with respect to working with peers and disciplinary methods have been challenged (Smith, Salmivalli, and Cowie 2012). Pearce et al. (2011) conclude that raising awareness and educating the whole school community is one of the key strategies to help reduce cyberbullying in schools. The transition to secondary school provides an opportune period in which to intensify whole-school bullying intervention programmes.

Conclusion

Problem Behaviour Theory is supported for traditional direct bullying but not for cyberbullying. Students engaging in cyberperpetration behaviours did not also engage in higher levels of other problem behaviours. While this study supports the correlation between cyberbullying and traditional forms of bullying, it found that levels of traditional victimisation and perpetration at the beginning of secondary school (grade 8) predicted levels of engagement in problem behaviours at the end of grade 9. Cyberbullying was not found to represent an independent risk factor over and above levels of traditional victimisation and perpetration for higher levels of engagement in problem behaviours. The results suggest that it will be most beneficial to focus interventions on traditional bullying, specifically reducing direct bullying during the first few years of secondary school.

Acknowledgements

We thank Melanie Epstein and Stacey Waters for their contributions to the Supportive Schools Project (SSP), and the SSP study schools and their staff, parents and students. The SSP Project and this study were funded by the Western Australian Health Promotion Foundation (Healthway) and the research supported by the Child Health Promotion Research Centre (CHPRC) at Edith Cowan University,

Western Australia. This research was funded through a Western Australian Health Promotion Foundation Scholarship and supported by the Department of Industry, Innovation, Science, Research and Tertiary Education. Special thanks are given to all CRN partners for the contribution to the development of this work.

References

Archer, J., and S. Coyne. 2005. An integrated review of indirect, relational, and social aggression. *Personality and Social Psychology Review* 9: 212–230.

Ary, D., T. Duncan, A. Biglan, C. Metzler, J. Noell, and K. Smolkowski. 1999. Development of adolescent problem behavior. *Journal of Abnormal Child Psychology* 27: 141–50.

Bandura, A. 1991. Moral disengagement in the perpetration of inhumanities. *Personality and Social Psychology Review* 3: 193–209.

Barrera, M., A. Biglan, D. Ary, and F. Li. 2001. Replication of a problem behavior model with American Indian, Hispanic, and Caucasian youth. *Journal of Early Adolescence* 21: 133–57.

Bartlett, R., D. Holditch-Davis, and M. Belyea. 2007. Problem behaviors in adolescents. *Paediatric Nursing* 33: 13–18.

Bender, D., and F. Lösel. 2011. Bullying at school as a predictor of delinquency, violence and other anti-social behaviour in adulthood. *Criminal Behaviour and Mental Health* 21: 99–106.

Chung, H., and M. Elias. 1996. Patterns of adolescent involvement in problem behaviors: Relationship to self-efficacy, social competence, and life events. *American Journal of Community Psychology* 24: 771–84.

Cross, D., T. Shaw, L. Hearn, M. Epstein, H. Monks, L. Lester, and L. Thomas. 2009. *Australian Covert Bullying Prevalence Study*. Child Health Promotion Research Centre, Edith Cowan University, Perth.

Dooley, J., J. Pyżalski, and D. Cross. 2009. Cyberbullying versus face-to-face bullying: A theoretical and conceptual review. *Zeitschrift fur Pyschologie/Journal of Psychology* 217: 182–8.

Dukes, R., J. Stein, and J. Zane. 2010. Gender differences in the relative impact of physical and relational bullying on adolescent injury and weapon carrying. *Journal of School Psychology* 48: 511–32.

Hampela, P., S. Manhalb, and T. Hayera. 2009. Direct and relational bullying among children and adolescents: Coping and psychological adjustment. *School Psychology International* 30: 474–90.

Hay, C., R. Meldrum, and K. Mann. 2010. Traditional bullying, cyber bullying, and deviance: A general strain theory approach. *Journal of Contemporary Criminal Justice* 26: 130–47.

Hayatbakhsh, M., J. Najman, K. Jamrozik, A. Al Mamun, W. Bor, and R. Alati. 2008. Adolescent problem behaviours predicting DSM-IV diagnoses of multiple substance use disorder. *Social Psychiatry and Psychiatric Epidemiology* 43: 356–63.

Hinduja, S., and J. Patchin. 2007. Offline consequences of online victimization: School violence and delinquency. *Journal of School Violence* 6, no. 3: 89–112.

Hinduja, S., and J. Patchin. 2008. Cyberbullying: An exploratory analysis of factors related to offending and victimization. *Deviant Behaviour* 29: 129–56.

Jessor, R., and S. Jessor. 1977. *Problem behavior and psychosocial development: A longitudinal study of youth*. New York: Academic Press.

Li, Q., D. Cross, and P.K. Smith, eds. 2012. *Cyberbullying in the global playground: Research from international perspectives*. Chichester: Wiley-Blackwell.

Menesini, E., V. Sanchez, A. Fonzi, R. Ortega, A. Costabile, and G. Lo Feudo. 2003. Moral emotions and bullying: A cross-national comparison of differences between bullies, victims and outsiders. *Aggressive Behavior* 29: 515–30.

Mitchell, K., M. Ybarra, and D. Finkelhor. 2007. The relative importance of online victimization in understanding depression, delinquency, and substance use. *Child Maltreatment* 12: 314–24.

Mouttapa, M., T. Valente, P. Gallaher, L. Rohrbach, and J. Unger. 2004. Social network predictors of bullying and victimization. *Adolescence* 39: 315–35.

Nansel, T., M. Overpeck, D. Haynie, W. Ruan, and P. Scheidt. 2003. Relationships between bullying and violence among US youth. *Archives of Pediatric Adolescent Medicine* 157: 348–53.

Nansel, T., M. Overpeck, R. Pilla, J. Ruan, B. Simons-Morton, and P. Scheidt. 2001. Bullying behaviors among US youth: Prevalence and association with psychosocial adjustment. *Journal of the American Medical Association* 285: 2094–100.

Niemelä, S., A. Brunstein-Klomek, L. Sillanmäki, H. Helenius, J. Piha, K. Kumpulainen, I. Moilanen, T. Tamminen, F. Almqvist, and A. Sourander. 2011. Childhood bullying behaviors at age eight and substance use at age 18 among males. A nationwide prospective study. *Addictive Behaviors* 36: 256–60.

Olweus, D. 1996. *The Revised Olweus Bully/Victim Questionnaire*. Bergen: Mimeo, Research Center for Health Promotion (HEMIL), University of Bergen.

Pearce, N., D. Cross, H. Monks, S. Waters, and S. Falconer. 2011. Current evidence of best practice in whole-school bullying intervention and its potential to inform cyberbullying interventions. *Australian Journal of Guidance and Counselling* 21, no. 1: 1–21.

Petterson, A. 1993. Creating adolescents: The role of context and process in developmental trajectories. *Journal of Research on Adolescence* 3: 1–18.

Resnicow, K., D. Ross-Gaddy, and R. Vaughan. 1995. Structure of problem and positive behaviors in African American youths. *Journal of Consulting and Clinical Psychology* 63, no. 4: 594–603.

Rigby, K., and P. Slee. 1998. *The Peer Relations Questionnaire*. Point Lonsdale, VIC: Professional Reading Guide for Educational Administrators.

Smith, P.K. 2004. Bullying: Recent developments. *Child and Adolescent Mental Health* 9: 98–103.

Smith, P.K., C. Salmivalli, and H. Cowie. 2012. Effectiveness of school-based programs to reduce bullying: a commentary. *Journal of Experimental Criminology*, Published Online 12 February 2012, 1–9.

Sutton, J., and P.K. Smith. 1999. Bullying as a group process: An adaptation of the participant role approach. *Aggressive Behavior* 25: 97–111.

Tokunaga, R. 2010. Following you home from school: A critical review and synthesis of research on cyberbullying victimization. *Computers in Human Behavior* 26: 277–87.

Vandebosch, H., and K. Van Cleemput. 2009. Cyberbullying among youngsters: Profiles of bullies and victims. *New Media and Society* 11: 1349–71.

Walrave, M., and W. Heirman. 2011. Cyberbullying: Predicting victimisation and perpetration. *Children and Society* 25: 59–72.

Ybarra, M., and K. Mitchell. 2004. Youth engaging in online harassment: Associations with caregiver–child relationships, Internet use, and personal characteristics. *Journal of Adolescence* 27: 319–36.

Index

Page numbers in *Italics* represent tables.
Page numbers in **Bold** represent figures.

acceptance: social 28, 36
acculturative stress model 51, 55, 57, 61, 63, 64
Adam, R.E.: Fredstrom, B.K. and Gilman, R. 149
ADHD (attention deficit hyperactivity disorder) 30
adolescents: Australian 148, 162, 207; Czech 92; Finnish 35, 103; German 119, 122; Israeli 133, 142; Italian 147; Jewish Israeli 136; Norwegian *see* peer groups and victimisation
Agatston, P.W.: Kowalski, R. and Limber, S. 142
age 125, 165, *165*
aggression 20, 24, 26, 107, 108, 114; cyber 80; new media 79–82; reactive 108, 114, *see also* electronic aggression
aggressor 15, 148
Aiken, L.S.: and West, S.G. 183
ambivalence 13
anger 162, 170
anonymity 96
anxiety: chronic 135; Depression Anxiety Stress Scale (DASS-21) 164–5, 167–9; social 67, 74
ASD (autism spectrum disorder) 30
Asher, S.: Hymel, S. and Renshaw, P. 67; and Wheeler, V. 67
assertiveness 186
attention deficit hyperactivity disorder (ADHD) 30
attitude: to school 84–5; self-enhancing 20
audio tape recordings 10
Austin, S.: and Joseph, S. 20
Australia: adolescents 148, 162, 207; Western, Catholic Education Office (CEO) 208
Austria: migration situation 63; studies 62, 104
autism spectrum disorder (ASD) 30

bad conscience 127, *127*, 129
Bakken, A.: and Nordahl, T. 49
Bandura, A. 121
Beckman, L.: Hagquist, C. and Hellström, L. 4
behavioural characteristics 119
Beirens, K.: and Fontaine, J.R.J. 63
belongingness 134
Belschak, F.: Fetchenhauer, D. and Katzer, C. 104, 114
blame: self- 180
Bohli, G.: Hagekull, B. and Rydell, A-M. 25
Bollmer, J.M.: *et al* 44
Bolman, C.: Dehue, F. and Vollink, T. 176
Boulton, M.J.: *et al* 15
boys: emotional and behavioural problems 111–12, *112*, **113**
Brighi, A.: *et al* 3
buffering: effects 186–7; hypothesis 177
bully 11–12, 176, 186–7, *see also* victims
bullying: definition 1, 19, 52, 93, 207; subtypes 19, 20
Burgess, A.W.: Cavanaugh, D.J. and Dowell, E.B. 80
Burk, W.J.: Kerr, M. and Stattin, H. 157
Bussey, K.: and Singh, P. 177
bystanders 7, 128–9, 134

Cairns, R.B.: *et al* 53
Campbell, M.: *et al* 4
Campfield, D.C. 148
CAPI (Computer Assisted Personal Interview) 124
Carter, J.M. 115
Catholic Education Office (CEO) of Western Australia 208
Chi, C.W.: and Frydenberg, E. 176
Child Depression Inventory (CDI) 66, 137
Cohen, R.: and Schoffstall, C.L. 115
Coie, J.D.: and Dodge, K.A. 24
communication technologies 79, 80
competence: social 25, 28
Computer Assisted Personal Interview (CAPI) 124
conduct problems 29

conscience: bad 127, *127*, 129
Cook, C.R.: *et al* 148
coping strategies 174–88; avoidant and emotion-focused strategies 176; buffering effects 186–7; cybervictimisation 175–6, 185–6; depressive symptoms 181; descriptive statistics 180, *181*; longitudinal association 181–3; moderating effects 183–4, **184**; multivariate analyses 181–4, *182*, *183*; productive 35; research questions 178; results 180–4; retaliation 176, 185–6; self-reporting 178, 187; victimisation 178–9, 185
coping theory 176
Corbin, J.: and Strauss, A. 95
Cowan, K.C.: and Lieberman, R. 43
Cowie, H.: and Jennifer, D. 1; Smith, P.K. 15
Crick, N.R.: and Grotpeter, J.K. 155
Cross, D.: Lester, L. and Shaw, T. 4
cyberaggression 80
cyberbullies 114: 122; victims 103, 115, 186
cyberbullying 107, 114; definition 1, 102–3, 148, 164, 203, 207; Germany 102, 103
cybervictimisation 113–15, 142, 155; coping strategies 175–6, 185–6; loneliness and depressive mood 137–9, *138*, 139–42, *140*, *141*, *142*; and perpetration 209, 214
cybervictims 103, 115, 186
Czech adolescents 92

Dalgleish, J.: and Price, M. 134, 176
DAPHNE III questionnaire 107
DASS-21 (Depression Anxiety Stress Scale) 164–5, 167–9
de-individualisation theory 99
defensive egotism 20
Dehue, F.: Bolman, C. and Vollink, T. 176
Dempsey, A.G.: *et al* 103, 115
depression 50, 66, 137, 163; symptoms 50–1, 53–5, *54*, 104, 107, 115, 179, 181
Depression Anxiety Stress Scale (DASS-21) 164–5, 167–9
depressive mood 135, 142, *see also* loneliness and depressive mood
deviant behaviour 207
differential item functioning (DIF) 197
Dinelli, S.: Pacilli, M.G. and Prezza, M. 154
direct bullying 19, 21, 82, 164
direct and indirect bullying 213–14, *213*
Dishion, T.J.: and Wang, M.T. 154
dissociation effects 98
DiStefano, C.: and Finney, S.J. 108
Dodge, K.A.: and Coie, J.D. 24
Dogan, A.: and Strohmeier, D. 2
Dooley, J.J.: *et al* 177
Dowell, E.B.: Burgess, A.W. and Cavanaugh, D.J. 80
Due, P.: *et al* 34

Eden, S.: Heiman, T and Olenik-Shemesh, D. 3
egotism: defensive 20
electronic aggression 79, 83, 85–6, *87*, 88; Lodz Electronic Aggression Prevalence Questionnaire 83
electronic aggression typology 79–89; attitude towards school 84–5; discussion 87–8; former romantic partner 87, 88; gender differences 86, 87–8; implications 88–9; instruments 83–5; results 85–7; risk and protective factors 83–4; study sample 82–3; victims 83, *84*, 87
emotional and behavioural problems 102–16; conclusions 115–16; cyberbullying 107, 114; cybervictimisation 113–15; data analysis 108; discussion 112–15; externalising problems 104; gender differences 104, 110; implications 116; internalising problems 103–4; measures 107–8; participants 106; questionnaire 106; research objectives 105; results 108–14, *108*, *109*; results for boys 111–12, *112*, **113**; results for girls 110–11, *110*, **111**, 112–13, 114; self-reports 107, 116, *see also* problem behaviours; social difficulties
emotional difficulties 20, 58, 103–5, 123, 126
emotional loneliness 134–5
emotional well-being 177
emotions: understanding of others 6–7
Erdur-Baker, O. 194
ethnic homophily 50, 57
ethnic minority students 49
ethnicity and victimisation 193
EU Daphne II Programme 150
exclusion: social 30

face-to-face bullying 19, 21, 82, 164
family: conflicts 84; relations 156; self-esteem 154
Fandrem, H.: Strohmeier, D. and Jonsdottir, A. 2; Strohmeier, D. and Roland, E. 49
Farrington, D.P.: and Loeber, R. 37; and Ttofi, M.M. 7, 216
Fekkes, M.: Pijpers, E.I.M. and Verloove-Vanhorick, S.P. 34
Feldman, S.S.: and Lodge, J. 177
Fetchenhauer, D.: Belschak, F. and Katzer, C. 104, 114
Finkelhor, D.: Mitchell, K.J. and Wolak, J. 148; Mitchell, K.J. and Ybarra, M. 175; Ormrod, R. and Turner, H. 192
Finland: KiVa programme 130, 171
Finney, S.J.: and DiStefano, C. 108
Finnish adolescents 35, 103

Fischer, U.: Jäger, R.S. and Riebel, J. 119, 123
follower character 13, 14
Fontaine, J.R.J.: and Beirens, K. 63
Fredstrom, B.K.: Adam, R.E. and Gilman, R. 149
friendlessness (chronic) 121
friendship 36, 42–3, **42**, 135, 147–8; and mental health 42–3, **42**; mixed-mode 147–8; networks 74; quality 36, 43, 44
Frisén, A.: Slonje, R. and Smith, P.K. 129
Frydenberg, E.: and Chi, C.W. 176
Fuchs, D. 44

gateway behaviours 208
gender differences 21, 35, 104, 110, 125, 142, 154–5; and age 165, *165*; bullying types 149; depressive symptoms 50; electronic aggression 86, 87–8; involvement types study 40–2, *41*; loneliness and depressive mood 137–9, *138*; retaliation 185–6; and victimisation 170
German adolescents 119, 122, *see also* emotional and behavioural problems
Germany: cyberbullying 102, 103
Gilman, R.: Adam, R.E. and Fredstrom, B. K. 149
Gini, G.: and Pozzoli, T. 35, 148
girls: emotional and behavioural problems 110–11, *110*, **111**, 112–13, 114
Goodman, R. 38, 39; *et al* 44–5
Goossens, L.: and Marcoen, A. 149
Gradinger, P.: Strohmeier, D. and Spiel, C. 104, 115, 194, 202
Graham, S.: Juvonen, J. and Nishina, A. 49; Juvonen, J. and Schuster, M.A. 35
Greca, A. La: and Lopez, N. 67
Gross, E.F.: and Juvonen, J. 175, 176
Grotpeter, J.K.: and Crick, N.R. 155
grounded theory method 95
group norms 15
Guerra, N.G.: and Williams, K.R. 105
Guess Who measure 23, 24

Hagekull, B.: Bohli, G. and Rydell, A-M. 25
Hagquist, C.: Beckman, L. and Hellström, L. 4
Hazler, R.S. 7
health: psychological problems 48, 57; somatic symptoms 103, 161, *see also* mental health; psychosomatic health problems; psychosomatic health problems
Health Behaviour in School-aged Children (HBSC) 195
Heiman, T.: Eden, S. and Olenik-Shemesh, D. 3
Hellström, L.: Beckman, L. and Hagquist, C. 4
Higgins, K.: McCrystal, P and Percy, A. 44
Hinduja, S.: and Patchin, J. 193; and Patchin, J.W. 81, 148–9, 176
Hodges, E.V.E.: Malone, M.J.J. and Perry, D. G. 36, 135; Peets, K. and Salmivalli, C. 82, 88
Hoff, D.L.: and Mitchell, S.N. 175, 176
Holahan, C.J.: *et al* 186
home: online activities 85
homophily 49
Hopkins Symptom Checklist 53
humiliation: visual material 93
Hymel, S.: Asher, S. and Renshaw, P. 67
hyperactivity 29, 30
hypothetical cyberbully scenario 16, 179–80, 186

Iannotto, R.: Nansel, T. and Wang, J. 194, 202
ICQ instant messenger 95
imbalance of power 12, 93
indifference 12
indirect bullying 19, 21, 213–14, *213*
instant messenger (ICQ) 95
instrumental aggression 107
internalising problems 103–4
interventions (anti-bullying) 88–9, 130, 156–7, 171, 208, 215
interviews: online 95
involvement types study 34–45; bully, victim, bully-victim 37–9, *39*, 43; conclusions 45; discussion 43–4; gender differences 40–2, *41*; mental health 38, 39–40, **39**; participant characteristics 37; results 38–43; self-report questionnaire 37; study limitations 44–5
Israel: social networks 133
Israeli adolescents 133, 142; Jewish 136
Italian adolescents 147

Jäger, R.S.: Fischer, U. and Riebel, J. 119, 123
Jennifer, D.: and Cowie, H. 1; and Shaughnessy, J. 16
Jessor, R.: and Jessor, S. 206
Jewish Israeli adolescents 136
Jones, S.E.: Manstead, A.S.R. and Livingstone, A.G. 7
Jonsdottir, A.: Fandrem, H. and Strohmeier, D. 2
Joseph, S.: and Austin, S. 20
Juvonen, J.: Graham, S. and Schuster, M.A. 35; and Gross, E.F. 175, 176; Nishina, A. and Graham, S. 49

Kaltiala-Heino, R. 193; *et al* 34–5, 202

Kärnä, A: *et al* 49
Katzer, C.: Fetchenhauer, D. and Belschak, F. 104, 114
Kerr, M.: and Stattin, H. 157; Stattin, H. and Burk, W.J. 157
KiVa programme (anti-bullying, Finland) 130, 171
Klomek, A.B. 43
Kochenderfer-Ladd, B. 177
Kokkinos, M.: and Panayiotou, G. 44
Kowalski, R.: Agatston, P.W. and Limber, S. 142
Kumpulaien, K.: and Räsänen, E. 35

Law, D.M.: *et al* 148
Leary, M.R.: and Downs, D.L. 155
Lester, L.: Cross, D. and Shaw, T. 4
Li Lei, Y.: and Wu, M.A. 156
Lieberman, R.: and Cowan, K.C. 43
Limber, S.: Agatston, P.W. and Kowalski, R. 142
Livingstone, A.G.: Jones, S.E. and Manstead, A.S.R. 7
Lodge, J.: and Feldman, S.S. 177
Lodz Electronic Aggression Prevalence Questionnaire 83
Loeber, R.: and Farrington, D.P. 37
loneliness 67, 74, 107, 115, 151; emotional 134–5; Louvain Scale for Children and Adolescents (LLCA) 151; perceptions and gender 149; questionnaire 137; and school climate 154; social 134
loneliness and depressive mood 133–44; cause and effect 143; cyberbullying questionnaire 136–7; cybervictimisation 139–42, *140*, *141*, *142*; cybervictimisation and gender differences 137–9, *138*; data analysis 137; discussion 142–4; measures 136–7; participants 136; research objectives 135; results 137–42
Lopez, N.: and La Greca, A. 67
Louvain Loneliness Scale for Children and Adolescents (LLCA) 151

McCrystal, P.: Higgins, K. and Percy, A. 44
McGilvray, A. 135
Machmutow, K.: *et al* 4
maladjustment: psychosocial 36
Malone, M.J.J.: Hodges, E.V.E. and Perry, D. G. 36, 135
Manstead, A.S.R.: Jones, S.E. and Livingstone, A.G. 7
Marcoen, A.: and Goossens, L. 149
media: new 66, 79–82
Mellor, D. 45
Melotti, G.: *et al* 149
mental health 38, 39–40, **39**, 166–7, 174, 193; and friendship 42–3, **42**; somatic symptoms 103, 161, *see also* psychosomatic health problems
migration and victimisation 61–75, **65**, *70*; demographic information *69*; depression 66; discussion 73–5; emotional problems 62, 63, 68–72, *71*; experiences 67–8; indirect effects 72–3; measures 66–7; new media access 66; research 64–5, 67; results 68–73; risk factors 72–3, *73*; self-reports 65, 66, 75; Turkey 63–4
Millward, L. 10
mind: theory of 21
Mitchell, K.J.: Finkelhor, D. and Wolak, J. 148; and Ybarra, M.L. 104, 114; Ybarra, M.L. and Finkelhor, D. 175
Mitchell, S.N.: and Hoff, D.L. 175, 176
mixed-mode friendship 147–8
mood: depressive 135, 142
moral disengagement 15, 119–30; age and gender 125; bad conscience 127, *127*; bullying roles 123; cyber and traditional roles 125; discussion 128–9; emotional and social difficulties 120–1, 123, 125, *126*; measures 123–4; methodological limitation of study 129; participants 122; participants' roles 124, *125*, 128; practical implications 130; research 122, 124; research results 124–8; social difficulties 123–4
moral emotional attribution 6–17; data analysis 10–11; discussion 14–17; interviews 9–10; materials 8–10; negative emotions 14; participants 8; pictorial vignettes *9*, **9**; procedure 10; results 11–13; study design 8

Nansel, T.: *et al* 215; Iannotto, R. and Wang, J. 194, 202
networks: social 98, 133
new media 66, 79–82
Nishina, A.: Graham, S. and Juvonen, J. 49
Nordahl, T.: and Bakken, A. 49
Nordhagen, R.: *et al* 192
norms: group 15; peer group 84
Norwegian adolescents *see* peer groups and victimisation

Olenik-Shemesh, D.: Heiman, T. and Eden, S. 3
Olweus Bully/Victim Questionnaire (OBVQ) 195
Olweus, D. 93, 119, 121, 123, 209; and Solberg, M.E. 164
online activities: school and home 85
Ormrod, R.: Finkelhor, D. and Turner, H. 192

Ortega, R. 104; *et al* 170
Otavová, M.: Ševčíková, A. and Šmahel, D. 3

Pacilli, M.G.: Dinelli, S. and Prezza, M. 154
Panayiotou, G.: and Kokkinos, M. 44
participant roles (cyberbullying) 133–4
Patchin, J.W.: and Hinduja, S. 81, 148–9, 176, 193
Pearce, N.: *et al* 216
peer groups and victimisation 48–58; depressive symptoms 53–4, *54*, 55; discussion 55–7; group affiliation 53; measures and procedure 52–3; participants 51–2; peer group characteristics 54–5, **55**, *56*; research questions and hypotheses 51; results 53–5; self-report 52; study limitations 57–8
Peer Relations Questionnaire (PRQ) 37
peers: group norms 84; rejection 30; relations 36; support systems 15
Peets, K.: Hodges, E.V.E. and Salmivalli, C. 82, 88
Percy, A.: McCrystal, P. and Higgins, K. 44
perpetration: and victimisation 209, 210–11, *212*, **212**
perpetrators 133–4, 211
Perren, S.: *et al* 104, 149, 194, 202
Perry, D.G.: Hodges, E.V.E. and Malone, M. J.J. 36
pictorial vignettes *9*, **9**
Pijpers, E.I.M.: Fekkes, M. and Verloove-Vanhorick, S.P. 34
Poland: electronic aggression typology 80–1, *81*
Pouwelse, M.: *et al* 177
power: imbalance 12, 93
Pozzoli, T.: and Gini, G. 35, 148
Prezza, M.: Pacilli, M.G. and Dinelli, S. 154
Price, M.: and Dalgleish, J. 134, 176
pride 12
Priest, H.: Roberts, R. and Woods, L. 10
Problem Behaviour Theory 206, 214, 215, 216
problem behaviours 206–16; cybervictimisation and perpetration 209, 214; data collection 210; direct and indirect bullying 213–14, *213*; discussion 214–16; measures 209; perpetrators 211; results 210–14, *211*; study sample and procedure 208; victimisation and perpetration 209, 210–11, *212*, **212**, *see also* emotional and behavioural problems; social difficulties
PRQ (Peer Relations Questionnaire) 37
PSP (PsychoSomatic Problems) scale 197, 198
psychological difficulties 19
psychological health problems 48, 57
psychosocial maladjustment 36
psychosocial outcomes 34
psychosomatic health problems 192–203; analysis 198–9, *199*; background data 195; discussion 202–3; group differences 198, 201–2, *201*; linear regression analysis 199, 202; measurements 195, *196–7*; methodological issues 203; multinominal logistic regression analysis 198, 199–201, *200*; participants 194, *196–7*; results 199–202, *see also* mental health; somatic symptoms
PsychoSomatic Problems (PSP) scale 197, 198
publicity 179
Pyżalski, J. 3

Raine, A.: *et al* 24
Rappoport, L. 134
Räsänen, E.: and Kumpulaien, K. 35
Raskauskas, J. 163
reactive aggression 108, 114
Reijints, A.: *et al* 161–2
rejection: peer 30; social 29–30
reliance: self- 175
Renshaw, P.: Asher, S. and Hymel, S. 67
repetition 93
resettlement 62
Resnicow, K.: *et al* 209
retaliation 176, 185–6
Riebel, J.: Fischer, U. and Jäger, R.S. 119, 123
Rigby, K. 121, 177; and Slee, P. 209
risk: behaviours basket 82; factors 154
Roberts, R.: Priest, H. and Woods, L. 10
Roland, E.: Fandream, H. and Strohmeier, D. 49
Rosenberg Self-Esteem Scale 66
Rydell, A-M.: Hagekull, B. and Bohli, G. 25

sadistic bullying 6
Şahin, M. 135, 149
Salmivalli, C.: *et al* 7, 20, 128; Hodges, E.V. E. and Peets, C. 82, 88
Scheithauer, H.: and Schultze-Krumbholz, A. 103, 104
Schoffstall, C.L.: and Cohen, R. 115
school: attitude to 84–5; bullying conceptualisation 80; online activities 85; satisfaction 121, 128, 155; secondary (UK) 35; Supportive Schools Project 208
school climate 82, 136, 149, 150, 155; and loneliness 154
Schultze-Krumbholz, A.: *et al* 3; and Scheithauer, H. 103, 104
Schuster, M.A.: Graham, S. and Juvonen, J. 35
Seals, D.: and Young, J. 20
secondary schools (UK) 35
self-assessments 129

self-blaming 180
self-enhancing attitude 20
self-esteem 29, 66–7, 82, 85, 149, 150–1, 155; bullies 88; family 154; level 85; Rosenberg Scale 66
self-evaluation 156
self-perception 20, 26–8
self-reliance 175
self-reporting 52, 107, 116, 178, 187; migration and victimisation 65, 66, 75
self-worth 29
Ševčíková, A.: and Šmahel, D. 92; Šmahel, D. and Otavová, M. 3
shame 12, 13, 14
Shaughnessy, J.: and Jennifer, D. 16
Shaw, T.: Cross, D. and Lester, L. 4
Singh, P.: and Bussey, K. 177
Skrzypiec, G.: *et al* 2
Slee, P.: and Rigby, K. 209
Slonje, R.: and Smith, P.K. 99, 169, 175, 195; Smith, P.K. and Frisén, A. 129
Šmahel, D.: Otavová, M. and Ševčíková, A. 3; and Ševčíková, A. 92
Smith, H.: *et al* 2
Smith, P.K.: Cowie, H. 15; *et al* 35, 102, 162, 195; Frisén, A. and Slonje, R. 129; and Slonje, R. 99, 169, 175, 195; Sutton, J. and Swettenham, J. 21, 30
social acceptance 28, 36
social anxiety 67, 74
social cognition skills 21
social cognitive mapping (SCM) 53
Social Cognitive Theory 206, 214
social competence 25, 28
Social Deficit Model 21, 30
social difficulties 19–31, 123–4, 127; discussion 28–31; gender differences 29; hypotheses for investigation 21–2; measures 23–5; participant characteristics 25, *25*; participants 22; research procedure 22–3; results 25–8, *27*, *see also* emotional and behavioural problems; problem behaviours
social exclusion 30
Social Inclusion Survey 23–4
social loneliness 134
social networks 98, 133
Social Perception Profiles 24–5, 26
social protection layer 144
social rejection 29–30
social status 214
social success 14
social support (buffering hypothesis) 177
socio-ecological perspective 55, 57
Solberg, M.E.: and Olweus, D. 164
somatic symptoms 103, 161, *see also* psychosomatic health problems
Sontag, L.M.: *et al* 104
Sourander, A.: *et al* 103, 104, 149, 193–4
Spears, B.A.: *et al* 162
Spiel, C.: Gradinger, P. and Strohmeier, D. 104, 115, 194, 202
Spriggs, A.L.: *et al* 121
Stattin, H.: Burk, W.J. and Kerr, M. 157; and Kerr, M. 157
status: social 214
Stefanek, E.: *et al* 49
Strauss, A.: and Corbin, J. 95
Strengths and Difficulties Questionnaire (SDQ) 24, 37, 38, 164, 167; abnormal range 36, 42, 43, 44; bullies 19, 20; gender differences 26; subscales 40, *40*; victims 35, *168*
stress: acculturative model 51, 55, 57, 61, 63, 64
Strohmeier, D.: and Dogan, A. 2; Fandream, H. and Roland, E. 49; Fandrem, H. and Jonsdottir, A. 2; Gradinger, P. and Spiel, C. 104, 115, 194, 202
students: ethnic minority 49
success: social 14
support: peer systems 15; seeking 175–6, 180; social 177; teacher 175
Supportive Schools Project 208
Sutton, J.: and Smith, P.K. and Swettenham, J. 21, 30
Switzerland 178

teacher: support 175
technical solutions 176
technologies: communication 79, 80
text-messaging 7
Tokunaga, R.S. 102–3, 120, 155, 176
Ttofi, M.M.: and Farrington, D.P. 7, 216
Turkey: migration situation 63–4
Turner, H.: Finkelhor, D. and Ormrod, R. 192

UCLA Loneliness Scale-8 (ULS-8) 107
United Kingdom (UK): secondary school 35

Verloove-Vanhorick, S.P.: Fekkes, M. and Pijpers, E.I.M. 34
victim character 11
victimisation: contextual factors 49–50; coping strategies 178–9, 185; cyberbullying 82; depressive symptoms 50–1; and ethnicity 193; gender differences 170; known offline offender 99; and perpetration 209, 210–11, *212*, **212**; protective factors against 121; traditional 142, *see also* cybervictimisation; migration and victimisation; peer groups and victimisation

victimisation predictors 147–57; demographic data 150; descriptive analyses 152, *152*; discussion 154–7; gender differences 154, 155; participants 150; questionnaire 150–1; research 151; results 152–4, *152*, *153*; statistical analyses 151–2
victims 134; bully 31, 193, 202; cyberbullying 103, 115, 186; electronic aggression 83, *84*, 87
victims' perceptions: aggressor (known) 97; aggressor (unknown) 96; cyberbullying 92–100; data analysis 95; discussion 98–9, 169–70; ethics of research 95–6; gender and age 165, *165*; harshness 166; impact 166, *167*; implications 171; measures 164–5; participants 94, *94*, 163; research goals 93; research limitations and strengths 170–1; results 96–8, 165–9; traditional and cyberbullying 161–71
Viding, E.: *et al* 20, 44
violence 85
visual material (humiliating) 93
Vollink, T.: Bolman, C. and Dehue, F. 176

Wachs, S. 3; and Wolf, K. 120
Wang, J.: Nansel, T. and Iannotto, R. 194, 202
Wang, M.T.: and Dishion, T.J. 154
Weiss, R.S. 134
well-being: emotional 177
West, S.G.: and Aiken, L.S. 183
Wheeler, V.: and Asher, S. 67
Williams, K.R.: and Guerra, N.G. 105
Wolak, J.: Mitchell, K. and Finkelhor, D. 148
Wolf, K.: and Wachs, S. 120
Wolke, D.: *et al* 20
Woods, L: Priest, H. and Roberts, R. 10
worry 12, 14
Wu, M.A.: and Li Lei, Y. 156

Ybarra, M.L. 143; Finkelhor, D. and Mitchell, K.J. 175; and Mitchell, K.J. 104, 114
Young, J.: and Seals, D. 20
Youth Internet Survey 209